This textbook investigates definiteness both from a comparative and a theoretical point of view, showing how languages express definiteness and what definiteness is. It surveys a large number of languages to discover the range of variation in relation to definiteness and related grammatical phenomena: demonstratives, possessives, personal pronouns. It outlines work done on the nature of definiteness in semantics, pragmatics and syntax, and develops an account on which definiteness is a grammatical category represented in syntax as a functional head (the widely discussed D). Consideration is also given to the origins and evolution of definite articles in the light of the comparative and theoretical findings. Among the claims advanced are that definiteness does not occur in all languages though the pragmatic concept which it grammaticalizes probably does, that many languages have definiteness in their pronoun system but not elsewhere, that definiteness is not inherent in possessives, and that definiteness is to be assimilated to the grammatical category of person.

CAMBRIDGE TEXTBOOKS IN LINGUISTICS

General editors: S. R. ANDERSON, J. BRESNAN, B. COMRIE, W. DRESSLER, C. EWEN, R. HUDDLESTON, R. LASS, D. LIGHTFOOT, J. LYONS, P. H. MATTHEWS, R. POSNER, S. ROMAINE, N. V. SMITH, N. VINCENT

DEFINITENESS

In this series

P. H. MATTHEWS *Morphology* Second edition
B. COMRIE *Aspect*
R. M. KEMPSON *Semantic Theory*
T. BYNON *Historical Linguistics*
J. ALLWOOD, L.-G. ANDERSON and Ö. DAHL *Logic in Linguistics*
D. B. FRY *The Physics of Speech*
R. A. HUDSON *Sociolinguistics* Second edition
A. J. ELLIOTT *Child Language*
P. H. MATTHEWS *Syntax*
A. RADFORD *Transformational Syntax*
L. BAUER *English Word-Formation*
S. C. LEVINSON *Pragmatics*
G. BROWN and G. YULE *Discourse Analysis*
R. HUDDLESTON *Introduction to the Grammar of English*
R. LASS *Phonology*
B. COMRIE *Tense*
W. KLEIN *Second Language Acquisition*
A. J. WOODS, P. FLETCHER and A. HUGHES *Statistics in Language Studies*
D. A. CRUSE *Lexical Semantics*
F. R. PALMER *Mood and Modality*
A. RADFORD *Transformational Grammar*
M. GARMAN *Psycholinguistics*
W. CROFT *Typology and Universals*
G. G. CORBETT *Gender*
H. J. GIEGERICH *English Phonology*
R. CANN *Formal Semantics*
P. J. HOPPER and E. C. TRAUGOTT *Grammaticalization*
J. LAVER *Principles of Phonetics*
F. R. PALMER *Grammatical Roles and Relations*
B. BLAKE *Case*
M. A. JONES *Foundations of French Syntax*
A. RADFORD *Syntactic Theory and the Structure of English: a Minimalist Approach*
R. D. VAN VALIN, JR. and R. J. LAPOLLA *Syntax: Structure, Meaning and Function*
A. DURANTI *Linguistic Anthropology*
A. CRUTTENDEN *Intonation* Second edition
J. K. CHAMBERS and P. TRUDGILL *Dialectology* Second edition
C. LYONS *Definiteness*

DEFINITENESS

CHRISTOPHER LYONS

LECTURER IN LINGUISTICS
UNIVERSITY OF CAMBRIDGE

CAMBRIDGE
UNIVERSITY PRESS

PUBLISHED BY THE PRESS SYNDICATE OF THE UNIVERSITY OF CAMBRIDGE
The Pitt Building, Trumpington Street, Cambridge, United Kingdom

CAMBRIDGE UNIVERSITY PRESS
The Edinburgh Building, Cambridge CB2 2RU, UK   http://www.cup.cam.ac.uk
40th West 20th Street, New York, NY10011-4211, USA   http://www.cup.org
10 Stamford Road, Oakleigh, Melbourne 3166, Australia

First published 1999

Typeset in Times 9/13   [GC]

A catalogue reference for this book is available from the British Library

Library of Congress Cataloguing in Publication data

Lyons, Christopher.
Definiteness / Christopher Lyons.
   p. cm. — (Cambridge textbooks in linguistics)
Includes bibliographical references and index.
ISBN 0 521 36282 2 (hardback). — ISBN 0 521 36835 9 (paperback)
1. Definiteness (Linguistics) 2. Grammar, Comparative and
general – Syntax. 3. Semantics. 4. Pragmatics. I. Title.
II. Series.
P299.D43L97   1998
415—dc21   98–24724   CIP

ISBN 0 521 36282 2 hardback
ISBN 0 521 36835 9 paperback

Transferred to digital printing 2004

To the memory of my parents,
Edith and Patrick Lyons

CONTENTS

Contents

Contents

PREFACE

This book is primarily a survey, but, unlike some other topic-based books in this series, it surveys two areas. First, it offers an account of the range of variation displayed by languages in relation to definiteness and related grammatical concepts. Most languages do not have "articles", and in those that do they vary strikingly in both their form and their range of use. All languages have demonstratives, personal pronouns, possessives, and other expressions which either seem to be inherently definite or to interact in interesting ways with definiteness; but again, there is considerable variation in the ways in which these expressions relate to definiteness. Second, the book gives a (very selective) outline of the theoretical literature on definiteness. This literature is vast, consisting both of direct accounts of definiteness and of work mainly concerned with other phenomena on which definiteness impinges. Both the cross-linguistic survey and the theoretical survey are introductory and far from complete, and many of the choices I have made in reducing the material to manageable proportions are no doubt arbitrary. This is true particularly as regards the literature, where I have had to omit much which I see as important, and it is essential that the reader follow up further references given in the works I do refer to.

This is not just a survey, however. I am much too interested in the topic not to want to present my own view of what definiteness is, and I believe the work gains in coherence from the aim of reaching and defending (if in outline) a preferred account. Chapters 7 to 9, in particular, contain much discussion of the approach I believe to be the most promising. But in the earlier chapters too, I have not hesitated to advance far-reaching claims anticipating this approach. The view of definiteness I propose may be wrong, of course, but it will have achieved its purpose if a student reading my proposals is spurred to investigate further and show their inadequacy. My aim in this book is not to present a set of facts and analyses to be learned, but to offer a body of ideas to be thought about and improved upon.

The investigation of definiteness necessarily takes the reader into several domains of inquiry, some of which (like semantics and syntax) are highly technical. While I assume some familiarity on the part of the reader with the principles and methods of linguistics, I do not assume advanced competence in these domains, and I have given at appropriate points brief outlines of essentials and references to further reading, where possible at an elementary level. But it must be stressed that the interested reader would need to follow up these references, sometimes to a fairly advanced point, in order to come fully to grips with the issues in question. I have in general maintained neutrality between different theoretical frameworks, except as regards syntax, where I assume the principles-and-parameters approach which is the most highly developed and best known. Most of the text of this book was written at a time when the current "minimalist" version of this approach was in its infancy and there were few accessible accounts available of this framework to refer the reader to, so I have taken little account of minimalism. But there is little in the syntax discussed here which cannot be easily recast in this paradigm.

There has been much debate over the years on the relative merits of, on the one hand, the wide-ranging descriptive work of typological studies, and, on the other, the deep analysis of a smaller range of languages done in theoretical work. I firmly believe that descriptive breadth and analytical depth benefit one another, but that the latter must be the ultimate goal, and I hope that the gulf between these two approaches to language is narrower now than it was. The "new comparative linguistics" in generative work indicates a recognition among theorists of the value of cross-linguistic investigation, though some of it can be criticized as too selective in scope. But, to repeat a familiar point, our understanding of the way language works is deepened by bringing to bear serious analyses of languages, not mere observational facts. And even the best descriptive grammars are rarely adequate by themselves to provide the basis for an analysis of any depth of a specific aspect of linguistic structure. Indeed, even the descriptive observations and generalizations made in typological work must be treated with great caution, partly because the descriptive grammars on which they are based are often unclear on crucial points or analytically unsophisticated, partly because the typologist looking at unfamiliar languages in pursuit of a generalization is prone to the same inaccuracy as the theorist aiming to prove a point of theory. In my own cross-linguistic survey here, I too will certainly have included inaccuracies, and I urge the reader to treat it as a guide and starting point, not as fully reliable data.

Many people have helped me in various ways in the course of my writing this book, and I wish to thank in particular the following friends and colleagues who have read and commented on the manuscript or sections of it, or discussed particular points with me: Nigel Vincent, Deirdre Wilson, Noel Burton-Roberts, Kasia Jaszczolt. Most special thanks to Ricarda Schmidt for constant intellectual and moral support.

A couple of points concerning the presentation of the material should be noted. Where items of literature discussed exist in different versions, I have tried to refer to the most easily accessible version. In the case of doctoral theses subsequently published this means the formal publication. The effect is sometimes that my reference is to a version dated several years later than the version most commonly cited. Finally, a note on my use of gender-marked personal pronouns in describing conversational exchanges: I follow the convention that the speaker is, unless otherwise stated, female, and the hearer or addressee male.

ABBREVIATIONS

1	first person
1EXC	first person exclusive
1INC	first person inclusive
2	second person
3	third person
ABL	ablative case
ABS	absolutive or absolute case
ACC	accusative case
ADESS	adessive case
ANA, ana	anaphoric
ART	article
ASP	aspect
ASS1, Ass1	associated with first person
ASS1EXC	associated with first person exclusive
ASS1INC	associated with first person inclusive
ASS2, Ass2	associated with second person
ASS3	associated with third person
AUX	auxiliary
C	common gender
CL	clitic
CLASS	classifier, class marker
CONT	continuous aspect
DAT	dative case
DECL	declarative
DEF, Def	definite
DEM, Dem	demonstrative
DIR	direction
DIST	distal
DU	dual number
ELAT	elative case

ERG	ergative case
EXP	experiential aspect
F	feminine gender
FUT	future tense
GEN	genitive case
GENR	generic aspect
HAB	habitual aspect
HON	honorific
IMP	imperative
IMPF	imperfect, imperfective aspect
IMPRS	impersonal
INAN	inanimate
INDEF	indefinite
INESS	inessive case
INST	instrumental case
INTR	intransitive
IRR	irrealis
LINK	linker
LOC	locative case
M	masculine gender
N	neuter gender
NEG	negative
NOM	nominative case
NONPAST	non-past tense
NUN	nunation
OBJ	object
OBL	oblique case
PART	partitive case
PASS	passive voice
PAST	past tense
PERS	person
PL	plural number
POSS	possessive
PRES	present tense
PRF	perfective aspect
PRI	primary case
PROX, Prox	proximal
PRT	particle
REFL	reflexive
REL	relative marker

Abbreviations

SG, Sg	singular number
SUBJ	subject
TNS	tense
TOP	topic
WH	interrogative

The standard labels are used for syntactic categories (N, V, D and Det, Agr etc.). Any idiosyncratic or non-standard labels used are explained at the appropriate point in the text.

1
Basic observations

This chapter sets the scene by presenting some basic issues and ideas, which will be investigated in greater depth in the rest of the study. It begins by examining the concept of definiteness itself, to establish a preliminary account of what this concept amounts to. This is followed by consideration of the various types of noun phrase which are generally regarded as definite or indefinite – since definiteness and indefiniteness are not limited to noun phrases introduced by *the* or *a*. Finally, some basic ideas concerning the syntactic structure of noun phrases are presented in outline. English is taken as the starting point, with comparative observations on other languages where appropriate, because it is easier and less confusing to outline basic issues as they are instantiated in one language, where this can be done, than to hop from one language to another. For this purpose, English serves as well as any language, since it has readily identifiable lexical articles, which make definite and indefinite noun phrases on the whole easy to distinguish. It is important to bear in mind that the discussion in this chapter is preliminary, and aims at a tentative and provisional account of the points examined. Many of the proposals made here and solutions suggested to problems of analysis will be refined as the study progresses.

1.1   What is definiteness?

I begin in this section by attempting to establish in informal, pre-theoretical terms what the intuitions about meaning are that correspond to our terming a noun phrase "definite" or "indefinite".

1.1.1   Simple definites and indefinites

In many languages a noun phrase may contain an element which seems to have as its sole or principal role to indicate the definiteness or indefiniteness of the noun phrase. This element may be a lexical item like the definite and indefinite articles of English (*the*, *a*), or an affix of some kind like the Arabic definite prefix *al-* and indefinite suffix *-n*. I shall refer to such elements by the traditional label **article**, without commitment at this stage to what their grammatical status actually is. Of course not all noun phrases contain an article – probably in any language – though the definite–indefinite distinction is never thought of as applying only to those that do. This is clear from the fact that in English *this house* would usually be judged (at least by linguists and grammarians) to be definite and *several houses* indefinite; judgments would probably be more hesitant over *every house*. Noun phrases with *the* and *a* and their semantic equivalents (or near-equivalents) in other languages can be thought of as the basic instantiations of definite and indefinite noun phrases, in that the definiteness or indefiniteness stems from the presence of the article, which has as its essential semantic function to express this category.[1] I shall refer to such noun phrases as **simple definites** and **simple indefinites**, and I limit the discussion to them in this section to avoid any possibility of disagreement over the definite or indefinite status of example noun phrases.

So the question we are concerned with is: What is the difference in meaning between *the car* and *a car*, between *the greedy child* and *a greedy child*, between *the hibiscus I planted last summer* and *a hibiscus I planted last summer*? Many traditional grammars would give answers like the following: *The* indicates that the speaker or writer is referring to a definite or particular car etc., not just any. But apart from being rather vague, this answer is quite inaccurate. If I say *I bought a car this morning*, I am not referring to just any car; the car I bought is a particular one, and is distinguished in my mind from all others. Yet *a car* is indefinite. There is in fact no general agreement on what the correct answer is, but two major components of meaning have been much discussed, and I introduce these in 1.1.2 and 1.1.3 in relation to some illustrative English data.

1.1.2 *Familiarity and identifiability*

Continuing with the example just considered, compare the following two sentences:

(1)   I bought **a car** this morning.

(2)   I bought **the car** this morning.

The car here is in some sense more "definite", "specific", "particular", "individualized" etc. than *a car*, but, as noted above, *a car* certainly denotes a particular or specific car as far as the speaker is concerned. The difference is that the reference of *the car* in (2) is assumed to be clear to the hearer as well as the speaker. This is the first crucial insight; whereas in the case of an indefinite noun phrase the speaker may be aware of what is being referred to and the hearer probably

---

[1] We will see, however, that articles can encode more than definiteness or indefiniteness, and that they have been argued to have a quite different principal function, at least in some languages.

not, with a definite noun phrase this awareness is signalled as being shared by both participants. One would typically utter (1) where the car in question has no place yet in the hearer's experience, and is being newly introduced to it. (2) would be used where the hearer knows or has seen the speaker's new car. She may be at the wheel right now, or they may be standing looking at it together in her drive; or it may be that the hearer has not yet seen the car in the speaker's possession, but was aware that she had been looking over a particular car in a showroom recently.[2]

Examples like these have led to a view of definiteness known as the **familiarity hypothesis**. *The* signals that the entity denoted by the noun phrase is familiar to both speaker and hearer, and *a* is used where the speaker does not want to signal such shared familiarity. The familiarity hypothesis has a long history, and its first full presentation is in Christophersen (1939), a work which has greatly influenced much subsequent writing on the subject. The major recent work in this tradition is Hawkins (1978), and the discussion I give here owes much to this account.

As further illustration, consider (3)–(12):

(3)   Just give **the shelf** a quick wipe, will you, before I put this vase on it.

(4)   Put these clean towels in **the bathroom** please.

(5)   I hear **the prime minister** behaved outrageously again today.

(6)   **The moon** was very bright last night.

(7)   An elegant, dark-haired woman, a well-dressed man with dark glasses, and two children entered the compartment. I immediately recognized **the woman**. **The children** also looked vaguely familiar.

(8)   I had to get a taxi from the station. On the way **the driver** told me there was a bus strike.

(9)   They've just got in from New York. **The plane** was five hours late.

(10)   **The president of Ghana** is visiting tomorrow.

(11)   **The bloke Ann went out with last night** phoned a minute ago.

(12) a.   **The fact that you've known them for years** is no excuse.
      b.   We were rather worried by **the prospect of having to cook for six for two weeks**.

---

[2] This is something of a simplification, skirting a number of issues subject to debate. First, there is dispute over whether definite noun phrases can be referring expressions, or whether it is rather speakers who sometimes refer using them. Second, if definites can refer or be used to refer, it is less clear that reference is involved in the case of indefinites like *a car* here. Nevertheless, the distinction drawn captures a clear intuition, and its expression in terms of speaker's and hearer's familiarity with a referent is standard in at least the less technical literature. I return to this in Chapter 4.

Basic observations

Examples (3)–(5) show **situational** uses of *the*, in that the physical situation in which the speaker and hearer are located contributes to the familiarity of the referent of the definite noun phrase. In (3) the situation is the immediate, visible one; the shelf is familiar to speaker and hearer in that it is before their eyes. In (4) the situation is still relatively immediate, though the referent of the definite noun phrase is probably not visible; in a particular house, the hearer would most naturally take it that the reference is to the bathroom of that house. In (5) the relevant situation is wider; in a particular country, the reference to *the prime minister* would normally be taken to be to the prime minister of that country; the individual concerned is not personally known to the hearer, but is familiar in the sense of being known to exist and probably known by report. (6) can be regarded as a situational use in which the situation is the whole world, or as a use in which familiarity stems from **general knowledge**. Thus *the moon* is taken to refer to the particular moon associated with this planet, or to a unique entity forming part of the hearer's general knowledge.

In (7) we have examples of **anaphoric** *the*. The referents of *the woman* and *the children* are familiar not from the physical situation but from the linguistic context; they have been mentioned before. In this example the previous mention takes place in an earlier sentence uttered by the same speaker, but it could equally well occur in part of the discourse spoken by another person, as in the following exchange:

(13) A: An old man, two women and several children were already there when I arrived.
     B: Did you recognize **the old man**?

It is significant that in (7) and (13) the earlier mentions of the woman, the children and the old man take the form of indefinite noun phrases; new referents are introduced into the discourse in this form because they are so far unfamiliar to the hearer.

Examples (8) and (9) are **bridging cross-reference** or **associative** uses, and can be thought of as a combination of the anaphoric and general knowledge types. In (8) the driver has not been mentioned before, but there has been mention of a taxi, and it is part of our general knowledge that taxis have drivers. The idea is that the mention of a taxi conjures up for the hearer all the things that are associated with taxis (a driver, wheels, seats, the fare etc.), and any of these things can then be referred to by means of a definite noun phrase. So the referent of *the driver* is familiar through association with the antecedent *a taxi*. (9) is particularly interesting because the antecedent which warrants the definite *the plane* is not even a noun phrase. But travelling from New York to most places necessarily involves some form of conveyance, with an aircraft being the most likely if the present conversation is taking place in, say, Manchester.

4

There are two possible ways of characterizing (10). The hearer may not know the president of Ghana personally, nor even have heard of him, but will know from his knowledge of the world that there probably is such an individual. The alternative characterization involves taking the definite article to be modifying not *president of Ghana*, but just *president*, so that *of Ghana* is a phrase added to provide clarifying information and not itself within the scope of *the*. On this view, the prepositional phrase has the same function as the previous mention of *a taxi* in (8): to provide a trigger for the association that familiarizes the definite noun phrase. If this is correct, then it is possible for an associative use of *the* to be based on following as well as preceding information. A similar treatment seems appropriate for (11). In this example, the familiarity of *the bloke* depends on the following relative clause. Assume that the hearer did not even know that Ann had gone out last night. The relative clause informs him of this, and also informs him that she went out with someone. The familiarity of *the bloke* then consists of its association with this succeeding information.

Finally, consider (12). Here, *that you've known them for years* is the fact in question, and *having to cook for six for two weeks* is the prospect. So these clauses, again following rather than preceding the definite noun phrase, act as "antecedent" for *the fact* and *the prospect*, which are therefore anticipatory anaphoric (or "cataphoric") uses.

It may be already clear from this presentation that the concept of familiarity as an explanation for the definite–indefinite distinction is not unproblematic. It is fairly straightforward for examples like (3)–(6), where the hearer is genuinely acquainted with the referent, (7), where previous mention makes the referent familiar (by report rather than direct acquaintance), and even (8), where the fact that taxis always have drivers affords the same sort of familiarity as in (7). But getting from New York to Manchester does not necessarily involve flying; the association appealed to in (9) is certainly real, but can one really say that the plane was in any sense known to the hearer before the utterance of the second sentence of this example? In (10), the hearer would normally be prepared to accept that Ghana has a president, but that is not the same as knowing this person. In (12), where cataphoric information is appealed to, one can claim that the necessary familiarity is established after the utterance of the definite noun phrase, but in (11), the fact that Ann went out with a man is not expressed in the relative clause; in fact, *the bloke* can be replaced by *a bloke*, without changing the referent, which seems to make it clear that the information in the relative clause is not such as to establish the familiarity that would make *the* obligatory.

Because of considerations like these, many linguists basically sympathetic to the familiarity thesis prefer to see definiteness as being about **identifiability**. The idea is that the use of the definite article directs the hearer to the referent of the noun phrase by signalling that he is in a position to identify it.[3] This view of definiteness does not altogether reject familiarity. Rather, familiarity, where it is present, is what enables the hearer to identify the referent. In such cases the hearer is invited to match the referent of the definite noun phrase with some real-world entity which he knows to exist because he can see it, has heard of it, or infers its existence from something else he has heard.

In the examples discussed above where familiarity seems rather forced, it is generally the case that the definiteness of the noun phrase confirms an association which is only probable or possible rather than known. In (9), the journey mentioned makes the involvement of an aircraft likely, and then the definite noun phrase *the plane* authorizes the hearer to associate its referent with this journey, confirming the possible association. It does this by indicating that its referent can be identified by the hearer, and the most straightforward identification is with a plane the travellers probably came on from New York. A similar association is involved in (10); Ghana probably has a president, and it is with this probable individual that the reference of *the president* is identified. But in this example, the phrase which provides the probable referent occurs after the definite noun phrase and is attached to it in such a way as to make the association certain rather than probable. In (11) the relative clause provides a context in which a referent for *the bloke* can be found. Ann went out last night with someone, and the referent of *the bloke* is that someone, even though the relative does not provide any information about the person (that it was a man, for example).

So while on the familiarity account *the* tells the hearer that he knows which, on the identifiability account it tells him that he knows or can work out which. Let us now consider a case where an explanation in terms of familiarity would be impossible. Back in the sitting-room which was the setting for (3), Ann is trying to put up a picture on the wall, and, without turning round, says to Joe who has just entered:

(14)   Pass me **the hammer**, will you?

Joe looks around and, sure enough, sees a hammer on a chair. The difference between (14) and (3) is that, whereas the hearer in (3) knows there is a shelf in the room which provides an obvious referent for the definite noun phrase, Joe does not know at the time of Ann's utterance that there is a hammer in the room. He has to look

---

[3] Note that the article itself does not identify the referent; *the* is a "grammatical word" with no descriptive lexical content, and therefore contains nothing which can itself identify a referent. The most it can do is invite the hearer to exploit clues in the linguistic or extralinguistic context to establish the identity of the referent. The article has been said by many writers to "pick out" an entity, but this is inaccurate; *the* may be about identifiability, but not identification.

for a referent, guided by the description *hammer*.[4] The definite article tells Joe that he can identify the hammer Ann is talking about, and the verb *pass* (which tends to take things immediately available as complement, by contrast with *fetch, get, buy*) makes it almost certain that he will find it in the room. The referent of the definite noun phrase is unfamiliar to the hearer, but he is able to find a referent for it.

1.1.3   Uniqueness and inclusiveness

Identifiability certainly offers a more comprehensive picture than does familiarity, but there are also cases of definites for which an account in terms of identifiability is either not fully convincing or simply inadequate.

Associative uses of the definite article in general are problematic for identifiability; consider the following example:

(15)   I've just been to a wedding. **The bride** wore blue.

The definite reference *the bride* in (15) is successful because the hearer knows that weddings involve brides, and makes the natural inference that the reference is to the bride at the particular wedding just mentioned. But is it accurate to say that the hearer identifies the referent in any real sense? He still does not know who she is or anything about her. If asked later who got married that morning he would be in no position to say on the basis of (15), and if he passes the newly-wed in the street the next day he will not recognize her as the person referred to.

Many situational uses are also associative; they work because the hearer is able to associate a definite noun phrase with some entity which he expects to find in or associates with the situation. This is the case with the following:

(16)   [Nurse entering operating theatre]
            I wonder who **the anaesthetist** is today.

A definite is possible because we take it for granted that operations involve anaesthetists. But it is clear from what is said in (16) that the speaker cannot identify the referent of the definite noun phrase, and does not necessarily expect the hearer to be able to. Both participants know there is or will be such an individual, but that is not identification. The point becomes all the clearer if we replace the definite article in (16) by a demonstrative:

(17)   I wonder who **that anaesthetist** is.

---

[4] In the semantics literature, the term "description" is used of all material that ascribes properties to entities – including nouns as well as, more obviously, adjectives. A particularly important use of the word, especially in the philosophical literature, is in the term **definite description**, meaning an expression which ascribes a property or properties to a particular entity – in other words, a definite noun phrase. *The hammer*, then, is a definite description.

Again the speaker does not know the identity of the person referred to, but she
is referring to a particular individual and expects the hearer to be able to pick out
precisely which individual she means. This is not the case with (16), indicating
that while demonstratives may require identifiability, definites do not.

Consider also a cataphoric case, where the definite article is sanctioned by a
relative clause following the noun:

(18)   Mary's gone for a spin in **the car she just bought**.

In (18) the relative tells the hearer something about the car (the fact that Mary
just bought it), but it does not help him identify it. He still would not know the
car in question if he saw it (unless Mary was driving it).

What can be claimed about all these examples is that they involve the idea of
uniqueness: the definite article signals that there is just one entity satisfying the
description used. This uniqueness is generally not absolute, but is to be understood relative to a particular context. Thus in (15) there is just one bride at the
wedding which triggers the association. In (16) the assumption is that there is just
one anaesthetist taking part in the operation about to begin, but who it is is not
known. And in (20) *the* conveys that Mary bought one car.

In the associative examples an indefinite article would seem unnatural, for various reasons; in (15), for example, the general knowledge on which the association is based includes an assumed normal pattern of one bride per wedding. But
in (18) it is perfectly possible to substitute *a* for *the*:

(19)   Mary's gone for a spin in **a car she just bought**.

The most natural interpretation is still that only one car is involved, but the possibility is left open that Mary may have just bought more than one car. So the
indefinite article does not signal non-uniqueness; rather it does not signal uniqueness. Indefinites are neutral with respect to uniqueness (though this will be
qualified below).

As observed, the uniqueness of the definite article is usually relative to a particular context, but it can be absolute. This is the case with nouns which are inherently unique, denoting something of which there is only one. We can speak of *the
sun* and *the universe*, but not normally of *a sun* or *a universe*; the qualification is
important, because although for most purposes we think of our sun and our universe as the only entities to which those names apply, there are situations in which
we might speak of our sun as one of many or entertain the possibility of there
existing another universe. Nouns like *Pope* are also often thought of as inherent
uniques, because there is usually only one at any given time; but of course if one
looks across history there have been many Popes, and with this perspective it is
reasonable to speak of *a Pope*. The fact that one can always find a context in which

8

a noun ceases to be uniquely denoting does not invalidate the point. Just as it is possible to claim that the count–mass distinction is basically valid despite the possibility of recategorizing any noun (as in the count use of the basically mass *milk* in *He strode up to the bar and ordered three milks*), so there is a class of inherently unique nouns. And such nouns, used as uniquely denoting, require the definite article.

Consider also the following immediate situation definite:

(20)　　　Beware of **the dog**.

This is intended to inform the reader that there is a dog in the vicinity, and that he is likely to meet it if he waits long enough or proceeds any further. One could argue that identifiability is involved, in that if he sees a dog nearby he is likely to connect it with the one mentioned in the notice. But there is no expectation that he will seek a referent for *the dog*; rather, (20) is equivalent to *There is a dog*. Uniqueness, on the other hand, does seem to offer an adequate account here, since an intrepid intruder could reasonably claim to have been misled if he found he had to deal with two dogs.

The uniqueness criterion is particularly attractive in cases where the referent is hypothetical, potential, or in the future:

(21)　　　**The winner of this competition** will get a week in the Bahamas for two.

(22)　　　**The man who comes with me** will not regret it.

Assuming the competition in (21) is not yet over and no one has yet agreed to accompany the speaker in (22), the winner and the man are certainly not yet identifiable. But they are unique, in that a single winner and a single male companion are clearly implied.

Finally, there are certain other modifying constituents of the noun phrase which are incompatible with the indefinite article; among these are superlatives, *first*, *same*, *only* and *next*:

(23)　　　Janet is **the/(*a) cleverest child** in the class.

(24)　　　You are **the/(*a) first visitor** to our new house.

(25)　　　I've got **the/(*a) same problem** as you.

(26)　　　He is **the/(*an) only student** who dislikes phonology.

(27)　　　I offered a discount to **the/(*a) next customer**.

Uniqueness offers an explanation for these facts, according to Hawkins (1978), since the unacceptability of the indefinite article seems likely to stem from a semantic incompatibility between an element of uniqueness in the meaning of the modifier and the non-uniqueness of *a*. For although I have said that the indefinite article is neutral with respect to uniqueness, there are cases where choosing *a* rather than *the* implies non-uniqueness; this is a point I will return to. For the moment it will suffice to look at it in this way: if the descriptive material in the noun phrase indicates that the referent is unique, then the only appropriate article is the one that encodes uniqueness. This is the case with inherently unique nouns, and noun phrases containing superlatives etc. *Cleverest* means 'cleverer than all the others', and *first* means 'before all the others'; so uniqueness can be argued to be involved here, as it obviously is with *only*. In (25), if the hearer has a single problem, or a single salient problem, as seems to be implied, then the speaker can have only one problem which is the same as the hearer's. *Next* means 'immediately following', and given that customers are generally dealt with one by one, there can be only one customer who immediately follows the preceding one.

All the examples so far considered in this section have involved count nouns in the singular. But the definite article can occur equally well with plural count nouns and mass nouns, and the obvious question is: How can a definite noun phrase which is plural or mass have a referent which is unique (in the context)? The noun phrases *the pens* and *the butter* (the latter occurring with its usual mass value and not recategorized as count) cannot refer to just one pen and just one butter. Let us look at examples corresponding to those examined above, but with plural (the (a) sentences) and mass (the (b) ones) definite noun phrases:

(28) a. We've just been to see John race. The Queen gave out **the prizes**.
   b. We went to the local pub this lunch time. They've started chilling **the beer**.

(29) a. [Nurse about to enter operating theatre]
      I wonder who **the anaesthetists** are.
   b. [Examining restaurant menu]
      I wonder what **the pâté** is like.

(30) a. We're looking for **the vandals** who broke into the office yesterday.
   b. I can't find **the shampoo** I put here this morning.

(31) a. Beware of **the dogs**.
   b. Beware of **the electrified wire**.

(32) a. We're offering several prizes, and **the winners** will be invited to London for the presentation.
   b. Fred's decided to take up home brewing. He plans to sell **the beer** to his friends.

(33) a. Janet and John are **the cleverest children** in the class.
   b. This is **the best muesli** I've ever tasted.

(34) a. You are **the first visitors** to our new house.
   b. This is **the first rain** to be seen here for five months.

(35) a.   I've got **the same problems** as you.

     b.   All the family used to take their bath in **the same water**.

(36) a.   They are **the only students** who dislike phonology.

     b.   This is **the only water** you're likely to see for miles.

(37) a.   I offered a discount to **the next three customers**.

     b.   **The next water** is beyond those hills.

As a first attempt at a solution, one might propose that uniqueness still applies, but to sets and masses rather than to individuals. Thus the set or mass referred to by a definite noun phrase is the only set or mass in the context satisfying the description. But this does not work. In (28a), suppose there are three prizes. These form a set, but there is also the set consisting of the second and third prizes, that consisting of the first and second prizes, and so on; these, of course, are subsets of the set of three – and this is the point. Our intuition about (28a) is that the Queen gave out all the prizes, not some subset of the total; similarly in (28b), we assume that all the beer at this pub is now served chilled.

This points us to the proposal that definiteness, at least with plural and mass noun phrases, involves not uniqueness but **inclusiveness** (a term due to Hawkins (1978)). What this means is that the reference is to the totality of the objects or mass in the context which satisfy the description. So in the (a) examples of (29)–(32) the reference would be taken to be to all the anaesthetists about to take part in the operation, all the vandals involved in the break-in, all the dogs guarding the property, and all the winners in the competition. In the (b) examples, it is to all the pâté on offer in the restaurant, all the shampoo left there, the electrified wire surrounding the property as a whole, and all the beer Fred brews. In (33), Janet and John are the only children in the class meriting the description *cleverest*, and the muesli praised is the totality of the muesli in the speaker's experience deserving to be called the best. I leave the reader to work out how inclusiveness accounts for (34)–(37).

It appears, then, that with plural and mass nouns *the* is a universal quantifier, similar in meaning to *all*. As support for this position, consider the following:

(38) a.   I've washed the dishes.

     b.   I've washed all the dishes.

(39)   No you haven't, you've only washed some of them.

Our intuition is that (38a) and (38b) are equally false if there are still some dishes unwashed, and in that case (39) would be a reasonable retort to either. So *the* (in some uses) and *all* are very close in meaning, and the difference between them may be that *all* is simply more emphatic. But it seems unsatisfactory to say that *the* signals uniqueness with singular noun phrases and inclusiveness with plural and mass noun phrases. In fact uniqueness can be assimilated to inclusiveness. When the noun phrase is singular, inclusiveness turns out to be the same as uniqueness, because the totality of the objects satisfying the description is just one. For example, the speaker in (16) is assuming there will be only one anaesthetist; so the total number of anaesthetists assumed to be involved is one.[5]

1.1.4 Identifiability, inclusiveness and indefinites

The relationship of the indefinite article to identifiability and inclusiveness is rather complex. We saw in relation to (18)–(19) that *a* is neutral with respect to uniqueness rather than signalling non-uniqueness. Where *the* is used the referent has to be unique: Mary bought one car. *A* allows this same interpretation, while also permitting an interpretation in which the car referred to is one of several. This picture is reinforced by sentences like the following:

(40)   I went to the surgery this afternoon and saw **a doctor**.

The doctor the speaker saw may have been one of several in the surgery, but not necessarily; (40) is perfectly compatible with there having been only one doctor there.

But there are other cases where *a* signals non-uniqueness and the choice of *a* rather than *the* makes a significant difference:

(41)   Pass me **a hammer**.

(42)   Janet ran well and won **a prize**.

These sentences clearly imply that there is more than one hammer in the situation to choose from, and Janet won one of a number of prizes.

It appears that, while *the* logically entails uniqueness with singular noun phrases, *a* is logically neutral with respect to this. But it carries a weaker implication of non-uniqueness. How this can be formalized will be discussed more fully in Chapter 7, but for the moment the point is that *a* may imply that the referent is non-unique, but this implication may be overridden. This can be illustrated in relation to (42), where it is possible to add material indicating that the referent is, after all, unique:

(43)   Janet ran well and won **a prize** – the only prize in fact.

---

[5] It should be noted, however, that with singulars *the* is not (near-)synonymous with *all*. We use *the table* to refer to the only table in a certain context, but *all the table* denotes every part of the table, and **all table* is not a well-formed noun phrase.

There have been various reformulations of the basic insight behind inclusiveness, for example as "maximality" (Sharvy 1980, Kadmon 1987): the reference of a definite description is to the maximal set satisfying the description.

The fact that there is no contradiction in this sentence makes it clear that although in (42) the indefinite *a prize* strongly implies non-uniqueness, this implication is less central to the meaning of *a* than is uniqueness to that of *the*: (44) is much less acceptable than (43):

(44)   ?Janet ran well and won **the prize** – one of several in fact.

We can summarize by saying that when a referent is inclusive in the context, *the* is normally used rather than *a*, because *a* implies non-inclusiveness (equivalent to non-uniqueness, since *a* only occurs with singulars). This implication can be overridden, however, making it clear that non-inclusiveness is not an entailment of the indefinite article. When the referent is not inclusive in its context, *a* must be used and *the* may not be, as (44) makes clear.

But there is a further use of *a*. This is when the entity referred to is not associated with what I have been calling a "context" – a physical situation or the previous discourse. First-mention uses exemplify this:

(45)   I met a lion-tamer this morning.

Where there is no contextual set (other than perhaps the whole world) within which inclusiveness may or may not apply, *a* is used. And in such cases it seems to be a matter of non-identifiability rather than non-inclusiveness. The referent is taken to be unfamiliar to the hearer because it has not been mentioned before. This is probably also the best explanation for the indefinite in (19), where the referent may well be unique. This use is probably not to be seen as cataphoric (the relative postmodifier establishing a domain for uniqueness or familiarity); rather, the entire noun phrase, including head noun and relative, is treated as non-identifiable, and is therefore indefinite.

1.1.5 A unified account?

We have seen that familiarity can be subsumed under identifiability, and that uniqueness is merely a special case of inclusiveness, resulting from the singularity of the noun phrase. So the question now is: Can we make a choice between identifiability and inclusiveness? Is one of them right and the other wrong, or are there two kinds of definiteness?

In section 1.1.3 we examined a number of uses of *the* which can be accounted for by inclusiveness but not (or not very convincingly) by identifiability. Indeed the inclusiveness account could be extended to many other examples that are not problematic for identifiability. If certain uses can be handled by inclusiveness and not by identifiability, and other uses can be handled by either hypothesis, then inclusiveness must be preferred. Consider for example (14), repeated here:

13

(14)   Pass me the hammer, will you?

This example is unproblematic for the identifiability account. The hearer was not previously aware of the presence of a hammer in the room, but takes it from the definite noun phrase that there is one which he can identify; he looks around and finds the referent. But inclusiveness works equally well. If on looking around the hearer saw three hammers, he might have to ask back which one was meant; the definite reference would have failed, because the hearer could not identify the referent. Identification is thus only possible in (14) if the desired hammer is unique in the context. So both identifiability and inclusiveness work here as explanations for the appropriateness of *the*.

However, there are cases where identifiability works and inclusiveness does not. Consider the following:

(46)   [In a room with three doors, one of which is open]
         Close **the door**, please.

(47)   [In a hallway where all four doors are closed. The speaker is dressed
         in coat and hat, and has a suitcase in each hand]
         Open **the door** for me, please.

(48)   [Ann, fixing her motorbike, is examining a large nut. Behind her, just
         out of reach, are three spanners, two of them obviously far too small
         for the nut]
         Pass me **the spanner**, will you?

(49)   [Two academics]
  A: How did the seminar go?
  B: Fine. **The student** gave an excellent presentation, which generated a
         really good discussion, with all the other students contributing well. ·

In (46), an immediate situation use, the door referred to is not unique; but it is easily identified because of the verb – you can only close an open door. (47) is similar; the door is not unique, but the speaker's state of preparedness for a journey makes it obvious that the street-door is meant. In (48) the hearer is expected to be able to work out that only one of the three spanners can possibly fit the bill and identify that as the intended referent. And in (49), the nature of a seminar makes it clear that one student in the group stood out as having a special task, and this individual will be taken to be the referent of *the student*. All these examples represent perfectly normal uses of *the*, and they cannot be adequately accounted for by inclusiveness.

We have, then, some usage types which can only be accounted for by identifiability, some which can only be accounted for by inclusiveness, and some which both theories account for equally well. This is not a satisfying conclusion, and I shall return to the matter in Chapter 7. But for the moment let us settle for a view of definiteness as involving either identifiability or inclusiveness, or both: if the reference of a noun phrase is characterized by either property, then that noun phrase should be definite. Bear in mind, however, that the two properties are in principle independent of one another, even if in many examples the presence of one follows from the presence of the other; the two theories make quite distinct claims.[6]

It is also possible that what we are calling definiteness is in fact two or more distinct semantic categories, which happen to have the same lexical or morphological realization in English. A way to test this possibility would be to look for languages in which different kinds of "definiteness" are expressed in different ways, by different articles for example. Or it may be that definiteness is a unified phenomenon, but that neither identifiability nor inclusiveness is the correct characterization. We will come back to these speculations, assuming for the present that definiteness is a single category.

1.2 Types of definite noun phrase

This section surveys, still informally, and still using mainly English data, the range of noun phrase types which have definiteness as part of their meaning. Including the definite article in a noun phrase is not the only way of making definite reference to some entity. There are several other kinds of noun phrase which appear either to express the inclusiveness of the referent or to indicate that the referent is identifiable. The following noun phrases all have much in common semantically with definite noun phrases containing *the*: *that man, these houses; Ann, Venice; my car, a friend's house; they, us; all writers, every shop.*

1.2.1 *Testing for definiteness*

Articles like *the* and *a* are part of the larger class of **determiners** – another term used here informally, without commitment to the grammatical category of the items concerned, to cover non-adjectival noun phrase modifiers such as *this, several, our, all*. Some of these are definite determiners, differing from *the* in that they combine definiteness with some other semantic content. The

---

[6] A number of writers present definiteness in terms which suggest an attempt to combine or reconcile the two accounts, characterizing definites as "uniquely identifying". One should not be misled by this; it either represents a failure to appreciate the difference between uniqueness and identifiability, or is merely equivalent to "identifying", or "identifying unambiguously". A good example is the account of definiteness given by Leech (1983: 90–3). Leech says that the use of *the* conveys that there is a referent that can be uniquely identified by speaker and hearer. He adds that "uniquely" means that "we should be able to select the one X concerned from all other X's". There is nothing here about the referent being unique (in the context). But then he refers back to this characterization as "the uniqueness implicature associated with *the*", which ensures that *the postcard I got from Helen last week* implies that there exists only one such postcard. This is by no means an isolated instance of confusion of identifiability and uniqueness.

combination may be a necessary one, because this other semantic content entails definiteness or is incompatible with indefiniteness. Or it may be that two semantic properties, in principle independent of one another, happen to be jointly encoded by a portmanteau morpheme. I shall follow the established practice of representing the grammatical and semantic content of lexical items and morphemes by features. So *the* is [+ Def] and *a* is [− Def]. Other determiners may be characterized as [+ Def] along with other feature specifications.[7] I have adopted the term "simple definites/indefinites" to describe noun phrases with *the* or *a*; so other definite noun phrases, in which [+ Def] is present as a consequence of, or otherwise in combination with, another feature, are **complex definites.**

It has long been recognized that a number of syntactic environments either do not admit or admit only with some difficulty a definite, or conversely an indefinite, noun phrase. These environments have been used as diagnostics, to determine whether a given noun phrase type is definite or not. The following examples show how some of these "definiteness effects" distinguish between simple definites and simple indefinites; the constructions in (50)–(53) were first exploited by Postal (1970) and that in (53) is discussed in detail by Milsark (1979).

(50) a.   Big as the boy was, he couldn't lift it.
     b.   ?Big as a boy was, he couldn't lift it.

(51) a.   The house is mine.
     b.   ?A house is mine.

(52) a.   which/some/all of the women
     b.   *which/some/all of (some) women

(53) a.   Is there a dictionary in the house?
     b.   ?Is there the dictionary in the house?

These diagnostics are not foolproof, and not too much reliance should be placed on them. For example, the structure in (50) admits an indefinite noun phrase interpreted generically (as referring to an entire class), and similar counterexamples can be devised to some of the other tests:

[7] Although writers are commonly noncommittal as to whether features are grammatical (morphosyntactic) or semantic, my discussion so far (with examination of usage types and the attempt to characterize definiteness in terms of notions like inclusiveness and identifiability) implies that I take the features I introduce to be semantic. Indeed nearly all discussion in the literature of definiteness and related concepts like demonstrativeness takes these to be semantic or pragmatic. I will in fact argue in later chapters that definiteness (though not necessarily demonstrativeness) is a grammatical category, not a semantic one (though it is related to a semantic/pragmatic concept). For the moment, I assume that [+ Def] is a defining characteristic of certain determiners, so that a noun phrase with one of these determiners is definite, even if neither inclusiveness nor identifiability seems to be involved in the interpretation. This assumption will be important in 1.2.4 below.

(54)   Big as a bus is, it can easily pass through this gap.

(55)   A house is mine if I pay for it.

Nevertheless, the examples (50)–(53) do draw a recognizable distinction, and these diagnostics offer a rough guide. If applied to a range of putative complex definites, they range these clearly with *the*:

(56) a.   Big as **that boy** was, he couldn't lift it.
     b.   **That house** is mine.
     c.   which/some/all of **those women**
     d.   ?Is there **that dictionary** in the house?

(57) a.   Tall as **Nuala** is, she won't be able to reach it.
     b.   **Fido** is mine.
     c.   (*which)/some/all of **Paris**
     d.   ?Is there **Peter** in the house?

(58) a.   Big as **my cousin** is, he can't lift it.
     b.   Make yourself at home – **my house** is yours.
     c.   which/some/all of **the students' essays**
     d.   ?Is there **Rachel's racket** in here?

(59) a.   Clever as **you** are, I bet you won't solve it.
     b.   **I** am yours.
     c.   which/some/all of **us**
     d.   *Is there **him** here yet?

(60) a.   Strong as **every contestant** is, they'll never shift it.
     b.   **All hats** are yours.
     c.   (?which)/(?some)/(*all) of **all the men**
     d.   ?Is there **every visitor** here?

The partitive structure in the (c) examples shows some deviations from the pattern seen with *the*; *which of* cannot be followed by a proper noun because these are always singular, and noun phrases with *all* do not readily occur at all in partitives, for reasons which are not obvious. Otherwise the only point of note is that personal pronouns are even less acceptable in the *there is/are* construction than are other definites. In the following sections we will look more closely at demonstratives, proper nouns, possessives, personal pronouns, and determiners like *all* and *every*.

1.2.2 Demonstratives

Demonstratives are generally considered to be definite, but it is clear that their definiteness is not a matter of inclusiveness. A sentence like *Pass me that book* is likely to be used in a context where there is more than one possible referent corresponding to the description *book*, and the utterance may well be

17

accompanied by some gesture indicating which book the speaker has in mind. Hawkins (1978) argues that demonstrative reference always involves a contrast, clear or implied, between the actual referent and other potential referents. On the view so far adopted here, identifiability is what links demonstratives with the definite article. In uttering *Pass me that book*, or *I've read this book*, the speaker assumes that the hearer can determine which book is intended, by contrast with *Pass me a book* or *I've read a book* (the former not involving any intended referent).

But identifiability is only part of the semantic content of demonstratives. They are often grouped with the varied class of words which express **deixis**. Deixis is the property of certain expressions and categories (including tense and grammatical person) of relating things talked about to the spatio-temporal context, and in particular to contextual distinctions like that between the moment or place of utterance and other moments or places, or that between the speaker, the hearer, and others. Demonstratives like *this* and *that* are deictic because they locate the entity referred to relative to some reference point in the extralinguistic context. The contrast between *this/these* and *that/those* is to do with distance from the speaker; *this book* denotes something closer to the speaker than does *that book*. This distance is not necessarily spatial; it may be temporal (*that day* referring to some past or future occasion, as opposed to *this week*, meaning the present week), or emotional (*There's that awful man here again*, *What about this present you promised me?*). For discussion of these possibilities see Lakoff (1974). *This* and *that* are often termed **proximal** and **distal** demonstratives, respectively. But it is possible to relate this distance contrast to the category of person. *This* is used to refer to some entity which is close to or associated in some way with the speaker, or with a set of individuals which includes the speaker; so *this article* could be 'the article which I am reading', 'the article which you and I are discussing', or 'the article which you, I and they are interested in', among other possibilities. Now this concept of a set of one or more individuals which includes the speaker is the definition of "first person"; it corresponds to the pronouns *I* (set of one) and *we* (set of more than one). *That* is used where the referent is associated with a set including hearer but not speaker (second person) or a set including neither speaker nor hearer (third person):

(61)   Show me **that** (?**this**) letter you have in your pocket.

(62)   Tell her to bring **that** (?**this**) drill she has.

This is certainly possible in these examples, but it would imply that the letter or drill is in some way associated with the speaker (or a set including the speaker). Thus, for example, the letter may have already been the subject of discussion between speaker and hearer; and the speaker may have been previously thinking about the amazing drill she has recently heard one of her friends has acquired. But in the absence of such factors (or of the speaker's desire to communicate such factors), *that* is the appropriate demonstrative: in (61) the letter is in the possession of the hearer (second person), and in (62) it is someone not present in the discourse situation (third person) who has the drill. So it would be reasonable to speak of *this* as a first-person demonstrative and *that* as a non-first-person demonstrative.

An important question is whether this deictic element is the defining characteristic of demonstratives, distinguishing them from the definite article. An affirmative answer is given by many writers. Sommerstein (1972) and J. Lyons (1975, 1977) assume that the distance component is the only thing that distinguishes *this* and *that* from *the* (so that *this* marks proximity, *that* marks distance or non-proximity, and *the* is neutral with respect to distance); and Anderson and Keenan (1985) comment that a demonstrative system with only one term "would be little different from a definite article". But there are good reasons for rejecting this view.

English *that* is sometimes neutral with respect to distance or person, as when used pronominally in relative constructions:[8]

(63)   She prefers her biscuits to **those** I make.

(64)   I want a coat like **that** described in the book.

Taking the deictic opposition to be expressed by a feature [± Prox], then either these demonstrative occurrences do not carry this feature, or the negative value [− Prox] characterizing *that* and *those* can include neutrality with respect to distance. On the assumption that *the* too is either unmarked for [± Prox] or redundantly [− Prox], there must be some other feature distinguishing *the* and *that*.

More striking evidence is afforded by languages which have a demonstrative unmarked for any deictic contrast which is either the only form in the system or is distinct in form from the terms which are deictically marked. Egyptian Arabic has basically a one-demonstrative system with no deictic contrast: *da* 'this' or 'that'

---

[8] Stockwell, Schachter and Partee (1973) regard *that* and *those* in such sentences as forms of the definite article rather than demonstratives, because of a supposed complementary distribution between these forms and the usual simple definite form – *that* and *those* occurring with mass and plural value before a post-nominal modifier, and *the one* occurring with singular count nouns. They would disallow *the ones* for *those* in (63) and *that* (as opposed to *the one*) in (64), but they are simply mistaken in this. The claim of complementary distribution fails particularly clearly in the case of plurals like (63), where *the ones* and *those* are equally acceptable. Stockwell, Schachter and Partee do have a point as regards singulars like (64), for which the distribution they present does represent the general tendency; and there is no obviously simple definite alternative to *that* relating to a mass noun phrase (as in *I prefer this butter to that you got from the market*), unless we propose that the "free relative" *what* is this alternative (*I prefer this butter to what you got from the market*). But the fact that the complementary distribution claimed is only partial and optional indicates that an analysis in which the demonstrative forms really are demonstratives cannot be ruled out. But if we take the forms in (63)–(64) to be true demonstratives, it is evident that they do not express any degree of distance or association with person.

19

(Mitchell 1962). There are ways of indicating the relative distance of an object from the speaker, but such information is not lexicalized in the demonstrative system. But *da* is not a definite article; Egyptian Arabic has a definite article *ʔil*, distinct from the demonstrative. Another case is French, where distance is expressed by a suffix *-ci* or *-là* on the noun, so that the information usually thought of as belonging to the demonstrative is divided between two morphemes: *ce bateau-ci* 'this boat', *ce bateau-là* 'that boat'. But this suffix can be freely omitted, so that no information about distance is conveyed: *ce bateau* 'this/that boat'. But again, *ce* is still distinct, in form and meaning, from the definite article *le*.[9]

So deixis is a usual but not invariant property of demonstratives. There must be some other property, then, that distinguishes them from the definite article. Let us call it [± Dem].[10] So *this/these* is [+ Def, + Dem, + Prox]. Views differ very widely, however, on what the [± Dem] distinction amounts to; put differently, writers who agree that demonstratives have some distinctive property apart from deixis are divided on what it is.[11] Hawkins (1978) claims that demonstratives are distinguished by a "matching constraint", which instructs the hearer to match the referent with some identifiable object, that is, some object which is visible in the context or known on the basis of previous discourse. This constraint captures the observation that, whereas with a simple definite the referent may be inferrable on the basis of knowledge of the world (as in (65), cars being known to have engines), with a demonstrative the referent must be given in the linguistic or non-linguistic context – thus the impossibility of (66):

(65)   I got into the car and turned on **the engine**.

(66)   *I got into the car and turned on **this/that engine**.

Hawkins's matching constraint looks rather like identifiability, though a more restricted notion of identifiability than is involved in definiteness. See also Maclaran

---

[9] Harris (1977, 1980) argues that *ce* is rivalling *le* as definite article, the latter form tending to become an unmarked determiner with the function of carrying agreement features (number and gender), but this process is certainly not complete yet. The sentences *Passe-moi le marteau* 'Pass me the hammer' and *Passe-moi un marteau* 'Pass me a hammer', in immediate situation use, show the same contrast as the English glosses.

[10] The conclusion that the deictic content of demonstratives that have it is not what distinguishes them from the definite article becomes inescapable in view of the fact, which will emerge in Chapter 2, that there are languages in which non-demonstrative definite articles show these deictic distinctions.

[11] It is important to be aware of a certain variation in the literature in the use of the term "deixis". I have been using it here to denote the distinctions of proximity to the speaker or association with a particular person which make it possible to locate entities in the context of utterance relative to others. But the term is also often used to denote the basic property common to all demonstratives, the property expressed here by the feature [+ Dem]. On this use, "deictic" is equivalent to "demonstrative", being applied to forms which "point out".

(1982) for a modified version of this account. The position I adopt here is that a demonstrative signals that the identity of the referent is immediately accessible to the hearer, without the inferencing often involved in interpreting simple definites. This may be because the work of referent identification is being done for the hearer by the speaker, for example by pointing to the referent. The deictic feature typically expressed on a demonstrative plays a similar role to pointing, guiding the hearer's attention to the referent. This suggests a necessary connection between [+ Dem] and [+ Def], the former implying the latter. I take demonstratives, then, to be necessarily definite.

very imp.

1.2.3 *Proper nouns*

The term "proper noun", or "proper name", is applied to a very heterogeneous set of expressions, including *John*, *The Arc de Triomphe*, *South Farm Road*, some of which have internal grammatical structure and contain descriptive elements, and some of which do not. I limit my attention here to names like *John* and *Paris*, which (though they have an etymology) are not generally thought of as having any descriptive semantic content, or as having any meaning independent of the entity they name. The name *Paris* is applied to a particular city, but tells us nothing about that city; of course we would normally expect the bearer of the name *John* to be male, but it is argued that this is not part of the meaning of the name. By contrast, the common noun *man*, in being applicable to a particular individual, is so in virtue of the fact that that individual satisfies certain descriptive criteria (being human, male, adult). Proper nouns are often said to be referring expressions but to have no sense. They are also sometimes said to be logically equivalent to definite descriptions, in being uniquely referring expressions.

There may be millions of people called *John* and there are several towns called *Paris*, so context is important for the identification of the referent, as with definite descriptions. But a common view is that we use proper nouns as if they were absolutely unique, corresponding more closely to inherently unique definites (like *the sun*) than to possibly contextually unique definites (like *the man*). When we are conscious of there being more than one possible referent for the name *John* we can either expand it to a fuller proper noun (*John Smith*) or recategorize it as a common noun and add some descriptive material (*the John I introduced you to last night*). I shall assume this to be correct as an outline of how proper nouns are used; for a detailed and clear discussion of the complexities of proper nouns see J. Lyons (1977: 177–229).

It is clear that the uniqueness of reference of proper nouns is what aligns them with definites, though it may be added that this very uniqueness will generally ensure the identifiability of their referent. But a number of questions arise at this point. How do proper nouns differ from inherently unique nouns like *sun*? They

21

have in common that they are both generally used as though they denote a unique entity, but they differ grammatically: *sun* behaves like a common noun in that it takes the article, or some other definite determiner (*the sun, that lucky old sun*); *John*, unless recategorized, generally does not, and in fact is not only a noun, but also a complete noun phrase. One answer is that nouns like *sun* denote singleton sets, while proper nouns denote individuals; this would be in keeping with the view that proper nouns have reference but not sense. Another, implying that proper nouns do have sense, is that both types of noun denote singleton sets, but in the case of *sun* the set just happens to have only one member, while the set satisfying *John* is by definition a single-member set.

This latter proposal goes some way towards answering the question why proper nouns in English do not take the definite article. If by definition they denote a singleton set, there is no need to signal the uniqueness of their referent. But are they then in fact definite, or merely semantically similar in some way to definite noun phrases? In other words, is the feature [+ Def] present in proper nouns, and if so, where? If proper nouns are [+ Def], this feature would appear to be on the noun, given the lack of a determiner. But it seems to be clearly a determiner feature in common noun phrases. It would be preferable to be able to say that the definiteness feature occurs in one place only, and in general the determiner seems the most probable locus (unless we say a grammatical feature can have its locus in a phrasal category, so that it is the noun phrase, not the noun or the determiner, which carries [± Def]). If we assume that the feature [+ Def] pertains only to determiners, it may be that proper nouns are accompanied by a phonetically null determiner, or that the feature does not after all appear on proper nouns. One proposal along these lines is Lyons (1995c), where it is argued that proper nouns in English are in fact indefinites, and their apparently definite behaviour comes from their being generics – generic noun phrases anyway (whether definite or indefinite) showing similar distributional behaviour to definite non-generics. This idea will be taken up again in Chapter 4.

In a number of languages, at least some types of proper noun (most typically personal names) do regularly take the definite article. Examples are Classical Greek (*ho Sōkratēs* 'Socrates', *hē Hellas* 'Greece'), Catalan (*l'Eduard, la Maria*). It may be that these names should be treated as no different from uniques like English *the sun* – and thus unlike English proper nouns. It is clear that they are definite noun phrases, with [+ Def] encoded in the determiner.

1.2.4   Possessives

Under this heading I include determiners like *my, their* (together with their pronominal forms *mine, theirs*), and also "genitive" forms like *Fred's, the woman's, that man next door's*. These genitives are clearly full noun phrases, and the *'s* ending (which may be a genitive case morpheme or a postposition, among other possibilities) appears right at the end of the whole phrase. Possessives like *my* are also formed from noun phrases, since they are derived from personal pronouns. These possessive forms of noun phrases occur as modifying expressions within other noun phrases, as illustrated in (67), where each of the bracketed expressions is a noun phrase (or a derivative of a noun phrase):

(67) a. [[my] cousin]
b. [[Fred's] only friend]
c. [[that man next door's] car]

Now, in English at least, possessives render the noun phrase which contains them definite, as shown by the diagnostics introduced in 1.2.1. And the phrases in (67) could be roughly paraphrased by the expressions *the son/daughter of my aunt and uncle, the only friend Fred has, the car belonging to that man next door* – clearly definite noun phrases, beginning indeed with the definite article.[12] The same applies to many other languages; as a further example, with a different word-order

---

[12] It might be supposed that what makes these noun phrases definite is that the noun phrase underlying the possessive expression (*me, Fred, that man next door* in (67)) is definite – the definiteness of the embedded noun phrase is somehow transferred to the matrix noun phrase. Precisely this explanation has been offered by a number of writers for the definiteness of the corresponding structures in Semitic languages; we will return to this in Chapter 3. This would mean that if an indefinite noun phrase (such as *a woman*) were made the basis of the possessive (thus *a woman's*), the matrix noun phrase (*a woman's drink* for example) would be indefinite. And this may seem to be the case, since such noun phrases occur fairly readily after existential *there is/are*:

(i)   There's a woman's drink on the shelf here.

But this impression is mistaken. Noun phrases like *a visitor's hat, a friend of mine's cousin*, containing an indefinite possessive, are definite, and are naturally paraphrased by the clearly definite *the hat of a visitor, the cousin of a friend of mine*. The impression of indefiniteness comes from the fact that examples like *a woman's drink* are structurally ambiguous, as indicated in (ii)–(iii), where the possessive phrase is bracketed:

(ii)   a [woman's] drink

(iii)   [a woman's] drink

The structure we are interested in here is the one in (iii), where the possessive is the indefinite *a woman's*. The matrix noun phrase is definite, natural paraphrases being *the drink belonging to a woman, the drink left behind by a woman*, etc. In (ii) the possessive expression *woman's* is probably not a full noun phrase, and is therefore not indefinite. The indefinite article *a* is not part of the possessive expression, but is a modifier of the matrix noun phrase and accounts for its indefiniteness. The sense of (ii) is something like 'a drink suitable for women'. For a detailed discussion of this distinction between "inner genitives" (as in (ii)) and "outer genitives" (as in (iii)) see Woisetschlaeger (1983). The observation stands, then, that in English a possessive noun phrase, whether itself definite or indefinite, renders its matrix noun phrase definite.

pattern, consider Irish, in which possessives derived from pronouns appear pre-nominally (*mo/do hata* 'my/your hat'), and those based on "full noun phrases" are genitive case forms occurring to the right of the head noun (*hata an fhir* (hat the+GEN man+GEN) 'the man's hat'). In neither case can the head noun be modified by the definite article (**an mo hata*, **an hata an fhir*), yet the matrix noun phrase must be understood as definite; these examples are equivalent to 'the hat belonging to me/you/the man'. But in many other languages possessives do not impose a definite interpretation on the matrix noun phrase. Italian has only pronoun-derived possessive determiners (*mio* 'my' etc.); possession with full noun phrases is expressed prepositionally (*il libro di Carlo* (the book of Carlo) 'Carlo's book') – a structure which does not seem to impose definiteness in any language. Now the Italian translation of the definite *my book* is *il mio libro* (the my book), in which the definiteness is conveyed by the article *il*; this article may indeed be replaced by the indefinite article *un*, and the matrix is then indefinite: *un mio libro* (a my book) 'a book of mine'. The point is that the presence of the possessive *mio* has no bearing on whether the matrix noun phrase is definite or indefinite. The situation is similar in Classical Greek, which uses genitive case forms for full noun phrase possessives. To express the definite 'the man's horse', the possessive noun phrase 'the man's' (itself definite and therefore having the definite article) is preceded by the article which renders the matrix noun phrase definite, with the result that two articles occur in sequence: *ho tou andros hippos* (the+NOM the+GEN man+GEN horse+NOM).

This difference between English and Irish on the one hand and Italian and Greek on the other is discussed by Lyons (1985, 1986a), in terms of a typological distinction between "DG languages" (English, Irish) and "AG languages" (Italian, Greek).[13] The difference between the two types is claimed to reside in the structural position occupied by the possessive; what it amounts to essentially is that in DG languages possessives appear in a position reserved for the definite article and other definite determiners, but in AG languages they are in adjectival or some other position. This claim is controversial, and I shall return to a more detailed discussion of it. For the moment we can say that in some languages a possessive induces definiteness in the matrix noun phrase while in other languages it does not. The traditional assumption that possessives are definite determiners, stated without further comment in many descriptive grammars and in much recent theoretical work – presumably because possession is assumed to entail definiteness – is misguided. It reflects a lack of awareness of the AG phenomenon. We have seen above that

[13] "DG" and "AG" stand for "determiner-genitive" and "adjectival-genitive", respectively (though it is not claimed that possessives are necessarily determiners in the first type and adjectives in the second).

[+ Dem] is always accompanied by [+ Def], apparently because demonstrativeness is semantically incompatible with indefiniteness. But this is not the case with possession.[14] We shall return to the "definite constraint" on possessives in DG languages in Chapters 3 and 8.

There is one circumstance in which this definite constraint can be suspended, at least in some DG languages; this is when the noun phrase is in predicative position:

(68)   Mary is **Ann's friend**.

(69)   I was once **Professor Laserbeam's student**.

The noun phrases indicated may be understood as either definite or indefinite. There is not necessarily any implication that Ann has only one friend and Professor Laserbeam has only had one student; rather, the bold phrases in (68) and (69) are likely to be interpreted as equivalent to *a friend of Ann* and *a student of Professor Laserbeam*. But notice that this same interpretation is possible even where the predicative noun phrase with possessive modifier is marked as definite by the article: *I was once the student of Professor Laserbeam.*[15]

There is also a use of non-predicative noun phrases with possessive modification which cannot be characterized as either inclusive or identifiable:

---

[14] This is easily demonstrated, even limiting the discussion to DG data. Note first that possessives do not necessarily express possession in the sense of ownership. The phrases *John's house, John's club, John's annoyance, John's son* may mean 'the house John lives in', 'the club John is a member of', 'the annoyance John feels', 'the boy John has fathered'. Possessives express merely that there is a relationship of some kind between two entities (represented by the possessive noun phrase and the "possessum" – the matrix noun phrase). The nature of that relationship may be dictated lexically by the head noun, if it is relational or a body part for example; or it may be determined pragmatically, the context and background determining whether *John's team* is the team John owns, the team John supports, or the team John plays in. Now, assume for the sake of argument that *John's car* is 'the car belonging to John' and *John's team* is 'the team John supports'. If "possession" is semantically incompatible with indefiniteness in the possessum, the phrases *a car belonging to John* and *a team John supports* should be semantically anomalous. But they are not. In fact English has a possessive construction which can be indefinite, the "postposed possessive"; *a car of John's, a team of John's*. So the fact that a prehead possessive in English imposes a definite interpretation on the matrix noun phrase has nothing to do with the semantics of possession.

[15] This phenomenon is probably to be distinguished from the ambiguity as regards definiteness of predicative possessives with no overt possessum. In *That pen is mine, mine* is either merely the predicative form of *my* or a pronoun. If it is the latter, it is a definite noun phrase ('That pen is the one belonging to me') because the definite constraint applies to possessive pronouns. If it is the former, then the definite constraint does not apply, because the possessive is not part of a noun phrase ('That pen belongs to me'). In Spanish these two readings would be clearly distinguished, and indeed the definiteness of the pronoun clearly marked by the article: *Esa pluma es **mía*** (predicative non-pronominal possessive), *Esa pluma es **la mía*** (pronominal possessive).

(70)   I'm going to stay with **my brother** for a few days.

(71)   Joe has broken **his leg**.

(72)   Oh, I've just torn **my sleeve** on that bramble.

There is no implication in these sentences that the speaker has only one brother and Joe only one leg, or that the hearer is in a position to tell which of the speaker's sleeves has been torn. In all these cases, an indefinite (*a brother of mine*) or a partitive (*one of my sleeves*) could have been used, but the definite structure is usually preferred. The referent is in each case one of a small number (people have only two legs or sleeves, and generally a limited number of brothers), and it is perhaps unimportant which of this number is at issue; nevertheless, neither inclusiveness nor identifiability applies. Since true indefinites can be used, there is no reason to consider the bold noun phrases in (70)–(72) to be indefinite. It seems rather that what we are dealing with here is definite noun phrases used where the conditions for definiteness do not strictly hold. This use is limited to noun phrases where the head noun is one of a small lexical class denoting mainly body parts, clothing, and family and other personal relationships – thus, inalienable and other intimate possession. It is not at all clear what lies behind these facts, but what makes them interesting is that they are not specific to English. Compare the following French example:

(73)   Jacques s'est cassé la jambe.
         'Jacques has broken his leg.'

In fact this example does not contain a possessive, French generally using the definite article and a dative pronominal form to express possession with body parts (thus literally 'Jacques has broken to himself the leg'). The point is made all the more clearly here, given the definite article, that the "possessed" body part, though not unique or identifiable, is referred to by a definite noun phrase.

1.2.5 *Personal pronouns*

The personal pronouns are traditionally so called because they express grammatical person, but they have also long been recognized as definite and are often referred to as "definite pronouns" (by contrast with indefinite pronouns like *one* and *someone*). Postal (1970) proposes to account for the definiteness of personal pronouns by deriving them transformationally from definite articles, and I will adopt the essence of this account, though with some modifications first proposed in C. Lyons (1977).

Such an account has obvious attractions. In general English pronouns are part of determiner–pronoun pairs; so *this, that, one, some, all, each, several* and numerous other items can occur both pre-nominally (as determiners) and independently (as pronouns). Two obvious exceptions to this are the definite article, which only occurs as a determiner (*Pass me the book*, but **Pass me the*), and third-person personal pronouns, which are always pronominal (*Pass me it*, but **Pass me it book*). A neat solution to this oddity would be to pair these together, and say that *he, she, it* and *they* are the pronominal correlatives of the determiner *the* (which is therefore third person). This idea is strongly supported by the observation that the first- and second-person plural pronouns *we* and *you* also occur pre-nominally:

(74) a. **We Europeans** are experiencing some strange weather patterns.
  b. I don't trust **you politicians** an inch.

So *we* and *you* can be regarded as forms of the definite article, differing from *the* only in respect to person, but occurring both as determiners and as pronouns; suppletive variation is limited to the third person. In the singular, *you* does not occur freely as a determiner (**You linguist are relying on some pretty odd data*), but it is so used in exclamations: *You idiot!, You lucky bastard!*. The first-person singular pronoun does not occur at all in English pre-nominally (**I wish you'd leave me foreigner alone; *I idiot!*). I can suggest no reason for this restriction, but it is, at least in part, a language-specific fact; German permits both the exclamatory use and the more general use with *ich* 'I':

(75) Ich Esel!
  I donkey
  'Silly me!'

(76) Ich Vogelfänger bin bekannt bei Alt und Jung . . .
  I birdcatcher am known to old and young . . .

Postal derives pronouns from an underlying full noun phrase consisting of an article plus a minimal noun head (with the form *one* in English). The latter is generally deleted, but surfaces in the third person when the noun phrase contains a restrictive modifier:

(77) a. I met the one who/that Lucille divorced.
  b. I know the one with brown hair.
  c. I bought the green one.

The fact that normal third-person pronouns are (at least in colloquial standard) excluded with such modifiers (*?him who/that Lucille divorced, ?her with brown hair, *it green*), is further support for the analysis. The hypothetical noun *one* also shows up with first- and second-person articles in the presence of a preposed modifier: *us clever ones*.

  Contesting this account, Sommerstein (1972) points out that while *we* and *you* can be stressed or unstressed (with a reduced vowel) when used pronominally (thus [wiː] and [wɪ], [juː] and [jə]), when they are used as determiners they are always stressed and with a full vowel, except in the exclamatory use. Thus the reduced form [jə] may occur in *You fool!*, but not in (74b). This ties in with the point made by Hawkins (1974) that pre-nominal *we* and *you* have as their third-person correlative, not *the*, but demonstratives, because of distributions like the following:[16]

(78) a.   the strongest/only soldiers in the army
     b.   *we/you/these strongest/only soldiers in the army

The point that personal pronouns often have more in common with demonstratives than with *the* is taken up by C. Lyons (1977), who argues that Postal is basically right but that the English personal pronouns are forms both of the definite article and of the [− Prox] demonstrative. This claim is based on a case of complementary distribution between demonstratives and third-person pronouns.

Is this the case in ʋraⁿ

The various uses and forms of English demonstrative pronouns must first be distinguished. There are two kinds of anaphoric use, **strict anaphora** as in (79), where the demonstrative is coreferential with a previously occurring noun phrase, and **identity of sense anaphora** as in (80), where there is no coreference but the previously occurring noun phrase supplies the understood descriptive content of the demonstrative.

(79)   Jim finally found a flat with a view over the park, and bought **that (one)**.

(80)   I could never follow our first coursebook, and I'm glad we now use **this one**.

Then there is the non-anaphoric use, typically indicating something in the immediate situation. In fact the identity of sense example (80) is also situational, in that the demonstrative gets its reference from the immediate situation, but we need to distinguish this from non-anaphoric situational uses like the following:

(81)   Bring **that** along with you.

One only appears in singular count use, where it is near-obligatory in identity of sense use, optional in strict anaphoric use, and absent in non-anaphoric use. Now,

---

[16] Hawkins's claim is that noun phrases like *we soldiers* are appositive structures, consisting of a pronoun with a full noun phrase in apposition with it. This is also the position of Delorme and Dougherty (1972), who see *we men* as identical in structure with *we, the men*, the only difference being that the appositive noun phrase is indefinite, with the zero determiner normal in plural indefinites. They point out that Postal's account fails to explain the impossibility of singular **I boy*, which falls out naturally on their analysis since *boy* is not a possible singular indefinite noun phrase. But their own analysis fails equally to account for the impossibility (in standard English) of *they men*.

the forms without *one* – *this, that, these, those* – in non-anaphoric and strict anaphoric use can only have non-human reference (while *these/those* can be human in identity of sense use). Human reference in sentences like (79) and (81) would be made by stressed *him, her* or *them*. The claim is that these pronouns used in this way are forms of a demonstrative. Further evidence comes from the following paradigms; the noun phrases are to be understood as non-anaphoric, and the capitalized forms as stressed:

(82) a.   Take a look at the car/teacher.
     b.   Take a look at him.
     c.   Take a look at her.
     d.   Take a look at it.
     e.   Take a look at them.

(83) a.   *Take a look at THE car/teacher.
     b.   Take a look at HIM.
     c.   Take a look at HER.
     d.   *Take a look at IT.
     e.   Take a look at THEM.

THE and *IT* here are replaced by *that* (or *this*). Moreover, in standard English, *THEM* must be human, and for non-human reference would be replaced by *those* (or *these*). There is thus a neat complementary distribution between third-person personal pronouns and demonstratives, the latter filling certain gaps in stressed occurrences of the former.[17]

The conclusion is that the third-person pronouns *he, she, it, they*, when unstressed, represent pronominal forms of the definite article, but in addition some of them, when stressed, also represent forms of a demonstrative. Since they do not encode any degree of distance or proximity to any person, these demonstrative forms can be regarded as belonging to the deictically unmarked, or perhaps [– Prox], demonstrative already identified for English in 1.2.2. The forms of this demonstrative are, then, in the third person: singular pre-nominal *that*; singular pronominal *he, she, that*; plural pre-nominal *those*; plural pronominal *they* (human), *those* (non-human). Turning to first- and second-person pronouns, it is natural to conclude that the stressed forms of these are also demonstrative – first- and second-

---

[17] *The* and *it* are both capable of bearing stress, to express contrast, for example, as in *I'm THE owner of this house, not one of the owners* and *I just met Julia walking her poodle; SHE looked fed up, but IT was chirpy enough.* What is impossible is the kind of demonstrative stress likely to be accompanied by pointing or some equivalent gesture appropriate to (83).

Among other qualifications to the pattern observed is the fact that *this* and *that* do occur with human reference in subject position in copular sentences: *Who's this?, That's Jill's husband.* But this exception may be only apparent because *it* is used in the same way, suggesting that a demonstrative used in this way is neuter: *Who is it?, It's Jill's husband.*

person forms of the non-deictic demonstrative – while the unstressed forms are simple definite. And the demonstrative-like behaviour of pre-nominal *we* and *you*, shown in (78), is straightforwardly accounted for; these too are demonstrative, the corresponding third-person form being *those*.[18] I take personal pronouns generally, then, to be determiners. When unstressed they are forms of a definite article, and in some, but probably not all, stressed occurrences they are forms of a demonstrative.

What distinguishes personal pronouns from full definite (or demonstrative) noun phrases is their lack of descriptive content (beyond partly descriptive grammatical features like gender in some forms). A pronoun is therefore used, in general, where the associated descriptive content can be readily recovered from the discourse or the non-linguistic context. But there is much more to pronouns than this, and their grammar is enormously complex, involving some of the most central issues in syntactic theory. The theory of **binding** sets out the anaphoric possibilities of different types of noun phrase, dividing these into three categories accounted for by three binding principles. Reflexive pronouns (like *myself*, *themselves*) and reciprocals (like *each other*) are handled by Principle A, which says that these expressions (labelled **anaphors**) must be "bound" by an antecedent, and that the anaphor and its antecedent must both appear within a particular syntactic domain, called the anaphor's "governing category". The governing category is typically the minimal clause, but it may sometimes be a noun phrase or other phrase, and can be a complex clause; in the simplest cases, an anaphor and its antecedent must be in the same minimal clause (thus ***The gangster*** *shot* ***himself***, but *****The gangster** *is afraid the police will shoot* ***himself***). Ordinary personal pronouns are the second category of nominal expression, and Principle B says they may be bound by an antecedent but need not be, and if they are the antecedent cannot be in their "governing category". Thus, in *The gangster shot him*, the pronoun *him* may take its reference from some noun phrase occurring earlier in the discourse, but *the gangster*, which is in the same minimal clause, cannot function as its antecedent. Principle C is concerned with all remaining referential noun phrases (full noun phrases essentially), and these are not subject to binding. We have seen, of course, that definite full noun phrases may be anaphoric, but it is important to realize that binding is a technical concept defined partly in terms of structural configuration;

---

[18] There are gaps in the paradigms of the deictically neutral or [– Prox] demonstrative and of the definite article, for these plural forms as well as for *I* and singular *you*. *We* cannot occur in the exclamatory use: *You fools!* but **We fools!*. And in non-exclamatory uses the pre-nominal simple definite article only occurs in the third person: **The linguist(s)** but (with unstressed pronunciation of the determiner) **I/you/we linguist(s)*. By contrast, in their pronominal use *I*, *you* and *we* show the full range of occurrence available to the third-person forms, and can appear with full or reduced pronunciation fairly freely.

it does not just mean "having an antecedent".[19] For an accessible account of the binding theory, see Haegeman (1994: chapter 4).

Work on the semantics of pronouns has identified further complexities in their behaviour which might be taken to argue against their being merely determiners without the descriptive content found in full noun phrases. As well as the straightforward referential uses of pronouns in which they get their reference either from a linguistic antecedent or from the situation, we can distinguish the **bound-variable** use, the **E-type** use, and the **lazy** use. For discussion of these and of the semantics of pronouns more generally see Cooper (1979), Hausser (1979), Evans (1980), Reinhart (1983). Bound variable pronouns are dependent on (or "bound" by) a quantifying expression (such as one expressible in terms of the logician's universal quantification), and, though singular, do not have a specific referent but rather denote a range of individuals. For example:

(84)   **Every girl** thinks **she** should learn to drive.

(85)   **Every student** thinks **they** have passed the exam.

Note that *they* in (85) is the vague singular use, becoming increasingly common nowadays where the antecedent is of mixed gender. These examples are anaphoric in that the pronoun has an antecedent, *every girl* and *every student*, but this antecedent defines a range of entities and the pronoun refers to each of these individually. E-type pronouns are similar, but the antecedent of the pronoun is itself a variable bound by a quantifier, and the configurational relationship between pronoun and antecedent is not the one defining binding (because the antecedent does not **c-command** the pronoun: for explanations of c-command see Radford (1988: chapter 3) and Haegeman (1994: chapter 2)):

(86)   **Every man** who bought **a car** crashed **it**.

Lazy pronouns are so called because they relate somewhat sloppily to an antecedent, agreeing with it in descriptive content rather than referential identity:

---

[19] It is nevertheless important not to overstate the difference between personal pronouns and full definite noun phrases. There is in fact a class of full definite noun phrases sometimes termed "epithets", typically with affective content showing something of the speaker's attitude to the referent, with behaviour resembling that of third-person personal pronouns:

   (i)   Finally **John** arrived, and you could see **he** was pleased with himself.

   (ii)   Finally **John** arrived, and you could see **the lad/bastard/little darling** was pleased with himself.

The inherent definiteness of personal pronouns may, in fact, be an important factor in their behaviour as regards binding.

31

(87)   I keep **my car** in the garage but my next-door neighbour keeps **it** in his drive.

The pronoun *it* here refers, of course, to my neighbour's car, not mine. But most of these uses are not, in fact, restricted to pronouns. Kempson (1988) shows that full definite noun phrases can have the bound-variable and E-type uses:

(88)   Of **every house** in the area that was inspected, it was subsequently reported that **the house** was suffering from subsidence problems.

(89)   **Everyone** who bought **a house** discovered too late that **the house** was riddled with damp.

The lazy use seems to be a purely pronominal phenomenon,[20] but otherwise personal pronouns are strongly parallel in behaviour and range of use to definite full noun phrases. The claim stands that pronouns are definite noun phrases minus the description – thus determiners.

1.2.6   *Universal quantifiers*

Determiners like *all*, *every* and *each* can be thought of as approximating to universal quantification in logic. In fact these determiners differ in important ways from the logician's universal quantifier, and from each other, but this need not concern us here. For discussion see McCawley (1981: 98–101). It seems obvious that the behaviour of these expressions in the diagnostics in 1.2.1, aligning them with definites, is to be related to inclusiveness, since they express totality, either within a context or absolutely.

It is to be noticed, however, that some other determiners which do not express totality show similar behaviour to *all* etc. in at least some of the diagnostic environments:

(90) a.   Strong as **most** contestants are, they can't shift it.
     b.   **Most** hats are yours.
     c.   ?Are there **most** visitors here?

---

[20] Interestingly, in Kempson's discussion this use, peculiar to pronouns, is paralleled by a use peculiar to full definite noun phrases, the bridging cross-reference or associative anaphoric use discussed above in 1.1.2. Kempson does not suggest this, but it is tempting to argue that lazy pronouns are the pronominal equivalent of bridging cross-reference. Examples like the following suggest a case can be made for this view:

(i)   I glanced into **the kitchen** and saw that **the windows** were filthy; in **the bathroom**, on the other hand, **they** were quite clean.

The pronoun is interpreted, in terms of description, on the basis of the preceding noun phrase *the windows*. But while *they* refers to windows, it does not refer to the same windows; this is what makes it a lazy pronoun. It gets its reference from association with *the bathroom*, just as *the windows* gets its reference from association with *the kitchen*. The suggestion is, then, that *it* in (87) is similarly an associate of *my next-door neighbour*. But, being a pronoun, it also needs a full noun phrase "antecedent" to permit recovery of the description to be assigned to its referent; *my car* serves this function.

32

What *most* has in common with *all* is that it expresses a proportion of some whole – as indeed does *the* if it is inclusive. This has led to the suggestion that the inclusiveness of the definite article is one case of a broader concept of **quantification**, characterizing determiners which denote a proportion. This is an issue I will take up in Chapters 6 and 7.

1.3 Simple and complex indefinites

The article *a* is the obvious signal that a noun phrase is indefinite, but just as definites need not involve the definite article, so there are indefinites which do not contain the indefinite article. We here consider the range of indefinite noun phrase types, and look more closely at the indefinite article itself and its role in the expression of indefiniteness.

1.3.1 Indefiniteness and cardinality

An important question is whether indefiniteness is a function of the presence of certain indefinite determiners in a noun phrase, or whether it is simply a matter of the absence of definite determiners. The indefinite article *a* suggests the former, on the assumption that *a* encodes [− Def]; and of course *a* and *the* are mutually exclusive. But the object noun phrases in the following sentences are also indefinite, involving neither identifiability nor inclusiveness:

(91)   I bought **three books** this morning.

(92)   I wonder if Helen has read **many books**.

These indefinite noun phrases do not contain the indefinite article however. So perhaps they should be considered to be complex indefinites, with indefiniteness being signalled by some other determiner. Indeed determiners like *three* and *many* which denote **cardinality** – that is, a number or an amount, as opposed to a proportion – have been characterized as indefinite determiners. But it is clear that they do not encode [− Def]. Unlike *a*, they can co-occur with definite determiners:

(93)   Pass me **those three books**.

(94)   I've only read a few of **the many books** she's written.

These cardinality terms are obviously neutral with respect to (in)definiteness. There are some determiners which only appear in indefinite noun phrases; *some* and *enough* are examples, and these could reasonably be categorized, together with *a*, as indefinite determiners. But what makes the noun phrases in (91)–(92) indefinite is the absence of any definite determiner. Notice also that count nouns in the plural and mass nouns can occur without any determiner, and are then (at least where not interpreted generically) indefinite:

Basic observations

(95)   John has gone out to buy **milk**.

(96)   I've already put **spoons** on the table.

The indefinite article *a* only occurs, in fact, in singular count noun phrases – an
odd limitation – and this has led many grammarians to suppose that its place is
taken in examples like (95)–(96) by a "zero" variant of the indefinite article. But
notice that even singular indefinite count noun phrases do not necessarily take *a*:
one orange. This is not because *one* is an indefinite determiner; it is a cardinality term like *three* and *many*, and, like them, can appear in definite noun phrases:
the one orange, this one ticket. So the idea that there is in English a zero plural
and mass indefinite article finds little support; the reality seems to be that a noun
phrase is indefinite if it has no definite determiner, whether or not it has an indefinite
determiner. Another determiner traditionally regarded as being a plural and mass
variant of *a*, or at least as complementing *a*, is *some*. In fact it is necessary to distinguish stressed *some*, with a full vowel, from a form which is usually (though
probably not always) unstressed and with reduced vowel, thus pronounced [səm]
– and often represented for convenience as *sm* (a convention I shall adopt). *Some*
can occur with singular count nouns (*There's some man at the door*), and it is *sm*
which partially complements *a* and is reasonably taken to be an indefinite article.
But again, plural and mass noun phrases do not need to take *sm* to be indefinite,
as seen from (95)–(96) (and (91)–(92)).

In view of these facts, one must ask whether *a* and *sm* really are indefinite articles. They are not in full complementary distribution with definite determiners, since
we can have noun phrases with neither; in fact *a* does not co-occur with either
the definite article or with any numeral, though *the* and numerals can co-occur. There
is in fact good reason to classify *a* and *sm* as cardinality expressions. *A* is derived
historically from the same ancestral form as the numeral *one*, and while few writers
now recognize a synchronic link, an exception is Perlmutter (1970), who argues
that *a* is derived from *one* by a phonological rule of reduction operating in the
absence of stress. I prefer to regard *a* and *one* as distinct items, but if they are
assigned to the same lexical class (both being cardinality terms, perhaps even numerals), it is clear that there is a particularly close relationship between them.[21]

This position is strengthened by the fact that in many languages the semantic
equivalent of *a* is identical to the equivalent of *one*: German *ein*, French *un*, Turkish
bir. In these languages, although descriptive grammars do tend to make a distinction
between an indefinite article and a singular numeral, they are mainly distinguished

---

[21] There are many contexts in which they are interchangeable, with little difference of meaning:
a/one fifth, a/one mile away, a/one week from now, not a/one bit. A is also numeral-like in
only occurring with count nouns, though this is not true of *sm*, which aligns with vague cardinality terms like *much/many* rather than numerals.

34

by stress; it may be, therefore, that in these languages the "article" is merely the unstressed variant of the singular numeral. But the differences are more substantial in English, where *a* can be contrastively stressed and is then realized as [eɪ], not as *one*. I take *a*, therefore, to be a cardinality term, perhaps even a kind of numeral, but a distinct lexical item from *one*. I suggest that the semantic difference between them is that *one* is in contrast with *two*, *three* etc., while *a* is in contrast with 'more than one'. *A* thus encodes no more than [+ Sg], while *one* has some additional content besides. *Sm* can be thought of as expressing a vague quantity, but (if the noun is count) more than one; it may therefore stand in opposition to *a*, encoding [− Sg] (this specification applying both to plurals and, redundantly, mass noun phrases). But whereas *a* obligatorily accompanies singular indefinites in the absence of some other determiner, this is apparently not so of *sm* and non-singular indefinites.[22]

The treatment of *a* as a cardinality expression, closely related to *one*, while attractive, does leave unexplained the fact that it cannot co-occur with *the* or other definite determiners. Since numerals can follow these determiners, **the a house* or **this a car* should be possible. On Perlmutter's view that *a* is simply the unstressed form of *one*, one might claim that this numeral can only be unstressed and reduced when initial in the noun phrase, so that after another determiner the full form is appropriate; thus *the one house*, *this one car*. But *one* is purely optional here, whereas in the absence of a definite determiner a cardinality expression is obligatory in the singular, with *a* as the default form (the one that must occur if no other does). So for the Perlmutter analysis the problem is to explain why some cardinality expression is required if there is no definite determiner but optional otherwise. For my analysis the problem is to explain why a particular cardinality term, *a*, is obligatory

---

[22] The distribution of *sm* in relation to plural and mass noun phrases such as those in (95)–(96) is a complex and controversial matter. It has been claimed, by Carlson (1977), that *sm* is the plural correlate of *a*, and the "bare plural" (as in (96)) is something radically different – not an alternative indefinite plural. We will return to a more detailed discussion of this in Chapter 4, and for the present it will suffice to note that in some contexts a plural or mass noun phrase may occur either in bare form or with *sm* with little difference in meaning, whereas in other contexts there may be a more substantial difference. Consider the following:

(i)   I'm looking for a record.

(ii)   I'm looking for sm records.

(iii)   I'm looking for records.

Sentence (i) is ambiguous between a reading on which the speaker is looking for a particular record and one on which she does not have a particular record in mind. Pairs of readings of this sort, commonly available with indefinites, are termed **specific** and **non-specific**, respectively. Turning to the plurals, the same ambiguity appears in (ii). But (iii) is different: here, with the bare plural, the specific reading, that the speaker has particular records in mind that she hopes to find, is either unavailable or at least difficult to get.

with singulars in the absence of any other determiner but impossible after a determiner. *The* and *a* are both phonologically weak forms, and this shared characteristic can be taken to reflect their both being the unmarked or basic members of their respective classes; *the* is the basic definite determiner and *a* is the basic cardinality determiner. These basic items act as default forms. A definite noun phrase must normally contain a definite determiner, and *the* is the one that occurs in the absence of some other with more semantic content. Indefinite noun phrases are characterized by the non-occurrence of a definite determiner, but both definites and indefinites should normally contain, in principle, an expression of cardinality. The fact that this can be dispensed with much more easily in plural and mass noun phrases may be related to the fact that plurals do have an expression of cardinality in the plural inflection on the noun, and cardinality is intrinsically less central, if indeed relevant at all, to mass expressions. With singulars, since the noun carries no number inflection, a cardinality determiner is in principle required, and *a* is the default form. But I suggest the issue is complicated by a phonological constraint that weak forms can only occur initially in the phrase.[23] The result is that in definites the initial definite determiner blocks the expected appearance of *a* in second, cardinality, position.

The basic, unmarked nature of *the* and *a*, with their minimal semantic content ([+ Def] and [+ Sg] respectively), reflected in their phonological weakness and default behaviour, I shall take to be what defines the term **article**. *The* is, then, the **definite article**, and I adopt the label **cardinal article** for *a* and *sm*. Notice though that the suggested phonological constraint blocking the appearance of *a* and *sm* after another determiner ensures that these items only appear in indefinite noun phrases. For this reason they can be said to signal indefiniteness indirectly. An article that does this, while not itself encoding [– Def], I shall describe by the further label **quasi-indefinite article**.

1.3.2 Complex indefinites

I use the term "complex indefinite", informally, to denote noun phrases in which some determiner other than one of the quasi-indefinite articles seems to compel indefiniteness and render a definite determiner impossible. Cardinality terms other than *a* and *sm* tend to be compatible with definiteness as well as indefiniteness. But there are some cardinality expressions which show either a strong preference for indefiniteness (*several*) or incompatibility with definiteness (*enough*). *Several* is rarely used in company with a definite determiner (*the several trees*, *those several visitors*), but such sequences are not impossible and it

---

[23] The major exception to this is that "pre-determiners" such as *all* and *half* can occur before articles: *all the way*, *half an hour*.

may be simply that the meaning of *several* is such that it occurs more commonly in indefinites. But *enough* is incompatible with definiteness (**the enough sugar*, **those enough cups*).[24]

There are other determiners which are not self-evidently cardinality expressions and which occur only in indefinite noun phrases. Most prominent in this group are *some* (as distinct from *sm*) and *any*. These determiners are traditionally labelled "indefinite", and indeed must be serious candidates for consideration as encoding [– Def]. We shall see that determiners corresponding closely to these are identifiable cross-linguistically, many languages showing indefinite expressions forming a cline of specificity. We have observed that English *a* and *sm* can be specific or non-specific, and we will discuss *some* below in relation to this distinction. But it is clear that *any* expresses a kind of extreme non-specificity, in which the speaker does not merely have no particular entity in mind corresponding to the description, but does not care what is taken to satisfy the predicate. To express specificity unambiguously English has *a certain*, but there seems to be no reason to see this as a separate determiner. Rather, the adjective *certain* compels the specific interpretation available anyway to *a*.

Determiners in English can be used pronominally as well as pre-nominally, and we have seen in 1.2.5 that there can be substantial difference in shape between pronominal and pre-nominal forms. The pronoun corresponding to *a* is *one*, as illustrated by the following:[25]

---

[24] It is not obvious why this is so. A synonym such as *sufficient* does seem to be acceptable in a definite context (though barely), which suggests that the incompatibility is not entirely semantic. There may be some syntactic constraint peculiar to the item *enough* behind the restriction. This determiner is unique in being able to follow the noun (*enough money* or *money enough*), a characteristic shared by its German equivalent *genug*. Now *genug* (which is equally excluded from definite noun phrases) also has the peculiarity of being uninflected. There are some other cardinality determiners in German, such as *viel* 'much', 'many' and *wenig* 'little', 'few', which can occur pre-nominally either with or without the normal inflection: *viel-er Kummer* or *viel Kummer* 'a lot of trouble', *wenig-e Freude* or *wenig Freude* 'little joy'. But these cardinality terms must be inflected if preceded by a definite determiner: *der viele Kummer*, **der viel Kummer*; *die wenige Freude*, **die wenig Freude*. So the impossibility of *genug* after a definite determiner may be linked to its inability to take inflection. And this suggests the incompatibility with definiteness of *enough* may be an idiosyncratic syntactic property of this lexical item, left over from a constraint (similar to that in German) applying in an earlier stage of English when adjectives were inflected. This is speculation, and I will not pursue the point.

[25] Note that the *one* in (97) is distinct from that in (i):

(i)   I'm looking for a white hydrangea but I can only find a pink **one**.

Here *a pink one* is a complete noun phrase, with *a* as determiner and *one* as the head noun. This is the same minimal noun as in *the blue one* or *the one who Lucille divorced*, discussed above, and clearly has nothing to do with *a*. But if the *one* in (97) were this same minimal noun we would expect it to be preceded, like any count noun, by the article *a*; and this is impossible.

(97)   I'm looking for a white hydrangea but I can't find **one**.

Turning to *some* and *any*, these determiners, together with *sm*, can function pre-nominally and pronominally with no change in form, except that the pronominal form of *sm* is unreduced, thus *some*:

(98) a.   Joan met **some** man today.
     b.   Could you pass me **sm** broccoli, please?
     c.   I don't want **any** noise.

(99) a.   Give me **some**.
     b.   You haven't taken **any**.

But there are restrictions. Pronominal *some* can only be mass or plural, like *sm*; thus the occurrence in (99a) cannot be interpreted as singular count; pronominal *any* also tends to be mass and plural. Pronominal *some* and *any* are restricted to identity of sense anaphoric use.[26] In other functions they are replaced by fuller forms, *someone/somebody* and *anyone/anybody* for human reference (singular only), *something* and *anything* for non-human reference.[27]

But while *anyone* and *anything* clearly correspond as pronouns to the determiner *any*, it is not obvious whether *someone* and *something* correspond to *some* or *sm*. The fact that *someone* is singular count suggests it includes *some*, not *sm*; but there is a striking difference in interpretation between *someone* and *some*. *Some*, with a singular count noun, implies that the referent is unfamiliar to the speaker, thus non-specific, as the following make clear:

(100) a.   There's some book lying on the table.
      b.   ?I've spent the afternoon reading some book.

But *someone* and *something* show the same ambiguity with regard to specificity as *a* and *sm*:

---

[26] Sentence (97) illustrates identity of sense anaphora (see 1.2.5 above), which is a major use of indefinite pronouns. The anaphoric expression relates to an antecedent with which it shares descriptive content, but the two are not coreferential. Note that with identity of sense anaphora the "antecedent" can be provided by the non-linguistic context, as when Mary is silently offered cake and says *Yes, I'll have some* or *I don't want any, thanks*. This, of course, is not really anaphora, but rather a kind of immediate situation use; I will, however, continue to use the term loosely to cover such cases.

[27] These complex forms combine the determiner with a noun, but they cannot be regarded as full, non-pronominal, noun phrases which happen to be represented orthographically as single words. This is clear from the position of adjectives: *someone important*, not *some important one* (which would only occur as an identity of sense anaphoric use of *some*, not necessarily human); and *something big* as distinct from the equally possible but not synonymous full noun phrase *some big thing*.

(101) a.   I'm looking for someone/something – but she/it doesn't seem to be here.

      b.   I'm looking for someone/something – but I can't find anyone/anything I like.

Yet while *sm* is mass or plural, *someone* is singular, and *something* is singular or mass. So these pronouns do not correspond closely to either *some* or *sm*. They seem to correspond in fact to *sm* and *a* jointly. These articles between them cover the range singular, plural and mass; and they show the ambiguity between specific and non-specific. The fact that *someone* and *something* cannot be plural can be attributed to the incorporated noun.

The main uses of *any* and the pronouns based on it are illustrated by the following:

(102) a.   You can borrow **any** book you wish.

      b.   **Anyone** could paint a picture like that.

      c.   I'm not choosey; I'll eat **anything**.

(103) a.   Have you bought **any** vegetables?

      b.   I don't want **any** wine; I've drunk enough.

      c.   Have you had **anything** to eat?

      d.   I don't think John's in his room; at least, I can't hear **anyone**.

Sentences (102) illustrate what I shall term the "random" sense, indicating an unrestricted choice. Examples (103) show the use of *any* in interrogative and negative contexts (which we can term jointly "non-assertive" contexts), where it tends to be preferred to *sm*. Non-assertive *any* tends to be unstressed and may be reduced (with pronunciations like [n̩] or [nɪ], and similarly [n̩θɪŋ] etc.), while random *any* has to have some degree of stress and is phonologically full. But *sm* and related forms are also possible in non-assertive contexts, and, in particular, are perfectly good in interrogative sentences like (103a) and (103c). This suggests that non-assertive *any* may represent no more than a less emphatic use of random *any* rather than a distinct sense. On the other hand the two uses distinguished behave differently with regard to the diagnostic environments for definiteness; I illustrate this from the *there is/are* construction:

(104)   ??There is/are any book(s) in this library.

(105) a.   Are there any books in this library?

      b.   There aren't any books in this library.

Any is perfectly good in non-assertive sentences with *there is/are*, but in positive declarative sentences, like (104), where it must be given the random interpretation, it is of very low acceptability. This seems to indicate that only non-assertive *any* is indefinite, and random *any* definite, which would presumably mean we have two distinct senses, if not two distinct homophonous items. And this distinction correlates with another observation. *Any* seems to differ in position from cardinals in being able to precede numerals (*any three books*, *any one man*); but in this position (which could be definite determiner position) it can only have the random interpretation. So it may well be that random *any* is a definite determiner, occurring in the same "slot" as definites like *the* and *that*, while non-assertive *any* is a cardinality term, a variant of *a* and *sm* restricted to negative and interrogative contexts, occupying the same position in the noun phrase as other cardinals.

The discussion so far seems to leave the hypothesis that no determiner is specified [– Def], and that indefiniteness amounts to absence of a [+ Def] determiner, still plausible. Let us examine one further determiner which is a candidate for indefinite status, in that it never modifies definite noun phrases. *Such* has two principal uses, illustrated in the following sentences:

(106) a.   Mary is such a clever girl.
      b.   I was given such lovely flowers.

(107) a.   We don't need such a man here.
      b.   I'd love to have such colleagues.

Whatever the syntactic status of *such* in (106), it is (on one interpretation) semantically a variant of *so*, and modifies the adjective. But in (107) it modifies the noun (an interpretation also possible in (106)), meaning something like 'of that kind' or 'like that'. We need consider only the second use, which, it will be noticed, involves a demonstrative element.[28] We could simply say that *such* means 'of that kind' or 'of this kind', so that demonstrativeness is one element in its meaning. But it is interesting to observe at this point that noun phrases generally can have a "variety interpretation". Consider the following sentences:

(108) a.   I wish I could afford to buy that car.
      b.   I don't like those boots.

As well as comments about a particular car and a particular pair of boots, these sentences could be used to refer to a type of car and a style of boots exemplified by the entity indicated (thus equivalent to *that type of car* or *a car of that type*, and *that style of boot* or *boots of that kind*). Now notice that *a car of that type* and *boots of that kind* are indefinite, and, moreover, very close in meaning to *such*

---

[28] *Such* is almost certainly an adjective, and a complete adjective phrase. It follows most cardinality expressions (*one such person*, *three such people*), but behaves like adjectives accompanied by degree modifiers in preceding the article *a*: *such a man*; *so/how/too clever a man*. The fact that *a* appears here in second position, which we have seen it is generally unable to do, suggests strongly that *such* and *so clever* etc. come to be in pre-article position as a result of a movement process, having originated in normal post-article adjective position.

a car and *such boots*. So *such* is synonymous, or near-synonymous, with a variety interpretation of a demonstrative. But perhaps one can go yet further, and propose that *such* is an indefinite demonstrative. On this proposal, *such* is synonymous with *this/that* (though not showing the proximal–distal distinction), but *this* and *that* occur only in definite noun phrases while *such* is the demonstrative form used in indefinite noun phrases. This would mean that demonstrativeness is not, as I have so far assumed, inherently definite. Interesting as this suggestion is, we will see in Chapter 3 that it does not seem to be supported by cross-linguistic evidence. It may, however, merit further investigation.

1.4 The noun phrase

No investigation into the nature of definiteness can proceed far without consideration of the place of articles and other determiners within noun phrase structure. The question of how noun phrases are structured will be examined in more depth in Chapter 8, but it will be useful to establish some preliminary notions at this point.

The general view within generative syntactic theory is that the structure of phrases is determined by the principles of X-bar theory, according to which a phrasal category, an XP, is projected from a **head** X. Between these two is an intermediate level X′. XP immediately dominates, besides X′, the position of **specifier** (which is therefore sister to X′). And the head may take one or more **complements** as sister, depending on its lexical properties. The specifier and complement positions are occupied by phrasal categories. This gives the following schema, in the linear order generally appropriate for English; linear order varies from language to language, and superficial (S-structure) order may differ from the underlying order of D(eep)-structure.

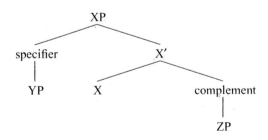

In addition, it is possible for other expressions, typically phrasal categories, to be **adjoined** to some or all of the projections of X (X itself, X′, and XP). If A is adjoined to B, it is attached to it in this way:

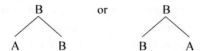

For example, modifying expressions such as adjective or adverb phrases have been taken to be adjoined to X′ or XP in the phrases they modify.

Given this general framework, the usual view until recently was that the noun phrase is a maximal (that is, phrasal) projection of the head N, with determiners in specifier position, adjectival expressions adjoined mainly to N′, and any complements typically expressed by prepositional phrases. Some examples will make this clear:

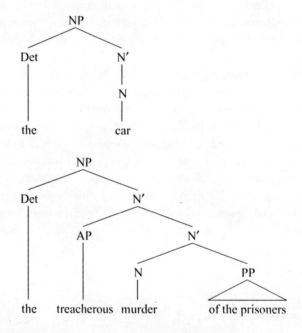

For a clear and much fuller exposition of the general principles of X-bar theory and NP structure as just outlined, the reader is referred to Radford (1988: chapters 4 and 5).

A different account has recently come to prominence, and achieved almost general acceptance. This is that the "noun phrase" is a phrasal projection, not of the noun, but of the determiner (Det or D). It is therefore DP, not NP. There still exists a category NP, projected from N, but this is within DP, as complement of the head D, and corresponds more or less to N′ on the older analysis. The general principles

of X-bar theory still apply, though it is now commonly assumed that adjunction
to X′ is not permitted. The following exemplify DP structure:

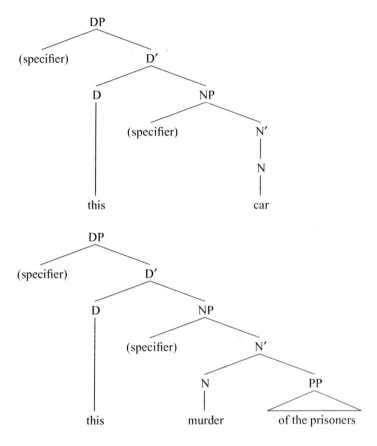

The position of adjectives has been the subject of much debate. They have been
claimed to be adjoined to NP, but a currently influential view is that they are specifiers
of some phrasal category between NP and DP.

The DP analysis arises from an interest in "functional" categories. These are
grammatical categories as opposed to "lexical" or "substantive" categories like
N(oun), V(erb), A(djective), P(reposition) (which can be thought of as denoting
real-world entities, states, activities, properties, relations etc.). In clause structure,
functional categories like T(ense) and Agr(eement) (representing subject–verb agreement) are treated as heads of phrases, and the DP analysis extends this trend to
the "noun phrase", taken to be a projection of the functional category of D(eter-
miner). Other functional heads, each projecting a phrase, have also been claimed
to be involved in nominal structure; examples are Num(ber) and K (for case).

The question of which is the correct framework for nominal expressions will be taken up in Chapter 8 (where I will propose a substantially modified version of the DP hypothesis). For the present I will use the label Det to denote the formal category to which the English definite article and other determiners belong, but will leave open the question of whether it is the head or the specifier of the "noun phrase".[29] The position of the definite article in English I will term non-committally "Det position" – which is either specifier of NP or head of DP depending on the framework chosen. The overall phrase, which is formally either NP or DP depending on the framework, I shall continue to term informally "noun phrase".

English demonstratives and possessives apparently occupy the same slot in the noun phrase as *the*, and the definite quantifiers *all*, *both*, *every*, *most* tend to occur in this position too. *All* and *both* are sometimes termed "pre-determiners" because they may appear before definite Dets, to express a proportion of the whole denoted by the definite noun phrase: *all the girls*, *both your friends*. The phrase is equivalent to a partitive, and indeed an overtly partitive construction is available as an alternative: *all of the girls*, *both of your friends*. For reasons which are far from clear, *all* and *both* (at least in the pre-determiner construction) do not quantify over indefinites: **all sm girls*, **all a potato*, **both sm boys*. But they may occur with no following determiner:

(109)   All three defendants were acquitted.

All here is probably in Det, rather than pre-determiner, position. *All three defendants* does not denote the totality of an indefinite group of three defendants, but of a definite group; it is synonymous with *all the three defendants*, not *all of three defendants* (if this is possible). Given the absence of *the*, the definiteness of the domain of quantification must come from *all*. The simplest explanation is that *all* is in Det position; when in this position it allows the noun phrase to be definite without *the*. *Most* has been argued to be a definite Det, and it is probably in Det position in *most men*, though it could be claimed to be in a cardinality position deeper inside the noun phrase, since it co-occurs neither with definite Dets nor with cardinality expressions. *Most* can also head a partitive construction, but cannot be a pre-determiner: *most of those men*, **most those men*. *Every* clearly occupies the same position as *the*; it cannot occur with it either as pre-determiner or (normally) in some more interior position, and it can precede numerals: **every the chair*, **the every chair*, *every one chair*, *every three chairs*. The only complication here is that it can, somewhat marginally, follow possessives: *his every whim*, *the king's every whim*. This is also possible after *the* but only with a possessive

---

[29] The convention has grown up of using the label D within the DP framework, while Det is preferred within the older NP framework. But the two are equivalent.

PP: *the every whim of the king.* So *every* seems to be capable of occurrence not only in Det position (the normal case) but also in some position deeper in the noun phrase, but only in the presence of a possessive expression; the marginality of this construction lies in its being available only with a limited range of head nouns: **his every car, *the king's every castle, *the every carriage of the king.* So it is possible to say that, in English, Det position is the locus not only for the definite article but for definite determiners more generally.

Most writers assume that *a* occupies the same position in noun phrases as *the*, but this is because they take *a* to be an indefinite article. If it is in reality a cardinal article, closely related to *one*, it is natural to suppose that it occupies (or at least originates in) the same position as numerals. Numerals agree closely in distribution with various other cardinality expressions – all being mutually exclusive and apparently occupying the same place relative to other constituents such as definite determiners (where they are compatible with these) and adjectives: *the **one** good book*; *the **three/many/few** good books*; ***enough** good books*. I shall assume that the English noun phrase has a position for cardinality expressions between the definite Det position and the position of adjectival modifiers, and that all the above words appear in this position.[30] A general similarity in behaviour and distribution between numerals and other cardinality determiners is to be found in many languages, as well as a strong tendency for these expressions to stand closer to the noun than definite determiners. I will assume, therefore, that syntactic theory makes available to languages a cardinality position which is more internal to the noun phrase than Det position.

1.5 Definiteness beyond the noun phrase

I end this chapter with the suggestion (which I will not pursue in the rest of the study) that definiteness is not only a feature of noun phrases, but occurs more widely. Let us consider two possible instances of it.

The tense–aspect distinction between past historic or preterite *I read that book* and perfect *I have read that book* has sometimes been described in traditional grammars in terms of a distinction between "definite" and "indefinite" past. These may be mere labels, but it is arguable that the preterite does make a definite time reference. In the absence of a time adverbial which identifies the time of the

---

[30] It may also be that they belong to the same category – possibly a phrasal category QP (quantifier phrase); this label is taken from Bresnan's (1973) study of the comparative construction, though Bresnan does not include numerals in her treatment. She defines *much, many, little, few* as possible heads of QP, which also contains a Det position; possible QP Dets are *as, so, -er* (*-er much/many* underlying *more*). If numerals and *a* are QPs, they are probably heads of category Q, differing from *many* in not admitting a Det. In this they are like *enough* and *several*. On the idea of a cardinality position less peripheral than definite Det position see also Verkuyl (1981).

event (*I read that book yesterday*), the hearer is assumed to be able to locate the event temporally on the basis of contextual knowledge. The perfect also presents the event as past, but, while the speaker may know when she read the book, there is no implication that the hearer knows or can work out (or needs to) when the event occurred. Put this way, the distinction is closely parallel to that between *the car* and *a car*, with identification of time of event substituted for referent identification.[31]

The structural position of determiners in the noun phrase is paralleled in the adjective phrase (and in adverb and quantifier phrases) by "degree modifiers" (Deg): *as/so/that/too big*. These words can be treated as being also of category Det, and, like this, as being either specifiers of AP or heads of a functional phrase containing AP. Note in particular that *that* operates both as a definite Det in the noun phrase and as a Deg in the adjective phrase, and that *this* also occurs in both uses:

(110) a.   Tom is stupid but not that stupid.
      b.   The fish I almost caught was this big!

There is little reason to doubt that *this* and *that* have demonstrative meaning in this use; the degree they convey of the property expressed by the adjective is accessed anaphorically in (110a) and communicated by means of an ostensive gesture in (110b), exactly parallel to what happens with noun phrase demonstratives. *This* and *that* as Degs are colloquial, and their more formal counterpart is *so*. As their near-synonym, *so* must also be a demonstrative Deg, lacking only the deictic distinction. If this is correct, the obvious question is whether there is then also a simple definite Deg. I believe the Deg to consider for this characterization is *as*. It is phonologically weak, with a normally reduced vowel, and its use in examples like the following is close to that of *the*:

(111) a.   Joe is as bright.
      b.   Joe is as bright as Ann.
      c.   Joe is not as bright as you think.

In (111a) the degree of brightness referred to is accessed by the hearer from the context or the preceding discourse, and in (111b) and (111c) it is provided in a relative-like modifier.

---

[31] Partee (1984) discusses parallels, not exactly between tense and definiteness, but between tense and (definite) pronouns. She observes that, just as pronouns can relate to a referent introduced in the previous discourse or to a referent understood on the basis of the context, so tense can relate to an antecedent time or to an understood time.

2
Simple definites and indefinites

Having established a provisional (and clearly less than satisfactory) conception of what definiteness is, and with a picture of the kinds of determiner and noun phrase that are central to an understanding of definiteness, we are now in a position to survey the languages of the world to see how the definite–indefinite distinction is expressed. We begin this survey in this chapter by examining what I have called "simple" definite and indefinite noun phrases. These are noun phrases which correspond in terms of what they express, if approximately, to English noun phrases in which [± Def] is signalled by, at most, one of the articles *the*, *a*, *sm*. In the next chapter we will extend this survey to "complex" definites and indefinites. Bear in mind that the term "article" is being used here informally, to mean any linguistic form which has as its central function to encode a value of [± Def] (or [± Sg] in the case of cardinal articles). It thus covers affixal definiteness markers as well as free-form determiners. On the basis of what we have seen in English, we may expect articles more widely to act as default members of larger categories of definite or indefinite expressions, to be obligatory (except perhaps under certain generally specifiable conditions) in the absence of other such expressions, and to be unstressed and perhaps phonologically weak. We will in fact see that these expectations do carry over to many languages, but that they cannot all be taken as universal properties of articles. This chapter is concerned, then, with the range of lexical, syntactic and morphological devices used by languages to encode the distinctions in question, and with the general behaviour of the markers identified. Of course it cannot be assumed that what resembles definiteness in certain languages is exactly the same semantic category as observed in other languages, and we must examine the semantic content as well as the form of the articles considered. In fact it turns out that semantic distinctions very close to those identified for English do occur widely, but distinctions are also found which divide the general semantic area in question differently.

2.1 Definiteness and indefiniteness marking

Not all languages have definite or indefinite articles, and we here consider the extent to which the definite–indefinite distinction is overtly expressed before looking at the forms this expression may take. Moreover, among languages which do consistently distinguish definites and indefinites, there is an impression that the distribution between the two can vary, so that some languages seem to make more use of apparently definite noun phrases than others. I shall suggest some reasons for this impression in this section.

2.1.1   The occurrence of articles in languages

The most fundamental cross-linguistic distinction relating to the articles is, of course, that between languages which have them and languages which do not. All languages have demonstratives and personal pronouns, which are perhaps inherently definite, so it could be claimed that the feature [± Def] is represented in some form in all languages. This is debatable, and is a question I will return to. But the encoding of simple (in)definiteness is far from universal; indeed, languages marking it are in a distinct minority. The first-century Roman grammarian Quintilian, comparing Latin (which had no article) with Greek (which did have one), commented: *Noster sermo articulos non desiderat* 'Our language does not need articles', and indeed most of the world gets along quite well without being obliged to distinguish consistently *the article* from *an article*.[1]

The marking of simple definiteness is often an "areal feature". It is well known that languages which are geographically contiguous, even genetically unrelated languages, may develop common characteristics. The greatest concentration of languages marking definiteness today is in Western Europe and the lands around the Mediterranean (as well as parts of the world where languages from this region have been planted through colonization in recent centuries – for example English, Spanish and Portuguese in the Americas). This area is a big one, and it may be pure coincidence that Norwegian and Arabic both have a definite article. On a smaller scale, a classic example of a "Sprachbund" (an areal grouping of languages) is the Balkan region, and here the situation is clearer. Several Balkan languages belonging to different Indo-European sub-families (Slavonic, Romance, Hellenic and Albanian) have been shown to share features of syntax and morphology, including features not especially common outside this region. One of the shared features is a definite article, and two aspects of this situation are particularly striking. One is that Bulgarian and Macedonian are almost alone among the Slavonic

---

[1] The minority of languages showing articles is, however, not a small minority, and one can probably only speculate on why many languages express a distinction which many others do not. Definiteness marking is obviously not essential to communication. Yet many languages which do not mark simple definiteness can be argued to compensate by having other distinctions with a similar function. Definiteness may be thought of as one of a number of categories which serve to guide the hearer in working out how the discourse is structured and how entities referred to fit into it: markers of topic and focus come to mind here. This will be discussed further in Chapter 6.

languages in having a definite article (though it does appear also in some North Russian dialects). The other is that, apart from Greek in the south, all the languages involved – Bulgarian and Macedonian, Romanian (a Romance language) and Albanian – have a postposed article, appearing as a suffix on the head noun or on some other word in the noun phrase.

Another example of the involvement of definiteness in areal facts concerns the combined representation of definiteness and the direct object relation. This will be discussed in detail in Chapter 5, for it is not certain that what is represented is, strictly speaking, definiteness. For the moment I shall merely observe that the marking of something akin to definiteness on direct object noun phrases only is found in many languages, but the phenomenon is concentrated in a geographical area (again a huge one) covering mainly the Middle East and Central Asia. In this case too the languages involved are not always related to each other, Turkic, Semitic, Uralic and Indo-European languages being included. The converse, wide geographical areas where the marking of definiteness is absent, or almost absent, is also found. Australia and South America (as regards their older-established languages) are such areas.

It is by no means the case, however, that definiteness marking only occurs as an areal feature. There are numerous examples of languages, or small groups of related languages, which are distinguished from their neighbours in having a definite article. A good example is offered by Erzya-Mordva and Moksha-Mordva, two closely related Uralic languages spoken in a wide area to the west of the Urals (Krámský 1972, Comrie 1981b). These languages have a definite article, in the form of inflectional material on the head noun, and in showing this (as distinct from definite object marking, mentioned above) the Mordva languages differ from all their neighbours. And given that this article is thought to be a Mordva development rather than an inherited Uralic characteristic, it is clear that languages can develop a definiteness marker spontaneously.

In languages which distinguish simple definites and indefinites, there are three obvious ways in which the distinction can be expressed:

(a)   marker of definiteness only
(b)   marker of indefiniteness only
(c)   markers of both definiteness and indefiniteness

But the matter is complicated by the phenomenon of quasi-indefinite cardinal articles. I have argued that English *a* and *sm* are cardinality words, not indefinite articles; but they do indirectly signal indefiniteness while not encoding it: *a* is obligatory in singular indefinite noun phrases in the absence of any other determiner, and neither *a* nor *sm* ever appears in definite noun phrases. This "indirect signalling" of indefiniteness by a cardinality determiner, leading to a strong intuition that it contrasts with definite determiners, is widespread; we will consider further examples below. If we restrict "marker of indefiniteness" to forms which directly encode [− Def], then possibility (a) above is by far the most common. But if we allow quasi-indefinite articles to count as markers of indefiniteness, possibilities (b) and (c) are also frequent. Some examples of pattern (a), where there is no form like *a* which could even be argued to be an indefinite article, indefinite noun phrases being recognized simply by the absence of the definite article, are:

(1)   *Irish*
 a.   an bord   'the table'
 b.   bord   'a table'

(2)   *Classical Greek*
 a.   to dendron   'the tree'
 b.   dendron   'a tree'

Let us take pattern (b) to be satisfied by languages which do not have a definite article, but have either a true indefinite or a quasi-indefinite article. This article is found most commonly in the singular, an item closely related to the numeral 'one' occurring, with a vague cardinality term like *sm* sometimes occurring with plural and mass indefinites. Examples are:

(3)   *Turkish* (Lewis 1967)
 a.   ev   'house', 'the house'
 b.   bir ev   'a house'
 c.   bazı ev   'sm houses'

(4)   *Mam* (England 1983)
 a.   xiinaq   'man', 'the man'
 b.   jun xiinaq   'a man'
 c.   kab' xiinaq   'sm men' (also 'two men')

(In fact definiteness is indicated in Turkish when the noun phrase is a direct object, but not otherwise.) Pattern (c), with both definite and indefinite signalled by articles, is illustrated by the following (as well as English):

(5)   *Danish*
 a.   boggen (book+DEF)   'the book'
 b.   en bog   'a book'

(6)   *Standard Arabic* (Tritton 1977)
 a.   albaytu (DEF+house)   'the house'
 b.   baytun (house+INDEF)   'a house'.

(7)   *Lakhota* (Buechel 1939, Boas and Deloria 1939)
 a.   c'ą kį   'the stick'
 b.   c'ą wą   'a stick'

I will argue that markers of indefiniteness turn out in nearly all cases to be cardinal articles rather than true indefinite articles, so that the pattern of only the positive value of the feature [± Def] being directly encoded is very general. If it is completely general, then on a strict interpretation of the terms pattern (a) is the only one occurring.

2.1.2   The distribution of definites and indefinites

There are considerable differences across languages in the relative distributions of what look like definite and indefinite noun phrases. Minor differences are to be expected, and it is not particularly odd that, for instance, translating *in bed* into Spanish gives *en la cama* (in the bed), where a Spanish definite seems to correspond to an English indefinite. English has a number of set prepositional expressions of this kind in which a state or direction is expressed rather than a relationship to a particular entity, and it is arguable that since *bed* here is not referential it is not indefinite in the way that *a bed* would be. Spanish also has some expressions of this kind (*en casa* (in house) 'at home', for example), and they do not always coincide with the English ones. But there are, for example, languages in which the definite article is systematically omitted after a preposition. This is the case in Romanian (Murrell and Ştefănescu-Drăgăneşti 1970): *sub o masă* (under a table) 'under a table'; but *sub masă* (under table), not **sub masa* (under table-DEF), 'under the table'. The reason for this pattern is quite mysterious.

Another striking observation is that the definite article seems to have a much wider range of use in French than in English, for example. The main reason for this impression is that generic noun phrases (those denoting a whole class or mass rather than an individual member, a plurality of members, or a part) tend to take the definite article in the former language but not in the latter. For example:

(8) a.   *English*   She loves **detective novels**.
    b.   *French*   Elle adore **les romans policiers**.

(9) a.   *English*   **Cotton** is easy to wash.
    b.   *French*   **Le coton** est facile à laver.

This is a major difference between languages, and will be discussed in detail when we come to examine generics in Chapter 4. Until then I will confine my attention largely to non-generics. For the moment it will suffice to note that there are many languages like French in which generics take definite form, and many like English in which they are typically bare. Rather than assuming that the article occurring in generics in languages such as French is a special generic article that happens to be homophonous with the definite article, I will adopt the simpler view that generics are (typically) definite in some languages and indefinite in others.

51

2.2 Definites: semantic content and behaviour

2.2.1 Optional definite articles

Among languages that have a definite article, the dominant pattern is for this article to act as a default form that must occur in a definite noun phrase in the absence of a semantically fuller definite determiner, as in English. Thus a "simple" noun phrase with no definite article will normally be indefinite. But there are numerous languages in which the definite article can be omitted where the situational or discourse conditions for definiteness do apply (and therefore where translation into a language such as English would require a definite article). This is the case in Hausa (data from Kraft and Kirk-Greene 1973, Jaggar 1985):

(10) a. Wani yaro ya   zo.
         a   boy AUX come
         'A (certain) boy has come.'
     b. Yaro-n   ya   zo.
         boy-DEF AUX come
         'The boy has come.'
     c. Yaro ya   zo.
         boy AUX come
         'The/A boy has come.'

The definite suffix is principally used anaphorically, where the referent has previously been mentioned in the discourse, and associatively, where the referent is related to something previously (or subsequently) mentioned, as in the following example:

(11)   To, ashe ya   bar hula-r-sa   a **wuri-n**   da   aka yi
         OK really AUX leave cap-DEF-his at place-DEF REL AUX do
         karo-n,   sai wani yaro ya   ga **hula-r**.
         collision-DEF then a   boy AUX see cap-DEF
         'OK, he had left his cap where the collision had happened, then a boy
         saw the cap.'

Two of the definite noun phrases indicated in (11) are second mentions; *hular* 'the cap' has its antecedent *hularsa* 'his cap' in the same sentence, while the previous mention of *karon* 'the collision' is considerably further back in the discourse. The third, *wurin* 'the place', is definite because it is an associate of the trigger *karon*, making this a case of associative cataphora. But the definite suffix is optional even in such clearly anaphoric or associative cases, as the following shows:

(12)   Sarki ya   tashi, ya   shiga gida duk rai   a bace ...
         emir AUX get-up AUX enter house all mind at spoil
         'The emir got up, entered the house most distressed ...'

The emir and the house have been mentioned before, so only definite translations are appropriate, but both nouns occur in bare form in the Hausa.

In a detailed study of this phenomenon in Hausa, based on a statistical analysis of texts, Jaggar (1985) argues that, while the appearance or omission of the article cannot be fully predicted, it is largely determined by the accessibility of the referent. If the previous mention of a referent is considerably far back in the discourse it is less easily activated by the hearer; and if other, similar, referents have occurred in the intervening discourse, these can interfere with the hearer's identification of the intended referent. In such circumstances the speaker tends to use the "heavier coding" of an article-marked noun phrase as a way of alerting the hearer to the need to find the referent and thus helping him in the task. In other words, a bare noun phrase is used when the referent is judged to be easy to access, and a definite-marked noun phrase when more effort seems to be required. If the task of referent identification appears yet greater, a demonstrative is used. It may not be obvious how the article (or demonstrative) helps the hearer, but if the article is essentially anaphoric rather than general definite, then one can see that it serves to direct the hearer to the preceding discourse rather than seeking a situational referent for a description which does not immediately activate a referent. For a detailed study of accessibility, see Ariel (1990).

2.2.2 *Anaphoric articles*

I have suggested that the Hausa definite article suffix -*n*/-*r* is used principally for anaphoric definites (and associative definites, which are closely related to anaphora). Hausa has another, free-form, definite article, *ɗin*, used specifically when the referent has been previously mentioned, and in most cases occurring as an alternative to -*n*/-*r*:

(13)   Ina   son   fensir ɗin.
         AUX want pencil the
         'I want the pencil.'

(14)   Na   kawo keke   ɗin-ka.
         AUX bring bicycle the-2SGM
         'I brought your bicycle (previously mentioned).'

This phenomenon is not unusual. Hidatsa (Matthews 1965) has a single definite article, -*s*, restricted to anaphoric use. Interestingly, Hidatsa also has an indefinite, or perhaps cardinal, article *wa*, which acts as a generally obligatory default form with indefinites; the result is that noun phrases with no article or other determiner are usually to be understood as non-anaphoric definite. Other languages have two definite articles dividing the overall field of definiteness into anaphoric and non-

Simple definites and indefinites

anaphoric. Lakhota has a general definite article *kį* and a specialized anaphoric form *k'ų* used when the referent has already been mentioned: *wowapi kį* 'the book' (situational), *wowapi k'ų* 'the book (mentioned before)'. The article *kį* appears not to be totally excluded from anaphoric use, which suggests this form is general definite rather than non-anaphoric, and that the two forms overlap in meaning.

It is possible in most languages to refer to something previously mentioned using a demonstrative, and we will examine this phenomenon more closely in Chapter 3. But this means that it may be unclear whether a determiner specialized in anaphoric use is an article or a demonstrative. Indeed Buechel (1939) says that the Lakhota anaphoric form *k'ų* corresponds to English *that* (as well as giving *the above-mentioned*, *the aforesaid* as renderings). But there is rather strong evidence that some anaphoric determiners are definite articles rather than demonstratives. First, Lakhota *k'ų* is, like *kį*, unstressed – a normal characteristic of articles but not of demonstratives. Second, it can co-occur with demonstratives, and it is not normal cross-linguistically for distinct demonstratives to appear together modifying a single noun phrase. In Lakhota attributive demonstratives must be accompanied in the noun phrase by the definite article, and this requirement can be met by either the general definite *kį* or the anaphoric *k'ų*:

(15) a. He wic'aša kį ksape'.
         that man   the wise
         'That man is wise.'
     b. He wic'aša k'ų ksape'.
         that man   the wise
         'That man (previously mentioned) is wise.'

A very similar argument works for Hausa *ɗin*, despite the complication that this is a free-form determiner by contrast with the definite affix *-n/-r*. The attributive demonstratives *nan* 'this/these' and *can* 'that/those' normally follow the noun, which has *-n/-r* suffixed to it:[2] *abinci-n nan* 'this food', *gona-r can* 'that farm'. Now *nan* may co-occur with *ɗin*, in which case *ɗin* replaces the article suffix:

(16) Yaro ɗin nan bai   dawo ba.
      boy the this NEG-AUX return NEG
      'That boy (previously referred to) has not returned.'

Lakhota *k'ų* and Hausa *ɗin* do, therefore, appear to function as anaphoric articles.

[2] Some descriptive grammars treat this suffix as a mere "linker" (a meaningless morpheme found in some languages linking a noun to its modifiers) rather than a definiteness marker. But I see little justification for this view, which would involve a linker, which happens to be homophonous with, and showing the same allomorphy as, the definite article, occurring precisely in a construction in which many languages do require the definite article to occur.

2.2.3 Deictic distinctions

The kind of deictic distinctions which typically occur in demonstratives (distinctions of distance from the speaker, association with different persons, for example) are occasionally found in simple definites. That is, features like the [± Prox] postulated for English can appear independently of [± Dem] – a point which gives further support for the existence of this latter feature in demonstratives, particularly since in some languages the same deictic features appear both on demonstratives and on the definite article. An example is Wolof (Mbassy Njie 1982, Malherbe and Sall 1989), in which nouns are accompanied by a marker indicating the noun's membership of a particular class. This class marker forms the basis of any accompanying articles or demonstratives. Thus, indefiniteness is marked by *a-* prefixed to the class marker, preceding the noun; definiteness is marked by *-i* or *-a* suffixed to the class marker, following the noun; and demonstratives are also formed by suffixation to the class marker, usually following the noun. But the point is that the two-way proximity contrast found in the demonstratives also shows in the definiteness marker:

(17) a. ab xale   'a child'
     b. xale bii   'this child'
     c. xale bee   'that child'
     d. xale bi   'the child (nearby)'
     e. xale ba   'the child (further off)'

A three-way person-based distinction, common in demonstrative systems, is found in the suffixed definite article as well as the demonstrative of Classical Armenian (Meillet 1936, Jensen 1959, Minassian 1976):

definite article		demonstrative	
-s	'the (near me)'	ays	'this (near me)'
-d	'the (near you)'	ayd	'that (near you)'
-n	'the (near him etc.)'	ayn	'that (near him etc.)'

Interestingly, the Modern Armenian forms descended from the article of the classical language have been partly reinterpreted as possessive suffixes: *-s* 'my', *-t* 'your' (Feydit 1969). The third form, modern *-n/-ə*, descended from classical *-n*, serves both as the third-person possessive and as the definite article. So Modern Armenian, while maintaining a three-way person-based deictic contrast in demonstratives, has lost it in the definite article. Another language showing a three-way deictic contrast in both demonstratives and the definite article is Macedonian (Lunt 1952, de Bray 1980). The demonstrative system is as follows:

M SG	F SG	N SG	PL	
ovoj	ovaa	ova	ovie	'this (near me)'
toj	taa	toa	tie	'that'
onoj	onaa	ona	onie	'that (yonder)'

The middle term of this system, *toj*, is unmarked or general in value, not express-ing a particular degree of distance; it can, however, contrast with either of the other two, and then would express lesser proximity in contrast with *ovoj* and lesser dis-tance in contrast with *onoj*. The definite articles are bound forms, derived from these demonstratives with the reduction typical of articles (though exhibiting a gender contrast in the plural not found in the demonstratives):

M SG	F SG	N SG	M/F PL	N PL
-ov	-va	-vo	-ve	-va
-ot	-ta	-to	-te	-ta
-on	-na	-no	-ne	-na

The three terms of this system are close in meaning to the morphologically cor-responding demonstratives, so that *-ov* is 'the (near me)' and *-on* is 'the (at a dis-tance)'; *-ot* is the unmarked article form, occurring much more commonly than the others and with no "second-person" or other deictic value; it is simply 'the'. Thus *čovek-ot* 'the man', *čovek-ov* 'the man here', *čovek-on* 'the man over there'.

A particularly interesting example of this phenomenon is Bella Coola (Newman 1969, Nater 1984), in which indefinites as well as definites are deicti-cally marked. Nouns are accompanied by a proclitic or prefixed particle, perhaps best regarded as a class marker, which encodes number, gender, and location rel-ative to the speaker:

	singular		plural
	female	*non-female*	
proximal	tsi-	ti-	wa-/a-/Ø
distal	lha-/ʔilh-	ta-	tu-/ta-

A noun marked only with one of these prefixes is generally understood as indefinite: *tsi-cnas* 'a woman (proximal)', *lha-cnas* 'a woman (distal)'. "Proximal" can be interpreted to mean close to the speaker, present in the speech situation, or simply visible; "distal" can mean remote from the speaker, absent from the speech situation, or invisible. The prefix is not itself an indefinite article, since it appears also in definites; rather, indefiniteness is indicated by absence of definiteness marking. Definiteness is marked by a set of enclitic or suffixed particles encoding the same distinctions of number, gender, and relative location, which can occur in addition to the prefixes and must agree with these in the features encoded. These suffixes also encode a distinction of simple definite versus demonstrative. The combined prefixal and suffixal marking works as follows, with *N* representing the noun stem (and omitting prefix and suffix variant forms):

	female	*non-female*	*plural*
PROX DEF	tsi-N-tsc	ti-N-tc	wa-N-ts
PROX DEM	tsi-N-ts'ayc	ti-N-t'ayc	wa-N-ʔats
DIST DEF	lha-N-ʔilh	ta-N-tx	tu-N-txw
DIST DEM	lha-N-ʔilhaʔilh	ta-N-t'ax	tu-N-t'axw

So definite article and demonstrative are both suffixal and involve the same deictic distinctions:

(18) a.   ti-ʔimlk-t'ayc   'this man'
     b.   ti-ʔimlk-tc   'the man (close to speaker)'
     c.   lha-cnas-ʔilhaʔilh   'that woman'
     d.   lha-cnas-ʔilh   'the woman (remote)'

2.2.4 *Definite and specific*

The material discussed in the last two sections is compatible with a conception of definiteness close to that outlined in Chapter 1. Languages with an anaphoric article divide the range of uses covered by [+ Def] into two parts, and either use a separate article for each part, or encode only one part of the field. And where a language expresses deictic distinctions in the definite article, these are simply additional to [+ Def]. We now come to the phenomenon of a language encoding something which resembles definiteness, but not very closely. A category is expressed, typically by a particle with the positional and morphophonological characteristics of an article, which is either distinct from definiteness yet cuts across it, or is broader than, and inclusive of, definiteness. The category in question corresponds in part to the concept of specificity which we have discussed informally. It is found in a number of Polynesian languages, which I exemplify here from Samoan (Mosel and Hovdhaugen 1992) and Maori (Bauer 1993).

Samoan distinguishes a "specific" article *le* and a "non-specific" article *se* (both showing several allomorphic variants). A noun phrase introduced by *le* may be definite or indefinite, in that its reference need not be familiar to or identifiable by the hearer:

(19)   Sa   i ai **le**   ulugāli'i 'o   Papa **le**   tane   a   'o
         PAST exist ART couple   PRES Papa ART husband but PRES
         Eleele **le**   fafine.
         Eleele ART woman
         'There was **a** couple, Papa, **the** husband, and Eleele, **the** wife.'

Se indicates that no specific referent is intended, but any member or part of what is denoted by the noun and associated descriptive material:

(20)   'Au-mai **se**   niu.
         take DIR ART coconut
         'Bring me a coconut.'

It is also used where there is a particular referent but the identity of this is either not known exactly to the speaker or considered unimportant or uninteresting:

(21)   Sa   fesili mai **se**   tamaitai po-o   ai l-o   ma
         PAST ask   DIR ART lady   WH PRT who ART POSS 1EXCDU
         tama.
         father
         'A lady asked us who our father was.'

The non-specific article is required in a negative or interrogative context, and this applies equally to generics, which are usually expressed in positive statements with the specific article:

(22)   E   ai-na **le**   gata.
         GENR edible ART snake
         'Snakes are edible.'

(23)   E   le tagi **se**   agelu.
         GENR not cry ART angel
         'Angels do not cry.'

Bauer (1993) discusses the meaning and use of articles in Maori in some detail, and is doubtful whether definiteness or specificity offers a consistent basis for the distinctions occurring. The article *te*, plural *ngaa*, is standardly described as definite, though some writers regard it as specific. *He*, invariable for number, appears to be non-specific indefinite. A third item, *teetahi* (made up of *te* and *tahi* 'one'), with plural *eetahi*, is specific indefinite. The following examples illustrate the use of these articles:

(24)   Kei te   ruku raaua i   **te**   kooura
         TNS-ASP dive 3DU OBJ ART crayfish
         'They are diving for crayfish.'

(25)   Ka   hoko-na e ia **he** hikareti, **he** pepa, **he** wai
        TNS-ASP buy PASS by 3SG ART cigarette ART paper ART water
        reka, **he** aha, **he** aha.
        sweet ART what ART what
        'He bought cigarettes, paper, soft drinks, and other things.'

(26)   Kei-te   maatakitaki a   Mere . . . i **eetahi** koti.
        TNS-ASP gaze   ART Mere OBJ ART   coat
        'Mere . . . is looking at some coats.'

The article *he* is severely limited in distribution. It cannot follow a preposition, and in fact only occurs in intransitive subjects; it is replaced with direct objects by the "incorporation" structure in which a bare noun, with no determiner or case marker (and consequently no number marking), occurs:

(27)   E   tuhi-tuhi   reta ana   ia.
        TNS-ASP write write letter TNS-ASP 3SG
        'She is writing letters/a letter.'

Bauer suggests that *he* (which does not distinguish number) is used when the kind of entity (that is, the descriptive content of the noun phrase) is crucial, and *tee-tahi/eetahi* when the number is significant. She sees *te* as a "default" article, used when the particular senses of the other articles are not appropriate. It is clear that the meanings and patterns of use of the Maori articles are not yet established and call for further investigation, and the reader is referred to Bauer's discussion. But definiteness–indefiniteness does not seem to be a consistent distinction in this language, and the article system seems to relate at least partly to the distinction between specific and non-specific – though this too may not be fully adequate to describe it.

Articles marking specificity, or something close to specificity, rather than definiteness are fairly widespread. Two further probable instances are Shuswap (Kuipers 1974) and Sango (Samarin 1967). Shuswap distinguishes "actual-determinate" and "hypothetical-indeterminate" articles *y/l* and *k*. The former indicates that the referent is "uniquely determined for the speaker". Sango has a post-nominal particle *ní*, used "to identify and single out a particular object". It can be used anaphorically in reference to an object already mentioned in the discourse, and can co-occur with demonstratives. It can also be used pronominally, to replace a personal pronoun, and tends especially to occur instead of the third-person pronoun for inanimate reference. But examples like the following, in which it co-occurs with *mbéni* 'some', 'a certain', make it clear that *ní* need not be definite:

(28)   Auto afáa   mbéni méréngé ní.
        car had-killed certain child   ART
        'A car had killed a child.'

It seems that this article combines definite with specific indefinite, contrasting with non-specific indefinite. For a complex interaction of definite and specific, expressed by variation in a class prefix, see the discussion of Dzamba in Bokamba (1971).

2.2.5 Nominalizing and other functions

An important aspect of the behaviour of definite articles is their use other than with nouns. It is common for articles and other determiners, definite and indefinite, to occur with adjectives (and other noun modifiers), so that the latter constitute the descriptive core of a noun phrase: English *the rich*, Spanish *un pobre* (a poor) 'a poor person', *lo difícil* (the difficult) 'the difficult thing/part' or 'what is difficult' (where *lo* is the "neuter article", a form of the definite article unmarked for gender). Verbs can also be nominalized, and in many languages an infinitive, or other basic verb form, can occur with the definite article: Spanish *El hacer esto fue fácil* (the to-do this was easy) 'Doing this was easy', 'It was easy to do this'; Lakhota *ktepi kį wąyake* (kill the saw) 'He saw the killing'.

More strikingly, a definite article can sometimes serve to introduce an entire finite clause, thus functioning somewhat as a complementizer – and this may well be the correct analysis of such uses. This applies particularly to subordinate clauses with an argument function – that is, clauses behaving like noun phrases, as subject or object of a higher sentence for instance – as in this example from Huixtan Tzotzil (Cowan 1969, Suárez 1983):

(29)   Ivʉunaʃ   ti   ʃka?   ti   te?.
         it-appeared the is-rotting the wood
         'It appeared that the wood is rotting.'

This phenomenon may be particularly characteristic of polysynthetic languages (in which the verb can incorporate all the information necessary for a complete clause), as observed by Mithun (1984). She gives this example from Mohawk:[3]

(30)   Teionatonhwentsó:ni **ne** aontakontiráthen.
         they-want(-it)   the they-would-climb-up-here
         'They want to climb up here.'

Consider also the following example from Lakhota (Buechel 1939) in which the complementizer-like article (occurring post-clausally, in keeping with the post-nominal position of articles in the noun phrase in Lakhota) is reinforced by the demonstrative *he*:

---

[3] On the other hand, there is reason to believe that the Mohawk particle *ne* is not a definite article; see Baker (1996), who argues, furthermore, that there is no definiteness marking in polysynthetic languages.

(31)   Wic'aša kį he tok'el ic'ikte   kį he tuweni slolye śni.
         man   the that how killed-REFL the that anyone know NEG
         'Nobody knows how that man killed himself.'

Andrade (1933) reports that in Quileute both definite and indefinite articles can occur before a subordinate clause in an argument function. The definite article is used if the fact expressed in the clause is "related to previous experience" (meaning, presumably, either familiar to the hearer or relatable by the hearer to what is familiar); otherwise the indefinite article is used.

In Lakhota the anaphoric article *k'ų* is used at the end of direct reported speech (Boas and Deloria 1939):

(32)   "Oyakapi k'ų", 'eyapi'.
         tell-3PL   the   said-3PL
         ' "They tell it", they said.'

Articles, definite and indefinite, can also be appended to a sentence in Lakhota with the conversational function of expressing the speaker's attitude to some part of the content of her utterance or to a preceding utterance to which she is responding. The indefinite *wą* expresses approval or agreement, and the definite *kį* and definite anaphoric *k'ų* express disapproval or disagreement. *Wą* and *kį* may be intensified by the addition of a particle -*š*. Thus two possible replies to *Nį kta he?* 'Are you going?' are:

(33) a.   Hiya, m.nįkteśni kįš.
           'No, I am not going!'
     b.   Toš, m.nįkta wąš.
           'Yes, of course I am going!'

The *wąš* in (33b) can be interpreted as implying that the question was unnecessary, the questioner should have known better than to ask. On Lakhota see also Van Valin (1985).

The use of definite articles, and also demonstratives, to introduce (or close, depending on the language's word-order pattern) relative clauses is very common, and in some cases is probably to be explained in terms of the close relationship between determiners and pronouns. In the following examples the relative element or pronoun (indicated as *REL*) is identical morphologically to the definite article of the language illustrated.[4]

---

[4] The Homeric Greek example is complicated by the fact that at this stage of the language the "article" forms tended to have demonstrative value. By the time of Classical Greek, when these forms were unambiguously a definite article, the relative pronoun was clearly distinguished from this. In German the relative pronoun is in most forms identical to the definite article (which can also have demonstrative value, and can be used pronominally). In the genitive forms and in the dative plural the relative pronoun is morphologically fuller than the article, an extra syllable -*en* being added.

(34)   *Homeric Greek* (Goodwin 1992)
         dōra ta   hoi   xeinos   dōke
         gifts REL-NPL him-DAT stranger gave
         'gifts which a stranger gave him'

(35)   *German*
         Der Mantel, den   er trägt, ist zu groß.
         the coat   REL-ACC he wears is too big
         'The coat he is wearing is too big.'

The following example from Miskito (Thaeler and Thaeler undated, Suárez 1983) illustrates the "internal-head relative" construction, in which the noun modified by the relative occurs within the relative clause. This being so, the relative particle *ba* is probably to be seen as simply the article modifying the entire relative "noun phrase". The article in Miskito is post-nominal anyway; in the relative construction it appears at the end of the phrase and a demonstrative (here *baha*) may appear at the beginning.

(36)   baha waikna naiwa balan ba   baku win.
         that man   came today REL said so
         'The man that came today said so.'

See Comrie (1981a) for discussion of the internal-head relative and other types of relative structure; see also 6.3.4 below.

2.3 Definite article types

The form and position of definite articles show considerable variation across the world's languages. This variation does, however, fall within certain limits, and a small handful of types of expression occurs repeatedly. A typological distinction has often been drawn in traditional descriptive work between preposed articles, appearing before the head noun, and postposed articles, following the noun:

Preposed article		
Hungarian **a** nö	(the woman)
Arabic	**al**baytu	(the-house)
Catalan	**l'**ampolla	(the-bottle)
	la noia	(the girl)
Postposed article		
Wolof	nenne **bi**	(child the)
Romanian	carte**a**	(book-the)
Hausa	kujera**r**	(chair-the)
	fensir **ɗin**	(pencil the)

But such a distinction of position in relation to the noun is not necessarily of profound significance. Much more important is the question of whether an article is an independent word or a bound morpheme. It is primarily this distinction which is to be observed in contrasting Spanish *el hombre* (the man) with Romanian *omul* (man-the) 'the man'. In addition to this both independent, free-form articles and bound articles may precede or follow the head, perhaps depending on other factors present in particular languages. The Hausa examples above show that this language has both a free-form and a bound article, though both are "postposed". Catalan looks similar, with free and bound "preposed" articles, but *l'* is almost certainly not bound but merely a reduced independent form required before a vowel.

Among bound forms there is an important distinction between inflectional affixes and clitics, but I shall not attempt to draw this distinction systematically for all cases discussed, since it is often far from clear. Detailed analysis of the facts of a particular language are usually required to determine the status of a given form, and writers often disagree. The term "clitic" is itself a pre-theoretical one, and has been used to denote a variety of possibly distinct phenomena; for discussion see Zwicky (1977), Zwicky and Pullum (1983), Klavans (1985). Many of the bound articles I shall consider are attached to the lexical head of the appropriate phrase, the noun; some of these are inflections and some clitics – I shall use the term "affix" for both. These "head affixes" are to be distinguished from "phrasal clitics", a type of clitic which attaches, not necessarily to a head or to any specified constituent, but to one of the boundaries of a phrase. They are proclitic or enclitic to either the first or the last word or constituent of the phrase; an example might be English possessive *'s*, attaching enclitically to the last word of a noun phrase (as in *[[the man I spoke to's] car]*).

Quite apart from the issue of whether an affixal form is an inflection or a clitic, it is not always a simple matter to decide even whether the article occurring in a particular language is an independent lexical item or an affix, given that all article types tend to be phonologically weak. It may well be that, for example, an article I here class as lexical could be argued to be affixal.

2.3.1 Free-form articles

One of the most common ways of expressing simple definiteness is by means of an article which is a free form, an independent lexical item, like English *the*. *The* is a member of the category Det, along with other "determiners" (a term I continue to use informally).

2.3.1.1 *Structural position*

In the great majority of languages where a lexical article occurs, it is closely comparable to English *the* in terms of its position in the noun phrase.

That is, it precedes modifying expressions such as adjectives, numerals and cardinality expressions (but frequently not the equivalent of *all*, which in many languages takes the whole noun phrase as sister). It is likely, therefore, that a free-form definite article is usually, if not always, a Det appearing in the same Det position as in English. A few examples are: Portuguese *as duas casas* (the two houses); Kekchi *li cha.b'il wi.nk* (the good man) (Eachus and Carlson 1966); Samoan *le aso muamua o le vāiaso* (ART day first POSS ART week) 'the first day of the week' (Mosel and Hovdhaugen 1992). Ewe shows the mirror image of the English pattern, with adjectival modifiers following the head noun and the article *lá* (one of two article forms, the other being an affix) coming last (Westermann 1960): *atí nyuí lá* (tree beautiful the) 'the beautiful tree'. Lakhota is similar: *wowapi wašte ki* (book good the) 'the good book' (Buechel 1939).

Cases like Ewe and Lakhota notwithstanding, there is a strong tendency for the definite article, if a free form, to occur initially in the noun phrase, independently of a language's general constituent-order pattern. This can be taken as evidence against the assumption that Det position is NP specifier; since subjects of clauses are generated in a specifier position, one might expect VSO languages, for example, to show noun phrase specifiers also in post-head position. This expectation is commonly borne out as regards genitive expressions, while the definite article is pre-nominal: Irish *hata an fhir* (hat the-GEN man-GEN) 'the man's hat', but *an rothar* (the bicycle). To take a different word-order pattern, Malagasy is a VOS language, yet has the article preceding the head noun: *ny zazavavy* (the girl) (Keenan 1976). On the other hand, it is perfectly possible for a language to show one structural pattern in clauses but a different one in noun phrases, and I limit myself here to the observation that the generalization of phrase-initial position for the definite article is a rather strong one. It does seem possible, moreover, to advance the strong hypothesis that lexical definite articles are generated universally in some "Det position", whatever this turns out to be structurally.

2.3.1.2 Some characteristics

Definite articles show a strong tendency to be unstressed (though they are often capable of being stressed for emphasis or contrast, as English *the* can be, with its "strong" pronunciation [ðiː]). This fact shows itself in many languages which have phonological reduction processes, in the article's being a weak form. This is exemplified in the reduced vowels occurring in English *the* ([ðə] or [ðɪ]), Irish *an* ([ən] or [ə]), Dutch *de* [də], *het* [ət]; the French masculine singular form *le* [lə] is the result of the same kind of vowel reduction in Old French. Articles are, moreover, almost always monosyllabic, in accordance with the strong tendency for unstressed words to be monosyllabic and for stress reduction to be accompanied by reduction of polysyllabic items to monosyllabicity (see Selkirk 1984). This tendency is particularly evident in the many examples of definite articles being derived historically from demonstratives and the development being accompanied by syllable reduction – for example Latin demonstrative forms *ille, illum, illa, illam* yielding Romance article forms *el, il, lo, le, la.*

It may be that many instances of the definite article fall into the class of what Zwicky (1977) calls "simple clitics". A "simple clitic" is a weak or reduced item which is phonologically dependent on an adjacent "host", the two together forming a word-like unit, but which nevertheless occupies the same position in the sentence or phrase as the corresponding full form (if there is one). A clear example is English *'s*, the reduced form of both *is* and *has*, in expressions like *John's ill*, *Mary's found it*. Not all simple clitics have a corresponding full form, however, and this would usually be the case with the definite article, since it is normally unstressed. There are instances, though, of articles, already weak and unstressed, being further reduced in particular environments, by processes which are idiosyncratic to the items in question rather than instantiating general phonological rules. An example is the reduction of the French feminine singular article *la* to *l'* pre-vocalically: *la femme* 'the woman', but *l'autre femme* 'the other woman'. We saw an instance of the same phenomenon above from Catalan: *la noia* 'the girl', but *l'ampolla* 'the bottle'. Apart from its obligatoriness, this can perhaps be compared with the reduction of English *has*, which may itself already be unstressed and with a reduced vowel, [həz], to *'s* [z]. But apart from cases like these, where an item occurs in different forms, varying in degree of reduction, it is often far from obvious whether a weak item is a clitic or whether its weakness follows merely from its being a "function word" (in the sense of Selkirk 1984), that is, a "grammatical word" as opposed to a member of one of the major lexical classes.[5] An interesting manifestation of article reduction is exhibited by Ewondo, a North-West Bantu tone language (Redden 1979). A great deal of vowel elision and contraction occurs in Ewondo, and the tone of an elided segment may pass to the adjacent syllable. This kind of assimilation occurs not only within words; some monosyllabic function words can be completely elided by it. Thus *á oŋgóla* (to fence) 'to the fence' contracts to *óŋgóla*, the high tone of the preposition *á* transferring to the assimilating syllable following; the loss of the low tone of the first syllable of *oŋgóla* then leads to downstepping of the next high tone to mid. Now the definite article is *é*, which is likewise elided at

---

[5] Selkirk, discussing the English definite article along with other function words, claims that its weak, stressless nature can be accounted for in terms of its being a monosyllabic function word (particularly one consisting of an open syllable with a lax vowel), without the need to appeal to cliticization. On the other hand, Nespor and Vogel (1986) give one argument for treating the definite article of Modern Greek as a clitic. A rule of nasal deletion, which applies under certain segmental conditions within words and within host-clitic combinations, but not across word boundaries, applies within the group consisting of the article and a following noun: [tin θéa] → [ti θéa] (the-ACC view-ACC).

conversation speed before an immediately adjacent syllabic segment, its high tone passing to the next syllable. So *é oŋgóla* 'the fence' becomes *óŋgōla*, downstepping of the second high again occurring under the influence of the suppressed low.[6]

A very commonly occurring process is for noun phrase-initial definite articles to combine with a preceding preposition. This is presumably a kind of cliticization, but it is particularly striking because it is operating across a phrase boundary; it is, moreover, not immediately obvious which is the clitic and which is the host, since both articles and prepositions tend to be weak items. A common analysis within the DP framework is that D, the article, moves by a transformational process of "Head Movement" to attach to the higher P head. Examples are: French *de le → du* 'of the', *à le → au* 'to the'; Italian *in il → nel* 'in the', *con il → col* 'with the'; German *in dem → im* 'in the', *zu der → zur* 'to the'. In many of these "contractions", there seems to be more phonological material remaining from the preposition than from the article, which suggests that the latter is phonologically enclitic to the former. In some instances the changes following the cliticization have been so far-reaching that neither component is recognizable in the combination; in Irish, the preposition *i* 'in' and the article *an* yield the combined form *sa* [sə] (via a still extant *insan*).

The tendency for definite articles to be unstressed is not universal, however, because it depends on the suprasegmental phonological structure of the language. A distinction between fully stressed "lexical" words and frequently unstressed "function" words can only exist in languages which have word stress. French has phrasal rather than word stress, the stress tending to fall on the last syllable of phrases, but sometimes on the first syllable – whatever the status of the word occurring at that point. An effect of this is that articles are stressed in some contexts. One such context is that of enumerations, as in the following, where it would be normal for the articles to carry the main stress of their noun phrase:[7]

(37)　　Tous nos produits alimentaires sont importés: **la** viande, **les** légumes, **les** fruits, **le** blé, **les** produits laitiers – enfin tout.
'All our food products are imported: meat, vegetables, fruit, wheat, dairy products – in fact everything.'

---

[6] The downstepping is due to Ewondo being a "terraced-tone" language, in which a high is normally lower than a preceding high by the same interval as a mid is, when a low intervenes. The intervening low may be elided, but its effect remains, the second high still being lower than the first by the same interval as a mid – it thus becomes superficially a mid.

[7] This may seem odd in view of the fact, noted above, that the French article exhibits clitic-like behaviour in attaching in a reduced form to a following vowel-initial word (*l'autre femme*) and in entering into contractions with prepositions (*du, au*) – behaviour associated with reduction of weak forms. But these cliticized and contracted articles are the result of reductions which occurred at a time when French had a very different stress system; such reductions do not occur synchronically in Modern French. This is particularly clear from the fact that the orthographic *u* of *du* [dy] and *au* [o] is the result of a process of vocalization of [l] which occurred in the medieval period.

The definite article is, in most languages having one, an invariable word, in the sense that it is not inflected (though it may undergo some allomorphic variation, as with Hungarian *az* pre-vocalically and *a* pre-consonantally). For this reason it is often labelled in descriptive grammars a "particle". Thus Pocomchi *re* (Mayers and Mayers 1966), Tzotzil *ti* (Suárez 1983), Akan *no* (Schachter 1985), Lakhota *kį* and *k'ų*, Hausa *d'in*, English *the* show no agreement with the head noun or other constituents of the noun phrase. This is often the case even in languages with a fairly high degree of inflection, in which a related demonstrative does show inflection. Thus in Hungarian, the demonstrative *az* takes case inflections as does the head noun, but the article *az*, *a*, derived historically from it, does not.

In many other languages, however, the article is an inflected form, encoding features such as number, gender and case. This is the case particularly in Indo-European languages, as illustrated in the following paradigms:

Classical Greek

	singular			*dual*			*plural*		
	M	F	N	M	F	N	M	F	N
NOM	ho	hē	to	tō	tō	tō	hoi	hai	ta
ACC	ton	tēn	to	tō	tō	tō	tous	tās	ta
GEN	tou	tēs	tou	toin	toin	toin	tōn	tōn	tōn
DAT	tō	tē	tō	toin	toin	toin	tois	tais	tois

German

	singular			*plural*
	M	F	N	
NOM	der	die	das	die
ACC	den	die	das	die
GEN	des	der	des	der
DAT	dem	der	dem	den

Catalan

	M	F
SG	el	la
PL	els	les

In many languages the inflection of the article assumes a particular importance, since some nominal features are only encoded, or only consistently encoded, on the article (or on the determiner more generally); this point will be discussed in detail in Chapter 5.

2.3.2 Bound articles

A second commonly encountered device for representing definiteness is affixation, to the head noun or elsewhere. Many definite affixes are known to derive historically from lexical determiners (and ultimately, like these, from demonstratives). A particularly clear example is that of Icelandic (Einarsson 1949, Glendening 1961), where the determiner from which the definite suffix is probably (though not certainly) derived still exists as a free-form definite article, and the two articles differ from each other only slightly, as can be seen in the following paradigms:

	masculine		feminine		neuter	
NOM SG	hinn	-(i)nn	hin	-(i)n	hið	-(i)ð
ACC SG	hinn	-(i)nn	hina	-(i)na	hið	-(i)ð
DAT SG	hinum	-num	hinni	-(i)nni	hinu	-nu
GEN SG	hins	-(i)ns	hinnar	-(i)nnar	hins	-(i)ns
NOM PL	hinir	-nir	hinar	-nar	hin	-(i)n
ACC PL	hina	-na	hinar	-nar	hin	-(i)n
DAT PL	hinum	-num	hinum	-num	hinum	-num
GEN PL	hinna	-nna	hinna	-nna	hinna	-nna

The free-standing article rarely occurs in spoken Icelandic, but is used in writing and elevated spoken style when the head noun is modified by a preceding adjective; otherwise the suffix occurs: *hestur-inn* 'the horse', *hinn sterki hestur* 'the strong horse'. The determiner *hinn* is, moreover, still used also as a demonstrative (with contrastive value: 'the/that other'), differing in form from the article only in that the neuter nominative singular is *hitt* rather than *hið*. The suffixed article of the other Scandinavian languages is cognate with that of Icelandic, but the independent determiner and demonstrative from which it derives no longer exists, having been replaced by a rival form. I exemplify from Danish:

	singular		plural	
common	den	-(e)n	de	-(e)ne
neuter	det	-(e)t	de	-(e)ne

A particularly interesting feature of the Icelandic suffixal article is that it is itself inflected for number, case and gender (like the determiner it derives from), while being attached to a noun which is also separately inflected for these categories. Consider the paradigms for the definite forms of *hestur* 'horse', *borg* 'town' and *fjall* 'mountain', exemplifying each gender:

	masculine	*feminine*	*neuter*
NOM SG	hestur-inn	borg-in	fjall-ið
ACC SG	hest-inn	borg-ina	fjall-ið
DAT SG	hesti-num	borg-inni	fjalli-nu
GEN SG	hests-ins	borgar-innar	fjalls-ins
NOM PL	hestar-nir	borgir-nar	fjöll-in
ACC PL	hesta-na	borgir-nar	fjöll-in
DAT PL	hestu-num	borgu-num	fjöllu-num
GEN PL	hesta-nna	borga-nna	fjalla-nna

The form of the noun to which the article suffix is attached is in fact almost identical to the corresponding unsuffixed form (the form used when indefinite or with a free-form determiner). The only difference is in the dative plural, where *hestu-*, *borgu-*, *fjöllu-* correspond to unsuffixed *hestum*, *borgum*, *fjöllum* – clearly a simple case of allomorphic reduction triggered by the article suffix *-num*. The point is that the suffixed article, itself fully inflected to agree with the noun, is added to the inflected form of the noun, with the result that number, case and gender are each encoded twice. The article suffix is not simply one inflectional morpheme, encoding definiteness, among others on the noun. It seems plausible to treat it rather as an independently inflected lexical item – probably, in fact, the definite Det *hinn* – which under certain circumstances is cliticized onto the noun. The other Scandinavian languages present the same phenomenon, though with a much reduced inflectional system. I exemplify again from Danish:

	singular		*plural*
mand-en	'the man'	mænd-ene	'the men'
kone-n	'the women'	koner-ne	'the women'
barn-et	'the child'	børn-ene	'the children'

Again the form of the noun to which the article suffix is added, in both singular and plural, is identical to the corresponding form of the noun without article suffix. It is clear that the noun and the article suffix are separately inflected items, so that in these definite forms number is encoded twice. The main difference between Icelandic and Danish is that in the latter language the suffixal article cannot so plausibly be argued to be a cliticized form, with some reduction, of the free-standing article. The two are diachronically distinct and synchronically not particularly similar in form. In fact the suffixed definite article closely resembles, in the singular, the quasi-indefinite article *en/et*, but can hardly be taken to be a cliticized version of this! We saw similar facts in 2.2.3 above in Bella Coola, where the noun is accompanied by a prefix expressing number, gender, and location relative to the speaker, but these features are also encoded on the definite suffix.[8]

Affixal definite articles are also frequently invariable. Examples are the Abkhaz prefix *a-* (Hewitt 1979) and the Ewe suffix *-á*. Uninflected affixal articles may, of course, show allomorphic variation, as in Modern Armenian (Feydit 1969), where the article is *-ə* after a consonant (*kirk'-ə* 'the book') and *-n* after a vowel (*gadou-n* 'the cat'). Another instance is Vai (Welmers 1976), in which the suffixal article has the forms *-ă* (after *-a*), *-ĕ* (after *-e* and *-o*) and *-ĕ̌* otherwise. There are also affixal articles which do encode more than [+ Def], varying for number, gender and/or case for example, but without duplication of the encoding of these additional categories; this is because these categories are only encoded on the noun when the definite article is attached. This is partially the case for the category of number in Erzya-Mordva (data from Feoktistov 1966, given in Spencer 1992). In this language definiteness is encoded suffixally along with other inflectional categories, but the indefinite form of nouns only encodes number in the nominative whereas the definite form distinguishes singular and plural throughout the paradigm. I give here a partial paradigm (Erzya-Mordva has a system of ten cases in all):

	kudo 'house' *indefinite*	*definite*
NOM SG	kudo	kudo-s'
GEN SG	kudo-n'	kudo-nt'
DAT SG	kudo-n'en'	kudo-nt'-en'
ABL SG	kudo-do	kudo-do-nt'
INESS SG	kudo-so	kudo-so-nt'
NOM PL	kudo-t	kudo-t-n'e
GEN PL	kudo-n'	kudo-t-n'e-n'
DAT PL	kudo-n'en'	kudo-t-n'e-n'en'
ABL PL	kudo-do	kudo-t-n'e-d'e
INESS PL	kudo-so	kudo-t-n'e-se

Since the definiteness morpheme varies between *-nt'-* in the singular (except in the nominative where it takes the form *-s'*), and *-n'e-* in the plural, it can be claimed to express number. The plural variant is always preceded by *-t-*, which encodes plural;

---

[8] Before an inflection analysis of these definiteness markers is dismissed, on the grounds that an inflection cannot itself be inflected, and articles of the sort discussed assumed to be clitics of some kind, it is worth considering Spanish verb morphology, in which uncontroversially inflectional material is, for the most part, fairly readily segmented into discrete morphemes expressing verb class, tense–aspect, and person–number. But in one tense paradigm, the preterite, it can be reasonably argued that the tense–aspect morpheme also varies for person, so that person is encoded twice. See also the discussion of Erzya-Mordva below.

so, for the nominative plural, it is fair to say that Erzya-Mordva is like the Scandinavian languages in that number is doubly expressed. But in the other plural case forms the -*t*- only appears with the definiteness morpheme (and could perhaps be argued to form a single morphological element with this).

There is considerable variation in the relationship between definite affixes and other affixal material occurring on nouns. Albanian offers a good example of inflectional definiteness marking in which it is not possible to identify a discrete morpheme representing [+ Def] – definiteness, gender and case being inextricably combined. The article suffix encodes the gender of the noun, with masculine -*i*/-*u*, feminine -*a*/-*ja*, neuter (which is rare) -*t*, and general plural -*t*/-*të*. (The variation between -*i* and -*u* etc. is predictable on phonological grounds.) But the suffix also varies for case, so that nouns have distinct definite and indefinite declensions; these are illustrated here for a masculine and a feminine noun (Pipa undated, Newmark, Hubbard and Prifti 1982):

| | Masculine 'boy' | | Feminine 'sister' | |
	INDEF	*DEF*	*INDEF*	*DEF*
NOM SG	djalë	djali	motër	motra
ACC SG	djalë	djalin	motër	motrën
DAT SG	djali	djalit	motre	motrës
ABL SG	djali	djalit	motre	motrës
NOM PL	djem	djemtë	motra	motrat
ACC PL	djem	djemtë	motra	motrat
DAT PL	djemve	djemve(t)	motrave	motrave(t)
ABL PL	djemsh	djemve(t)	motrash	motrave(t)

It seems impossible to further segment the inflection -*in*, for example; it is a portmanteau morpheme encoding simultaneously definite, accusative, masculine and singular. Such inseparability of categories is common in inflectional systems. We will, however, return to the Albanian definiteness marker in 2.3.3, since, despite the inflection-like characteristics just pointed out, there is good reason to treat it as a phrasal clitic (or perhaps a "phrasal inflection").[9]

[9] Another article of uncertain morphological status is the Standard Arabic definite prefix *al*-. This is clitic-like in that there are no idiosyncrasies displayed by any combination of it with a host noun; any morphological variation shown by *al*- is determined by general rules. But there is one respect in which definiteness behaves in a way normally associated with inflectional categories. Attributive adjectives agree with their noun in definiteness, as well as in number, gender and case; and definiteness agreement takes the form of the article prefix appearing on the adjective as well as on the noun: *al-bustan-u l-kabir-u* (DEF-garden-NOM DEF-big-NOM) 'the big garden'.

2.3.3 Phrasal clitics

Most of the bound definite articles discussed in the last section attach necessarily to the head noun. Another type of bound item consists of elements which attach, not necessarily to the head of the phrase, and not obligatorily to any one specific host category, but to a host specified by its position in the phrase. I term these bound forms "phrasal clitics". It is not certain whether they are a distinct phenomenon from the clitics already discussed; they may be simply clitics whose position of attachment makes them more clearly distinct from inflections – the lexical head of a phrase being merely one of the phrase "positions" that may, host clitics. Two examples of phrasal clitics have achieved some prominence in the literature (for example Anderson 1985, Klavans 1985). In Kwakw'ala, the definite article *da*, *a*, together with case morphemes, occurs at the initial boundary of the noun phrase. But while it immediately precedes the first word of the noun phrase to which it relates (and thus the noun phrase as a whole), it encliticizes phonologically to the preceding word:

(38)   kʷixz?id-i-da   bagʷanəma-x̱-a q'asa-s-is   t'alwagayu
       clubbed SUBJ DEF man OBJ DEF otter INST his club
       'The man clubbed the otter with his club'

The article is thus, as argued by Klavans, syntactically proclitic to the following noun phrase and phonologically enclitic to whatever word precedes the noun phrase. In Nootka, the definite article *?aq* is a clitic appearing in phrase-second position; that is, it is enclitic to the first word of the noun phrase, whatever that word is:

(39) a.   bowatc ?aq
          deer   the
          'the deer'
    b.   ?ix̱ ?aq bowatc
          big the deer
          'the big deer'

This pattern is more general in Nootka, in that clause-level clitics, such as the tense-mood "auxiliary", are similarly enclitic to the first word of the clause.

The behaviour of the Kwakw'ala article is obviously of great importance to the theory of cliticization if it indeed shows cliticization (of different kinds) in two directions. The Nootka article is particularly interesting because it represents a very common pattern of phrasal cliticization, that of second-position attachment. The second position in a phrase or clause is sometimes known as "Wackernagel position" and second-position clitics as "Wackernagel clitics", after the nineteenth-century linguist who investigated such clitics in the Indo-European languages (Wackernagel 1892). In some languages, like Nootka, Wackernagel clitics attach suffixally strictly to the first word of the phrase or clause. In others attachment is to the first constituent – itself possibly a phrase – as an enclitic to the final word of this constituent. And some languages allow a choice between these two interpretations of second position. In fact, recent work by Adams on weak pronoun position in Classical Latin (Adams 1994) indicates that some cases of what have been thought to be second-position clitics actually involve attachment, not to the first word or constituent, but to a focussed or prominent host; the impression of second-position attachment is due to the tendency of focussed expressions to be initial. Nevertheless, it is clear that many cases of phrasal cliticization do involve Wackernagel position. Second-position clitic definite articles are in fact rather common. Further instances of languages showing them are Amharic, Bulgarian and Romanian.

The Amharic article (Armbruster 1908, Leslau 1968, Hartmann 1980) varies for gender and number, the most common forms being: masculine singular -*u*/-*w* (*färäs-u* 'the horse', *geta-w* 'the master'); feminine singular -*wa* (*gäräd-wa* 'the maid', *doro-wa* 'the hen'); plural -*u* (*nəgus-očč-u* (king-PL-DEF) 'the kings', *nəgəst-očč-u* (queen-PL-DEF) 'the queens'). But when the noun is modified by a preceding adjective or numeral, the article is attached to this:

(40) a.   təlləq-u bet
        big DEF house
        'the big house'

     b.   dähna-wa set
        good DEF woman
        'the good woman'

     c.   amməst-u kəfl-očč
        five DEF room-PL
        'the five rooms'

Bulgarian has a definite article varying for gender and number (but without the deictic distinctions of the closely related Macedonian, discussed in 2.2.3); in addition it distinguishes nominative and oblique case forms in the masculine singular, a distinction not made in the absence of the article (de Bray 1980, Scatton 1983):

	masculine	*feminine*	*neuter*
	'city'	'earth'	'field'
NOM SG	grad-**ət**	zemja-**ta**	pole-**to**
OBL SG	grad-**a**	zemja-**ta**	pole-**to**
PL	gradove-**te**	zemi-**te**	poleta-**ta**

If the noun is pre-modified, the article attaches to the first element:

(41)   Viždam golemi-**ja** xubav grad.
         see-1SG big DEF fine   city
         'I see the big, fine city.'

73

But Bulgarian differs from Nootka in that its article is not always enclitic to the first word of the noun phrase. If a pre-nominal adjective is itself pre-modified by an adverb or degree word, this initial word cannot host the article, which must attach to the adjective:

(42)   mnogo xubavi-**jat** grad
         very   fine DEF   city
         'the very fine city'

In other words, the article is enclitic to the whole adjective phrase, indicating that Wackernagel position in the Bulgarian noun phrase is after the first constituent of this phrase, not the first word.

   The Romanian definite article, too, is a Wackernagel form enclitic to the first constituent of the noun phrase. But, by contrast with Bulgarian, Romanian shows rather severe limitations on what can host the article, possible hosts being almost exclusively nouns and adjectives. The Romanian article is, moreover, particularly interesting since, while it is clearly clitic in character (being strictly a second-position form and attaching to more than one possible host category, and being added to a separately inflected host), it is at the same time relatively well integrated morphologically with its host, not always allowing easy segmentation, and (in common with free-form determiners like demonstratives and the quasi-indefinite article) it carries the main burden in the noun phrase of expressing grammatical information, especially case. The article varies for number, gender and case ("primary" case being a combined nominative–accusative form and "oblique" a combined genitive–dative form – these finer distinctions being made only in personal pronouns), as follows (data from Murrell and Ştefănescu-Drăgăneşti 1970):

	masculine	*neuter*	*feminine*
PRI SG	-(u)l, -le	-(u)l, -le	-a
OBL SG	-(u)lui	-(u)lui	-i
PRI PL	-i	-le	-le
OBL PL	-lor	-lor	-lor

The noun or adjective hosts to which these are added are separately inflected for number, gender and case, but in a much more impoverished way. Case in particular is only marked in the feminine singular, with an oblique form consistently identical to the plural. This marking is shown for both nouns and adjectives in the following paradigms:

	masculine	neuter	feminine
	'good dog'	'good train'	'good book'
PRI SG	cîine bun	tren bun	carte bună
OBL SG	cîine bun	tren bun	cărţi bune
PRI PL	cîini buni	trenuri bune	cărţi bune
OBL PL	cîini buni	trenuri bune	cărţi bune

The usual, unmarked order is for adjectives to follow the noun, but adjective–noun order is also possible, and fairly common with some adjectives. The definite article attaches to whichever element comes first, and both nouns and adjectives independently take the inflections shown above. I illustrate for a feminine noun:

(43) a.   cartea bună *or* buna carte   'the good book'
     b.   cărţii bune *or* bunei cărţi   'of/to the good book'
     c.   cărţile bune *or* bunele cărţi   'the good books'
     d.   cărţilor bune *or* bunelor cărţi 'of/to the good books'

Most numerals, despite commonly being the first noun phrase constituent, cannot host the article. But a noun following a numeral cannot take the article either, as this would violate the strict second-position rule. Instead a free-form determiner *cel* is used: ***cei patru prieteni*** 'the four friends'.

Let us return to Albanian, in which the article offers a good example of something which is not straightforwardly classified as inflectional affix or phrasal clitic, and perhaps gives reason to call into question the validity of the distinction. It shows very definite Wackernagel behaviour, disguised in part by the fact that adjectives rarely occur pre-nominally in Albanian. But they can, for emphasis or contrast, and commonly do when in the superlative degree; and then it is the adjective, not the noun, which carries any definiteness marking (which is necessarily present with the superlative). Consider the paradigms for a feminine noun followed by adjective, without and with definiteness marking. The particles *e, të, së* can be ignored for the moment; they will be discussed in 2.3.4. Note also that I conflate the dative and ablative cases distinguished in 2.3.2, as "oblique", since the separate ablative forms are becoming obsolete.

	indefinite	definite
	'good girl'	'the good girl'
NOM SG	vajzë e mirë	vajza e mirë
ACC SG	vajzë të mirë	vajzën e mirë
OBL SG	vajze të mirë	vajzës së mirë
NOM PL	vajza të mira	vajzat e mira
ACC PL	vajza të mira	vajzat e mira
OBL PL	vajzave të mira	vajzave(t) të mira

The adjective takes plural inflection, but is otherwise invariable. But when the order is reversed, the noun becomes invariable except for number marking. The adjective, now in initial position, carries the case endings as well as the definiteness marking:

	indefinite	*definite*
NOM SG	e mirë vajzë	e mira vajzë
ACC SG	të mirë vajzë	të mirën vajzë
OBL SG	të mire vajzë	së mirës vajzë
NOM PL	të mira vajza	të mirat vajza
ACC PL	të mira vajza	të mirat vajza
OBL PL	të mirave vajza	të mirave(t) vajza

So both definiteness and case in Albanian are encoded as second-position forms. Or, more accurately perhaps, given the inseparability of the definiteness morpheme from the case morpheme pointed out in 2.3.2, it may be that case and definiteness constitute together a single formative, a kind of noun phrase "auxiliary", which is enclitic to the first constituent of the noun phrase.

But the Albanian definite article does not always appear in second position. It may appear on the noun following demonstratives and numerals. Demonstratives may be followed by nouns in either definite or indefinite form, the former being more likely when the reference is anaphoric or when the noun is followed by an identifying modifier:

(44)   këto vajzat   e   Agimit
          these daughters-DEF PRT Agim-GEN
          'these daughters of Agim's'

Cardinal numerals cannot host the definite article or case marking, but these categories can appear on a noun following a numeral; in a definite noun phrase the numeral is, in addition, preceded by a particle *të* (about which more below):

(45) a.   katër vajza   'four girls'
     b.   të katër vajzat 'the four girls'

So the Albanian definiteness–case morpheme does not always show clear phrasal clitic behaviour. The distinction between clitic and inflection is not a simple one, and the reader is referred to Börjars and Vincent (1993) for discussion of a number of borderline phenomena and a proposal for accounting for them in terms of distinctions within the concept of host.

As a final example of a phrasal clitic article I take Basque, in which the definite article is attached to the right boundary of the noun phrase, an enclitic on the last word (de Arrigaray 1971, Saltarelli 1988):

(46)   elur zuri, otz ta lodi-**a**
          snow white cold and thick-DEF
          'the white, cold and thick snow'

But, again, this article is not always identifiable as a discrete element. In some forms, definiteness, case, and possibly number, are inseparably encoded (for example, *-ek*, encoding definite ergative plural). It is clear that placement characteristic of phrasal clitics is compatible with other aspects of behaviour which are inflection-like – giving rise to what are sometimes called "phrasal affixes" or "phrasal inflections".

2.3.4 Mixed systems and double determination

We have seen that a number of languages have both a bound definite article and a free-form one. In most cases the two are complementary to each other; either one or the other occurs in a given definite noun phrase, depending on various factors. In some languages there are grammatical rules governing the distribution of the two article forms; in others it is a matter of free choice or stylistic preference. This is the case in Hausa, where *-n/-r* and *d̃in* are simply alternatives, though the free-standing article is preferred with nouns of foreign origin, especially those ending in a consonant, contrary to the normal Hausa pattern. Ewe is another language in which two articles are, in part, simply alternatives (Westermann 1960). Ewe has a lexical article *lá*, occurring finally in the noun phrase: *atí lá* 'the tree'. There is also an affix *-á*, attaching to the noun, and preceding the plural affix: *atí-a* 'the tree', *atí-a-wo* (tree-DEF-PL) 'the trees'. But while *-á* and *lá* are in free variation in the singular, only *-á* is possible in the plural. In Danish and written Icelandic the choice between the suffixal article and the free-form determiner is grammatically conditioned. The free-form article is used whenever the noun is preceded by modifying material, and the suffix otherwise:

(47)   *Danish*
   a.   hus**et**   'the house'
   b.   **det** gamle hus   'the old house'
   c.   **de** tre huse   'the three houses'

(48)   *Icelandic*
   a.   bátur**inn**   'the boat'
   b.   **hinn** fallegi bátur 'the beautiful boat'
   c.   **hinn** eini bátur   'the one boat'

The explanation for this distribution is not obvious, though some possibilities suggest themselves. One is that the suffix expresses agreement with a null article in Det position, and that this agreement, which licenses the null definite determiner, is subject to an adjacency condition, so that it is blocked by any intervening modifier;

when this happens, an overt free-form article must occur in Det position. Another possibility is that the bound article is actually a Wackernagel clitic, with the complication that only the noun can host it. This means it can only appear when the noun is initial in the phrase; otherwise the alternative free-form article must be used.

Swedish also has two definite articles, a suffix and a free form, cognate with those of Danish, but differs in that the two can co-occur (Holmes and Hinchliffe 1994). The free-form article is used, as in Danish, in the presence of a prenominal modifier,[10] but the affix also appears in this case:

(49) a. resa**n**   'the journey'
     b. **den** långa resa**n**   'the long journey'
     c. **de** fyra resor**na**   'the four journeys'

This phenomenon is termed 'double determination' or 'double definition', among other labels, in the literature, and the reader is referred to Börjars (1994) for more detailed discussion of it. Double determination is reminiscent of clitic doubling, in which a clitic object pronoun appears as well as an overt noun phrase object in some languages, and is of considerable importance for the theory of definiteness and determiners. Within the NP analysis of noun phrases, one would presumably have to say that in *den långa resan* the determiner *den* is in NP specifier position and *-n* is an affix on the head N, perhaps representing agreement with the determiner. In the DP analysis, one might argue that *den* is the head D and *-n* is an affix on the noun, again expressing agreement. But the principle widely accepted within this framework that inflectional categories generally originate as independent functional heads, combining with lexical items through movement of one or the other, would lead rather to the assumption that both *den* and *-n* are functional heads. Since they express the same category, definiteness, it seems we need two head D positions – and this is the analysis adopted, implicitly at least, by a number of writers, including Taraldsen (1990). This is a less than desirable conclusion, and I take double determination to be evidence for the analysis I will propose in a later chapter, that definite articles are to be found cross-linguistically originating in one or both of two positions, a head and a specifier. Specifically, Swedish *-n* here, and suffixal articles more generally, are realizations of a D head, while free-form articles tend to stand in a DP specifier position.

---

[10] In fact the suffixal article can occur alone on a pre-modified noun, in both Swedish and Danish, when it is a matter of a commonly occurring adjective–noun combination or a fixed expression. Some of these have (near-)proper name status or can be argued to function as single lexical units, though in others it seems to be merely the fact that the adjective is one of a set of frequently occurring ones ('old', 'young', 'big', 'small' etc.) that licenses the construction. I exemplify from Swedish: *katolska kyrkan* 'the Catholic Church', *stora flickan* 'the big girl'.

Further possible instances of mixed free-form and affixal article systems, and perhaps of double determination, are offered by the Balkan languages Albanian and Romanian, though the situation in these languages is much less straightforward than in the Scandinavian languages. Recall from 2.2.3 that adjectives in Albanian are accompanied by a particle which varies in form for number, gender and case. This particle is termed in some descriptive grammars the "adjectival article", and it appears with most, though not all, adjectives: Albanian has "articulated" and "non-articulated" adjectives. To avoid confusion and to avoid the risk of prejudicing the issue, I shall prefer to call it the "adjectival particle". But the point is that this particle is cognate with the definite article suffix and derived historically from a definite article. The similarity is evident in phrases such as: *i mir-i djalë* 'the good boy (NOM)', *të miri-t djalë* 'the good boy (OBL)', *së mirë-s vajzë* 'the good girl (OBL)'. But this particle is quite clearly not a definite article today, because it appears also in indefinite noun phrases:

(50) a.   një djalë i   mirë
        a   boy PRT good
        'a good boy'
    b.   disa të   mira vajza
        sm   PRT good girls
        'sm good girls'

The adjectival particle is probably best analysed as an agreement morpheme associated with the adjective – though it is interesting for diachronic linguistics that a definite determiner should develop into such a morpheme. In fact this particle accompanies not only adjectives but a wider range of modifiers, including possessives and oblique (or "dative") case nouns used attributively. This last use makes particularly clear the agreement function of the adjectival particle: *drejtori i shkollës* 'the principal (M NOM) of the school'. The form of the particle is determined by the number, gender and case of the head noun, the possessum, not of the modifying attributive noun to which it is attached. It therefore expresses the agreement of a modifier with grammatical features of the expression modified. But the adjectival particle is sensitive to definiteness. Consider its paradigm (omitting the rare neuter):

	M SG	*F SG*	*PL*
NOM	i	e	të (e)
ACC	të (e)	të (e)	të (e)
OBL	të	të (së)	të

The bracketted forms are used only with an attributive modifier when the nominal head is definite and immediately precedes. Thus:

79

Simple definites and indefinites

(51) a.   E   gjeta   një shtëpi **të**   pastër.
           CL found-1SG a   house PRT clean
           'I found a clean house.'

      b.   E   gjeta   shtëpin   **e**   pastër.
           CL found-1SG house-DEF PRT clean
           'I found the clean house.'

      c.   E   gjeta   shtëpin   **e**   pastër e   **të**   këndshme.
           CL found-1SG house-DEF PRT clean and PRT pleasant
           'I found the clean and pleasant house.'

      d.   E   gjeta   shtëpin   **të**   pastër.
           CL found-1SG house-DEF PRT clean
           'I found the house clean.'

Examples (51a) and (51b) show the indefinite–definite contrast. In (51c) the second adjective takes *të* because it is not directly adjacent to the definite noun, and in (51d) *të* is used because the adjective is not attributive (thus not in the noun phrase) but predicative. But these observations do not amount to seeing a definite article in Albanian distinct from the suffixal one. It is simply that the adjectival particle, an agreement morpheme attached to modifiers, expresses partial agreement for definiteness as well as other categories.

Romanian has a similar particle occurring with certain kinds of modifier, also expressing agreement with the noun modified, and also of definite article origin though occurring now in indefinites. It is used to link a genitival or possessive modifier to its head noun when the latter is either indefinite or has another modifier:

(52) a.   prietenul   meu
           friend-DEF my
           'my friend'

      b.   un prieten **al**   meu
           a   friend PRT-M-SG my
           'a friend of mine'

(53) a.   cartea   scriitorului
           book-DEF writer-DEF-OBL
           'the writer's book'

      b.   noua   carte **a**   scriitorului
           new-DEF book PRT-F-SG writer-DEF-OBL
           'the writer's new book'

It is also used with predicative possessives (*Cartea e a mea* 'The book is mine'), and with ordinal numerals: *studentul al doilea* or *al doilea student* 'the second student'. Notice that in the second alternative, where the ordinal precedes the noun, no definite article appears. The noun cannot carry the article because this would then not be in second position, and an ordinal (above 'first') cannot host the article.

So here one might argue that the particle *al* is functioning as definite article, but it is at least as plausible to argue that there simply is no article here expressing the definite value which is inherent in the ordinal.

These Albanian and Romanian particles are comparable to forms, descended historically from determiners or pronouns, found accompanying modifiers in various languages. In Hausa, possessive expressions are linked to the modified head by such a particle: *na/ta*, usually shortened to *-n/-r* (which, recall, is the definite article suffix) attached to the head.

(54) a. gida **na** sarki *or* gida-**n** sarki
      house PRT-M chief   house PRT-M chief
      'the chief's house'

    b. riga **ta** Garba *or* riga-**r** Garba
      gown PRT-F Garba   gown PRT-F Garba
      'Garba's gown'

The variation in the form of the particle between *na* and *ta*, *-n* and *-r*, again expresses the gender and number of the modified head. It may well be that Hausa *na/ta* is a variant of the definite article, but their occurrence in indefinites makes this less likely for the Albanian and Romanian particles discussed.

But Romanian has another free-standing form, *cel*, a reduced form of the remote demonstrative *acel* 'that', which does alternate with *-(u)l* etc. as a definite article, and indeed sometimes "doubles" the latter. This determiner, which varies for the number, gender and case of the expression modified, occurs only in definite phrases. It is used with adjectives in the superlative, in addition to the bound article when the adjective is post-nominal, and instead of the bound article when the adjective is pre-nominal (because an article bound enclitically to the adjective would fail to be in second position):

(55) a. clădirile cele mai mari
      buildings-DEF the-F-PL more big
      'the biggest buildings'

    b. cele mai mari clădiri
      the-F-PL more big buildings
      'the biggest buildings'

Cel is optional more generally with post-nominal adjectives in definite noun phrases: *bulevardele cele mari* 'the big boulevards'. Finally, *cel* is used in place of the bound article with most numeral modifiers (which appear pre-nominally but cannot host the clitic article): *cei doi băieţi* 'the two boys'. The examples of *cel* with a post-nominal modifier do look like candidates for treatment as double determination. But in these cases the free-form article appears from its position to be part of the adjective phrase rather than qualifying the noun phrase as a whole. The post-nominal superlative structure in particular is closely paralleled in French, where, however, the two articles occurring are of the same type, both (probably) free-form determiners: *l'étudiant le plus doué* (the student the more gifted) 'the most gifted student'. Here we obviously do not have a bound form and a free form jointly expressing definiteness, and the second article must be taken to be part of the super-lative modifier. Similarly, while Romanian does have two article forms, a clitic and a free-form determiner, it does not have the kind of double determination seen in Swedish – both forms occurring together to express the definiteness of a noun phrase. For further discussion, on a theoretical level, of these issues, see Cornilescu (1992) and Giusti (1994).

2.3.5 Definite adjectives

A phrasal clitic article may appear attached to an adjective if this is in the appropriate position, and adjectives (and other modifiers) may be more systematically marked for definiteness in agreement with the modified noun (or noun phrase) as in Arabic, Albanian, and, to a limited degree, Romanian. There is also evidence of a distinction between definite and indefinite adjective declen-sions in a number of Indo-European languages (principally Slavonic, Baltic and Germanic), either in combination and agreement with a definite marker elsewhere in the noun phrase or as the only marker.

The South Slavonic languages Serbo-Croat and Slovene show relics of an older system of indicating definiteness inflectionally on adjectives. This system is found in Old Slavonic (a South Slav language dating back to the ninth century), which has two adjective declension patterns, definite and indefinite (de Bray 1980). A noun phrase can be indicated as definite by the inclusion of a definite attributive adjective: *novə bogə* (new god) 'a new god', *novyj bogə* (new-DEF god) 'the new god'. The definite inflection is derived from an old demonstrative stem *j-*. The dis-tinction between the two adjective declension patterns survives in Serbo-Croat: *mladi student* 'the young student', *mlad student* 'a young student' (Javarek and Sudjić 1963). But it is falling into disuse, the "definite" form being now used far more than the "indefinite", and no longer necessarily conveying definiteness; many adjectives, indeed, have only a definite form. For adjectives that do have the two forms, the distinction has partly become grammaticalized, the definite form being obligatory after demonstratives and possessives and with vocatives, and the indefinite form in predicative use. Insofar as the distinction does still survive, it is made segmentally only in the masculine and neuter singular; in the feminine singular and the plural, the difference is one of tone (rising in the indefinite and falling in the definite), or, in some adjectives, by the position of the stress (second syllable for indefinite, first syllable for definite). In Slovene (Svane 1958, Lencek 1982), the definite–indefinite distinction in adjectives is expressed mainly by tone, and again, the indefinite form is tending increasingly to be restricted to predicative use. But the distinction between the two declensions seems to be still meaningful to a greater extent than in Serbo-Croat. In some cases where an adjective lacks a definite form, there is another, synonymous, adjective available to fill the gap; thus *majhen* 'little' is indefinite only, but is replaced by *mali* for definite function. Bulgarian and Macedonian have completely lost the Old Slavonic definite–indefinite distinction in adjective declension, and, as seen above, have developed a clitic definite article (Bulgarian *-ət*, *-ta*, *-to*, Macedonian *-ot*, *-ta*, *-to*) derived from a demonstrative. But when this second-position article is attached to an adjective, it takes a different form in the masculine singular, the adjective stem being extended: *-ijat* rather than *-ət* in Bulgarian, *-iot* rather than *-ot* in Macedonian. This *-i-* extension to the stem is a relic of the older South Slavonic definite adjective ending.

The definite adjective declension of Lithuanian is cognate in structure with the Slavonic one, being the result of affixation of a demonstrative with stem *j-* (Dambriūnas, Klimas and Schmalstieg 1972). This demonstrative is still extant in the language as the third-person personal pronoun. It is apparent from the following paradigm that the affix is added to the inflected forms of the adjective (with some modification), with consequent dual encoding of some grammatical features – rather as in the addition of the article suffix to the noun in Icelandic. I give here the masculine forms of one adjective, *báltas* 'white', and, for comparison, those of the personal pronoun *jìs* 'he':

	indefinite	*definite*	*pronoun*
NOM SG	báltas	baltàsis	jìs
ACC SG	báltą	báltąjį̇	j̇į̇
GEN SG	bálto	báltojo	jõ
DAT SG	baltám	baltájam	jám
INST SG	báltu	baltúoju	juõ
LOC SG	baltamè	baltájame	jamè
NOM PL	baltì	baltíeji	jiẽ
ACC PL	báltus	baltúosius	juõs
GEN PL	baltų̃	baltų́jų	jų̃
DAT PL	baltíems	baltíesiems	jíems
INST PL	baltaĩs	baltaĩsiais	jaĩs
LOC PL	baltuosè	baltuõsiuose	juosè

But, as with Serbo-Croat, the Lithuanian definite adjective declension has largely, if not entirely, lost its original definite value, according to Dambriūnas, Klimas and Schmalstieg. Definite forms are used pronominally ('white one' etc.), and, when attributive, simply emphasize the characteristic denoted by the adjective; they are often therefore merely alternatives to the indefinite form, the use of one or the other being a matter of subjective choice. On the other hand, Schmalstieg (1987) presents the definite adjective declension as still expressing definiteness.

In the related Latvian, the definite–indefinite distinction in adjectives is fully meaningful (Budiņa-Lazdiņa 1966), and, since Latvian has no other definite article, simple definiteness is expressed only in noun phrases containing an adjective:

(56) a.   koks   'tree', 'a tree', 'the tree'
     b.   liels koks   'a big tree'
     c.   lielais koks   'the big tree'

As well as expressing definiteness itself, the definite form of adjectives is required after definite determiners, like demonstratives and possessives or genitives: *tas lielais koks* 'that big tree', *mūsu mīļā māte* 'our dear mother'. The Latvian definite adjective declension also differs morphologically from that of Lithuanian, though of similar origin. The definite morpheme is more fully integrated into the adjective inflection, with no duplication of the encoding of case etc. As the following paradigm shows, a discrete definite morpheme cannot be consistently identified (though a form *-ai-* or *-aj-* can be discerned in several cells preceding the case morpheme, and it may be possible to posit this as an underlying form in the paradigm more generally). To facilitate comparison with Lithuanian, I take the adjective *balts* 'white' in the masculine; Latvian no longer has an extant determiner based on a stem *j-*.

	indefinite	*definite*
NOM SG	balts	baltais
ACC SG	baltu	balto
GEN SG	balta	baltā
DAT SG	baltam	baltajam
LOC SG	baltā	baltajā
NOM PL	balti	baltie
ACC PL	baltus	baltos
GEN PL	baltu	balto
DAT PL	baltiem	baltajiem
LOC PL	baltos	baltajos

In most of the languages so far considered, showing either fully functional definiteness marking on adjectives or the morphological relics of an earlier system of such marking, the simple definite–indefinite distinction (or its residue) is expressed only in noun phrases containing adjectival modification, because there is no other definite article. Bulgarian and Macedonian show a development in which a distinct definite article has arisen, but in these languages the earlier definiteness marking on adjectives has fallen into disuse. For definite adjective forms co-occurring with other encodings of definiteness in the noun phrase, we must turn again to the Scandinavian languages, which I exemplify from Swedish. Here again, adjectives show two declensions, traditionally termed either "strong" and "weak", or "indefinite" and "definite":

	klok 'wise', ny 'new'			
	strong/indefinite		*weak/definite*	
C SG	klok	ny	kloka	nya
N SG	klokt	nytt	kloka	nya
PL	kloka	nya	kloka	nya

The distribution of the two declensions correlates precisely with the definite–indefinite distinction.[11] Thus the strong form of the adjective is typically used predicatively, and attributively with no determiner or after the quasi-indefinite article or other indefinite determiner: ***kloka*** *vänner* 'wise friends', *en **ny** vän* 'a new friend'. The weak form occurs with definite determiners such as demonstratives and the free-form definite article, with the affixal definite article, and with genitives and possessives (Swedish being a DG language):

(57) a.   *den **nya** bilen*   'the new car'
     b.   *denna **kloka** vän*   'this wise friend'
     c.   *hennes **nya** man*   'her new husband'
     d.   ***svenska** folket*   'the Swedish people'

Less commonly, it can occur in the absence of other definite marking with vocatives and proper nouns and when the adjective itself is inherently definite: *käre Peter* 'dear Peter', *i **sista** stund* 'at the last moment'. But, apart from these last cases, the definite adjective ending alone does not suffice to encode the definiteness of a noun phrase (and even here it can be argued that the definiteness lies essentially in the proper noun or in the lexical content of the adjective *sist* 'last'). In general the definite adjective form must be accompanied by a definite determiner or article, and, given that one of these can mark a noun phrase as definite in the absence of any adjective, it is clear that the adjective ending plays only a secondary role in the expression of definiteness. Definiteness marking on adjectives in Swedish is essentially an agreement process; adjectives agree in (in)definiteness, as in gender and number, with whatever component of the noun phrase is the principal exponent of these categories.

---

[11] German too distinguishes strong and weak adjective declensions, but they do not correlate with indefiniteness and definiteness.

2.4 Other ways of expressing definiteness

Many languages have less direct ways of expressing definiteness than the encoding of [+ Def] by some morpheme within the noun phrase. These devices will be examined in greater detail in later chapters, and only a brief survey is given here.

2.4.1 *Adpositional marking*

A number of languages have a prepositional or postpositional object marker which only occurs with "definite" object noun phrases, though the noun phrase so marked is often "referentially prominent" rather than strictly definite, as pointed out by Comrie (1978). I shall return to the relationship between definiteness and the object relation, and two examples will serve here to illustrate the adpositional marking of something close to definiteness. In Tadzhik, the object-marking postposition *-ro* is cliticized to the final word of the noun phrase (Comrie 1981b):

(58)   xona-i   surx-ro
         house LINK red OBJ
         'the red house'

Hebrew has a preposition *'et* as definite object marker, as well as a prefixal definite article on definite noun phrases generally:

(59)   'et   ha-mora
         OBJ the teacher
         'the teacher'

2.4.2 *Agreement*

While adpositional markers of definiteness are perhaps not within the noun phrase, they are certainly closely associated with it and in some cases cliticized to it. But in some languages the definiteness of a noun phrase is expressed by an agreement marker elsewhere in the sentence. In several of the Uralic languages there is object–verb agreement. Hungarian, for example, shows two paradigms for each transitive verb, the so-called definite and indefinite conjugations. The definite conjugation is used where there is a definite direct object, and the verb inflection, as well as indicating such an object, also encodes person and number subject agreement features; the object agreement and subject agreement features are inseparably fused together. Thus in the indefinite *olvas-ok* 'I read', the agreement morpheme *-ok* encodes first-person singular subject; in the definite *olvas-om* 'I read (it)', *-om* encodes first-person singular subject and definite object; similarly for indefinite *olvas-ol* and definite *olvas-od* 'you read'. The definite conjugation of Hungarian indicates merely that there is a definite object, and gives no further information about such an object. In this respect Hungarian shows the simplest of the Uralic object–verb agreement systems (Comrie 1981b). In related languages other features of the object are encoded on the verb, but in all the Uralic languages which have object–verb agreement, this agreement only applies to definite objects. In the Mordva languages, for example, the person and number of both subject and definite direct object are encoded on the verb.

Similar facts are to be observed in some Bantu languages. In Swahili, the verb shows agreement with the subject, definite or indefinite, and with definite direct objects (Ashton 1944, Perrott 1951):

(60) a.   U-me-leta   kitabu?
         2SGSUBJ PERF bring book
         'Have you brought a book?'
    b.   U-me-ki-leta   kitabu?
         2SGSUBJ PERF OBJ bring book
         'Have you brought the book?'

In fact this difference between subject and object "agreement" may reflect a deeper difference, the object marker *ki* being an incorporated pronoun rather than an agreement marker, and the associated noun phrase being a topic rather than an object. See Bresnan and Mchombo (1987) and 5.2 below.

The Australian ergative language Ngiyambaa does not generally show agreement (Dixon 1980: 365–6; Donaldson 1980). But if subject or object noun phrases are pronominal, they may appear as bound forms which make up a clitic complex attaching after the first word or constituent of the sentence. These bound clitic pronouns cannot in general co-occur with coreferential free pronouns or non-pronominal noun phrases; that is, there is no "doubling" of these clitics, and they are not mere markers of agreement with noun phrases occurring in the sentence. The one exception to this is a third-person bound form *-na*, which is absolutive in case (subject of an intransitive verb or object of a transitive verb). This form can co-occur with a co-referential full noun phrase, and this noun phrase is then understood as definite. Thus:

(61) a.   ŋaa-nhi-ju-na.
         see PAST 1SG-ERG 3SG-ABS
         'I saw him.'
    b.   ŋaa-nhi-ju   burraay.
         see PAST 1SG-ERG child-ABS
         'I saw a child.'
    c.   ŋaa-nhi-ju-na   burraay.
         see PAST 1SG-ERG 3SG-ABS child-ABS
         'I saw the child.'

2.4.3 Pronominal marking

Some languages allow non-bound personal pronoun forms to appear together with overt noun phrases, which are then interpreted as definite. In Yoruba (Rowlands 1969), the third-person plural pronoun *awọn* 'they' optionally accompanies noun phrases to mark them as plural (number not being encoded on nouns); in fact the resulting interpretation is of a plurality of individuals as opposed to a collectivity: *iwe mi* (book my) 'my book' or 'my books'; *awọn iwe mi* (they book my) 'my (various) books'. The interpretation is also definite:

(62) a.   ọpọlọpọ enia
           many   person
           'a lot of people'
     b.   ọpọlọpọ awọn enia
           many   they person
           'a lot of the people'

2.4.4 Word order

Definiteness can be signalled in Chinese by word order, since pre-verbal noun phrases are constrained to be definite (or generic). In general, subjects are pre-verbal, and therefore definite, though subjects of "presentational" verbs can also be post-verbal; these post-verbal subjects are normally understood as indefinite:

(63)   *Mandarin* (Li and Thompson 1981)
     a.   Rén   lái   le.
           person come PRF
           'The person has come.'
     b.   Lái-le   rén   le.
           come PRF person ASP
           'A person has come.'

(64)   *Cantonese* (Matthews and Yip 1994)
     a.   Jek   māau jáu-jó   yahp-làih.
           CLASS cat   walk PRF enter come
           'The cat came in.'
     b.   Jáu-jó   jek   māau yahp-làih.
           walk PRF CLASS cat   enter come
           'A/The cat came in.'

The verbs which allow a post-verbal subject are those of appearance or location, some verbs of motion, and a few others. These are "unaccusative" verbs, with which the subject has the thematic (semantic) role of theme rather than agent, being in a state or undergoing a change of state. Unaccusative verbs (or a subset of them) allow this argument to occur post-verbally in many languages, including English and French, and it is then constrained to be indefinite: French *Il est arrivé deux étudiants* 'There arrived two students', English *There came a big spider*. The post-verbal argument is probably not in fact a subject; the usual analysis of unaccusative verbs is that they take only an internal argument or complement in underlying structure, and have no external argument or subject at this level. The complement may move to subject position, and this is what yields the subject–verb order in French *Deux étudiants sont arrivés* 'Two students arrived', English *A big spider came*, and the Chinese (63a) and (64a). For a simple presentation of the concepts of argument structure and thematic roles (or 'θ-roles') and of the "unaccusative hypothesis", see Haegeman (1994: chapters 1 and 6).

The unmarked position for objects in Chinese is post-verbal, and in this position they are (in the absence of, for example, demonstratives or numerals) ambiguously definite or indefinite – the context usually making it clear which:

(65) *Mandarin*
      Wǒ mǎi-le   shuǐguǒ le
      I   buy PRF fruit   ASP
      'I have bought sm/the fruit'

(66) *Cantonese*
      Ngóh tīngyaht wúih wán   go   leuhtsī
      I   tomorrow will contact CLASS lawyer
      'I'll contact a/the lawyer tomorrow'

But there are ways of making objects pre-verbal, and thus definite; the constructions involved will be discussed in Chapter 6.

2.5 Indefinites

2.5.1 *Indefinite article*

Real indefinite articles – encoding [– Def], and in part identifiable by not being the same as or readily derivable from a cardinality word – are rare, if they genuinely exist at all. Many languages have determiners expressing something like indefiniteness or arbitrariness (like English *any, some . . . or other*), which can be optionally present in a noun phrase, and others indicating specific indefinite reference (Spanish *cierto* 'a certain'). In part because of their optionality, these are not what is generally understood as indefinite articles. The point has been made in the case of definites that such tests for deciding whether a particular determiner is an article or not are not foolproof; we have noted languages with optional definite articles, and the same is likely to be true of indefinite articles. But if we do find an expression which either obligatorily marks any indefinite noun phrase, or normally does so but is absent under certain specifiable conditions, we can take it to be an indefinite article. English *a* and *sm* are candidates for this status; *a* is obligatorily present in singular count indefinite noun phrases in the absence of some other indefinite determiner, and *sm* is normal (though not obligatory) in non-generic plural and mass indefinites in the same circumstance. Similarly, it is not certain that all articles show morphological or phonological weakness (occurring as bound forms or as unstressed, perhaps reduced, words). But most do, so again we have here a useful, if rough, criterion. And again, English *a* and *sm* qualify as articles on this test. But we have also seen that these determiners are probably best treated as cardinality terms. A determiner which looks more like a true indefinite article is Maori *he*, discussed above in 2.2.4. Recall that Maori has an article *te* (plural *ngaa*) of unclear semantic value, but perhaps definite-specific, and a non-specific indefinite article *he*. *He* does not vary for number, and can be used with plural and mass nouns as well as singular ones: *he whare* 'a house', *he tamariki* 'sm children', *he wai* 'sm water'. But *he* is believed to be diachronically related to the numeral *tahi* 'one', and, as we shall see, it is not unheard of for a quasi-indefinite article identical with the numeral 'one' to be compatible with non-singular nouns. Indefinite affixes occur in Persian and Standard Arabic, and I shall examine these more closely.

Persian has a suffix *-ī* which may be added to indefinite noun phrases (Mace 1971, Windfuhr 1979). It is not obligatory, however, and does not simply encode [− Def]; semantically, it marks the noun phrase as non-specific or arbitrary in reference, and is approximately equivalent to *any* in non-assertive contexts and *some . . . or other* in positive declarative contexts. It thus occurs with a subset of indefinites, and need not be present for a noun phrase to be indefinite; thus: *mard* 'the man', 'a man'; *mard-ī* 'a man', 'any man', 'some man or other'. Interestingly, this affix is believed to derive historically from a form of the singular numeral, but it is distinct from the modern *yek* 'one'. It does, however, react in an interesting way with *yek*.

Like some of the definite affixes we have seen, the suffix *-ī* does not necessarily appear on the noun, but may optionally appear on a modifier. Adjectives normally follow the noun in Persian, and are linked to it by a particle *-e-* called the *ezāfe*; thus *mard-e-khūb* 'the/a good man'. To mark the noun phrase as non-specific indefinite, *-ī* is most commonly suffixed to the entire phrase: *mard-e-khūb-ī*. It may alternatively appear on the noun, in which case it replaces the *ezāfe*: *mard-ī khūb*. But the determiner *yek* may also be used (pre-nominally), to express essentially the same meaning, either instead of, or in addition to, *-ī*. The result is that there are five ways of expressing 'any good man', 'some good man or other', with little appreciable semantic difference among them:

(67) a.   mard-e-khūb-ī
     b.   mard-ī khūb
     c.   yek mard-e-khūb-ī
     d.   yek mard-ī khūb
     e.   yek mard-e-khūb

The phonological difference between *-ī* and *yek* is, of course, considerable, but no greater than that between *a* and *one*; and since *yek* can express the same idea as *-ī*, it is reasonable to speculate that *-ī* actually represents a quasi-indefinite cardinal article. Against this view it has to be observed that, unlike English *a*, *-ī* occurs in plural as well as singular noun phrases: *ketāb-ī* 'a book', *ketābhā-ī* 'sm books'. Surprisingly, however, the numeral *yek* can also appear, with the same indefinite sense, in plural noun phrases, again either with or instead of *-ī*:

(68)   'a book'
   a.   ketāb-ī
   b.   yek ketāb-ī
   c.   yek ketāb
(69)   'sm books'
   a.   ketābhā-ī
   b.   yek ketābhā-ī
   c.   yek ketābhā

The occurrence of the equivalent of *one*, semantically weakened in this way, in a plural noun phrase is not particularly unusual, as we will see below. It is perhaps to be likened to the Spanish *unos* 'sm', plural of *un* 'a', 'one', and it may be significant that modifiers and determiners in Persian do not show morphological agreement for number. What this means is that appearance in a plural grammatical context does not by itself prove that a given item must be a real indefinite article as opposed to a quasi-indefinite article really encoding cardinality. On balance, *-ī* is most probably to be seen as a suffixed or clitic cardinal article, limited to non-specific use. Moreover, the fact that *yek* is not limited to singular occurrence suggests that this form, as well as being the singular numeral ('one'), can also be a cardinal article combining the senses of English *a* and *sm*.

Standard Arabic has a suffix usually described as marking indefiniteness, which does not show any such alternation with the singular numeral as is seen in Persian, and which probably cannot plausibly be argued to be a cardinality expression (Tritton 1977, Haywood and Nahmad 1962). It is largely in complementary distribution with the definite prefix and other definite modifiers, though it is systematically absent with certain noun classes (some singulars and some plurals), and is considered to be absent with dual forms generally. This putative article is usually presented as having a single form *-n* (traditionally termed "nunation"), which comes after the case inflection; like the definite prefix, it is present by agreement both on the head noun and on any modifying adjectives. Thus:

(70) a.   al-bustān-u   l-kabīr-u
           DEF garden NOM DEF big NOM
           'the big garden'

b.   bustān-u-n   kabīr-u-n
       garden NOM INDEF big NOM INDEF
       'a big garden'

In fact in those noun classes where *-n* does not occur, indefiniteness marking is not simply absent, for these nouns have separate definite and indefinite declensions. Whereas definites show the usual three-way case distinction (nominative *-u*, accusative *-a*, genitive *-i*), indefinites distinguish two cases morphologically (nominative *-u*, oblique *-a*). As a result, the marking of indefiniteness is absent only in the dual, and in the plural of a small class of nouns, those masculines forming an "external" (non-mutational) plural (inflections: nominative *-ūna*, oblique *-īna*).

It appears, then, on a superficial examination, that indefiniteness is directly encoded in Arabic, usually by *-n*, and sometimes by variation in case morphology. There is reason to believe, however, that this is not the correct conclusion, and that the indefinite form of nouns is an unmarked form, required in certain grammatical circumstances but not encoding anything. The evidence for this concerns the distribution of the forms of nouns with and without the *-n* morpheme.

In general, *-n* occurs when the noun phrase is not definite, and the noun phrase can be made definite in two ways: attachment of the definite article *al-*, and modification by a possessive (since Arabic is a DG language). When a noun is modified by a possessive it is traditionally said to be in the "construct state", but for the most part what this means morphologically is that it does not have *-n*, so it is identical to the form occurring with *al-*. The construct state only differs from the form following *al-* in the dual and in masculine external plurals. The dual is formed by adding the endings *-āni* (nominative) and *-ayni* (oblique) to the stem. There is no nunation in the dual, so the indefinite form is the same as the form occurring after *al-*. The construct state differs, however, in that the final *-ni* is dropped, leaving the dual endings as nominative *-ā* (undergoing shortening to *-a* before the article of the possessor noun phrase) and oblique *-ay* (modified to *-ayi* before the article). The forms are thus as follows:

(71) a.   ʔayn-u-n
            eye NOM INDEF
            'an eye'
     b.   ʔayn-āni
            eye NOM-DU
            'two eyes'

(72) a.   al-ʔayn-u
            DEF eye NOM
            'the eye'

b.   al-ʔayn-āni
DEF eye NOM-DU
'the two eyes'

(73)   ʔayn-a   l-bint-i
eye NOM-DU DEF girl GEN
'the (two) eyes of the girl', 'the girl's (two) eyes'

A similar situation obtains with the external plural, which is formed by addition to the stem of *-ūna* (nominative) and *-īna* (oblique), for both definites and indefinites; but the final *-na* is dropped (and resulting final *-ū* and *-ī* shortened before a following article) for the construct state:

(74) a.   xādim-u-n
servant NOM INDEF
'a servant'
     b.   xādim-ūna
servant NOM-PL
'servants'

(75) a.   al-xādim-u
DEF servant NOM
'the servant'
     b.   al-xādim-ūna
DEF servant NOM-PL
'the servants'

(76)   xādim-u   l-malik-i
servant NOM-PL DEF king GEN
'the servants of the king', 'the king's servants'

Now two things are striking here. First, the plural endings *-ūna*, *-īna* look bimorphemic; the first syllable, *-ū-*, *-ī-*, closely resembles the nominative or genitive inflection of the singular, differing only in length. Second, the second syllable of both the plural and the dual endings contains [n], thus closely resembling phonologically the "indefinite article" *-n* (nunation). Recall that nunation generally, just like the *-na* and *-ni* of external plural and dual endings, is dropped in the formation of the construct state. A plausible analysis is that the indefinite morpheme is not just *-n*, but occurs in three variants: *-n* (occurring in singulars, most "broken" or mutational plurals, and feminine external plurals), *-ni* (occurring in the dual), and *-na* (occurring in masculine external plurals). This morpheme is always dropped in one type of definite context: where the noun is the possessum of a genitive construction. Where the noun is made definite by attachment of the article *al-*, the "weaker" *-n* variant is dropped, but the phonologically fuller *-ni* and *-na* are not. But if this is correct, the *-n/-ni/-na* ending cannot encode indefiniteness, since it sometimes co-occurs with *al-*. It is probably a semantically empty marker of nominality, which (like quasi-indefinite articles) indirectly indicates indefiniteness because of its partial complementary distribution with definite determiners.

This analysis of nunation and the dual and plural endings differs from the accounts usually given in the manuals. But I believe it is plausible, and if it is correct, it puts Arabic among the languages which have a definite, but no real indefinite, article; see also Lukas (1968) and Schuh (1983). Let us briefly examine two more instances of possible indefinite articles, in Nama (Hagman 1973) and Hausa (Kraft· and Kirk-Greene 1973, Jaggar 1985).

Nama has a nominal inflectional suffix very similar in function to the Persian *-ī*. It indicates that the referent is arbitrary or hypothetical, and can be variously rendered by *a/sm, any, some . . . or other* etc.; it can therefore be characterized as an article expressing non-specific indefiniteness. Interestingly, it neutralizes gender distinctions. Nama distinguishes two genders and three numbers, with a third gender category, "common", in non-singular use only, applicable to groups containing individuals of more than one gender; thus *kxòe-ku* 'persons (male)', *kxòe-tì* 'persons (female)', *kxòe-ǹ* 'persons (male and female)'. The forms of the number–gender morpheme are:

	singular	dual	plural
masculine	-p/-i	-kxà	-ku
feminine	-s	-rà	-tì
common		-rà	-ǹ/-iǹ

Now the "indefinite" suffix replaces these suffixes, with the result that number, but not gender, is distinguished in the non-specific indefinite forms. But while there is an indefinite form for all three numbers, it is identical to the common gender form in the dual and plural:

singular	dual	plural
-'ì	-rà	-ǹ/-iǹ

So *kxòe-ǹ* means either '(the) persons (male and female)' or 'some persons or other'.

Hausa has a free-form determiner expressing specific indefiniteness ('a certain'): *wani* (masculine singular), *wata* (feminine singular), *waɗansu* or *wasu* (plural). Whether this is an article or a "complex indefinite" is not obvious – the latter is suggested by its not being monosyllabic, and by the fact that it shares a stem *wa-* with demonstratives. It is used with first-mention indefinite noun phrases, but is optional, being usual with human referents but much less frequent with non-human ones. Jaggar argues that its occurrence is determined by the "discourse salience" of the referent – roughly, it signals that the referent is important for the subsequent discourse and is likely to recur.

I have no evidence on the question of whether the Nama and Hausa forms discussed directly encode [– Def] (or a category hyponymous to [– Def]) or if they too are really cardinality terms. But the general point made in this section is that very many instances of "indefinite articles" derive from cardinality expressions and can be reasonably argued to be cardinal articles. True markers of indefiniteness are rare, and may not occur at all.

2.5.2 *Quasi-indefinite article*

What I have called the indirect signalling of indefiniteness by a cardinality word is extremely common and widespread. Phonological identity between the quasi-indefinite cardinal article and the numeral 'one' is found in many languages: German *ein*, French *un*, Albanian *një*, Turkish *bir*, Ashkun *ač* (Krámský 1972), Amharic *and* (Leslau 1968), Basque *bat*, Tagalog *isa* (Matthews 1949), Aymará *ma* (Ebbing 1965). English *a* exemplifies a cardinal article which is a reduced form of the singular numeral; *a* and *one* are now so dissimilar phonologically that they are not obviously related. Another example of this phenomenon is Kurdish (Kurdojev 1957), with a suffix *-ək* (reduced to *-k* after a vowel), derived from the numeral *jek* 'one' (which is a free lexical item); in this case numeral and article show a significant phonological similarity, but differ in position and grammatical status: *jek mal* 'one house', *malək* 'a house'. Many languages are like Kurdish in having a cardinal article which is a reduced form of, and recognizably related to, the numeral 'one'; further examples are Armenian *meg* 'one', *ma* 'a' (Feydit 1969), Samoan *tasi*, *se*, Lakhota *wą́ži*, *wą*, Calabrian *unu*, *nu*.

I have suggested above that English *a* encodes [+ Sg]; *one* is also [+ Sg], but encodes additional lexical content expressing its contrast with the other numerals. In languages where 'a' and 'one' are the same phonologically (segmentally at least), it is not so easy to motivate a semantic difference between them. But that there is such a difference, in many languages at least, is suggested by the fact that the item in question shows the same obligatoriness in singular indefinite noun phrases in the absence of another determiner as noted for English. There is, moreover, a strong tendency for this item, when it appears in accordance with this requirement, to be unstressed, like the definite article, whereas numerals tend to carry a non-zero degree of stress. Again this is not universal; as with the definite article, it does not apply to French and other languages not having word stress.

Let us examine more closely one language, Turkish, in which the quasi-indefinite article is segmentally identical to the numeral 'one', with the form *bir* (Lewis 1967, Dede 1986, Tura 1986). Plural indefinites may take the determiner *bazı* 'sm', but this is frequently omitted. Turkish also agrees with many other languages in that, generally, no determiner is used with predicative indefinites. *Bir* is, however, usually included when a singular noun used predicatively is modified:

(77)   Biz-im   misafir-imiz yaman   bir adam-dır.
          we GEN guest 1PL   remarkable a   man is
          'Our guest is a remarkable man.'

In general, *bir* is only used when the indefinite noun phrase refers to a particular entity, that is, when it is a specific indefinite (as in *I've just bought a superb car*). Where there is no specific referent (for example in *I'm looking for a reliable car*, where I do not have a particular car in mind), or where the identity of the thing referred to is of no importance for the discourse, Turkish has the option of using the bare noun, without determiner, and without number marking. The noun is therefore vague as to number in this "incorporation" construction. Consider (78), where the non-specific bare noun is a direct object:

(78)   Dün   mektup yaz-dı-m.
          Yesterday letter   write PAST 1SG
          'Yesterday I wrote a letter/letters.'

The speaker here is not referring to any particular letter or letters, but is reporting an activity, letter-writing. This incorporated object is clearly distinguished from the specific indefinite (with *bir* in the singular, *-ler* and perhaps *bazı* in the plural) and from the definite, which takes an accusative case suffix:

(79) a.   Dün bir mektup yaz-dı-m.
          'Yesterday I wrote a letter.'
     b.   Dün (bazı) mektup-lar yaz-dı-m.
          'Yesterday I wrote sm letters.'

(80) a.   Dün   mektub-u yaz-dı-m.
          yesterday letter ACC write PAST 1SG
          'Yesterday I wrote the letter.'
     b.   Dün   mektup-lar-ı   yaz-dı-m.
          yesterday letter PL ACC write PAST 1SG
          'Yesterday I wrote the letters.'

Non-accusative noun phrases, however, are not marked for definiteness, and so, as subject for example, a bare noun can be either definite or arbitrary indefinite. The two would usually be distinguished by word order; the restriction of sentence-initial position to topics in Turkish will ensure that a bare noun occurring initially is interpreted as definite, but in non-initial position ambiguity is possible:

(81)   Yer-de   çocuk yat-ıyor-du.
          ground LOC child lie CONT PAST
          'A/The child was lying on the ground.'
          'Children were lying on the ground.'

96

Bir 'a' is not excluded in cases where there is no specific referent. The use of the bare noun just discussed involves neutralization of the number distinction, but the speaker may wish to mark the noun phrase for number, and then *bir* may be used:

(82) a. Yer-de bir çocuk yat-ıyor-du.
         'A child was lying on the ground.'
    b. Bir kitap arı-yor-um.
        a   book look-for CONT 1SG
        'I am looking for a book.'

(82b), like its English gloss, permits two interpretations: the speaker may be looking for a particular book, or any book. But if she intends to convey the latter, it is clear that she will be satisfied on finding a single book, which might not have been the case in the absence of *bir*. For an alternative analysis to that just outlined see Enç (1991), who presents *bir* as fully ambiguous between specific and non-specific, like English *a*; the accusative case suffix is the marker of specificity, not (as suggested above) of definiteness.

We have observed above that in Persian the numeral *yek* 'one' can be used to express a vague indefiniteness ('some . . . or other'), and with this sense can occur with plurals as well as singulars. It is in fact fairly common for such vague indefiniteness to be expressed by a form related to or identical to the singular numeral. English *any* is derived from the same ancestral form as *one* with the addition of an adjective-forming suffix. Irish affords an interesting case. The singular numeral is *aon* (preceded by a particle *a* when not pre-nominal, to give *a haon*); that this word is 'one' is shown by the fact that it is used in arithmetical contexts (*A haon óna deich sin a naoi* 'One from ten leaves nine'). *Aon* is not used as a quasi-indefinite article; indefiniteness is indicated by absence of an article: *an leabhar* 'the book', *leabhar* 'a book'. But *aon* cannot occur alone pre-nominally to convey 'one' either. It must be accompanied by *amháin* 'only': *aon leabhar amháin* 'one book'. Indeed the *aon* is regularly omitted: *leabhar amháin* 'one book'. Used without *amháin*, *aon* means 'any', appearing mainly in non-assertive contexts with mass nouns:[12]

(83) Níl aon airgead agam.
     is-not any money at-me
     'I haven't any money.'

---

[12] Other "secondary" meanings can be found attaching to the singular numeral. In a number of languages it has the sense 'other'; an example is Ewondo: *mod m̀bóág* 'one man', *é mod m̀bóág* 'the other man' (Redden 1979). With this sense it can occur in the plural: *é bod bəvɔ́g* 'the other men'. In Lezgian, the numeral *sa* 'one' (which also occurs, optionally, as a quasi-indefinite article) can express 'only': *sa za-z* (one me DAT) 'only to me' (Haspelmath 1993).

Many languages make a distinction in their cardinality determiner system between specific indefinite and non-specific or vague indefinite, either by having a separate determiner or article for each or by having a single cardinal article which is restricted to one or the other sense. And, in the latter case, it is clear from a number of the languages considered that an article derived from the numeral 'one' may be restricted to specific or to non-specific use. The Persian numeral *yek* and article *-ī*, and Irish *aon*, illustrate the restriction of a cardinality term to non-specific, vague or arbitrary value. And Turkish *bir* tends to be limited to specific use. Several writers report on what appears to be a diachronic change in progress in a number of languages previously not having a cardinal article: the increased use of the numeral 'one', generally with stress reduction, in indefinite noun phrases. In other words, these languages are gradually acquiring a quasi-indefinite cardinal article derived from the singular numeral; and in this early stage where the article is optional it is commonly restricted to specific indefinite use. Examples are Hebrew (Givón 1981) and Mandarin Chinese (Li and Thompson 1981):

(84)　　*Hebrew*
   a.　　Hu mexapes isha-**xat**.
      he look-for woman one
      'He is looking for a woman.' (a particular one)
   b.　　Hu mexapes isha.
      'He is looking for a woman.' (not a particular one)

(85)　　*Mandarin*
   a.　　Mén-kŏu　zuò-zhe yi-ge　　　nán-háizi.
      door mouth sit DUR one CLASS male child
      'In the doorway was sitting a boy.'
   b.　　Wŏ méi yŏu qiānbĭ.
      I　not exist pencil
      'I don't have a pencil.'

But there are also languages in which an optional cardinal article does not show this restriction. In Cantonese the numeral *yāt* 'one' functions as an optional article, but it seems to be possible in at least some types of non-specific indefinite as well as in specific indefinites (Matthews and Yip 1994):

(86) a.　　*specific*
      Yáuh (yāt) ga　　chē jó-jyuh　　　go　　chēut-háu.
      have one　CLASS car block CONT CLASS exit mouth
      'There's a car blocking the exit.'
   b.　　*non-specific*
      A-Yīng　yiu　wán (yāt) go　　　leuhtsī.
      PRT Ying need find one　CLASS lawyer
      'Ying has to find a lawyer.'

Note also that specificity may be only one factor involved in the choice to use the singular numeral with indefinites where this is optional. In languages which lack number marking on nouns, the numeral may occur (in contexts where English would use *a*) because singular number is a significant feature of the referent. This is the case in Yoruba (Rowlands 1969):

(87)　　Mo ri　ọkunrin kan lode.
　　　　I　see man　　one outside
　　　　'I see a man outside.'

Finally, for a language combining some of the patterns exemplified, consider Lakhota, with generally obligatory articles, definite and cardinal. The quasi-indefinite article *wą*, related to *wążi* 'one', is limited to specific indefinites. But the numeral *wążi* itself is used for non-specific indefiniteness:

(88) a.　**C'ą wą** 'ag.li'
　　　　　'He brought **a stick**.'
　　　c.　**C'ą wążi** 'ąu wo.
　　　　　'Put **a stick** on [the fire].'

So here we see the determiner closest morphologically to the numeral 'one' expressing non-specificity (though only in the singular). The article resembling the numeral less (presumably because derived from it earlier), *wą*, continues to express specificity rather than having spread to cover both specific and non-specific indefinites as has occurred in the history of some languages.

A major reason for analysing English *a* as a cardinality expression is that it only appears in singular count noun phrases, alternating with *sm* (and zero) in plural and mass phrases. A similar pattern is seen in many other languages, such as Lakhota (*winųhcala wą* 'an old woman', *c'ą-hąskaska k'eya* (wood/trees tall sm) 'sm tall trees', *c'ą 'etą* (wood/trees from) 'sm wood'). But there are many cases where a cardinal article, clearly derived from and perhaps morphophonologically identical to the numeral 'one', occurs readily with plurals or mass expressions or both. We have seen this in Persian, and another example is Navaho, where *ła'* 'one' may express specific indefiniteness both singular and plural (Reichard 1951). In such cases it is hardly possible to claim that the article encodes [+ Sg] as proposed for English *a*. A language such as Spanish, in which a form of the same determiner, inflected for number, occurs in plural as well as in singular indefinites (*una botella* 'a bottle', *unas botellas* 'sm bottles'), is probably not problematic in this respect. We can say *un(a)* encodes [+ Sg] and *unos/unas* [− Sg]. But what do the Persian and Navaho quasi-indefinite articles encode? I will return to this point in Chapter 8, with the suggestion that it is possible for an article to be a cardinality term yet have no semantic content, acting as a kind of pleonastic.

2.5.3 Types of cardinal article

The morphological types of quasi-indefinite articles are essentially the same as the more commonly occurring definite article types: free-form lexical items and bound forms (inflectional or clitic). The former type is by far the more common. Further examples are unnecessary here, but notice that double determination is also found with cardinal articles, as in the Persian examples (67)–(69) above; to repeat the relevant data, 'a book' may be *ketāb-ī* with bound article, *yek ketāb* with free-form cardinal determiner, or *yek ketāb-ī* with both.

2.5.4 Partitive indefinites

Some languages in which a cardinal article is used with singular indefinites use a partitive structure for plural and mass indefinites. In French and Italian singular indefinites take an article identical to the singular numeral (French *un ami* 'one/a friend', Italian *una casa* 'one/a house'), and plural and mass noun phrases take a "partitive article": French *des journaux* (of-the newspapers) 'sm newspapers', *du pain* (of-the bread) 'sm bread'; Italian *delle case* (of-the houses) 'sm houses', *del vino* (of-the wine) 'sm wine'. A difference between the two languages is that Italian also permits plural and mass indefinites without any determiner, while French does not. This form is particularly favoured in non-assertive contexts (*Hai comprato pane?* 'Have you bought bread?'), but is not limited to such contexts (*Luigi ha comprato (del) pane* 'Luigi has bought (sm) bread'). While French does not in general admit such "bare" plural and mass indefinites, it should be noted that in negative contexts the partitive article tends to be replaced by the preposition *de* alone: *As-tu de la bière?* 'Have you sm/any beer?' – *Non, je n'ai pas de bière* 'No, I haven't any beer'. In the following remarks I limit myself to French data, but the discussion carries over to Italian too.

The partitive article is almost certainly best regarded as a genuine partitive structure, and not as an indefinite article, because the various forms it takes (*du, de la, de l', des*) are identical to sequences of the preposition *de* 'of' plus the various forms of the definite article. It can be analysed as a prepositional partitive structure with a null head and with the noun phrase following *de* interpreted as generic. Thus, *du pain*, representing *de+le pain*, could be glossed literally as 'some of the bread', where 'some' is expressed by a null element, and 'the bread' (representing the domain of the partitive) is generic – generics normally being of this definite form in French. Note that "genuine" partitives, by which I mean partitives over a non-generic domain, are also expressed in French by means of *de* and may also have a null head: *J'ai bu de ce vin* 'I have drunk some of this wine', *J'ai bu du vin que tu m'as apporté* 'I have drunk some of the wine that you brought me'. As the last example shows, *du vin* can mean both 'sm wine' and 'some of the wine'; the possibility of a "genuine" partitive interpretation supports the contention that the indefinite, partitive article, interpretation is also structurally partitive. The two interpretations of *du vin* match the two interpretations of *le vin*, as 'the wine' (simple definite) and 'wine' (generic).

The French partitive indefinite construction is probably to be related to the use of a partitive case for plural and mass indefinites in some languages. Finnish is an agglutinating language with a large number of grammatical cases realized suffixally, expressing much of what in such languages as French is expressed by prepositions (Whitney 1956). One of these cases is the partitive, which, among other uses, occurs after expressions of quantity: *litra maito-a* (litre milk-PART) 'a litre of milk'. Interestingly in view of the ambiguity as regards the domain of partitivity in French *du vin*, Finnish makes a clear distinction in such expressions of partitivity between a generic and a restricted domain. The partitive case is only used where the whole of which some part is being picked out is generic (as in the above example). Where the whole is a definite set or mass smaller than the generic, a different case is used – the elative (typically expressing "extraction"). Compare (89) and (90):

(89)   Saat   palase-n   juusto-a.
         get-2SG piece ACC cheese PART
         'You will get a piece of cheese.'

(90)   Saat   palase-n   juusto-sta.
         get-2SG piece ACC cheese ELAT
         'You will get a piece of the cheese.'

Thus the partitive is well suited to express the same as French *de*, in its partitive indefinite article use. An important difference between these two languages, however, is that Finnish has neither a definite article nor a cardinal article. Where languages mark indefiniteness in plural and mass noun phrases by a partitive expression, this need not be complemented by any obligatory (or regular) marking of definites and singular indefinites.

For plural and mass direct objects, the partitive case, indicating indefiniteness, stands in opposition to the accusative, indicating definiteness:

(91)   Poika   osti   kirjat.
         boy-NOM bought book-PL-ACC
         'The boy bought the books.'

(92)   Poika   osti   kirjoja.
         boy-NOM bought book-PL-PART
         'The boy bought sm books.'

The situation is not so simple, however. The use of the partitive for the object may, as well as indicating indefiniteness in the object, indicate that the action expressed by the predicate is incomplete in some way. It can thus correspond to the use of a progressive verb form in English; so (92) can mean 'The boy was buying sm/the books'. Note that when the partitive is interpreted as having the whole predicate as its domain in this way, the object noun phrase is not necessarily understood as indefinite. On this interpretation the object can also be singular count:

(93) a.   Tyttö   lakaisi lattian.
          girl-NOM swept floor-ACC
          'The girl swept the floor.'
    b.   Tyttö   lakaisi lattiaa.
          girl-NOM swept floor-PART
          'The girl was sweeping the floor.'

Plural and mass subject noun phrases may also be in the partitive, to indicate indefiniteness, but only if the verb is intransitive; subjects of transitives must be nominative (and may in principle be understood as definite or indefinite). An intransitive verb with partitive subject does not show subject agreement as it does with a nominative subject, but appears in an unmarked third-person singular form. The structure is evidently an impersonal or unaccusative one, the "subject" being in a non-subject position (as in English *There entered three strangers*) – this being no doubt what permits it to take a case other than nominative:

(94) a.   Kukat   ovat maljakossa.
          flower-PL-NOM are vase-INESS
          'The flowers are in the vase.'
    b.   Maljakossa on kukkia.
          vase-INESS is flower-PL-PART
          'There are sm flowers in the vase.'

The fact that the partitivity expressed by the Finnish partitive case does not necessarily take as its domain the noun phrase which bears this case, but may be interpreted relative to the predicate as a whole, makes it clear that there is no encoding of [– Def] here. In fact for French too there is no reason to suppose that the partitive structure encodes [– Def] any more than the "indefinite article" *un* does. The null head of the partitive (if this is the correct analysis) need only be marked for cardinality, as [– Sg], to ensure that *des voitures* means 'sm cars' (some of all the cars there are) and not 'a car' (one of all the cars there are). If the analysis I have suggested for the French partitive article is correct also for Finnish partitive indefinites, these too must involve a null head, the partitive noun phrase being a complement to this head. But the fact that partitive case is apparently restricted to noun phrases not in subject position argues against this view. This restriction would be hard to account for if partitive case were assigned within the subject/

object noun phrase by its head rather than to this noun phrase by an external case assigner, the verb. I leave this question open.

The material discussed here relates to a proposal in the syntax literature that unaccusative verbs (those like English *enter* which permit a post-verbal "subject" with pleonastic *there* in subject position, as above) are able, optionally, to assign an abstract partitive case to their complement in a number of languages. The point is that these verbs take a single noun phrase argument, which underlyingly is a complement, because it typically requires a theme or patient θ-role rather than, for example, agent. This complement may then advance to the vacant subject position (giving, for example, English *Three strangers entered* or French *Des étudiants sont arrivés* 'Sm students arrived'). Or it may stay in complement position, subject position then being filled by a pleonastic (*There entered three strangers*, *Il est arrivé des étudiants* 'There arrived sm students'). This latter option is made possible by the option of partitive case assignment to complement position, but is only available to indefinite complements, since partitive case (it is claimed) entails indefiniteness. For discussion see Belletti (1988), Haegeman (1994: chapter 6). But this hypothesis differs from the present account of the French and Finnish data discussed in that it assumes singular indefinites (*un ami*) and those with numeral determiners (*trois étudiants*) to be abstractly partitive, not just those with a partitive article (French) or overt partitive case (Finnish). The unaccusative facts and their relationship to indefiniteness will be further discussed in Chapter 6. For detailed discussion of definiteness and indefiniteness and of the range of functions of the partitive in Finnish, see Chesterman (1991) and Kiparsky (1996).

2.5.5 *Bare indefinites*

In languages that have a quasi-indefinite article, there are almost invariably some types of indefinite in which it does not occur. These are usually the less specific or less referential types. We have seen that there are languages in which the article only appears in non-specific or vague indefinite noun phrases, but the more common case is for the article to occur only in specific indefinites. There is then a diachronic tendency for such specific quasi-indefinite articles to spread into non-specific contexts, with the result that many languages show a cardinal article in specific contexts and in some, but not all, non-specific contexts. Let us exemplify this from Spanish (data partly from Butt and Benjamin 1994). Spanish has a cardinal article varying for gender and number:

	masculine	*feminine*
singular	un	una
plural	unos	unas

Unos/unas thus corresponds to English *sm*, the distinction between [+ Sg] and [−Sg] being encoded in the desinence rather than in the lexical stem. The article is used in singular count indefinite noun phrases with specific reference, and equally in many non-specifics. In the plural, the article is commonly omitted, in specific as well as non-specific indefinites, often with little if any difference of meaning: *Nos dieron flores* 'They gave us (sm) flowers', *Trae clavos* 'Bring (sm) nails'. *Unos/unas* tends to be included where some emphasis on the cardinality is desired: *Tomamos unas cervezas* 'We had sm/a few beers', *Todavía tenía unos restos de fe* 'He still had sm/a few vestiges of faith'. And it can indicate non-literal use of the noun: *Son payasos* 'They are clowns', *Son unos payasos* 'They are (like) clowns'. The article cannot be used with mass nouns, which are commonly therefore "bare": *Hay vino en la mesa* 'There's (sm) wine on the table'. Bare plural and mass noun phrases will be considered more closely in Chapter 4.

Turning to singulars, where the article is in general obligatory in the absence of another determiner, simple indefinites tend to be bare in two major circumstances, in both of which the emphasis is on the descriptive content of the noun. The first is when the noun phrase is predicative, and here Spanish is displaying a characteristic shared by a great many languages. Predicative noun phrases expressing the profession, social status, sex etc. of human beings particularly tend to be bare:

(95) a.　María se hizo **dentista**.
　　　　 'María became a dentist.'
　　 b.　Juan es **soltero**.
　　　　 'Juan is a bachelor.'

But if the noun is modified it usually takes the article (and this applies also to plurals):

(96) a.　Es **un actor** que nunca encuentra trabajo.
　　　　 'He is an actor who never finds work.'
　　 b.　Son **unos conservadores** arrepentidos.
　　　　 'They are repentant conservatives.'

And nouns denoting personal qualities rather than membership of a particular group or category take the article (compare *(unos) payasos* 'clowns' above):

(97) a.　Es **un genio**.
　　　　 'He is a genius.'
　　 b.　Es **un ladrón**.
　　　　 'He is a thief.' (not a professional one)

Omission of the cardinal article in predication is also normal (though not obligatory) with a number of other nouns not easy to characterize in general terms:

Es (una) cuestión de dinero 'It is a question of money', *Es (una) víctima de las circunstancias* 'He/She is a victim of circumstances'. But on the other hand: *Es una pena* 'It is a pity', *Es un problema* 'It is a problem'. With this last group, however, omission of the article is usual under negation: *No es problema* 'It isn't a problem'.

The second circumstance inducing bare simple indefinites is when certain nouns (again difficult to characterize, but said by Butt and Benjamin to typically denote things of which one normally has only one at a time) head the complement of a particular range of verbs ('have', 'carry', 'produce', 'seek' among others):

(98) a.   Ana tiene **coche**.
        'Ana has a car.'
    b.   Hay que pedir **hora**.
        'It is necessary to ask for an appointment.'

Again, the article tends to be included if the noun is modified.

In addition, the article is omitted after certain prepositions, such as *con* 'with', *sin* 'without', *por* 'by way of', 'instead of', *como* 'as': *una casa con jardín* 'a house with a garden', *utilizar su zapato como martillo* 'to use one's shoe as a hammer'.

Languages with cardinal articles vary greatly in the extent to which bare indefinites occur, and Spanish offers a good example of a middle-of-the-road language in this respect. The reader is invited to compare other languages known with Spanish to see whether the list of contexts allowing bare indefinites in one language is a subset of the corresponding list in the other. See also Van Peteghem (1989).

2.6 General remarks

This chapter has surveyed the forms and uses of articles which express definiteness and indefiniteness, taking articles to be typically weak forms with limited semantic content. Definite articles derive historically overwhelmingly from demonstratives (which are also definite determiners), while indefinite articles generally derive from the singular numeral, and I have claimed that the latter are in fact cardinal articles, which express indefiniteness only indirectly as a result of never co-occurring with definite determiners. A complication for this claim is presented by languages with a cardinal article but no definite article, definiteness being signalled by absence of the cardinal article; I will address this problem in Chapter 8. While definite articles, along with other definite determiners, are associated syntactically with some Det position (yet to be given a precise definition), my proposal is that cardinal, or quasi-indefinite, articles have their locus, along with numerals, in some more interior cardinality position in the noun phrase. Definite articles encode [+ Def], and cardinal articles may encode [+ Sg] (English *a*) or [– Sg] (English *sm*). But both may also carry agreement features (for gender, number etc.), and, more importantly, may be restricted to, for instance, anaphoric definite use or specific indefinite use.

This last point raises the question whether an anaphoric definite article is different in kind from a demonstrative. In other words, if a definite article carries a feature [+ Ana] or a cardinal article a feature [+ Spec], is this really "simple" definiteness or indefiniteness? And is there then any significance in the term "article"? This term is a traditional one, and the rough definition I have given – weak form and minimal semantic content – is one that most traditional grammarians would be prepared to go along with. But for some languages it is difficult to demonstrate phonological weakness in putative articles, and "minimal semantic content" is a little vague. I want to maintain the distinction, however, between articles and other ("complex") determiners. I think our intuition points to a real distinction here, however difficult to pin down. And I will argue in Chapter 8 that this intuition can be given content by treating articles as having a pleonastic function.

Cardinal articles tend to be free-standing determiners, but occasionally occur as bound forms. Free forms and bound forms are both frequent among definite articles, and these two types taken together are overwhelmingly more common than the other forms of expression discussed (adpositional marking, agreement etc.). In fact we will see in Chapter 5 that the adpositional and agreement types very often do not involve direct reference to [+ Def]. Moreover, bound articles turn out to be usually phrasal clitics, with the Wackernagel type being particularly common. So any impression that anything goes in the way definiteness is expressed would not be accurate. A particularly interesting observation is that some second-position phrasal-clitic articles form a clitic complex with other noun phrase features, such as case, suggesting that what we have here is the nominal counterpart of the clause-level auxiliary constituent.

A point which emerges indirectly from the discussion is that there seems to be no necessary relationship between definite article type and cardinal article type in a given language, or between either of these and salient typological features of the language. It is true that in English both articles are pre-nominal free forms and that in Lakhota both are (probably) post-nominal free forms; but Romanian and Amharic have pre-nominal free-form cardinal articles and suffixal definite articles. And it is not clear that the post-nominal position of the Lakhota articles follows from the SOV word order of this language. Issues such as this call for detailed investigation of the structures of individual languages, beyond the scope of this survey.

3
Complex definites and indefinites

The cross-linguistic survey continues in this chapter, in which we turn our attention to noun phrases whose definiteness or indefiniteness is due to something other than presence or absence of an article. The range of these "complex" definites (including proper nouns, personal pronouns, and noun phrases containing a demonstrative or possessive modifier) and indefinites was outlined in Chapter 1 in relation to English, and here we look at their forms, structures and behaviour more widely. Some of these expressions are central to an understanding of what definiteness is and how it works, and will play an important part in the discussion in subsequent chapters. The grammar of these noun phrase types is complex, and the discussion here will be limited to pointing out the most salient aspects, enough to enable us to consider how they fit into the general system of definite and indefinite noun phrases.

3.1 Demonstratives

Demonstratives are probably to be found in all languages, and they seem to be inherently definite – which is in part why definite articles almost always arise from them historically, presumably by some process of semantic weakening. Bear in mind, however, that in Chapter 1 I entertained the possibility that this assumption of inherent definiteness could be mistaken, an indefinite demonstrative existing in the form of *such*. This possibility will be examined below, and rejected; in this section I anticipate this finding, and continue to assume that demonstratives are universally definite in meaning. Note that if this is correct, it seems to mean that definiteness exists in some form in all languages.

3.1.1 Deictic distinctions

The point was made earlier that the two-way deictic contrast exhibited in English between *this* and *that* can in principle be characterized in terms of distance or in relation to the category of person. On both accounts the speaker forms the deictic centre; [± Prox] is understood in terms of proximity to the speaker, and the person analysis represents the contrast as association with first person or not.

Complex definites and indefinites

In fact, the speaker is central not only to the concept of first person, but to the entire category of person, since the presence of the speaker in a set of individuals defines that set as first person, regardless of whether or not the hearer(s) or others are also present. Cross-linguistically, this kind of demonstrative system, where the speaker is the primary reference point, is basic, being found in almost all languages. But languages vary on whether person or distance from the speaker is the organizing principle. For English, with a two-term contrast, it is not obvious whether distance or person is the relevant dimension. But many languages distinguish three demonstratives, and then the situation may be clearer.

Lezgian has a rather rich demonstrative system (Haspelmath 1993), but the core of it consists of the following three-way contrast:

proximal	i
medial	a
distal	at'a

The first term is used to indicate something which is close to the speaker, the second something not particularly close (but not necessarily close to the hearer either), and the third something quite distant. Other three-term distance-based systems are: Lakhota *le* (proximal), *he* (medial), *ka* (distal) (Buechel 1939, Boas and Deloria 1939); probably Lithuanian *šis*, *tàs*, *anàs* (Dambriūnas, Klimas and Schmalstieg 1972); and possibly Serbo-Croat *ovaj*, *taj*, *onaj* (Javarek and Sudjić 1963), though Frei (1944) claims this system is person-based.

This contrasts with the three-term system of Ewondo, a Bantu language in which nouns are grouped into a number of classes (some of these classes complementing each other as singular–plural pairs). Each class has a distinct root from which demonstratives are formed by the addition of suffixes (Redden 1979). I illustrate from classes 1 and 2, a singular–plural pair of mostly human nouns:

	class 1	class 2
assoc. 1 person	ɲɔ́	bá
assoc. 2 person	ɲɔ́lɔ	bálā
assoc. 3 person	ɲɔ́lí	bálí

ɲɔ́ 'this' indicates something near to or connected with the speaker, ɲɔ́lɔ 'that' something near to or connected with the hearer, and ɲɔ́lí 'that' something remote from or unconnected with both. Such three-term person-based systems are very common, other examples being Modern Armenian *ays* (first person), *ayt* (second person), *ayn* (third person) (Feydit 1969); Japanese *kono*, *sono*, *ano* (Dunn and Yanada 1958); and Maori *nei*, *naa*, *raa* (Bauer 1993).

Even with such three-term systems, however, it is not always clear whether distance or person is the principle involved, and some languages may mingle the two. The Latin demonstratives *hic, iste, ille* are traditionally considered to relate to person (for example Gildersleeve and Lodge 1895, Kennedy 1962), but Frei (1944) argues that *iste* does not necessarily relate to second person. Lewis (1967) describes the Turkish system *bu, şu, o* as based on three degrees of distance from the speaker, but Bastuji (1976) argues that *şu* is merely an emphatic variant of *bu*. Spanish offers an example of a possibly mixed system. The three forms *este, ese, aquel* are, like those of Latin, traditionally regarded as based on person (see for example Ramsden 1959), but Anderson and Keenan (1985) claim that distance is the basis. It seems in fact that *ese* can contrast with *este* as indicating connection with the hearer as opposed to connection with the speaker (*Ojalá que yo tuviera* **ese** *talento* 'I wish I had that talent (of yours)'), and can also contrast with *aquel* as indicating lesser versus greater remoteness, regardless of distance from the hearer (*¿No ves* **ese** *coche?* 'Can't you see that car?'). With many languages, it is simply unclear from descriptions what the basis is, as with Aymará *aka, uka, khaya/khuyu*, said by Ebbing (1965) to correspond to Spanish *este, ese, aquel*.

Languages may even have more than one demonstrative system, and in this way make use of both the distance and the person basis. Shuswap has one series expressing a three-way distance contrast, and another showing a two-way person-related contrast (Kuipers 1974), though, curiously, the second term of the latter series relates to second person rather than being merely negatively specified with respect to first person:

proximal	ɣy-ʔén(e)	'this'
medial	y-ɣíne	'that'
distal	ɣy-lúne	'yonder'
assoc. 1 person	ɣy-ɣi?	'this (by me)'
assoc. 2 person	ɣy-ɣey	'that (by you)'

Surinam Carib is similar, but with two series each of two terms (Hoff 1968). The distance-based set distinguishes animate from inanimate reference, and has *mo:se* (animate) and *e:nï* (inanimate) to pick out something in the immediate vicinity of the speech event (thus apparently corresponding to both proximal and medial in standard three-term systems); and *mo:kï* (animate) and *mo:nï* (inanimate) to pick out something more distant. The participant-related set appears to have inanimate forms only, with *e:ro* for something near, relating to or concerning the speaker, and *mo:ro* for something not associated with the speaker. Thus the question *E: nï se maɲ?* 'Do you want this one here?' may receive an answer in which *e:nï* is repeated: *A:a, e:nï se wa* 'Yes, I want this one here'. But an answer to *E:ro se maɲ?* 'Do you want this one (near me)?' cannot make reference to the same object by means of another *e:ro*: *A:a, mo:ro se wa* 'Yes, I want that one (not near me)'. So, unusually, the "[Ass1]" form *e:ro* expresses association with the speaker only, first-person singular, not with first person in general as is standardly the case in person-related systems.[1]

The Catalan system resembles the Spanish one, but shows an interesting peculiarity. In principle there are three demonstratives: *aquest* (first person), *aqueix* (second person), *aquell* (third person). But the middle term, *aqueix*, has largely fallen into disuse, especially in the spoken language, and its function has been taken over by *aquest*, so that Catalan has effectively a two-term system. Now languages with two-way demonstrative contrasts nearly always follow the English pattern of a first-person or proximal form contrasting with a non-first-person or non-proximal one, where "proximal" is defined in terms of proximity to the speaker. But in Catalan, with the merging of the first- and second-person functions under one form, the contrast is between third person and non-third person, or distal and non-distal. Thus *aquesta galleda* may be 'this bucket' (which I have) or 'that bucket' (which you have), and *aquella galleda* is 'that bucket' (over there, or which neither you nor I have). Such a system is extremely unusual, though Carib, on Hoff's analysis, would have the same kind of contrast in its distance-based series, between distal and non-distal.

Catalan exemplifies a rather common diachronic phenomenon, the reduction of three-term demonstrative systems to systems of two terms. The three terms of Latin were reduced at a much earlier period in some other Romance varieties, Old French,

---

[1] This oddity suggests that Hoff's analysis of the Carib demonstratives may be mistaken, and that this language may have a single demonstrative system based on more elaborate person distinctions. I suggest the correct analysis distinguishes association with exclusive and inclusive first person as well as with second and third person. The evidence is that distinctions of this kind are made in the personal pronoun system (with some minimal similarities of form between pronouns and demonstratives which, on this analysis, correspond). I give demonstratives and personal pronouns together for comparison:

	demonstratives		personal pronouns	singular	plural
ASS1EXC	e:ro		1EXC	au	a?na
ASS1INC	e:nï (mo:se)		1INC	kïxko	kïxka:ro
ASS2	mo:ro		2	amo:ro	amïiyaro
ASS3	mo:nï (mo:kï)		3	moxko	moxka:ro

The distinction between inclusive and exclusive first person plural, made by many languages, amounts to having two expressions corresponding to *we*, one of which includes the hearer and the other not. Carib seems to have this distinction in singular as well as plural, with a "singular" inclusive pronoun form, *kïxko*, glossed by Hoff as 'you and I'; its plural, *kïxka:ro*, presumably refers to a set larger than two which includes speaker and hearer. For further discussion see 3.4.1.

for example, showing *cist* 'this' and *cil* 'that'. English too shows the relic of an earlier three-term system in the distal forms *yon, yonder* (archaic in modern spoken English though still in use in some dialects). German too has, in formal varieties, three demonstratives: proximal *dieser*, medial *der*, distal *jener*. But the last has largely fallen out of use in the spoken language.[2] In Lezgian, mentioned above as distinguishing three degrees of distance, the distal form *at'a* is rare (Haspelmath 1993), suggesting that the same process is at work here; here the medial form appears to have largely taken over the distal function. Two-term systems are, in fact, by far the most commonly occurring type. Some further instances are: Mandarin *zhèi* 'this', *nèi* 'that' (Li and Thompson 1981); Persian *īn, ān* (Mace 1971); Biblical Hebrew *zeh, hû'* (Lambdin 1973); Khalkha Mongolian *enə, terə* (Poppe 1970); Hidatsa *héo, ka* (Matthews 1965); Latvian *šis, tas* (Budiņa-Lazdiņa 1966); Albanian *ky, ai* (Newmark, Hubbard and Prifti 1982); Wolof *bii* or *bile, bee* or *bale* (Mbassy Njie 1982, Malherbe and Sall 1989).[3]

Despite this predominance of two-term systems, there are languages with four, five or even six demonstratives organized in the ways discussed. I suggested above that Carib may have a four-term person-related system. Tswana combines both distance and person in its system (Cole 1955), with the following forms being those used for nouns in class 1: *yôno* 'immediately next to the speaker', *yô* 'relatively near the speaker', *yôo* 'less close to the speaker, and usually near the hearer', *yôlê* 'remote from speaker and hearer'. Notice that the second term is morphologically basic, the others being formed by the addition of suffixes; the first term, *yôno*, is relatively infrequent. Navaho has a similar system, but with five terms (Young and Morgan 1987): *díí* 'near the speaker', *'eii* 'relatively near the speaker', *naghái* 'near the hearer or at some distance from the speaker', *ńléí* 'distant from both speaker and hearer', *'éí* 'remote and invisible'. Malagasy has a purely distance-based system, with six degrees of distance in relation to the speaker (Anderson and Keenan 1985): *ity, io, itsy, iny, iroa, iry*; these are supplemented

---

[2] Interestingly, the outcome of this reduction in spoken German is a system in which *der* functions as a general demonstrative without deictic content (like French *ce*), while *dieser* is used both as a proximal form and as a second general form without deictic restriction, especially in contexts where *der* might be confused with the definite article, which in careful speech is identical phonologically apart from its lack of stress (Durrell 1991).

[3] Classical Greek has three principal demonstratives, but distinguishing only two degrees of distance: proximal *houtos* and *hode*, distal *ekeinos* (Goodwin 1992). The distinction between *houtos* and *hode* is not clear cut, but the former is sometimes preferred for referring to something already mentioned, and the latter for referring to something about to be mentioned or something approaching or coming into view. Swedish, too, shows more forms than deictic distinctions, with *den här* (used in speech and informal writing) and *denna/denne* (essentially restricted to writing) for 'this'; and *den där* (speech and informal writing; preferred for concrete, perceptible referents) and *den* (stylistically unrestricted; preferred for abstract or non-present referents) for 'that' (Holmes and Hinchliffe 1994).

by an anaphoric form *ilay*. Hualapai also has a six-way system, but mixing distance and association with person: *va* 'close to the speaker', *ya* 'close to both speaker and hearer', *nyu* 'close to the hearer', *wa* 'close enough to point at', *ha* 'far away', *tha* 'very remote and perhaps invisible' (Watahomigie, Bender and Yamamoto 1982).

There are many languages in which the demonstratives involve other deictic categories, generally in addition to distance or person (or both). A fairly common one is visibility, as seen in some of the examples above. Some languages, like Dyirbal (Dixon 1972), make distinctions of height; see below. Lezgian, in addition to the three degrees of distance mentioned (largely reduced to two), has two demonstratives distinguishing "superiority" and "inferiority": *wini* 'that up there' and *aǧa* 'that down there' – though these too are falling into disuse. For useful surveys of demonstrative systems, with further examples, see Frei (1944) and Anderson and Keenan (1985).

The deictic distinctions illustrated in this section are not essential to demonstratives, and there are demonstrative systems in which no distance or person contrast is expressed. I have mentioned Egyptian Arabic, with a single demonstrative *da*; there is another form to be discussed below, *dukha*, expressing contrast, but this form too is devoid of deictic content. A similar general purpose demonstrative is found in Supyire: *ŋké kàn-he* (DEM village-DEF) 'this/that village' (Carlson 1994). This kind of system is unusual, and a much more common situation is where such a general demonstrative coexists with others which do make deictic distinctions. French is a case in point; the general demonstrative is *ce*, but this can be reinforced by the deictic enclitics (on the noun) *-ci* and *-là*: *ce jardin* 'this/that garden', *ce jardin-ci* 'this garden', *ce jardin-là* 'that garden'. Similarly, Czech has a general demonstrative *ten*, without deictic content, the most commonly occurring (Lee and Lee 1959). But where one needs to be more exact there are forms available incorporating the deictic particles *-to* and *tam-*: *tento* 'this', *tamten* 'that'. Polish has in theory a two-term system, *ten* 'this' and *tamten* 'that'. But the distinction, and the latter form, are largely limited to contrastive contexts; otherwise *ten* is used with the deictic contrast neutralized. Thus *tamten* is distal and *ten* deictically unmarked (Kryk 1987). In the same way Romanian uses *acest(a)* as a general deictically unmarked demonstrative, but has in addition a distal form *acel(a)* used when it is necessary to make a deictic contrast (Murrell and Ştefănescu-Drăgăneşti 1970). Other languages have a deictically unmarked demonstrative which is not basic in the sense of being the form generally used except in contrastive or otherwise special circumstances; rather it is additional to a fully specified deictic system such as those discussed. In such cases the unmarked demonstrative may be partly or fully restricted to particular functions. Latin has, in addition to its series expressing three degrees of deixis, *hic*, *iste*, *ille*, an unmarked form *is*, often labelled "anaphoric". Certainly one of the common uses of *is* is to pick out an entity recently mentioned, but it is also the usual form for the antecedent of a relative clause, as in *is vir quem vidisti* 'that man whom you saw'. A similar situation obtains in Swedish. As well as the four forms expressing two degrees of deixis discussed, Swedish has a deictically unmarked form *den* – identical to the distal demonstrative except that, unlike this, it is not accompanied in the noun phrase by the definite suffix on the noun, and distinguished from the free-form definite article only by being fully stressed. This demonstrative only occurs as antecedent to restrictive relatives: *de bilar som jag gillar bäst* 'those/the cars that I like best'. In other languages, the unmarked, general demonstrative occurs more freely, and serves simply as an alternative to the deictically marked forms. Lakhota, with its three-term distance-based system mentioned above, also has a general demonstrative *'e*. And Finnish supplements its two-degree series, *tämä* 'this', *tuo* 'that', with the unmarked demonstrative *se* (Whitney 1956).

A language with a single demonstrative which is not, however, deictically neutral is Dyirbal (Dixon 1972). Nouns in Dyirbal are usually accompanied by a class marker which encodes deixis: *yala-* (proximal visible, or deictically neutral), *bala-* (distal visible), *ŋala-* (invisible). But *yala-* is generally replaced in absolutive case by *giɲa-*, also encoding [+ Prox] and the only true demonstrative – and only occurring in absolutive case. However, Dyirbal also has several sets of secondary deixis markers, which can be added to this demonstrative or to any non-demonstrative noun marker. The first consists of *gala* 'vertically up', *gali* 'vertically down', *galu* 'out in front'. Then there are the sets *bayḏi, bayḏa, bayḏu* indicating short, medium and long distance downhill; *dayi, daya, dayu* indicating short, medium and long distance uphill; *balbala, balbalu* for medium and long distance downriver; *dawala, dawalu* for medium and long distance upriver. In addition there are *guya* 'across the river' and *bawal* 'a long way'. Interestingly, while the demonstrative *giɲa* by itself is proximal, it seems to lose this sense in combination with the secondary markers; so *giɲa-bawal* (this-long+way) expresses something like 'that over there'.

3.1.2 Non-deictic distinctions

Demonstrative systems may involve other, non-deictic categories in addition to a deictic basis. The most obvious of these is anaphora. It is nearly always the case that the distance distinctions discussed can relate to temporal and emotional distance as well as spatial distance, and that demonstratives expressing these can pick out referents in the preceding discourse. Thus proximal forms tend to serve for anaphoric reference to things very recently mentioned and distal forms to things mentioned further back in the discourse. Person-based systems too allow the same anaphoric use, with first-person forms admitting what is in effect an extended use as proximal, and non-first-person or (often) third-person forms a similar distal use. This is the case in Latin (generally taken to have a person-based system) where *hic* (first person) and *ille* (third person) are the deictic forms normally used (often in contrast with each other, as more versus less recently mentioned) for anaphoric reference. In this use, distal and proximal demonstratives frequently have the senses 'the former' and 'the latter'. It is also common for proximal or first-person forms to be used anaphorically to pick out something previously mentioned by the speaker, and non-proximal, medial, non-first-person, or second-person forms to pick out something mentioned by the person currently being addressed – and, of course, distal or third-person forms for a referent mentioned by some third party. Languages with a general, deictically unmarked demonstrative may also use this in the anaphoric function. Latin again illustrates this, with *is* frequently appearing anaphorically, especially where the distance back into the previous discourse of the earlier mention of the referent is not an issue.

But many languages have a special demonstrative for anaphoric use. Typically this does not prevent the deictically marked forms occurring anaphorically, especially where there is reason to indicate that the earlier mention was recent or remote or to make a recent–remote contrast between two referents. The anaphoric form can therefore be comparable in use with the anaphoric function of the general demonstrative in Latin, though in some cases it seems to have the more specific sense of 'just mentioned'. This is so of Surinam Carib, which, in addition to the complex deictic system discussed above, has an "immediate anaphoric" demonstrative *ino:ro* (animate), *i:ro* (inanimate). For a not necessarily immediate anaphoric form, consider Swahili, a Bantu language like Ewondo, with demonstratives formed on the root of class markers. Swahili has a two-way distance-based deictic system, formed by attachment to the class marker of the proximal prefix *h-* followed by reduplication of the root vowel, or the distal suffix *-le* (Ashton 1944, Perrott 1951). Thus, to take two classes representing singular and plural forms of inanimate nouns, with the class markers *ki* and *vi* respectively, we have proximal *hiki* 'this', *hivi* 'these', and distal *kile* 'that', *vile* 'those'. Now, the anaphoric demonstrative is like the proximal form but with a suffix *-o* (which triggers some changes to the root): *hicho*, *hivyo*. The basic *h-* and *-le* demonstratives can be used anaphorically, but the forms with *-o* can only be so used.

Yoruba also has a two-term deictic series, *yi* 'this', *yẹn* 'that', plus an anaphoric form *naa* (Rowlands 1969). Unusually, though, *naa* can co-occur with the deictic forms:

(1)   aṣọ ti   mo ra   lana   yi   naa
        cloth which I bought yesterday this ANA
        'this (already mentioned) cloth which I bought yesterday'

Demonstratives cannot usually co-occur, and indeed I used such co-occurrence in Chapter 2 as evidence for anaphoric determiners in some languages being articles rather than demonstratives. But it may be that Yoruba *naa* is not a determiner, since it does have some adverbial uses, with senses such as 'also', 'indeed', 'as has been said'. In Hausa, anaphoric demonstrative reference is indicated by tone (Kraft and Kirk-Greene 1973). Hausa too has a two-way deictic system, *nan* 'this', *can* 'that'. The tone on these forms is usually falling or low. But changing this tone to high (with a preceding high-tone syllable changing to falling) signals previous mention:

(2) a. rìgá-n   nàn
        gown DEF this
        'this gown'

   b. rìgâ-n   nán
        gown DEF this-ANA
        'this gown (previously mentioned)'

(3) a. kújèrá-r   càn
        chair DEF that
        'that chair'

   b. kújèrâ-r   cán
        chair DEF that-ANA
        'that chair (previously mentioned)'

A final observation on anaphoric demonstratives is that, particularly for those limited to immediately preceding mention, they often serve also as the expression for 'same'. This is the case with Lezgian *ha*, and Nama *//xaá* (Hagman 1973).

Demonstratives can also encode the fact that a referent is the current topic of the discourse. It is often difficult to distinguish such topic demonstratives from anaphoric ones, since a topic is likely to have been just mentioned. This is the case in Sarcee, where the proximal form *dìní* can be used in reference to something under discussion and the distal form *nùyú* for something mentioned earlier (Cook 1984). But a particularly clear instance is provided by Swahili, in which topic is expressed by the position of the demonstrative, and anaphoric reference quite differently. We have seen above that Swahili makes a two-way distance contrast and has an anaphoric demonstrative. These forms occur post-nominally, but the deictic *h-* and *-le* forms can appear pre-nominally, and then they indicate that the referent is the current topic. Ashton (1944) and Perrott (1951) comment that this use approximates to that of a definite article.

Contrast between referents is expressed in a variety of ways cross-linguistically. Swahili does not permit the use of the proximal and distal forms together for contrast (as in English *this and/or that*). The tendency is rather to use the proximal form twice: **Hii** *yafutika,* **hii** *haifutiki* 'That [*sc.* sin] can be blotted out, this one cannot be'. Some languages have a special demonstrative to express contrast. Egyptian Arabic has been mentioned as having a basic one-demonstrative system with no deictic distinctions: *da* 'this' or 'that'. But there is in addition a form *dukha* used mainly for contrast: *muʃ da lakin dukha* 'not this but that' (Mitchell 1962). Nama has a basic two-way distance contrast: *nee* 'this', *//nãá* 'that'. But it is not possible to use these two forms contrastively; instead a third form, *náú*, is used, and can contrast with either of the two basic terms. *Náú* expresses the further member of a contrasted pair, and so naturally occurs frequently with the proximal demonstrative: *nee kxòep tsĩ́ náú kxòep* 'this male person and that male person'. But if neither referent is near, *náú* can be contrasted with *//nãá*.

Finally, many languages have emphatic demonstratives. The process of reinforcing demonstratives morphologically, for example by the addition of further deictic particles, is common, and a reinforced form sometimes becomes the basic one when a previous basic form weakens semantically to become a definite article. But basic and reinforced demonstratives co-occur widely. Lithuanian has an emphatic demonstrative *šìtas* formed by combination of the basic proximal and medial forms. Swahili uses reduplication for emphasis: *hiki hiki* 'this', *kile kile* 'that'. But Swahili has another, more complex, emphatic structure, based on the anaphoric demonstrative; this form (*hivyo* in the plural class illustrated above) is preceded by a double reduplication of the root, but with the two vowels of the anaphoric form. Thus *vivyo hivyo* 'these very same'.

3.1.3 Forms and positions

Demonstratives overwhelmingly take the form of lexical items, as in English, and they are almost invariably stressed.[4] This is a major point of contrast between demonstratives and definite articles (for languages which have word stress), and is important in diachronic considerations, because definite articles in nearly all languages that have them are descended historically from demonstratives. It is in fact usually a deictically unmarked demonstrative, or a non-proximal or non-first-person one, which provides the source of a definite article. One consequence of this is that in many languages the definite article is segmentally identical or very similar to one of the demonstratives (though differing in stress). An example of this is German, where unstressed *der* is the article, and the same form with stress is a demonstrative unmarked for distance. In Danish, similarly, *den* is both a demonstrative and (with reduced vowel: [dən]) the free-form definite article. Recall, however, that definite articles occasionally show deictic distinctions, and then they may well derive from first-person or proximal demonstratives as well as others.

Not all demonstratives are free-form lexical items. It was observed in Chapter 2 that demonstratives in Bella Coola are enclitic on the noun, like the definite

---

[4] English provides a clear illustration of this point. The complementizer *that*, which serves to introduce certain types of subordinate clause, is normally unstressed and pronounced with a reduced vowel: [ðət]. But the demonstrative *that* never has this pronunciation; it always has a full vowel, because it is in principle a stressed form: [ðæt].

article (which shows the same deictic distinctions). Hualapai shows the curious phenomenon of three of its six demonstratives (those representing the second, fourth and sixth deictic degrees) being pre-nominal lexical forms and the remaining three being suffixes on the noun. Lango has phrasal-clitic demonstratives, suffixal to the final word of the noun phrase (Noonan 1992): *gwôkk à dwóŋ-ŋì* (dog LINK big+SG-this) 'this big dog'.

A number of languages have discontinuous demonstratives in which part of the information is conveyed by an affix or particle of some kind. In French the demonstrative *ce* is a pre-nominal determiner, but the optional deictic element is a suffix on the noun: *ce livre-ci* 'this book', *cette voiture-là* 'that car'. The two elements come together in the corresponding pronominal demonstrative, but with a different form for the determiner element: *celui-ci* 'this one' (masculine), *celle-là* 'that one' (feminine), and also *ceci* 'this', *cela* 'that' (forms not marked for gender). A somewhat similar situation is found in Irish, but the post-nominal particle is obligatory, and the pre-nominal determiner element is the definite article: *an leabhar* 'the book', *an leabhar seo* 'this book', *an leabhar sin* 'that book', *an leabhar úd* 'yonder book'. The pro-nominal forms consist (not surprisingly in view of the relationship assumed between pronouns and definite articles) of the appropriate third-person personal pronoun plus a form of the same particles: *sé seo* 'this one' (masculine), *sí sin* 'that one' (feminine), *siad siúd* 'those', 'yonder ones'. These Irish facts look at first sight like counterevidence to the claim that demonstratives involve (universally) more than a combination of the definite article and a deictic element. But the suffixal element can in certain circumstances occur independently of the article or personal pronoun, as a complete demonstrative equivalent to the French genderless forms *ceci*, *cela*, referring to a pro-position or an entity which cannot be assigned a gender: *Is trua sin* (is pity that) 'That's a pity'. This seems to indicate that *seo*, *sin* and *siúd*, unlike French *-ci* and *-là*, are not merely deictic particles (variants of *anseo* 'here', *ansin* 'there', and *ansiúd* 'over there', as *-ci* and *-là* probably are of *ici* and *là*). Rather they are complete demonstratives, marked [+ Dem] as well as with an appropriate deixis feature, but generally requiring to be accompanied by an expression of [+ Def]; this is not an unusual requirement, as we shall shortly see. It should not be ruled out, however, that there may be languages with expressions of deixis not marked [+ Dem] – perhaps, therefore, not having true demonstratives. We have seen that Dyirbal has only one genuine demonstrative, a proximal form, with no demonstratives expressing other deictic degrees. This is presumably possible in Dyirbal because three degrees of deixis are expressed anyway on most noun phrases, and because there is a large battery of secondary deixis markers which can be added. I suggested above that the anaphoric "demonstrative" of Yoruba could be an adverbial particle rather than a determiner; in fact the other forms too have adverbial uses: 'here' or 'now' as well as 'this', and 'there' or 'then' as well as 'that'. If all these Yoruba forms are adverbs or something similar rather than determiners, it may be that they express only deixis and are not true demonstratives.

Dyirbal and Yoruba are among the languages which do not express simple definiteness, and it would not be surprising if in such languages demonstratives (or the nearest thing to demonstratives) were not of the same syntactic category as articles (in other languages) and occupying a "Det position", as is the case in English. In Dyirbal the one demonstrative occupies the same position, and occurs in place of, the class marker which generally appears in noun phrases. In other languages demonstratives are accompanied by a classifier while themselves being in what may be a determiner position. This is the case in Chinese:

(4)   *Cantonese* (Matthews and Yip 1994)
        nī go   mahntàih
        this CLASS problem
        'this problem'

(5)   *Mandarin* (Li and Thompson 1981)
        nèi-liù-běn   shū
        that six CLASS book
        'those six books'

In Cantonese a linker morpheme *ge* may also occur: *nī go ge jitmuhk* (this CLASS LINK programme) 'this programme'. In Latin, another language with no expression of simple definiteness, demonstratives show considerable freedom of position, like adjectives, and there is probably little reason to treat them as categorially different from adjectives.

Turning now to languages which do have simple definiteness marking, these can be grouped informally, and roughly, into two types as regards the relationship of demonstratives to the definite article, and, I will suggest, the position of demonstratives in the noun phrase. There are languages like English in which demonstratives replace the definite article, and there are languages in which the two co- .
occur in the noun phrase. In fact the situation is complicated by the existence of (at least) two different types of definite article, free-form determiners and affixes, which appear to be of different syntactic categories and in different structural positions. But on the current assumption that demonstratives are [+ Def], it is not surprising that they should be in a paradigmatic relationship with the definite article in many languages, such as English. In these languages no co-occurrence is possible because demonstratives are of the category Det, like the definite article, and occupy the same structural position as the definite article. If there is a position, what I have termed "Det position", which free-form definite articles universally or generally occupy, it seems natural that demonstratives too, as definite determiners, should also appear there.

But then there is the second group of languages, in which demonstrative determiners co-occur with the definite article. Examples are Standard Arabic *hāðā al-bustānu* (this DEF-garden) 'this garden'; Ewondo *é mvú ɲí* (the dog this) 'this dog'; Swedish *den här bil-en* (the/that here car-DEF) 'this car'; Armenian *ajt gadou-n* (that cat-DEF) 'that cat'; and Irish, mentioned above. Care is needed in assessing the significance of these observations, because this second group of languages at least is very heterogeneous. In some of them, Arabic, Swedish and Armenian for example, the definite article is an affix, either on the head noun, or, as a phrasal clitic, attached to the noun or to some other element. These bound articles do not look like determiners in a structural position comparable to that of free-form articles (though they may be associated with such a position, perhaps via agreement). This Det position should then be available to be filled by a demonstrative. In other words, in some languages where a demonstrative co-occurs with a definite affix, it may be that the demonstrative is a determiner in the same Det position as in English (where the demonstrative replaces the article). This is probably the case in Swedish, where there is no obvious reason for drawing a difference of position between the free-standing definite article *den* and the demonstrative to which it is closely related. And since both co-occur with the definite affix, this must be in some other position. The only difference between these languages and the first type is that the article, or one of its variants, is something other than a determiner. On the view that this affixal article is a morpheme representing agreement with a Det (which may be phonologically null), a demonstrative in Det position would be the definite Det with which the affix displays agreement.[5]

But there are also clear cases of demonstratives co-occurring with a lexical definite article, which is itself probably in Det position. Irish and Ewondo exemplify this situation. In these languages the demonstrative is probably not of category Det. In Ewondo it is probably deeper inside the noun phrase than the article and may be adjectival, but not in Irish, where it can be shown to be external to the noun phrase. Noun phrases like Ewondo *é mvú ɲí* (the dog this) and Irish *an madra seo* (the dog this) 'this dog' look similar, but the formation of pronominal demonstratives is quite different. In Ewondo the pronominal form corresponding to *é mvú ɲí* is *é ɲí*, the article remaining in combination with the demonstrative. But the corresponding form in Irish involves a personal pronoun rather than the article: *sé seo* (it/he this).

---

[5] It is important to note that there is not always complete uniformity within a language. Whereas the demonstrative determiner of Armenian must be accompanied by the article suffix, in Swedish this varies from one demonstrative to another. The forms *den, den här* and *den där* are accompanied by the article suffix on the noun, but *denna* is not. This form, also presumably a Det, follows the pattern of Danish, in which the article suffix does not co-occur with any demonstrative. In Albanian too, demonstratives (also probably determiners) usually occur without the article suffix appearing on the noun; perhaps here and in Danish the article serves to license a null Det. But the suffix can appear in Albanian, as noted in 2.3.3.

Since personal pronouns constitute complete noun phrases, the demonstrative *seo* here must be outside the noun phrase.[6]

In some languages demonstratives co-occurring with the definite article are more clearly adjectival. In Spanish and Catalan this is the case optionally – the other option being that the demonstrative occur without the article, in typical pre-nominal Det position: Spanish *este país* (this country) or *el país este* (the country this) 'this country', Catalan *aquella ciutat* (that city) or *la ciutat aquella* (the city that) 'that city'. When the article is present the demonstrative must follow the head noun, in typical adjective position. A similar situation obtains in Maori and other Polynesian languages (Krupa 1982, Bauer 1993). Maori has a three-way demonstrative system based on the roots *nei, naa, raa*, which combine with a prefix *tee-* in the singular, *ee-* in the plural; *tee-* is a form of *te*, the singular definite-specific article, though the normal plural of this is *ngaa*. Thus: *teenei whare* 'this house', *eenei whare* 'these houses'. But there is an alternative, in which the demonstrative, without prefix, follows the noun, and the noun is preceded by the article (in its standard form): *te whare nei* 'this house', *ngaa whare nei* 'these houses'.

Adjectival demonstratives also occur in languages with affixal definite articles. Romanian shows the same kind of optionality as Spanish and Catalan, though the demonstrative differs in form as well as position according to the pattern used. The unmarked position is again before the noun, probably in Det position, and then the article suffix does not appear: *acest apartament* 'this flat'. The emphatic option is to place the demonstrative post-nominally, in adjectival position; it then takes a final *-a* (as in pronominal use) and the article suffix appears: *apartament-ul acesta*. Unlike ordinary adjectives, however, the demonstrative in this position takes case markers as it does when in Det position: *acestui domn* or *domnului acestuia* 'of/to this gentleman'. Hausa is another language in which demonstratives can be pre-nominal, in a fuller form in this case, without the article suffix appearing, or post-nominal, possibly in an adjectival position, accompanied by the suffixal article: *wancan gona* (that farm) or *gona-r can* (farm-DEF that) 'that farm'.

Let us summarize. Demonstratives, as inherently definite expressions, can occur in Det position. Here they normally replace a free-form definite article, though, as in Maori, they may occasionally be incorporated with it. In languages with an affixal article, this can co-occur with a demonstrative Det, as in Swedish and Armenian, but more commonly it is omitted when the demonstrative is in Det position (Danish, Albanian, Romanian, Hausa). Demonstratives can also occur in adjective position, or in other modifier positions such as the noun-phrase-external position of Irish. These are positions which have no particular association with definiteness,

---

[6] Irish demonstratives are in fact to be grouped with some other items, including the emphatic particle *sa/se* and *féin* 'self', 'even', of uncertain category status, and perhaps adjoined to the noun phrase (see McCloskey and Hale 1984, Lyons 1992b).

and an article (free-form or bound) is required to appear. This is for languages which have articles. For languages which do not, a similar range of positions seems to be available, though it may be that what can be interpreted as Det position is not. Finally, demonstratives occasionally occur as affixes, both in languages which express simple definiteness and in languages which do not.

These observations suggest that, in languages in which definiteness clearly exists as a category, as evidenced by encoding of simple definiteness, demonstratives must be associated syntactically with it. This association can take the form of the demonstrative occupying a position specialized in the expression of definiteness: Det position or the affix position where definite articles appear. Or it can take the form of the demonstrative occurring in some modifier position not associated with definiteness, but then with the noun phrase being marked as definite by the article. One might suppose that if demonstratives are inherently [+ Def] there should be no need for them to be accompanied by the definite article or otherwise to show a syntactic association with definiteness.[7] And indeed, at least some languages without simple definite markers manage without this association. A solution to this apparent redundancy is to propose that demonstratives are not lexically [+ Def], in any language, as so far assumed. Instead, they are merely constrained to appear only in definite noun phrases through being semantically incompatible with indefiniteness. This constraint may be met either by the demonstrative being in a structural position which expresses definiteness or by there being in the noun phrase a separate encoding of definiteness. This speculation will be developed in Chapters 7 and 8.

3.2   Proper nouns

Proper nouns show the general behaviour of definite noun phrases, though, as suggested in Chapter 1, it does not necessarily follow that they carry the specification [+ Def] in languages such as English in which they do not take the definite article. Most languages follow this pattern, but there are also languages in which proper nouns are obligatorily accompanied by the definite article, and in these cases it cannot be doubted that they are [+ Def]. One example is Modern Greek, as already noted: *ho Georgos* 'George'. Another is Albanian, in which it will be recalled that the definite article is a Wackernagel affix. Proper nouns, including names of persons and places, almost always occur in definite form: *Agim-i e pa Dritë-n* 'Agim saw Drita'. They only occur without the definite affix in a few contexts, in most of which common nouns too would be "bare": when complement to certain, mostly

---

[7] One might propose that those demonstratives which co-occur with the article are discontinuous items, with [+ Def] encoded separately from the main body of the demonstrative where the other features are expressed. But this is not an attractive idea. It would remain to explain why there are so many discontinuous demonstratives, and why non-discontinuous ones cannot occur in adjectival positions.

locative, prepositions (*në Tiranë* 'in Tirana'); when in apposition to a preceding. definite noun phrase (*në fshatin Dushk* 'in the village of Dushk'); when used as a vocative (*Prit, Lumtë!* 'Wait, Lumtë!'). Of course they are also "bare", though clearly not indefinite, when modified by a preceding adjective, which must carry the second-position article affix: *i zi-u Petrit* (PRT poor-DEF Petrit) 'poor Petrit'.

There is considerable language-internal variation, many languages using the definite article with proper nouns either optionally or in certain circumstances. In Modern Western Armenian, proper nouns in the accusative, dative and ablative must take the suffixal definite article (and it is used with genitives in speech), but the article is not permitted with proper nouns in the nominative and instrumental (and genitive in writing). In German, it is common in colloquial usage to use the article with first names (*die Claudia, der Hans*), and this usually conveys familiarity. With surnames the use of the article is not necessarily colloquial, and carries complicated pragmatic and socio-linguistic connotations. It is common, even in formal contexts, with the names of celebrities (actors, writers etc.), but tends to be limited to female ones (*die Dietrich, die Droste*, but *Schiller, Goethe*) – a point which many now find offensive. The colloquial use of the article with surnames more generally carries a connotation of assumed familiarity, which can be used to denigrate or praise (*Der Brandt ist doch ein Säufer* 'Brandt drinks', *Der Brandt ist ein ganz kluger Kopf* 'Brandt is very clever'). In Italian too it is common colloquially to use the article with names, but only female first names (*la Maria, l'Anna*, but *Luigi*); with surnames the article is used for prominent individuals both male and female. In Sissala the article is optional with names, and simply serves to emphasize the fact that the person named is known to the hearer (Blass 1990).

An important observation is that, even in languages like English where proper nouns are almost invariably bare, they can take determiners, as in *this Peter, my Annie*. As already noted, this may be a matter of the proper noun being recategorized as a common noun, no longer treated as unique; this would be the case if Peter and Annie are being picked out from others of the same names. But this is not necessarily the function here of *this* and *my*, which can be non-restrictive – with affective value for instance.[8] On this interpretation, *Peter* and *Annie* are probably still proper nouns. Longobardi (1994) points out that 'my John' can be expressed in three ways in Italian: *il mio Gianni, il Gianni mio, Gianni mio*; **mio Gianni* is impossible. Of these possibilities, *il Gianni mio* is strongly contrastive, and therefore probably involves recategorization; *il mio Gianni* need not be contrastive, so could correspond to the affective, non-restrictive English interpretation. This difference is expected, because post-nominal possessives in Italian tend to be contrastive, pre-nominal position being the unmarked one. But the most interesting

---

[8] This is particularly clear in the northern British usage *our Annie, your Peter*.

option is *Gianni mio*, with no article. The possessive here is post-nominal, but need not be understood contrastively; it has the same interpretation as the pre-nominal possessive of *il mio Gianni*. This point, together with the unacceptability of a pre-nominal possessive without article, leads Longobardi to propose (within a DP framework) that in *Gianni mio* the noun has moved into the Det position which the article would otherwise occupy – passing over the possessive, which is pre-nominal underlyingly. Generalizing from this, he argues that all articleless proper nouns in Italian involve movement of the noun to Det position; in this way the noun itself plays the role of the article, so that the phrase is structurally equivalent to one containing a definite article. Longobardi also claims that where a definite article does appear overtly with a proper noun (or with a generic), it is a mere pleonastic without substantive content – not [+ Def] therefore. I will return to this.

An interesting point is that many languages use a special article form with proper nouns. This is the case in many Austronesian languages, such as Tagalog (Krámský 1972): *ang gurō* (the-NOM teacher), but *si Marya* (the-NOM Mary). In Maori the "personal article" *ko* (distinct from the usual definite article *te*) is used with proper nouns and personal pronouns, but only in the nominative. Kekchi has *li* as the definite article with all common nouns (*li ixk* 'the woman', *li wi.nk* 'the man'), but distinct male and female article forms with personal proper names: *laj Manu'* 'Manuel', *lix Rosa* 'Rosa' (Eachus and Carlson 1966). In Catalan the definite article is optional with proper nouns, but a special form (*en* rather than *el*) is used before masculine proper nouns beginning with a consonant: *la Maria*, *l'Eduard*, but *en Pere*, *en Prat* (Yates 1975).[9] A final, curious,

---

[9] Romanian presents a complex picture (Murrell and Ştefănescu-Drăgăneşti 1970). Personal names occurring as subject and direct object do not require an article, but in "oblique" functions (essentially indirect object and possessive) they are preceded by a form *lui*, not used with common nouns (though it does occur with the names of months and years): *Sandu va trimite o scrisoare lui Petre* 'Sandu will send a letter to Petre'. This determiner *lui* is identical in form to the masculine oblique third-person singular pronoun, and almost identical to the oblique masculine singular definite article suffix of common nouns (*un prieten* 'a friend', *prietenul* 'the friend', *prietenului* 'to/for/of the friend'). It is not restricted to masculine proper nouns, however: *lui Ana* 'to/for/of Ana'. But despite this, and despite its only occurring in oblique functions, there is no doubt that *lui* is a special form of the definite article. The behaviour of feminine proper nouns makes this clear. Many feminine names end in *-a*, which happens to be identical to the feminine definite article suffix: *Ana, Maria*; compare *o gară* 'a station', *gara* 'the station'. Now, in oblique functions, feminine names ending in *-a* may optionally change the *-a* to *-ei* (one of the oblique forms of the feminine definite article suffix) instead of being preceded by *lui*. It seems that the final *-a* of such names is optionally interpreted as the nominative–accusative definite suffix. The ambiguous status of final *-a* in Romanian is supported by the behaviour of place names, which normally take the definite article – the common article, and not only in oblique functions: *Bucureştiul* 'Bucharest'. As with common nouns, the article is omitted following a preposition: *din Bucureşti* 'from Bucharest'. But most feminine place names keep the definite suffix *-a*: *Constanţa, din Constanţa*.

observation is that in Quileute all proper nouns must be accompanied in the oblique case by what seems to be the *indefinite* article (Andrade 1933).

3.3 Possessives

3.3.1 *Pronoun and full noun phrase possessives*

English has possessives corresponding to personal pronouns (*my*, *your*, *their* etc., and their pronominal and predicative forms *mine*, *yours*, *theirs*) and to full noun phrases (*Peter's*, *this woman's*). Apart from the distinction between attributive and pronominal/predicative, limited to the pronoun-based possessives, there is little reason to draw a major distinction between possessives based on pronouns and possessives based on full noun phrases, since their syntactic behaviour is essentially the same (though for some minor differences see Lyons (1986a)). Chomsky (1981) characterizes both as genitive case forms. The *'s* of full noun phrase possessives derives historically from a genitive inflection on the noun, though what it is now (case affix, postposition, even Det) is a matter of some debate. It is no longer tied to the noun, but appears right at the end of the noun phrase, where it may be attached to a word of any category (*the man I was talking to's dog*). This same historical development has occurred in some other Germanic languages, such as Danish: *Kongen af Danmarks hat* (king-DEF of Denmark-POSS hat) 'the king of Denmark's hat' – where the king, not Denmark, is the possessor of the hat. If *'s* is treated as a case affix, the pronoun possessives *my* etc. may well also be genitive case forms, since it is common for pronouns to be highly irregular in their morphology. Many other languages make no distinction between personal pronouns and full noun phrases as regards the formation of possessives. Japanese uses generally a structure which has been variously considered to involve a postposition or a case suffix: *watasi no nimotu* (me POSS luggage) 'my luggage', *gakusei no nimotu* (student POSS luggage) 'the student's luggage'. In Turkish personal pronouns and nouns inflect in essentially the same way (though see the discussion of Turkish possessive affixes below): *Ahmed'-in* (Ahmet-GEN) 'Ahmet's', *ben-im* (me-GEN) 'mine'.

The main reason for supposing *my* etc. may warrant a different analysis from the *'s* forms is that a common pattern, in inflecting languages, is for possessives derived from pronouns to be adjectives or determiners and those derived from full noun phrases to be genitive case forms. Examples are German, Russian, Latin, Greek, where the pronoun-derived possessives for the most part inflect to agree with the noun (or other noun phrase constituents) in number, gender and case, as do determiners and adjectives, while possessives based on full noun phrases are in an invariable genitive form. The dichotomy is far from watertight, however. For pronoun possessives, Greek permits a genitive case form *mou* as an alternative to the adjectival or determiner form *emos* 'my': *hoi emoi adelphoi* (the my brothers) or *hoi adelphoi mou* (the brothers me+GEN) 'my brothers'. Latin and Russian have adjectival/determiner forms in the first and second persons and third-person reflexive (Latin *meus* 'my', *tuus* 'your', *suus* 'his/her own'; Russian *moj, tvoj, svoj*), but genitive case forms are used in the third-person non-reflexive (Latin *eius* 'his/her'; Russian *jevo* 'his', *jejo* 'her'). Moreover, several Slavonic languages have possessive adjectives derived from full noun phrases (Corbett 1987): Upper Sorbian *Janowa kniha* (Jan's+F+SG book+F+SG), *mojeho bratrowe dźěći* (my+M+SG+GEN brother's+PL+NOM children+PL+NOM). Possession is expressed in Swahili by a particle *-a* which attaches suffixally to a class marker determined by the possessum noun, and is followed by the possessor expression: *kiti ch-a Hamisi* (chair CLASS-POSS Hamisi) 'Hamisi's chair'. So the possessive agrees with the possessum through its association with the class marker. It is exactly the same with a pronoun possessive, except that this takes a different form from the non-possessive personal pronoun, and fuses with the particle *-a* producing some morphophonemic modifications: *kiti ch-a-ngu* 'my chair', *kiti ch-e-tu* 'our chair'.

Another common pattern distinguishing personal pronouns and full noun phrases is for possessive determiners or adjectives to exist corresponding only to the former, and for the latter to have no genitive case form either; instead a prepositional construction is used – still with possessive meaning, but often differing in position (superficially at least) from the pronoun-derived forms. This is the pattern found in most of the Romance languages; for example French *son ami* 'his friend', with pre-nominal possessive determiner, but *l'ami de cet homme* (the friend of this man) 'this man's friend', with post-nominal prepositional possessive. A pattern which may be related is found in Nama, where full noun phrase possessives take a particle *tì* but are not obviously in a different position from pronoun possessives: *tíí 'oms* 'my house', *sáá 'oms* 'your house', *'aop tì 'oms* 'the man's house'. The prepositional construction is sometimes an optional alternative to genitive case, as in German: *das Haus des Mannes* and *das Haus von dem Mann* 'the man's house' (the prepositional option being more colloquial).

3.3.2 *Affixal possessives*

The possessives relating to personal pronouns are in many languages realized as affixes, nearly always appearing on the head noun, the possessum. Interestingly, these affixes are often phonologically identical to personal inflections or pronominal clitics appearing on the verb and representing a subject or object argument of the verb. Examples from Turkish are: *köy-üm* (village-1SG) 'my village', *el-in* (hand-2SG) 'your hand', *çocuk-lar-ımız* (child-PL-1PL) 'our children'. Turkish is a "null-subject language", subject personal pronouns only being used for emphasis; the person and number of the subject are adequately signalled

125

by inflectional material on the verb. In fact the verb affixes encoding this subject–verb agreement are, while showing a lot of allomorphic variation, very closely related morphologically to the possessive affixes. Egyptian Arabic also has personal suffixes, in this case occurring equally on nouns, verbs and prepositions. The suffixes are the same for all three categories, except that the first-person singular is *-ni* for verbs but *-i* (after a consonant) or *-ya* (after a vowel) for nouns and prepositions. A major difference from Turkish is that, attached to verbs (and prepositions), these personal suffixes represent the object rather than the subject. Examples are: *ʕarabiyyit-na* (car-2PL) 'our car', *fihmuu-na* (understand+PERF+3PL-2PL) 'they understood us', *wayyaa-na* (with-2PL) 'with us'. Carib has personal prefixes, but, again, uses the same forms for nouns, verbs and prepositions. A peculiarity is that they attach to an extended form of the noun, if the noun has such a form. Thus, *e:tï* 'name', *y-e:tï* 'my name'; *to:pu/to:puru* 'stone', *a-to:puru* 'your stone'. In other languages, such as Finnish, the possessive suffixes are distinct from the personal affixes appearing on verbs. Khalkha Mongolian has no personal morphemes on verbs relating to either subject or object, but does have possessive affixes. For the first and second persons they are reduced forms of the genitive of the corresponding personal pronoun (*-min* 'my', *-čin* 'your (singular)', *-man* 'our', *-tan* 'your (plural)'), and the third-person affix (*-n/-in/-ən*) is of demonstrative origin.

Languages with affixal possessives almost always have free-form possessives also, which can be used either instead of or in addition to the affixes. This is usually for emphasis, and is parallel to the use of a subject pronoun in null-subject languages to reinforce the personal marking on the verb. In some languages possessive affixes are purely pronominal in sense, while in others they can, or must, accompany full noun phrase possessives. Returning to Turkish, the possessive personal affixes can be reinforced, for emphasis, by a personal pronoun in the genitive case: *siz-in sokağ-ınız* (you-GEN street-2PL) 'your street'. The parallel with the use of nominative pronouns to emphasize a clausal pronominal subject suggests that the possessive affixes are to be analysed as agreement morphemes, encoding the agreement of the head noun with a genitive pronoun which, unless emphatic, is phonologically null. In current syntactic theory, the empty subject of null-subject languages is usually identified with *pro*, the phonologically null pronoun, and we can take it that Turkish possessive suffixes are also associated with *pro* in the absence of an overt free-form genitive form. See Haegeman (1994, chapter 8) for an elementary discussion of *pro*, and Jaeggli and Safir (1989) for a more advanced treatment. The Turkish personal affixes occur not only with pronominal possessors, but also with full noun phrase possessors: *çoban-ın kız-ı* (shepherd-GEN girl-3SG) 'the shepherd's daughter'. So we can assume that the personal affixes are not themselves pronoun possessives, but markers of agreement with lexical possessives (overt or null) which may or may not be pronominal. In Egyptian Arabic, on the other hand, the possessive suffixes do not in general "double" overt lexical possessives; thus if the possessor is a full noun phrase a suffix does not occur.[10]

The Lakhota possessive prefixes are attached directly to the noun only in cases of inalienable possession: *ni-c'iye* (2SG-elder+brother) 'your elder brother'. Otherwise they are attached to a particle *t'a*, and this is prefixed to the noun: *mi-t'a-ṣụka kị* (1SG-PRT-dog the) 'my dog'. The third-person form, incidentally, is zero, so 'his dog' is *t'a-ṣụka kị*. There are also fuller forms which are freestanding, formed by attaching the personal prefix to a fuller particle *t'awa*. These follow the noun: *ṣụkak'ạ mi-t'awa kị* (horse 1SG-PRT the) 'my horse', as well as being used pronominally and predicatively. These forms may be reinforced by a personal pronoun: *miye mit'awa* 'mine'. A full noun phrase possessor also occurs with one of the particles *t'a* and *t'awa*: *Peter t'a-ṣụkak'ạ kị* (Peter PRT-horse the) or *ṣụkak'ạ Peter t'awa kị* (horse Peter PRT the) 'Peter's horse'. Notice that, because the third-person affix is zero, it is unclear whether it occurs here to double the possessor noun phrase, as opposed to the possessive particle having no prefix attached.

Modern Armenian has a particularly interesting system of possessive suffixes, which are descended historically from a definite article distinguishing three degrees of person-related deixis; the form relating to each person in Classical Armenian (*-s*, *-d*, *-n*) has given the possessive of that person (*-s* 'my', *-t* 'your', *-n/-ə* 'his', 'her'). Corresponding plurals have been formed with a morpheme *-ni-*: *-nis* 'our', *-nit* 'your', *-nin* 'their'. If a free-form possessive occurs, in the form of a full noun phrase or a personal pronoun in the genitive, it must be doubled by a suffix; thus *Tikrani zkɛsd-ə* 'Tigrane's garment', *im sɛɣan-s* 'my table'. But agreement between the two possessive elements is limited to the singular; *-s* and *-t* are the suffix forms for first- and second- persons singular, but *-n/-ə* is used to double all plural possessors as well as third-person singular: thus *mɛr doun-ə*, not **mɛr doun-nis*, 'our house'. It may be that what is appearing on the noun in such instances with a plural free-form possessive is not a possessive suffix but the definite article (which is also *-n/-ə*).

---

[10] The same applies to Finnish as regards full noun phrases, but the possessive affixes may be accompanied by a genitive pronoun for emphasis: *hattu-nsa* (hat-3SG) 'his hat', *hän-en hattu-nsa* (him-GEN hat-3SG) 'his hat'. It is also possible for the plural pronouns in the genitive to occur without the corresponding personal suffix, where the possessive structure is expressing some relationship other than ownership: *meidän kylä* (us-GEN village) 'our village'. One language which allows a great deal of freedom in these respects, both free and bound possessor expressions being possible either alone or in combination, is Pirahã (Everett 1987). The same set of clitics can represent both objects and possessors, like the Egyptian Arabic suffixes: *Tí* **hi** *xibáobá* (I 3SG hit) 'I hit him', **hi** *kaiíi* (3SG house) 'his house'. Doubling is optional, so that for 'his house' with emphasis on the possessor, both *hiapió kaiíi* (him house) and *hiapió hi kaiíi* (him 3SG house) are possible. A full noun phrase possessor too may be doubled: *xaoói kaiíi* (foreigner house) or *xaoói hi kaiíi* (foreigner 3SG house) 'the foreigner's house'.

Phrasal clitic possessives are rare, but one clear case is Romanian, in which the pronoun-based possessives are Wackernagel forms: *maşina mea cea nouă* (car+DEF my the new) or *noua mea maşină* (new+DEF my car) 'my new car'. Notice that the Wackernagel article (which must be present in this definite structure) attaches to the first word of the noun phrase, and that the possessive is enclitic to this initial noun/adjective–article combination.

3.3.3 *Alienable and inalienable*

Numerous distinctions are made by languages between types of possession, in terms of the nature of the relation holding between possessor and possessum. For example, ownership may be distinguished from mere physical possession or from a general association, as shown for Finnish above. Dyirbal draws a distinction between present and past possession, expressed by two different genitive inflections, -*ŋu* for the former and -*mi* for the latter (Dixon 1972). Past possession may involve an implication that the object denoted by the head still belongs to the past possessor, having been lost or temporarily left, but not necessarily. Maori has two possessive or genitive particles, *a* and *o*, the first used where the possessor is in a position of dominance or control over the possessum, and the second otherwise (Biggs 1969, Bauer 1993). Most of these distinctions have no bearing on the question of definiteness in possessives, and I limit my attention to one of them (though a rather generally defined one) which may have some bearing.

The distinction between alienable and inalienable possession, the latter involving possessa which are more intimately or intrinsically tied to the possessor – body parts, items of clothing, family relations etc., is central to the possessive system of many languages. We have seen that in English and some other languages it is nouns of this type that permit a definite possessive structure with apparently indefinite sense (*my brother*, *your ear*, *Mary's sleeve* with no implication of uniqueness). In many languages nouns in this class involve different possessive structures from those with "ordinary" noun heads. The Lakhota examples above show a possessive particle to which personal prefixes are attached appearing in alienable possession, but the prefix being attached directly to the noun in inalienable possession. This illustrates the typical pattern, which is that in inalienable possession the structure is morphologically simpler or the possessive is in some way structurally closer to the head noun. Swahili shows an optional process of possessive reduction in inalienable possession, the effect again being closer integration of the possessive with the noun: *mwenzi wako* (companion your) 'your companion' reducing to *mwenzio*. It is important to bear in mind that what counts as inalienable for linguistic purposes varies considerably from one language to another, and that the term is an informal one which may cover a number of distinct categories of relation. In Italian, for example, 'my house' is *la mia casa* (the my house) but 'my mother' is *mia madre* (my mother). The difference may be stated in terms of the second phrase involving inalienable possession, but the head nouns allowing omission of the article in this way are limited in Italian to a small number of kinship terms.

Dyirbal, as well as having two genitive morphemes for present and past possession (both alienable), also distinguishes an inalienable possessive construction with no genitive marker. Possessor and possessum are simply juxtaposed in a noun phrase, with both nouns carrying the case inflection determined by the syntactic function of the noun phrase as a whole. But whereas nouns are generally accompanied by a class marker in Dyirbal, the possessum noun in this construction cannot be. I illustrate the two constructions in (6) (alienable) and (7) (inalienable):

(6) bayi   waŋal   baŋul   yaṟaŋu
     CLASS-ABS boomerang-ABS CLASS-GEN man-GEN
     'the man's boomerang'

(7) balan   ḍugumbil   mambu
     CLASS-ABS woman-ABS back-ABS
     'the woman's back'

Kinship terms, incidentally, are treated as alienable in Dyirbal. To see the relevance (though not the precise significance) of the distinction for definiteness, let us turn to two languages which have articles, Lakhota and Albanian.

In Lakhota the possessive prefix is attached directly to an inalienably possessed noun, without an intervening possessive particle: *ma-p'oge kị* (1SG-nose the) 'my nose'; a full noun phrase possessive is simply placed before the head noun: *John p'oge kị* (John nose the) 'John's nose'. But there are some interesting distinctions within the class of inalienable possession. Kinship terms and body-part terms take different prefixes for the first-person singular, *mi-* and *ma-* respectively; in the third person the prefix is always zero, but kinship heads usually take a suffix *-ku*: *hụ-ku kị* 'his/her mother', *John hụ-ku kị* 'John's mother'; and kinship heads with a first- or second-person prefix generally take no definite article: *ni-hụ* 'your mother'. In Albanian pronoun possessives (which are adjectives or determiners) follow the head noun except in the case of inalienably possessed heads (mainly kinship terms and some terms of social relationship), when first- and second-person forms generally precede; third-person possessives cannot precede, but instead the head can be preceded by an adjectival particle (with no possessive following), which conveys the sense of a third-person possessive: *e ëm-a* (PRT mother-DEF) 'his/her/their mother'. When a possessive follows the head the latter must carry the definite inflection unless there is a preceding indefinite determiner: *tren-i im* (train-DEF my) 'my train', *tem-a jote* (theme-DEF our) 'our theme'. But when a possessive precedes there is no definiteness marking: *im atë* 'my father', *jot gjyshe* 'our grandmother'. This pattern of the definite article tending not to occur in inalienable possession, though the sense may be definite, is shared by Albanian, Lakhota and Italian, and is widespread.

For further examples and discussion of the syntax of alienable and inalienable possession see Haiman (1985).

3.3.4 *Possessives and definiteness*

The most important issue arising from possessives for our concern is the (informal) distinction between "DG languages" and "AG languages". Recall that in the first type a possessive has the effect of inducing a definite interpretation in the noun phrase it modifies, and a definite article cannot also appear; in the second type a possessive does not have this effect, and the article must co-occur with it to get a definite interpretation (in languages that have an article). The central observation in this discussion is that possessives, unlike demonstratives, are not inherently definite or semantically incompatible with indefiniteness in the noun phrase they modify.

In DG languages possessives do not co-occur with articles, the reason traditionally assumed for this being that they are themselves definite determiners. Examples are English *my bicycle*, French *ma bicyclette*, German *mein Fahrrad*, all meaning 'the bicycle belonging to me'. In languages like English in which full noun phrase possessives have essentially the same distribution and behaviour as pronoun possessives, they too compel definiteness in the matrix phrase. And this fact makes it very clear that the DG phenomenon cannot be accounted for in terms of DG possessives being definite determiners. The phrases *the girl next door's bicycle* and *a girl next door's bicycle* are both definite ('the bicycle belonging to the/a girl next door'), despite the second having an indefinite possessor expression; *a girl next door's* is clearly not a definite determiner.[11] The same applies in, for example, Danish: *en vens kone* 'a friend's wife', 'the wife of a friend'. In French only pronoun possessives follow the DG pattern. Full noun phrases can only be used as possessives in a prepositional structure, and this is neutral with respect to definiteness, so that an article is also required: *la bicyclette de Jeanne* (the bicycle of Jeanne) 'Jeanne's bicycle', *une bicyclette à Jeanne* (a bicycle to Jeanne) 'a bicycle of Jeanne's'. In fact such a prepositional construction is the most common strategy used in DG languages to obtain the indefinite reading which is unavailable with the "basic" possessive structure. Some examples are French *un ami à moi* (a friend to me), German *ein Freund von mir* (a friend of me), Irish *cara liom* (friend with+me) 'a friend of mine'.

---

[11] It has been claimed that the morpheme *'s* is a definite determiner to account for the definiteness of *a girl next door's bicycle*. This will be discussed in Chapter 8.

A construction which has been the subject of much research in recent years is the traditionally termed "construct" of the Semitic languages (usually mislabelled "construct state" in the recent syntax literature, using a term, also from Semitic philology, with a different meaning; see 2.5.1 above). Essentially the same possessive construction characterizes also the Celtic languages. The construct is a DG construction in which the possessive follows the head, and the latter cannot take the usual definiteness marker. I illustrate from Standard Arabic and Irish:

(8) *Arabic*
  a. ʕayn-a   l-bint-i
      eye NOM-DU DEF girl GEN
      'the eyes of the girl', 'the girl's eyes'
  b. ʕayn-a   bint-i-n
      eye NOM-DU girl GEN NUN
      'the eyes of a girl', 'a girl's eyes'

(9) *Irish*
  a. muineál an   éin
      neck   the-GEN bird-GEN
      'the neck of the bird', 'the bird's neck'
  b. muineál éin
      neck   bird-GEN
      'the neck of a bird', 'a bird's neck'

In these examples the possessor phrase may be definite or indefinite; definiteness is marked by a prefixal article in Arabic and a free-form article in Irish, and indefiniteness by nunation in Arabic (see 2.5.1). The possessum is obligatorily bare, unmarked for definiteness or indefiniteness. But it is understood as definite. In fact it is stated in much of the literature that the possessum (or, more accurately, the matrix phrase) is interpreted as definite only if the possessor is definite, but this is almost certainly incorrect; see Lyons (1992b). For present purposes the point is that, apart from the difference in word order, the descriptive facts in relation to definiteness are exactly the same as for the DG structures of English and other languages. No article is associated with the possessum, but it is definite.

The AG–DG parameter applies as much to affixal possessives as to lexical ones. Many possessives of this kind are of the DG type, the matrix being interpreted as definite without the appearance of a definite determiner. The Egyptian Arabic example above, *ʕarabiyyit-na* (car-2PL) 'our car', is definite ('the car belonging to us') though the article prefix cannot appear: **ʔil-ʕarabiyyit-na*. Another example is Modern Armenian, with possessive affixes doubling free-form possessives (at least in the first- and second-persons singular): *im kirk'-s* (me+GEN book-1SG) 'my book'.

AG languages are those in which a possessive does not induce a definite interpretation. If the language has articles, these can co-occur with possessives to indicate definiteness or indefiniteness. An example is Portuguese (in which, as in the Romance languages more generally, only pronoun possessives are non-prepositional): *a nossa casa* (the our house) 'our house', *uma nossa casa* (a our house) 'a house of ours'. Other determiners than the articles can equally appear: *esta nossa casa* (this our house) 'this house of ours'. I have already observed that prepositional possessives are generally AG in effect, and have to be combined with an appropriate determiner to express definiteness or indefiniteness. This is the case with English *of* possessives (*that/a friend of Mary('s)*), and even in French, where there is a tendency to use a different preposition depending on the determiner (*de* with the definite article, *à* otherwise). AG languages in which full noun phrase possessors are expressed by a genitive case form and appear in the same position as pronoun possessives include Classical Greek (Goodwin 1992): *ho sos koinōnos* (the your partner) 'your partner', *sos koinōnos* (your partner) 'a partner of yours'; *ho tou andros koinōnos* (the-NOM the-GEN man-GEN partner-NOM) 'the man's partner', *tou andros koinōnos* (the-GEN man-GEN partner-NOM) 'a partner of the man's'. Albanian works similarly, but with an affixal definite article and a (free-form) cardinal article: *libr-i i saj* (book-DEF PRT her) 'her book', *një libër i saj* (a book PRT her) 'a book of hers'; *libr-i i vajzë-s* (book-DEF PRT girl-GEN+DEF) 'the girl's book', *një libër i vajzë-s* (a book PRT girl-GEN+DEF) 'a book of the girl's'. And in Mandarin Chinese, pronoun and full noun phrase possessives are formed in exactly the same way: *wǒ-de péngyou* (me-GEN friend) 'my friend' or 'a friend of mine'; *nèi-ge háizi-de péngyou* (that-CLASS child-GEN friend) 'that child's friend' or 'a friend of that child('s)'. Chinese lacks articles (though having optional incipient ones in the unstressed use of distal demonstrative and singular numeral), so these noun phrases are simply ambiguous between definite and indefinite (Huang 1987). This makes it clear that the AG type is not limited to languages . which have articles (though the DG type probably is).

Affixal possessives too can be of AG type. They are in Chamorro (Chung 1987, Krámský 1972), which has a definite article while simple indefinites are characterized by absence of an article: *i paine-kku* (the comb-1SG) 'my comb', *paine-kku* (comb-1SG) 'a comb of mine'. Lakhota too is AG, both in its prefixal possessives and free-form ones: *mi-t'a-ṡukak'ạ kị* (me-PRT-horse the) or *ṡukak'ạ mi-t'awa kị* (horse me-PRT the) 'my horse'; *mi-t'a-ṡukak'ạ wạ* (me-PRT-horse a) or *ṡukak'ạ mi-t'awa wạ* (horse me-PRT a) 'a horse of mine'; *Peter t'a-ṡukak'ạ kị* (Peter PRT-horse the) or *ṡukak'ạ Peter t'awa kị* (horse Peter PRT the) 'Peter's horse'; *Peter t'a-ṡukak'ạ wạ* (Peter PRT-horse a) or *ṡukak'ạ Peter t'awa wạ* (horse Peter PRT a) 'a horse of Peter's'. Mam has only a cardinal article, its absence implying definiteness, and is AG (England 1983): *n-jaa-ya* (1SG-house-1SG) 'my house', *juun n-jaa-ya* (a 1SG-house-1SG) 'a house of mine'. One language with affixal possessives and no articles which shows evidence of being AG is Nama.

The evidence is that the possessive prefixes can be attached to indefinite pronouns, which should be impossible if these prefixes induced definiteness: *y-o:tïrï* (1SG-something) 'something of mine'.

There are also mixed languages – in fact a great many languages combine elements of both patterns. It is therefore constructions, not languages, that are DG or AG. Spanish has both DG possessives (*mi casa* 'my house', definite) and AG possessives (*la casa mía* 'my house', *una casa mía* 'a house of mine'), the two differing somewhat in form; the AG forms, which are always post-nominal, inflect like adjectives for number and gender, while most of the DG forms are morphologically reduced (like many determiners) and inflect for number only. The AG forms are emphatic when used with the definite article; the DG structure is the unmarked one for expressing 'my house' and the like. As well as being normal and unmarked with the cardinal article, the AG possessives also occur with other determiners (as seen above in Portuguese): *aquella casa mía* 'that house of mine'. They also occur in predicative and pronominal use: *Aquella casa es mía* 'that house is mine'; *La mía es blanca* 'Mine is white', *Una mía es blanca* 'One of mine is white'.

The distinctions drawn in this section are remarkably similar to those seen among demonstratives, except that the latter rarely take the form of affixes. But demonstratives apparently differ from possessives in being inherently [+ Def], so while it seems odd that some demonstratives should appear with the definite article, in the case of possessives this co-occurrence involves no redundancy. The essential difference between DG and AG possessives, as with the two types of demonstrative, seems to be one of position. Free-form DG possessives behave like definite determiners, and it is reasonable to suppose that they occur in Det position, the standard position for such determiners; their position accounts for a free-form definite article not being able to accompany them, and their definiteness explains why a quasi-indefinite article cannot co-occur with them. Free-form AG possessives are typically adjectival and are positioned deeper within the noun phrase, they are not marked [+ Def], and since they leave Det position free this can be filled by the definite article or some other definite determiner – and has to be if the language has an article and a definite interpretation is required. This characterization is supported by the difference of position and form of the two possessive types in Spanish, where the AG possessive is in a typical adjective position and shows full adjectival agreement behaviour, while the DG possessive is in a paradigmatic relationship with the definite article and is, historically, a reduced form like the articles.[12]

This still takes DG possessives to be [+ Def], this being why they appear in Det position; and this is odd, since we have established that there is no logical

---

[12] See Lyons (1986b) for discussion of the phonological reduction of DG possessives in early Romance resulting from their being unstressed.

necessity for "possession" to be accompanied by definiteness (a point made clear anyway by the many AG languages). But it is not a necessary assumption, and I want to adopt the position that possessives are never lexically specified as [+ Def]. The definiteness of the DG structure is the consequence of the possessive being in Det position rather than the other way round. This point will be argued in Chapter 8, and for the moment it is enough to note that the facts relating to possessives (and demonstratives) support the idea that there is a special relationship between definiteness and some "Det position".

The AG–DG distinction for some, if not all, affixal possessives is readily accounted for in the same way as for lexical possessives, on the assumption that the affixes are markers of agreement with a lexical possessive, which may be phonologically empty. In the DG cases, the empty or overt possessor triggering agreement is in Det position; in the AG cases, the possessor phrase is in some other position within the matrix.

The discussion of inalienable possession above, for languages which distinguish it from possession more generally, like Lakhota and Albanian, showed a strong tendency for the definite article not to occur with this, even in strongly AG languages, despite the fact that the sense is probably mostly definite. In other words, inalienable possession constructions tend to be of DG type. Typical AG languages frequently also have DG forms, and these are often used with head nouns which fall into the inalienable possession category. Examples are Portuguese and Italian, in which possessa denoting family relationships (when in the singular and without modification) usually take a possessive with no article: Portuguese *o meu amigo* 'my friend', but *meu irmão* 'my brother'; Italian *la tua casa* 'your house', but *tua figlia* 'your daughter'. The same applies to Catalan, but with the possessive taking a different form: *el meu amic* 'my friend', *mon germà* 'my brother'.

3.4 Personal pronouns

The discussion here will focus on the claim developed in Chapter 1 that personal pronouns are the pronominal counterpart of definite articles, and sometimes of demonstratives. Given this, it is not surprising that, like definite articles, they are often descended historically from demonstratives; they also frequently resemble both definite articles and demonstratives phonologically.

3.4.1 *Semantic and grammatical content*

The basic category encoded by personal pronouns is grammatical person – whence their name. Person combines invariably with number, to give the distinctions which make possible reference to the various participants and to non-participants in the discourse situation. Thus first person singular denotes the speaker, first person plural a plurality which includes the speaker, second person plural a plurality which includes the hearer but excludes the speaker, and so on. It is fairly standard to distinguish three persons, based on the two participants, speaker and hearer, and any non-participant, as in most European languages. But a "fourth person" has been identified for some languages, Navajo for example (Akmajian and Anderson 1970). This category seems to be in a sense an extra third person, since it does not refer to speaker or hearer (though its referent must be human); its use is determined by complex grammatical and pragmatic factors. A similar distinction is that between "proximate" and "obviative" third-person pronouns in Algonquian languages (Hockett 1966). Different non-participants in a single sentence or limited discourse unit must be differently marked as regards person, and the general pattern is to use obviative for the entity less central to the current focus of concern.

Of course number systems vary, and it is fairly common for singular, dual and plural to be distinguished in each person. Take for example Warrgamay (Dixon 1980), shown here in intransitive subject forms, and Sanskrit (Coulson 1976):

Warrgamay

	first	*second*	*third*
singular	ŋayba	ŋinba	nyuŋa
dual	ŋali	nyubula	bula
plural	ŋana	nyurra	jana

Sanskrit

	first	*second*	*third*
singular	aham	tvam	saḥ
dual	āvām	yuvām	tau
plural	vayam	yūyam	te

Some languages distinguish more than three numbers, and sometimes not all persons distinguish the same numbers. In addition, a rather common phenomenon is the distinction between inclusive and exclusive in non-singular first person. In the former the hearer is included, in the latter not. Examples are Maori and Nama:

Maori

	first		*second*	*third*
	exclusive	*inclusive*		
singular	au		koe	ia
dual	maaua	taaua	koorua	raaua
plural	maatou	taatou	koutou	raatou

Nama

| | first | | second | third |
	exclusive	*inclusive*		
singular	tií-ta		saá-ts	//'ĩi-p
dual	sií-kxm̀	saá-kxm̀	saá-kxò	//'ĩi-kxà
plural	sií-ke	saá-ke	saá-ko	//'ĩi-ku

An interesting variant of this found in a number of languages, including Lakhota and Carib, is that dual number appears to exist only for inclusive first person, to denote just the speaker and hearer, 'you and I':

Lakhota

| | first | | second | third |
	exclusive	*inclusive*		
singular	miye		niye	'iye
dual		'ųkiye		
plural	'ųkiyepi		niyepi	'iyepi

Carib

| | first | | second | third |
	exclusive	*inclusive*		
singular	au		amo:ro	moxko
dual		kïxko		
plural	aʔna	kïxka:ro	amïiyaro	moxka:ro

A set of two including speaker but not hearer, in other words exclusive first person dual ('he and I' etc.), is expressed by the corresponding plural form, *'ųkiyepi* and *aʔna*. Notice also that whereas Carib distinguishes exclusive and inclusive also in the first person plural, Lakhota does not. The pattern shown by these paradigms and the morphology of plural formation certainly suggests strongly that these languages do not in fact have a dual number, and that the "inclusive dual" pronouns are grammatically singular. See the analysis of the Carib pronouns suggested above in 3.1.1. In some languages the inclusive–exclusive distinction may be expressed optionally. In Ewondo this is done by simply adding a second- or third-person pronoun (singular or plural) to the first-person plural pronoun: *bí wa* (we you+SG) 'you and I', *bí mĩnā* (we you+PL) 'you (plural) and I', *bí bɔ́* (we they) 'they and I'. Used as subjects, these combinations take a verb with the normal first-person plural marking.

Gender is often indicated in some or all forms: in third person singular only (English, German); in third person only (French); in third person and plural generally (Spanish); in all persons, singular and plural, except first (Standard Arabic). Gender marking is very rare for first person singular.

Distinctions are widely made, especially but not exclusively in second-person pronouns, to express respect versus familiarity or otherwise to encode the relative social status of referents. The second-person plural form is used for politeness to address a single individual in French (*vous*), Russian (*vy*), and Yoruba (*ẹ*). In Nama the second-person plural masculine form *saáko* may be used by a man to a single male equal to indicate closeness, while the common gender plural pronoun *saátú* is used as a highly respectful form of address to persons of either sex. Carib uses the third-person plural pronoun with an extra suffix, *moxka:ro-koɲ*, to refer respectfully to a third person. Yoruba too uses a plural form (*nwọn*) for polite third-person singular reference. Many languages use third-person forms for polite second-person reference. Italian uses the third-person feminine *Lei* for the singular and the general third-person *Loro* for the plural. German has the third-person plural *Sie* for singular and plural address. And Spanish has special forms for polite address, singular *usted*, plural *ustedes*, which are grammatically third person. See Cooke (1968) for a detailed study of the extremely elaborate systems operating in Thai, Burmese and Vietnamese.

Reflexive pronouns are commonly distinguished from non-reflexive personal pronouns. Classical Greek is like English in having distinct forms for all person–number combinations: *emauton* 'myself', *seauton* 'yourself', *heauton* 'himself', etc. Russian has a single reflexive pronoun, *sebja, -sja*, for all persons, as has Swahili (*-ji-*). In French and German a distinct form occurs in the third person only (French *se*, German *sich*); otherwise the ordinary personal pronouns are used reflexively.

3.4.2 *Strong, weak and null pronouns*

There is a general tendency for pronominal reference, when not emphatic, to take forms which are phonologically or morphologically weak – like the definite article. But these forms can be strengthened in various ways, to express emphasis or contrast, among other reasons. It is possible to say, therefore, that nearly all languages exhibit a strong–weak contrast in their personal pronoun systems, manifested in a number of different ways. It may be a distinction between stressed and unstressed occurrence, between phonologically full and reduced forms, between augmented and simple forms, between free-standing forms and clitics or affixes, or between overt and null forms. Most languages differentiate along one or other of these axes, and it will be recalled from 3.3.2 that possessives derived from personal pronouns show the same strong–weak distinction.

German is one language with free-form pronouns which are generally obligatory and may be stressed or unstressed. The unstressed forms are (like those of English) subject to reductions not indicated orthographically. Thus *du* [duː] 'you' and *sie* [ziː] 'she', 'they' are frequently reduced in speech when unstressed to [də] and [zə]. The unmarked pronouns of Irish are also free forms, and they have corresponding augmented forms used for emphasis, as follows (subject forms):

| | *weak* | | *strong* | |
	singular	*plural*	*singular*	*plural*
first	mé	sinn	mise	sinne
second	tú	sibh	tusa	sibhse
third	sé, sí	siad	seisean, sise	siadsan

As examples of clitic pronouns versus full, free-form pronouns, consider the Spanish object forms (direct object forms only for the clitics):

| | *clitic* | | *full pronoun* | |
	singular	*plural*	*singular*	*plural*
first	me	nos	mí	nosotros, -as
second	te	os	ti	vosotros, -as
third	lo, la	los, las	él, ella	ellos, ellas

It is not always the case that the strong forms simply replace the weak or clitic forms in emphatic or contrastive contexts. 'I see it' (referring to a table) in Spanish is *La veo* (CL see+1SG) – since *mesa* 'table' is feminine – with the clitic attached pre-verbally. Object position is normally post-verbal, so, since strong pronouns are free-standing noun phrases, one might suppose that the contrastive 'I see *it*' would be **Veo ella* (parallel to *Veo la mesa* 'I see the table'), but it is not. The strong object pronouns are purely prepositional object forms, which means that they normally occur after verbs only with human reference, since human direct objects require a preposition, the so-called "personal *a*": *Veo a la mujer* (see+1SG to the woman) 'I see the woman'. In fact a strong pronoun here would be accompanied by the clitic rather than replacing it: *La veo a ella* 'I see *her*'. This is the "clitic doubling" construction, the subject of a very extensive literature (see Lyons (1990) and references there).

Where a clitic pronoun is not reinforced by a strong form but is the only expression of the object argument, a widely held assumption is that the object position (where a full noun phrase or strong pronoun object would occur) is occupied by *pro*, the null pronominal. The clitic serves to "identify" (indicate the content of) this phonologically empty pronoun. Whether the clitic is generated in clitic position or moves there from the object position is a matter of debate (and a different analysis may be appropriate for different languages). But there are strong similarities between object clitic structures and the null subject phenomenon. Languages permitting phonologically empty pronouns in subject position are actually in a substantial majority. The "null subject parameter" is usually linked to agreement morphology on the verb (or elsewhere: many languages show an "auxiliary" constituent which hosts agreement) in the form of affixal or clitic material. The null subject is taken to be, in most cases, the null pronominal *pro*, which is licensed by agreement; that is, the agreement morphology identifies *pro* by encoding its person and number, and in effect renders an overt subject redundant. A typical example is Spanish *comemos* 'we eat', where the ending *-mos*, encoding first person plural, makes it possible to omit the overt pronoun *nosotros* 'we', which would only be included for emphasis. A number of studies (for example Suñer 1988, Lyons 1990) treat object clitics as representing precisely the same phenomenon syntactically as subject–verb agreement, and indeed, there is cross-linguistically no consistent morphological distinction between the agreement material identifying objects as opposed to subjects. Let us look briefly at Swahili, in which the two seem very similar. Swahili represents pronominal subjects and objects as prefixes on verbs, the subject forms being more peripheral:

| | subject | | object | |
	singular	*plural*	*singular*	*plural*
first	ni-	tu-	-ni-	-tu-
second	u-	m-	-ku-	-wa-
third	a-	wa-	-m-	-wa-

These are the forms used for human referents; for others, the third-person prefixes take the form of the appropriate class marker. Swahili also has a series of strong, free-standing pronouns, used only for emphasis:[13]

---

[13] In the examples so far considered, the strong pronouns corresponding to *pro* are, like those corresponding to overt weak pronouns, phonologically strong in the sense of being fully stressed, and perhaps polysyllabic. But it is possible for the "strong" form to be stronger than *pro* only in having some overt material, while actually being unstressed. I noted above that Irish has free-standing weak pronouns, and strong pronouns consisting of augmented forms of these. But Irish is also, in part, a null-subject language. The Irish verb is defective; in each tense paradigm, "synthetic" verb forms (displaying agreement morphology) are available for only some person–number combinations, and only with these is *pro* possible. Otherwise "analytic" (non-agreeing) forms occur, and a pronominal subject must be overt. Thus, to take the present tense, *tugaim* (give+PRES+1SG) 'I give', *tugaimid* (give+PRES+1PL) 'we give'; but *tugann tú* (give+PRES you+SG) 'you give', *tugann siad* (give+PRES they) 'they give'. Now in those parts of a tense paradigm where the availability of a synthetic verb form permits a pronominal subject to be null, emphasis on this subject is expressed by suffixing the same reinforcing

	singular	*plural*
first	mimi	sisi
second	wewe	ninyi
third	yeye	wao

In emphatic use, the strong forms reinforce rather than replace both subject and object prefixes: *Mimi nimekwisha* 'I have finished'; *Nilimwona yeye na Hamisi pia* 'I saw both *him* and Hamisi'. Where such "doubling" occurs, the pronominal clitic or inflection on the verb can be treated as encoding agreement with the free-standing pronoun.

The process of agreement which licenses null arguments may be constrained in a number of ways. First, the features involved, the so-called "φ-features", vary; they are typically some or all of person, number, gender, and case. Second, there are varying constraints on the noun phrase types that trigger agreement. In most Romance languages, for example, the verb agrees with any subject, but only with *pro* objects; where there is an overt object no clitic appears (Italian *Io lavoro* (I work+1SG) 'I am working', but **Mi vede me* (1SG sees me) 'He/She sees me'). Cross-linguistically, whether or not there is agreement may depend on whether the subject or object is overt or null, pronominal or full, definite or indefinite, and perhaps some other factors. For example, clitic doubling occurs in Macedonian, but only when the object is definite: *Ja vidov mačka-ta* (3SG+F saw+1SG cat-DEF) 'I saw the cat'.[14] All the points made here about *pro* in subject or object position can apply also to the position of object of a preposition. Languages in which prepositions show agreement morphology and may take a null pronominal complement include Welsh (*amdano* (about+3SG+M) or *amdano ef* (about+3SG+M him) 'about him') (Sadler 1988) and Berber (*zg-s* (from-3SG) 'from him') (Renisio 1932).

particle which is used to augment the free-form pronouns (in a form determined by person and number, with some phonologically conditioned allomorphy) to the verb. Thus, the emphatic forms of *tugaim* 'I give' and *tugaimid* 'we give' are, respectively, *tugaim-se* and *tugaimid-ne*. Given that the subject is post-verbal in Irish, the correct analysis of this form is almost certainly that the augment is attached to *pro* just as it attaches to overt pronouns: *tugaim pro-se, tugaimid pro-ne* (see McCloskey and Hale 1984). This means that the strong pronoun occurring with a synthetic verb form is still partly null, because it contains *pro*, though with an overt suffix. But this suffix is itself unstressed, so the whole pronominal form, though "strong" in function, is unstressed.

[14] In the kind of doubling noted in Spanish, where the overt object has to be associated with a pre-position (*La veo a ella* (3SG+F see+1SG to her) 'I see her'), it is far from certain that the verb is agreeing with the strong pronoun. The clitic may well represent agreement with a *pro* object, *ella* being in a prepositional phrase in some position other than that of object. For more detailed discussion of these points see Lyons (1990).

The licensing of null pronouns is actually less straightforward and less well understood than the discussion so far implies. It is not necessarily dependent on identification by rich agreement morphology. A number of languages permit null pronominal subjects or objects in the total absence of any agreement morphology; an example is Korean (Sohn 1994):

(10)   Minca-nun haikhing ka-ss-ta.   Keki-se sensayng-nim-ul
         Minca TOPhiking   go PAST DECL there   teacher HON ACC
         manna-ss-ta.
         meet PAST DECL
         'Minca went hiking. There she met her teacher.'

Cases like this, where an argument of a sentence which would naturally be rendered pronominally in other languages is not overtly expressed by either a pronoun or by any agreement material, may represent a radically different phenomenon from that of null arguments identified by agreement. For discussion see Huang (1984), Jaeggli and Safir (1989), Huang (1994). It is likely that *pro* is not involved in these languages, and that therefore the null arguments in sentences like (10) are not actually pronominal.

Since personal pronouns are assumed to be the pronominal counterpart of the definite article, and since both these entities can take the form of lexical items or affixes, an interesting question is whether there is a correlation within languages between the forms of pronouns and articles. Certainly many languages with a free-form definite article also have free-form pronouns (English, German), and many languages with an affixal or clitic article also have null subjects and/or objects identified by inflection or clitics (Albanian, Arabic). But many other languages, like Swedish and Lakhota (if the article in this language is a free form), show no such correlation. I will take this point up again in Chapters 8 and 9.

3.4.3   *Personal determiners*

By "personal determiners" I mean forms related to personal pronouns occurring within full noun phrases, of the type *we teachers, you students*. We have seen that these determiners are subject in English to two kinds of constraint. In their non-exclamatory use they are restricted (except in the third person) to strong, unreduced form (which I have claimed represents a demonstrative). And they are not available for all person–number values (being completely excluded from the first person singular: **I student*). The second constraint at least is language-specific, as can be seen from comparison of the following paradigms in English and German:

exclamatory use	argument use
*I fool!	*I boy disgraced myself.
You fool!	*You boy disgraced yourself.
The fool!	The/That boy disgraced himself.
*We fools!	We boys disgraced ourselves.
You fools!	You boys disgraced yourselves.
The fools!	The/Those boys disgraced themselves.
Ich Esel!	Ich Faulpelz muß mich beeilen.
I donkey	I lazybones must myself hurry
'Silly me!'	'*I lazybones must hurry', 'I must hurry, lazybones that I am.'
Du Esel!	Du Faulpelz mußt dich beeilen.
Der Esel!	Der Faulpelz muß sich beeilen.
Wir Esel!	Wir Faulpelze müssen uns beeilen.
Ihr Esel!	Ihr Faulpelze müßt euch beeilen.
Die Esel!	Die Faulpelze müssen sich beeilen.

Another language completely unconstrained in this respect is Warlpiri (Hale 1973), a language with no definite article and apparently only strong personal determiners (identical to personal pronouns):

(11) a. Ngarka ngatju ka-rna purlami.
man I AUX 1SG shout
'*I man am shouting.'
b. Ngarka njuntu ka-npa purlami.
man you-SG AUX 2SG shout
'*You man are shouting.'
c. Ngarka nganimpa ka-rnalu purlami.
man we AUX 1PL shout
'We men are shouting.'

On the other hand, there are languages much more constrained than English. In Spanish *yo estudiante* (I student), *tú estudiante* (you student), *nosotros estudiantes* (we students), *vosotros estudiantes* (you students) are all impossible. French permits only third-person forms in the exclamatory use, though these can have second-person reference: *Le salaud!* 'The bastard!', 'You bastard!'. And the argument use, limited to the same person–number values as English, is only possible (except in the third person) with the addition of *autre* 'other': *nous autres hommes* 'we men', *vous autres hommes* 'you men'.

In Nama, person is expressed inflectionally in the noun phrase, as a suffix on the noun. Nama is as unrestricted as German and Warlpiri as regards person–number:

tií	kxòe-ta	(I person-1SG+M)	'*I man'
saá	kxòe-ts	(you person-2SG+M)	'*you man'
	kxòe-p	(person-3SG+M)	'the man'
sií	kxòe-ke	(we person-1PL+M)	'we men'
saá	kxòe-kò	(you person-2PL+M)	'you men'
	kxòe-ku	(person-3PL+M)	'the men'

Notice that in first and second persons a free-standing personal determiner (identical to the corresponding pronoun) obligatorily co-occurs with the person–number–gender affix,[15] but not in the third person. The third-person pronoun may not occur in this construction. Instead, the noun can occur with affix only, or a free-standing demonstrative determiner could occur. Despite the difference in structure, this is remarkably similar to the English pattern, where it was seen that the personal determiner can be weak only in the third person (*the*), though a strong form (*this* or *that*) is also possible. Assuming that the doubling in the Nama first and second persons represents morphophonological strength, as doubling normally does, both languages are constrained to have strong determiners only (claimed to be demonstrative in English) in these persons. This constraint may, therefore, be a very general one.[16]

---

[15] Incidentally, Nama can express inclusive first person in this construction by having a second-person determiner doubled by a first-person dual or plural suffix: *saá tará-se* (you woman-1PL+F) 'we (inclusive) women'. This recalls the strategy pointed out for Ewondo in the clause.

[16] Another language displaying affixal personal determiners like Nama is Classical Nahuatl: *n-oquich-tli* (1SG-man-SG) '*I man'; for discussion see Andrews (1975). But this inflectional marking of person in the noun phrase is extremely rare. On the other hand, person–number affixes cross-referencing or identifying a possessor are common. And in some languages these possessive affixes can be used as if they were affixal "personal articles", apparently only in exclamatory use, as we would expect given the constraint just discussed. Similarly, some languages permit free-form possessives to have the sense of personal determiners in the exclamatory use; the Scandinavian languages exemplify this, as in Danish *Din idiot!* (your idiot) 'You idiot!' (Haugen 1976). That these constructions are genuinely possessive, rather than showing a person morpheme homophonous with the possessive morpheme, is suggested by the fact that Turkish has what looks like the same construction with an overt full noun phrase "possessor" and third-person possessive affix: *Bekir hırsız-ı* (Bekir thief-3SG) 'that thief Bekir'. But one language in which there is a case for claiming that there is an affixal person marker homophonous with the possessive marker (and not limited to the exclamatory use) is Armenian. This personal suffix occurs only to double a free-standing personal determiner (identical to the personal pronoun) in first and second person – exactly as in Nama. In the singular it is identical to the possessive suffix (first person -s, second person -t, third person -n/-ə); but the same forms are used for the plural, which means the suffix agrees with the determiner in person but not in number (perhaps because the noun's own plural morpheme makes this agreement redundant): *es ousoutsich-s* (I teacher-1) '*I teacher', *mɛnk' ousoutsich-nɛr-s* (we teacher-PL-1) 'we teachers'. But recall from 3.3.2 that the Armenian possessive suffix does not agree with a plural free-form possessive even in person, so this suffix does seem to be distinct.

Complex definites and indefinites

I observed above that Spanish does not allow first- and second-person pre-
nominal determiners at all. But, as is well known, Spanish compensates by permitting noun phrases third person in form to have first- or second-person reference,
this being shown by the appropriate agreement morpheme on the verb (so the phenomenon is limited to subject position):

(12) a.   Los estudiantes trabajan   mucho.
           the students   work-3PL much
           'The students work hard.'
    b.   Los estudiantes trabajamos mucho.
           the students   work-1PL much
           'We students work hard.'
    c.   Los estudiantes trabajáis   mucho.
           the students   work-2PL much
           'You students work hard.'

If the definite article is third person, or even if it is a default form unmarked for
person, it is clear that the verb's inflection need not agree in person with the subject in Spanish; it is presumably constrained merely not to disagree. Interestingly,
this possibility is only available in the plural, which means that the range of
references possible in terms of person–number values with full noun phrases (in
the argument use) is exactly the same as in English; *el estudiante* (the student)
cannot express '*I student' or '*you student'. A further important point is that,
whereas personal determiners are, like personal pronouns, invariably definite, this
structure can be indefinite:

(13) a.   Algunos estudiantes trabajamos mucho.
           some   students   work-1PL much
    b.   Tres estudiantes trabajáis   mucho.
           three students   work-2PL much

The sense here is a number of students including the speaker, and a group of three
students excluding the speaker but including the hearer. I return to this in Chapter 8.

Warlpiri, which has a full paradigm of personal determiners, also has the Spanish
construction (though without articles), and without the number constraint of Spanish:

(14) a.   Ngarka ka-rna   purlami.
           man   AUX 1SG shout
           '*I man am shouting.'
    b.   Ngarka ka-npa   purlami.
           man   AUX 2SG shout
           '*You man are shouting.'
    c.   Ngarka ka-rnalu   purlami.
           man   AUX 1PL shout
           'We men are shouting.'

This is actually much more commonly used in Warlpiri than the construction shown in (11). An interesting variant involves demonstratives. In Warlpiri these exhibit four degrees of deixis, on a mixed distance-person basis: proximal or associated with first person *njampu*, medial or second person *yalumpu*, distal or third person *yali*, ultra-distal *yinja*. Now the first two of these, as well as picking out something near speaker or hearer, can be used with reference to speaker or hearer; the agreement morphology on the auxiliary makes the sense clear:

(15) a.   Ngarka njampu ka   purlami.
            man   this   AUX shout
            'This man (near me) is shouting.'

      b.   Ngarka njampu ka-rna   purlami.
            man   this   AUX 1SG shout
            '*I man am shouting.'

(16) a.   Ngarka yalumpu ka   purlami.
            man   that   AUX shout
            'That man (near you) is shouting.'

      b.   Ngarka yalumpu ka-npa   purlami.
            man   that   AUX 2SG shout
            '*You man are shouting.'

It is arguable that the demonstratives in the (b) sentences here are functioning as first- and second-person determiners, and so trigger the appropriate agreement on the auxiliary. On this view these sentences show a variant of the construction (11). I think it is more likely that what we see in (15b) and (16b) is a variant of the "non-agreement" structure (14), with the non-person-marked subject noun phrase taking a demonstrative appropriate to its reference.

3.4.4 Definite and demonstrative personal forms

It is very common for demonstratives to serve as third-person personal pronouns, and for languages to have no personal pronoun in the third person distinct from a demonstrative. Often it is a demonstrative unmarked for deixis that fills this function. In Latin, for example, the general demonstrative *is* is used, especially in non-nominative cases where there is more need for an overt form (Latin being null subject). Similarly in Finnish, the general demonstrative *se* also serves as inanimate third-person pronoun, and sometimes replaces *hän* 'he', 'she'. Sometimes one of the deictically marked demonstratives supplies the personal pronoun. Again in Latin, the demonstrative related to third person, *ille*, frequently occurs rather than *is*. In Turkish too it is the third (distal) term of the demonstrative system, *o*, that supplies the personal pronoun. Persian uses the distal form of a two-term system, *ān*, for the non-human pronoun. In Lezgian the medial demonstrative *am*

Complex definites and indefinites

(in a three-term distance system) is used. Often there is no particular member of the demonstrative system that has this function (presumably becoming unmarked for deixis in the process), and whatever deictic choices apply to the demonstratives apply equally to the personal pronoun. Thus Albanian has the following personal pronoun system:

1SG	unë	'I'
2SG	ti	'you'
3SG-M-PROX	ky	'he', 'it', 'this one'
3SG-F-PROX	kyo	'she', 'it', 'this one'
3SG-M-DIST	ai	'he', 'it', 'that one'
3SG-F-DIST	ajo	'she', 'it', 'that one'
1PL	ne	'we'
2PL	ju	'you'
3PL-M-PROX	këta	'they', 'these'
3PL-F-PROX	këto	'they', 'these'
3PL-M-DIST	ata	'they', 'those'
3PL-F-DIST	ato	'they', 'those'

Equally in Khalkha, the two-term demonstrative series supplies the third-person pronoun: *enə* 'he', 'she', 'it', 'this one'; *terə* 'he', 'she', 'it', 'that one'; *edə* 'they', 'these'; *tedə* 'they', 'those'. Japanese uses a full noun phrase for the third-person pronoun:

1SG	watasi	'I'
2SG	anata	'you'
3SG	kono/sono/ano hito	'he', 'she'
1PL	watasitati	'we'
2PL	anatatati	'you'
3PL	kono/sono/ano hitotati	'they'

The third-person forms consist of the noun *hito* 'person' preceded by an appropriate choice from the three-term person-based demonstrative system. The form related to third person, *ano*, is the most common. Though *ano hito* 'that person' looks like a non-pronominal noun phrase, it follows the pronominal pattern of taking the number marker *-tati* in the plural, while nouns are otherwise invariable for number.

This use of demonstratives for the third-person pronoun is particularly evident in null-subject languages. In these languages personal pronouns are only overt, of course, in strong, emphatic use, which means that the demonstratives used for the third person are functioning as strong pronouns. The corresponding weak pronoun has the form of *pro* or an affix or clitic, which is non-demonstrative. But this pattern is not limited to null-subject languages. In languages in which personal pronouns are normally overt and free-standing, strong use may simply involve adding stress, but it may also involve a distinct form; and in this case the strong form is often a demonstrative. Consider the German system:[17]

1SG	ich	'I'	1PL	wir	'we'
2SG	du	'you'	2PL	ihr	'you'
3SG-M	er	'he', 'it'			
3SG-F	sie	'she', 'it'	3PL	sie	'they'
3SG-N	es	'it'			

These can all be stressed for emphatic or contrastive use, but there is a tendency in colloquial German for the third-person forms, when emphatic, to be replaced by the demonstrative forms *der/die/das/die*. A somewhat similar picture is suggested by the facts of the personal determiner system of Nama, discussed above. Recall that, in first and second persons, the person marker on the noun must be reinforced by a free-form personal determiner; I took this to suggest that the construction is strong, as in English. But in the third person the affix does not require this reinforcement (again recalling the English situation, where the personal determiner structure can be weak in the third person), and indeed a determiner of the form of the third-person pronoun stem cannot occur. A demonstrative can, however. What this suggests is that, in this construction, the third-person strong form is expressed by a demonstrative.

The generalization that these observations point to is that strong occurrences of personal pronouns and personal determiners are demonstrative. Whether they must express deixis too varies from one language to another. Consistency suggests that first- and second-person forms too, when strong, are demonstrative, though the deictic distinctions familiar in demonstratives are generally limited to third-person ones. This treatment is supported by the evidence presented in Chapter 1 that strong occurrences of personal pronouns and determiners in English are [+ Dem].

An interesting consequence of this analysis is that deictically unmarked demonstratives are more common than otherwise appears. Spanish, for instance, has the three-term deictically marked demonstrative series *este, ese, aquel*, already discussed, and no general demonstrative so far identified. But Spanish is a null-subject language, so that personal pronouns in subject position are generally emphatic (except that they may also appear non-emphatically to avoid ambiguity over the gender of a referent, for example). But, on the analysis proposed, emphatic *yo* 'I', *tú* 'you', *él* 'he', *ella* 'she' etc. are forms of a general, deictically unmarked demonstrative. In French, the emphatic third-person pronouns *lui*

---

[17] The glosses are simplified; *er* and *sie* correspond to English *it* when a non-human referent is denoted by a noun which is grammatically masculine or feminine, and in the same way *es* can occasionally be 'she'.

'he', *elle* 'she', *eux, elles* 'they' are the pro-nominal congeners of the deictically unmarked demonstrative determiner *ce, cette, ces*, while the deictically marked pronouns *celui-ci, celle-là* etc. correspond to *ce . . . -ci, cette . . . -là* etc.

3.5 Universals and other quantifiers

It was noted in Chapter 1 that quantificational expressions like *all* and *most* share some of the behaviour and distribution of definites. In English these determiners can stand outside a complete noun phrase, possibly (necessarily in the case of *most*) linked to it by a partitive construction: *all (of) the trees, most of these cars*. This is a common pattern cross-linguistically (French *tous les arbres* 'all the trees'), as is their occurrence in what looks like Det position inside the noun phrase (German *alle Autos* 'all cars'). Note that in the first pattern the noun phrase quantified over can sometimes be indefinite (French *toute une semaine* 'a whole week', English *most of a town*), though it does not follow that the combination is indefinite. The French equivalent of *most*, though linked to a noun phrase partitively, is definite in form: *la plupart des clients* (the most+part of+the customers) 'most customers', 'most of the customers'.

Within the noun phrase, the most interesting cross-linguistic observation is that quantifiers corresponding to *all* and *most* show the same pattern of distribution seen with demonstratives. They may occupy Det position as in English, in accordance with their apparent definite determiner status; or they may be in some more internal position, with something like adjectival status, but then with the definite article present (in languages that have one) to ensure the definiteness with which the quantifier must be associated: German *der ganze Wein in Kalifornien* (the all wine in California) 'all (the) wine in California', *die meisten Menschen* (the most people) 'most people'; Hungarian *a től-ed kapott valamennyi levél* (the from-2SG received each letter) 'each letter received from you' (Szabolcsi 1994).

3.6 Indefinites

Complex indefinites, noun phrases whose indefiniteness is due to some expression which is not an article, not typically weak, are not central to this study, and will not be investigated in detail. I am taking the determiners involved to be incompatible with definiteness, not necessarily themselves [– Def]; many of them seem to be to do with degrees of specificity.

We have seen that many so-called "indefinite" determiners are in fact cardinality expressions, and that cardinality does not entail indefiniteness. The numeral *one*, for example, appears in definites and indefinites. But it is appropriate to mention here one type of noun phrase containing the singular numeral which is in numerous languages indefinite in sense, despite being definite in form. In German *der eine Mann* (the one man) would normally mean 'one man' (out of a group) or 'one of the men'; this is especially so when there is a contrast expressed or implied with some other man or men. The same applies to the French *L'un est parti, l'autre est resté* 'One left, the other stayed'. The same phenomenon is probably at the root of the Albanian structure in which *një* 'a', 'one' is used with a noun in definite form accompanied by a possessive, the sense being again indefinite: *një motr-a ime* (a/one sister-DEF my) 'a sister of mine', 'one of my sisters'. Compare German *mein einer Sohn* (my one son) 'one of my sons'.

3.6.1 *Full noun phrases*

The cline of specificity illustrated by the English series *(a) certain, some, any* can be reproduced for many languages, if the correspondences are approximate. Thus Spanish *cierto, algún, cualquier,* Irish *áirithe, éigin, ar bith* (the last a prepositional phrase rather than a determiner), Latin *quidam, aliqui, quivis*. In other languages the cline makes fewer distinctions; Russian has specific ('certain') and general ('some') *njekij/njekotoryj* and random ('any') *vsjakij/ljuboj*.

Recall that English random *any* shows some grounds for being treated as definite, and it is common for a determiner with this random sense to function also as the equivalent of *every*; this is true of Russian *vsjakij*, French *tout*, German *jeder*, Hausa *kowane*. In English the random determiner serves also as a non-assertive or "negative polarity" form used in negative, interrogative, and similar contexts. Other languages distinguish a special form for this function, Latin *ullus* and Irish *aon* for example. French *aucun*, as well as occurring with purely negative sense as 'no' (*en aucune façon* 'in no way'), has this function: *sans faire aucun bruit* 'without making any noise'. It was also seen in Chapter 1 that *some* is in complementary distribution with *sm*, so they could be the same determiner, though occurring in strong and weak varieties. The strong form, which may have some additional semantic content, is the only one possible in singular count use. This situation is partly mirrored in Spanish, where *algún/algunos*, corresponding approximately to strong *some*, can occur in singular and plural (though not mass) contexts, but whereas in the plural it tends to express a vague cardinality, it cannot in the singular.

These indefinites are not only semantically extremely complicated and poorly understood, but also in all likelihood semantically very heterogeneous. This is reflected in considerable variety in structure and source. Some forms are clearly determiners, but others (like Irish *ar bith* 'any', more literally 'on earth', 'in the world') are prepositional, and others more complex (French *n'importe quel* 'no matter which', 'any'). Many indefinite determiners are (like most cardinal articles) of singular numeral origin, the Irish negative polarity *aon* 'any' for example. English *any* and German *einig* 'some' are derived from 'one' with an adjectival suffix added. Spanish *algún* consists of the singular numeral with an indefinite morpheme *alg-* prefixed.

Some random determiners contain a verbal element of the type *want* or *like*, often in combination with an interrogative element, the original sense thus being something along the lines of 'which . . . you wish'. Examples are Russian *lyuboj*, Spanish *cualquier*, Latin *quivis* and *quilibet*, and the Albanian pronominal *kushdo*. Indefinite determiners containing an interrogative element, or simply identical to an interrogative, are very common. The Spanish *cualquier*, Hausa *kowane* 'any' (from *wane* 'which'), Khalkha *alibaa* 'any' (from *ali* 'which'), and all the Latin forms mentioned containing the element *qui* exemplify the former; and the latter is illustrated by Maltese *xi* 'what', 'some' (Aquilina 1965) and Korean *enu* 'which', 'some'. A particularly interesting case is Lezgian (Haspelmath 1993), in which up to three separate elements co-occur, the numeral *sa* 'one', an interrogative modifier, and an indefinite particle *x̂ajit'ani* 'any' or *jat'ani* 'some': *hi waxt.und-a x̂ajit'ani* (which time-INESS any) 'at any time'; *sa hix̂tin jat'ani q̇alabulux* (one which some confusion) 'some confusion'.

3.6.2 Pronouns

It is common for indefinite determiners, like other determiners, to be also capable of pronominal occurrence, sometimes with slight variation in form. This is essentially the case with the complex indefinites of Lezgian, with *sa wuž jat'ani* (one who some) 'someone', *sa wuč jat'ani* (one what some) 'something', and *wuž x̂ajit'ani* (who any) 'anyone', *wuč x̂ajit'ani* (what any) 'anything'. But indefinite pronouns merit separate treatment because of special formations which are widely found. Like the determiners they are frequently based on interrogatives, often with an additional marker, and, more commonly than the determiners, they may be simply identical to interrogatives. Dixon (1980) observes that most Australian languages have a set of forms that have indefinite or interrogative sense, or both together; so a sentence containing a form of the root *ŋaan-* 'someone', 'who' may be understood as simultaneously predicating something of some individual and asking for this individual's identity. Similarly, in German *wer* is 'who' and 'someone', *was* is 'what' and 'something'; in Carib *no:kï* is 'who' and 'someone', *o:tï* is 'what' and 'something'; and in Sarcee *ādáyá* is 'who' and 'someone', *dit'á* is 'what' and 'something'. See also Ultan (1978). Examples of augmented interrogatives are: Russian *kto-to* and *nikto* 'someone', *čto-to* and *nječto* 'something', from *kto* 'who', *čto* 'what'; Hausa *kowa* 'anyone', *kome* 'anything', from *wa* 'who', *me* 'what'; Albanian *dikush* 'someone', *kushdo* 'anyone', from *kush* 'who'.

A common pattern in indefinite pronouns is the use of a noun of somewhat general sense (like 'person', 'thing'), either alone, modified by a determiner, or incorporated with a determiner. For 'someone' and 'something' Irish has, respectively, *duine éigin* (person some), *rud éigin* (thing some), but the determiner can be dropped leaving the noun alone; Persian has *kas-ī* (person-a), *chīz-ī* (thing-a); and Nama has *kxòe-'i* (person-INDEF), *xuu-'i* (thing-INDEF). Of course it is debatable whether these are pronouns or simply indefinite noun phrases. English *somebody* and *something* and French *quelque chose* 'something' exemplify the incorporated noun type. English *someone*, Persian *yek-ī* (one-a) 'someone', French *quelqu'un* 'someone', and Navaho *la'* (one) 'someone' illustrate the fact that, in all these types, 'one' often occurs in place of a noun in human forms.[18]

The English "arbitrary" human pronoun *one* has its equivalents in many languages, though sometimes, as in the case of French *on*, permitting indefinite as well as arbitrary reference (*On frappe à la porte* 'Someone is knocking at the door'). Many languages prefer an impersonal verb construction to express this idea, but one such language, Spanish, also has a pronoun used mainly in circumstances where the impersonal construction is excluded, and this also consists of the singular numeral. Other languages use a pronoun derived from (or identical to) a noun such as 'person' or 'man'. Irish again uses the noun *duine* 'person', and Turkish uses *insan* 'person'. German and Old English have *man*, and French *on* also has its origin in the word for 'man'.

For an excellent and much more detailed cross-linguistic survey of indefinite pronouns see Haspelmath (1997).

3.7 Indefinite demonstratives

In Chapter 1 we entertained two analyses of *such*. The first is that it is an indefinite demonstrative; that is, it is synonymous with *this/that* (though lacking the deictic contrast, being therefore of the "general demonstrative" type), differing only in that it is constrained to occur in indefinite noun phrases. The alternative analysis is that *such* is not a demonstrative, though it contains a demonstrative element as part of its meaning, which is something like 'of this/that kind' or 'like this/that'.

The close relationship of *such* to the demonstratives is evident in the fact that the corresponding term in other languages often does show the same deictic distinctions as the demonstratives do. Khalkha has a two-way demonstrative contrast, *ena* 'this', *tera* 'that', which is duplicated in *iima* 'such as this', 'of this kind', *tiima* 'such as that', 'of that kind'. Languages with three-term demonstrative

---

[18] That the noun is incorporated into the determiner to form a complex pronoun is clear for English and French, if uncertain for other languages. The French *quelque chose*, though based on a feminine noun, is grammatically masculine (that is, of unmarked gender), as shown by past-participle agreement (*quelque chose que j'ai fait/*faite* 'something I've done'). And in English, *someone nice, somebody big, something unexpected* are not synonymous with *some nice one, some big body, some unexpected thing*. For comparison, recall the Japanese definite pronoun *ano hito* (that person) 'he', 'she', which, while looking like a full noun phrase, behaves like a pronoun in taking number marking.

systems and corresponding three-way distinctions for 'such' are Turkish (*bu, şu, o; böyle, şöyle, öyle*), Japanese (*kono, sono, ano; konna, sonna, anna*), Lithuanian (*šìs/šìtas, tàs, anàs; šìtoks, tóks, anóks*). Albanian has a two-way contrast in demonstratives (*ky* 'this', *ai* 'that') and makes a corresponding contrast between *i këtillë* 'such as this' and *i atillë* 'such as that', but has in addition a deictically neutral form *i tillë* 'such' not corresponding directly to a specific demonstrative.

All these forms are limited to indefinite occurrence, while the corresponding demonstratives are definite. But if the first analysis, that *such* etc. are simply indefinite variants of the demonstratives, were correct, we would expect to find languages in which the complementary distribution were reflected in identity of form. That is, there should be languages with a single word for 'that' and 'such', the translation being determined by whether the noun phrase in which the word occurs is marked definite or indefinite. There appear to be no such languages, and I take this to point decisively to the second analysis. This means that the assumption that demonstratives are inherently definite is maintained.

3.8 Vocatives

We have not so far given any consideration to noun phrases used in direct address, in vocative function, but they are interesting in being of uncertain status in relation to definiteness. Proper names of persons are undoubtedly the noun phrase type most commonly used this way, but common nouns too can be vocative, and then they are typically bare in English (as in *Hello, **chaps*** or ***Children, what are you doing?***). Since vocatives are forms of direct address, we might expect them to be second person, and indeed second-person pronouns can be used this way (***You, come here!***), as can full noun phrases with second-person determiners (***You boys, follow me***). Since personal pronouns and personal determiners are inherently definite, vocatives involving these must be definite. But what about the bare noun type? It has no determiner, definite or cardinal, but since indefiniteness is a matter of absence of definite marking rather than presence of some other marking, these expressions should be indefinite. They may be of a similar status to proper nouns, also arguably indefinite if bare. English vocatives, then, can be definite and indefinite. In French common noun vocatives are always definite, taking either a definite article (*Salut, **les mecs*** 'Hello, chaps') or a possessive (*Bonjour, **mon général*** 'Good morning, general'). The problem in French is that at least the first of these looks third person. The answer to these difficulties, for both English and French, may be that the noun phrases involved are not formally vocative; that is, there is perhaps no grammatical category of vocative in these languages, but noun phrases of differing structure can be used in address function.

Many languages do have special vocative forms. Often this takes the form of a particle accompanying the noun (obligatorily, optionally, or only with certain categories of noun): Albanian *O bir* or *Biro* 'Son'; Egyptian Arabic *Ya wálad!* 'Boy!'; Cantonese *A-baak* 'Uncle' (addressing an older man). In Egyptian Arabic the particle is involved in agreement, appearing also before a modifier (as does the definite article). Sometimes the vocative particle is additional to a special vocative case form of the noun: Classical Greek *Ō andres Athēnaioi* 'Men of Athens!'; Irish *A Sheáin* 'John'. The vocative function is traditionally dealt with under the rubric of case (though see Blake (1994: 9), but where nouns do have a special form for the vocative (with or without a particle) there is a strong tendency for this to be a minimal form, often no more than the noun stem. This is so in the classical Indo-European languages Greek, Sanskrit and Latin, where most vocative forms which are distinct from the nominative consist of the mere stem (which may include a theme vowel indicating declensional class). In Turkish the form used for the vocative is the same as the nominative–absolutive, which is the stem with no case affix. In this morphological minimality the vocative resembles the imperative in verb conjugation, and I suspect that (in terms of the analysis of grammatical categories as functional heads) the vocative is the nominal counterpart of the imperative.

There is a strong tendency for vocatives to be bare, but it is no more than a tendency. In Albanian, where vocatives are identical in form to the nominative but take a particle, they do not normally take the definite affix; but some feminine names do, and all do when restrictively modified. Perhaps to be related to this last observation is the fact that in Serbo-Croat an adjective modifying a vocative takes "definite" form. In general, vocatives are not consistently definite or indefinite.

3.9 Non-configurational languages

This survey of the expression of definiteness and indefiniteness reveals variety which is compatible with the idea that definiteness is associated, perhaps universally, with a particular structural position, which I have termed "Det position", and cardinality with a different, lower, position. Affixal definite markers seem, in some cases at least, to be in a position distinct from that of free-form definite determiners, but it is arguable that they are in some position which enters into an agreement relationship with Det position. These ideas will be clarified in Chapter 8. The postulation of these generalizations exploits and depends on the hypothesis of a universal X-bar schema, subject to limited variation, and the discussion so far has implicitly taken all languages to be "configurational", that is, to be subject to the X-bar schema. But there is reason to believe that many languages are "non-configurational", and a great deal of work in recent years has been investigating a possible configurationality parameter. For a clear discussion of the issues see Hale (1983, 1989).

The properties thought to typify non-configurationality include: free word order, "flat" (as opposed to hierarchical) phrase structure, discontinuous expressions, extensive use of null arguments, absence of syntactic movement rules and (perhaps) of empty categories. In some putatively non-configurational languages these properties are accompanied, and arguably in part made possible, by a rich auxiliary system identifying the arguments of the sentence, and a rich case morphology. The phenomenon has been accounted for as consisting of a mismatch between a fully configurational level of "lexical structure" (expressing the predicate–argument structure of a clause) and a flat phrase structure with no VP node (Hale 1983, Mohanan 1983, Jelinek 1984, Austin and Bresnan 1996). It follows from the proposed absence of VP in syntactic structure that all arguments are on the same level, sisters to the verb, and this idea has led to an emphasis more recently in the literature on the investigation of "subject–object asymmetries" as offering more decisive criteria for configurational or non-configurational status. In a language like English where subjects are specifiers and objects are complements, so that the former c-command the latter, but not vice versa, there are numerous differences in behaviour between the two; for example, a subject can act as antecedent for a reflexive in object position, but not vice versa (*John shot himself*, but **Himself shot John*). Such asymmetries (in so far as they are due to the difference between specifier and complement positions) should be absent from languages in which subjects and objects are structurally equivalent. The results of investigation along this path are still indecisive, and the reader is referred to Marácz and Muysken (1989) for some good examples of the debate, and to Speas (1990: 123–201) for a strong argument against the existence of non-configurational languages. See also Baker (1995) for detailed investigation of the polysynthetic subtype of non-configurationality. An alternative account of languages appearing to require this characterization is that they are configurational in the underlying D-structure but subject to a process of "scrambling".

I will assume here, for expository purposes, that languages can be non-configurational. Languages are not necessarily configurational or non-configurational overall, however, but may vary in different parts of their grammars. For example, Hungarian and Lakhota have been argued to be non-configurational in clause structure (Kiss 1987, Williamson 1984), but both are highly configurational in noun phrase structure. There are probably, moreover, degrees of configurationality, languages showing some of the properties of each type or showing them to a limited extent.

Gil (1987) surveys a range of noun phrase properties for which languages may vary, and identifies two language types, which he terms A and B; it turns out that they are, respectively, configurational and non-configurational languages. These properties include the obligatory marking of (in)definiteness (characterizing type A but not type B), the use of numeral classifiers (type B but not type A), and the marking of plurality (type A but not type B). Gil argues that the first property reduces to the configurationality parameter. Type B languages do not mark (in)definiteness because they lack determiners; determiners require hierarchical structure because they have the function of mapping one bar-level into a higher one. The two other properties he explains in terms of the count–mass distinction. In type B languages all nouns are mass, so there can be no marking of plurality, and classifiers are necessary with numerals to establish units for enumeration. It seems likely, moreover, that the count–mass parameter is to be subsumed under the configurationality parameter, since the positive values of the two appear to coincide.

Gil's language sample is limited: he examines in detail only English (as a paradigm type A language) and Japanese (illustrating type B). But the properties observed for Japanese do seem to typify the most strongly non-configurational languages (such as Warlpiri and Korean). And languages may show a continuum of characteristics relating to configurationality; it seems unlikely, for example, that all configurational languages have obligatory marking of definiteness. Russian has no articles, but it does have number marking and does not use classifiers, and so seems to be basically configurational. There does, however, appear to be a tenable generalization that languages that are non-configurational in the noun phrase always lack definiteness marking. Within the present investigation, the temptation is to account for this in terms of absence in these languages, not of determiners generally, but of the hypothesized definite Det position.[19]

It is not clear how to reduce the count–mass parameter to the configurationality parameter, but the empirical evidence points to such a reduction. One possibility is that non-configurational languages have no cardinality position and so cannot have numerals except with classifiers. Whatever account is adopted, the question is important, because "indefinite articles", which I have claimed are cardinal, are absent in non-configurational languages according to Gil. If non-configurational languages do not have numerals (except with classifiers), for whatever reason, cardinal articles should be equally excluded, since they are in effect weak numerals. But then why should a quasi-indefinite article not take the form of a weak 'one' plus a classifier? In fact there is evidence for this possibility. In Cantonese classifiers are obligatory with numerals, and, as already observed, the numeral *yāt* is used optionally as an article, introducing new referents to discourse: *yāt ga chē*

---

[19] The claim that definiteness marking does not occur in languages which are non-configurational in the noun phrase because they lack the appropriate structure makes an interesting prediction that is easily tested: that these languages cannot have DG possessives. This is because, on the present account, DG possessives are associated with the same structural positions as definite articles. And, on a limited investigation, the prediction is borne out. In Japanese, for example, noun phrases with possessive modifiers are neutral with respect to definiteness: *anata no hon* (you POSS book) 'your book' or 'a book of yours'; *sensei no hon* (teacher POSS book) 'the teacher's book' or 'a book of the teacher's'.

(one/a CLASS car) 'a car' (Matthews and Yip 1994). If it is true that highly non-configurational languages cannot have definiteness marking but can have cardinal articles, this is additional evidence for the claim that articles like *a* really are cardinal rather than indefinite.

4

Some semantic and pragmatic distinctions

In the discussion of the nature of definiteness in Chapter 1, various distinctions apparently subsidiary to that between definite and indefinite were made: identifiable and inclusive, situational and anaphoric, specific and non-specific. We will examine these distinctions more closely in this chapter, with a view to determining whether they warrant splitting the concepts of definite and indefinite into a number of independent parameters of meaning, which just happen not to have distinct encodings in certain languages. In other words, could it be that English *the* expresses two or more separate semantic categories, misleading us into failing to see them as distinct? Or that "definite" is a broad, superordinate category embracing a number of distinct but related categories, which can be expected to be separately encoded in some languages? There are also semantic distinctions, like that between generic and non-generic, which appear to be independent of that between definite and indefinite, but which interact with the latter distinction. Generics are typically definite in form in some languages, but not in others. But generics do have a lot in common with definites in terms of behaviour, so the question arises: are they also a kind of semantically definite expression which does not necessarily appear in definite form in certain languages (like English) in which the encoding of [+ Def] by an article is limited to a more restricted version of definiteness? Finally, we return to the analysis of proper nouns, which we have seen resemble generics in being overtly definite in form in some languages but not in others. It will be suggested that proper nouns are a kind of generic.

4.1 One definiteness or several?

Here we consider the question whether it is merely a language-specific fact, though shared by a number of languages, that the range of noun phrase uses marked as definite shares this marking. That is, is the definite article, in English and other languages, ambiguous? Or is it rather simply polysemous or vague in meaning,

Semantic and pragmatic distinctions

the various uses we have distinguished being different manifestations of a single category of definiteness?[1]

4.1.1 *Identifiability and inclusiveness*

It appears that identifiability and inclusiveness are both required to account for the facts of the use of *the*, and it seems improbable that either one can be reduced to the other. Perhaps they are distinct features which overlap, so that a number of uses of *the* can be characterized by either, with little obvious difference in what is conveyed. One might imagine a language in which they are encoded by different articles, so that Art$_1$ and Art$_2$ are both translatable by *the* in English; but whereas some occurrences of *the* correspond to Art$_1$ and some to Art$_2$, others correspond ambiguously to either Art$_1$ or Art$_2$.

But the evidence for identifiability and inclusiveness being distinct features is lacking. Numerous languages are like English in expressing both by a single article, but there seems to be no language in which they are separately encoded by articles corresponding to Art$_1$ and Art$_2$ above, nor in which there is only one article encoding identifiability but not inclusiveness, or vice versa. The conclusion must be that the dichotomy between identifiability and inclusiveness does not reflect the reality, and that we must seek to unify them, either by deriving one from the other or by deriving both of them from some as yet undiscovered concept of which they are manifestations.

4.1.2 *Anaphoric and non-anaphoric definites*

The various uses of *the* identified in Chapter 1 (whether most readily accounted for in terms of identifiability or inclusiveness) fall into three main groups: anaphoric, situational, and general knowledge uses; a fourth major group, that of associative uses, cuts across the first three (so that, for example, situational uses may be associative or not). Of the first three groups, the anaphoric definites stand apart from the others, in that the context within which the referent is to be found, or within which the reference is inclusive, is linguistic, consisting of the discourse. The other groups of uses relate to the extralinguistic context, exploiting encyclopedic knowledge or knowledge of the immediate or wider situation.

The discussion in Chapter 2 showed that there is evidence from languages for drawing a line between anaphoric and other definites, treating them either as separate categories or as distinct sub-categories of definiteness, which happen to have the same encoding in English (and many other languages). Some languages have a definite article which is only used anaphorically (Hidatsa -*s*, Ewe *á* and

---

[1] For a clear discussion of the distinction between ambiguity and vagueness (and between homonymy and polysemy), see Kempson (1977), and for more recent and detailed work on polysemy see Ruhl (1989) and, especially, Pustejovsky (1995).

lá), while others distinguish an anaphoric article from a general definite article
(Lakhota *k'ų* and *kį* respectively). Of course it is important in making such observations on a language to make sure that the determiner used for anaphoric reference is a definite article rather than a demonstrative. In languages displaying both
an anaphoric and a non-anaphoric article, an interesting question is whether the
latter is excluded in anaphoric uses. The Lakhota article *kį* appears not to be so
excluded, though this is not entirely clear.

For languages like Lakhota it is not necessary to see the two categories,
anaphoric and extralinguistic, as unrelated; rather, they are hyponyms, sub-categories,
of a broader category of definiteness. Thus *k'ų* is [+ Def, + Ana] and *kį* is either
[+ Def, − Ana] or (if it can appear in anaphoric contexts) simply [+ Def]. English
the, in encoding just the broader category, is not ambiguous, but merely less
fine. That Lakhota *k'ų* and *kį* do share the specification [+ Def] is clear from their
behaviour in the internal head relative construction investigated by Williamson (1987)
and examined below in Chapter 6. The internal head in this construction is constrained to be indefinite, and noun phrases with either *k'ų* or *kį* (or other definite
determiners) are ruled out.

In languages with only an anaphoric article, it would appear that only one of
the categories hyponymous to definiteness is encoded: [+ Def, + Ana]. But this
feature specification would not be justified as a description of the content of this
article in the absence of any contrasting [+ Def, − Ana] article. Rather the article
should be simply [+ Def]. The problem then is to account for the restriction of
the definite article to anaphoric use. If definiteness is a semantic or pragmatic concept (as so far implied, and generally assumed), it seems not to be uniform across
languages. Perhaps [+ Def] always involves identifiability and/or inclusiveness,
but with varying characterization of the domain within which identifiability or inclusiveness may apply: the previous discourse in Hidatsa and Ewe, the previous
discourse or a range of situational and other domains in English.

Another possible approach is to take [± Def] to be a grammatical feature, whose
relation to meaning can vary from language to language, and which need not even
be semantically uniform within a single language. This is the treatment I shall
argue for in later chapters. Thus for languages in general there is a range of noun
phrase uses which can in principle be characterized as definite, because they can
be described in terms of identifiability or inclusiveness. These uses represent "semantic definiteness", but this is not what articles encode. A given language need not
treat the full range of these uses as grammatically definite; so the feature specification [+ Def] can segment the semantic field at different points in different
languages, its range in a particular language being shown by which uses require
the presence of a definite article or other definiteness marker. Thus (setting aside
complex definites), in Ewe only anaphoric noun phrases are [+ Def], in English

Semantic and pragmatic distinctions

anaphoric, situational and general knowledge noun phrases, in French anaphoric, situational, general knowledge and generic noun phrases. This means that a noun phrase may be definite in French and its translation equivalent indefinite in Ewe, though the two are referentially identical. I have already suggested something along these lines for proper nouns, possibly indefinite in English and definite in Greek, so that the same entity is represented in different ways by different languages. This point will be discussed further in 4.3 and 4.4, and in Chapter 7 an analysis of definiteness as a grammatical category will be proposed which is compatible with definiteness varying considerably across languages in the range of noun phrases it characterizes.[2]

4.1.3 *"Deictic" and non-"deictic" definites*

The picture just discussed, of anaphoric definites being separately encoded in some languages and being the only type of definite encoded in other languages, fits in well with the view of some theorists, notably Kempson (1975) and Heim (1989), that the anaphoric use is basic and other uses derivative. This view is based on the assumption that definiteness is about familiarity (and by extension identifiability), and anaphora represents the paradigm case of familiarity. But there is an opposing view, that the use of definites in the immediate situation where the referent is perceptible (often termed the "deictic" use) is basic, and the anaphoric use (and others) derived. This is the position of J. Lyons (1975, 1977: chapter 15), who claims that deixis is at the root of definite reference. The same view is held by Clark and Marshall (1981) and others. Recall that the term "deixis" is used in different ways by different writers. I have used it to denote distinctions involving closeness to or association with some centre (typically the speaker and the moment of utterance). Others use it to describe expressions which direct the hearer's attention towards a referent – essentially what demonstratives do. To keep the two concepts apart, let us adopt the label "ostension" for the latter use. J. Lyons, in the works referred to, unfortunately uses "deixis" in both senses, so that the definite article is said to be essentially deictic (that is, ostensive), and at the same time deictically neutral (expressing no distinction of the proximal–distal kind); I will substitute my labels in outlining his position.

An ostensive expression in J. Lyons's account, then, is one which draws the hearer's attention to a referent. Ostension is present in demonstratives, where it is typically complemented by deictic information such as distinguishes *this* and *that* in English. But a determiner may be ostensive without deixis (that is, it may be

[2] There seems less reason to interpret some of the other features introduced in Chapter 1, like [± Prox], as grammatical rather than semantic. But an inconsistency of treatment in this will turn out not to matter, since I will argue in Chapter 8 that there is no feature [± Def], definiteness being represented in the grammar as a functional head rather than a feature.

160

"deictically neutral", giving no information about the location of the referent), and then it is likely to be unstressed. This is the definite article. Ostension in its simplest form is reference to entities present in the physical situation of utterance, and this is the basis of all other uses of definite determiners. Deixis can, of course, be temporal as well as spatial, so that a distal demonstrative is likely to be used to refer to events further into the past or future than a proximal demonstrative. This is the link with anaphora. In many languages, two referents mentioned in the preceding discourse can be distinguished by the use of a distal demonstrative for the one mentioned earlier and a proximal demonstrative for the one mentioned more recently. The relationship between an anaphoric expression and its antecedent is itself a temporal one, and anaphoric reference involves the transference of basically spatial deictic concepts to the temporal dimension of discourse. The anaphoric use of demonstratives, and by extension the definite article, is thus derived from their situational, ostensive use.

If situational ostension rather than anaphora is the most basic kind of definiteness, one might expect that there are languages which have only this kind of definiteness, thus which have a definite article used only for referring to something physically perceptible. But we have seen no instances of this. Many languages have a demonstrative not marked for deixis, and Lyons might consider this meets the purpose, since he does not recognize a distinction between a deictically neutral demonstrative and a definite article. But I argued in 1.2.2 that they are distinct; French *ce livre* 'that book' and *le livre* 'the book' are not synonymous, and the latter as well as the former can be used situationally. Moreover, deictically neutral demonstratives are phonologically strong, unlike articles. The other phenomenon we might expect to find, a language in which two definite articles occur, one for situational ostension and the other for anaphoric and other derivative use, also does not occur.

But an interesting phenomenon does occur which bears some similarity to what we have just sought and not found. Demonstratives are the archetypal ostensive expression, and demonstratives occur freely in anaphoric as well as situational use, probably in all languages. Suppose we set up an extended notion of ostension (call it "textual–situational ostension") which includes anaphoric reference as well as reference to an entity perceptible in the physical situation. What these have in common is that the referent is immediately accessible. It is either directly perceived in the physical surroundings or straightforwardly recalled from the preceding discourse. All other uses are arguably more complex in that they require some inferencing to interpret; the hearer must calculate, using background knowledge and experience, what the referent is. A distinction of article form corresponding rather closely to this division is found in Fering, a North Frisian dialect studied in detail by Ebert (1971a, 1971b). Fering has two definite articles, the "A-article" and the "D-article", with the following principal forms:

	A-article	D-article
MSG	a	di
FSG	at	det
NSG	at	det
PL	a	dön

The D-article is used anaphorically as in (1), cataphorically, where the referent is identified in a following relative clause as in (2), and where the referent is visible in the physical context as in (3):

(1)   Oki hee an hingst keeft. **Di** hingst haaltet.
        'Oki bought a horse. **The** horse is lame.'

(2)   **Det** buk, wat hi tuiast skrewen hee, dochts niks.
        '**The** book that he wrote first is worthless.'

(3)   **Dön** kaater kleesi.
        '**The/those** cats are scratching.'

The A-article is used with uniques as in (4), generics as in (5), referents unique or identifiable in the wider situation as in (6), referents identified by a pre-nominal adjective as in (7), in associative occurrences as in (8), and (rather than a possessive) with inalienable properties as in (9):

(4)   **a** san
        '**the** sun'

(5)   **A** kaater kleesi.
        'Cats scratch.'

(6)   Ik skal deel tu **a** kuupmaan.
        'I must go (down) to **the** grocer.'

(7)   **A** fering spriik as det spriik, wat a feringen snaaki.
        '**The** Fering language is the language that the Föhrer speak.'

(8)   Jister wul wi deel an Sina bischük, an üüs wi diar uunkem, do as **a** dör feest.
        'Yesterday we wanted to go (down) and visit Sina, and when we got there, **the** door is locked.'

(9)   Hi ded ham **a** hun.
        'He gave him **his** hand.'

There are various contexts where both the D-article and the A-article are possible, sometimes with a difference in interpretation. In some cases it is because the usual conditions (above) for both articles are met, as when a generic noun has a relative modifier as in (10), or when a perceptible referent in the immediate situation is described with a pre-nominal adjective as in (11):

(10)   **Dön/A** foomnen, wat ei mulki kön, fu neen maan.
         'Girls who can't milk don't get a man.'

(11)   Wäl dü mi ans **di/a** brons dask auerda?
         'Will you pass me the purple bowl?'

Other cases are more intriguing:

(12)   Üüb't markels wul's mi an kü an an hingst üübdrei. **Di/A** hingst haa
         ik natüürelk ei keeft.
         'At the market they wanted to palm off a cow and a horse on me.
         The horse I naturally didn't buy.'

(13)   Ik hed **a/di** hiale daai a hunen fol tu dun.
         'I had my hands full all day.'

(14)   **a/di** prääster faan Saleraanj
         '**the** vicar of Süderende'

In (12), *a hingst* would mean the horse was being spoken of in contrast with the cow, while *di hingst* would imply a contrast with other horses. In (13), *di* is only possible when a particular day in the past is meant; *a* is possible on all interpretations, thus when a past day or today is meant. In (14), *di* is only possible where the conversation is not taking place in Süderende and the speaker does not live there; *a* is always possible.

In general, then, the D-article is used where the identity of the referent is to be found by searching the spatio-temporal or textual context. The referent, or a prior reference to it, is there to be picked out, and in some cases distinguished from other entities satisfying the same description (as in (12)). The A-article is used generically, and where, given the hearer's general knowledge or knowledge of the wider situation and of appropriate associations, the description is enough to single out the referent without the need for ostension. It might be suggested, therefore, that with the A-article, given the necessary knowledge and inferencing skills, the descriptive part of the noun phrase plays the major role in referent identification, while with the D-article the article itself has greater significance, signalling the presence of identifying information in the surroundings. This difference is reflected in the greater morphophonological substance of the D-article.

The difference just suggested between the two articles has been exploited recently as support for another putative distinction among article uses. Vergnaud and Zubizarreta (1992) and Longobardi (1994) argue for a distinction between substantive (meaningful) occurrences of the definite article and expletive or pleonastic occurrences in which the article has no semantic content. The substantive article is [+ Def] and functions semantically as an operator, while the expletive is not definite and merely fills a Det position which for various reasons may not be left empty. This expletive article occurs essentially in generic and proper noun phrases, in languages where these take the article – environments in which there is a long tradition of seeing the article as not semantically motivated; see 5.4 below. These two articles, distinct in content, are claimed to be neutralized in many languages, but Longobardi points to Fering as one language which distinguishes them morphologically. But (as he partly acknowledges in a footnote) the distinction between the two articles of Fering does not correspond closely to Longobardi's distinction. In particular, uniques like 'sun', associative uses, and all situational uses other than those involving the immediate situation where the referent is perceptible require the A-article. This article cannot be characterized as expletive in these uses. I will return to the expletive–substantive distinction in Chapter 8 and suggest reasons for rejecting it.

There is another way to interpret the Fering data, using the informal notion of textual–situational ostension suggested above. Recall from 1.2.2, 1.2.5 and 3.1.1 that many languages have a demonstrative unmarked for deixis and that English *that/those* can have this value. In several environments, particularly to refer to a perceptible entity, in anaphora, and before an identifying relative clause, either this deictically neutral demonstrative or the definite article can be used with very little difference in what is conveyed:

(15) [In a room where there is just one stool]
      Pass me **the/that** stool, please.

(16) I bought my first car, an old banger, when I was twenty, and for ten years it never occurred to me to move on to anything better. I had the means to get from A to B and that was all I cared about. I only replaced **the/that** car when my new husband refused to be seen dead in it.

(17) The exam results came out this morning, and **the/those** students who passed are already at the pub celebrating.

This does not mean that *the* and *that/those* are synonymous in these contexts, merely that their closeness of meaning produces an overlap in use (somewhat as on a particular occasion one might freely choose either *the car* or *the vehicle* to pick out the same object, with minimal difference in what the hearer understands). Now it is striking that in the English translations of Ebert's Fering data, *the* is almost always replaceable by *that/those* in rendering the D-article, but not the A-article. So if the Fering D-article represents textual–situational ostension, the extended version of J. Lyons's concept of ostension ("deixis"), it is precisely in this function that definite article and demonstrative overlap.

One possible account of the Fering facts is that the D-article is, in fact, a demonstrative. The D-article form certainly can be demonstrative, like the German and Scandinavian determiners with which it is cognate. Ebert notes that the D-article can be stressed and the A-article cannot. But if the D-article were always demonstrative, we would have to account for why the true definite article, the A-article, is excluded from a wide range of uses normally open to a definite article. It seems, moreover, that the D-article can be unstressed, so we should take it to be a genuine article. I assume, therefore, that Fering divides the field of definiteness along a line corresponding to a real semantic or pragmatic distinction, with textual–situational ostension on one side and all other uses on the other. The subcategory represented by my extended notion of ostension, hyponymous to definiteness, may well itself be superordinate to the lower subcategory of anaphoric, which we have seen is separately encoded in some languages. Textual–situational ostension is, moreover, the area of noun phrase use where simple definiteness and demonstrativeness overlap. I believe the facts of Fering have important implications for the diachrony of definiteness, reflecting some of the stages by which languages acquire or replace definite articles, and I will return to them in Chapter 9.

4.2 Specificity and referentiality

We have seen that indefinite noun phrases like the direct objects in the sentences *I bought a car* and *Pass me a book* differ in that, while neither involves a referent identifiable to the hearer, the first refers to something specific (and familiar to the speaker), but the second does not. An indefinite singular noun phrase may be used to denote a particular entity, or to speak of an arbitrary member of the class described by the noun phrase. This distinction is usually discussed under the heading of **specificity**, indefinite noun phrases being specific or non-specific. In fact, as will appear below, a similar distinction can be made for definites.

There is an ongoing debate in the semantics literature on the question of whether definite or indefinite descriptions can involve reference, so that the characterization of the specific–non-specific distinction just given would not be universally accepted (at least as a semantic account). On one view, non-specific *a book* above describes but does not refer, while specific *a car* is a referring expression (Donnellan 1978, Wilson 1978, Fodor and Sag 1982). A similar but "weaker" position is that definites may (but need not) refer, but that indefinites do not refer. This is precisely because the "referent" of a specific indefinite is not identifiable for the hearer; since understanding the sentence *I bought a car* does not involve picking out the car in question, the identity of this car cannot be part of the meaning of the sentence. On the other hand, if one says *I bought the car*, expecting the hearer to know or to work out which car is meant, so that identifying a referent is part of understanding the sentence, then the definite *the car* is referential. But, as will appear below, definites are not always referential, and may be ambiguous between a referential and a non-referential interpretation. An obvious assumption is that this is an ambiguity in the article.

The opposing view (which is probably the more widely held) is that neither definites nor indefinites are ever semantically referring (Kripke 1977, Neale 1990, Ludlow and Neale 1991). On this view, reference is limited to "singular terms", a class which includes proper nouns, demonstratives and personal pronouns, expressions whose meaning consists essentially of picking out an individual entity. Simple definites and indefinites describe, and denote whatever meets the description (definite) or something which meets the description (indefinite). They are analysed as quantificational rather than directly referring, following the account of Russell (1905) (to be discussed in Chapter 7). But it is recognized that definites (and, for at least some writers, indefinites) have referential **uses**, so that reference is treated as a matter of pragmatics rather than semantics. Thus while the proposition representing the literal meaning of a sentence containing a definite or indefinite description will involve quantification, this sentence may be used to convey a proposition involving direct reference.

For a clear and accessible discussion of the issues involved in this controversy see Larson and Segal (1995: chapter 9). I shall continue here to speak informally of both simple definites and indefinites as potentially referring, but without commitment as to whether the reference is semantic or pragmatic. In characterizing indefinites like *a car* above as referring, I mean no more than that there is a particular object which the speaker is thinking of as motivating the choice of description.

4.2.1 *Opacity and scope ambiguities*

Certain grammatical contexts have the effect of creating an ambiguity corresponding to the distinction drawn above. These contexts include those involving verbs of "propositional attitude" (such as *want, believe, hope, intend*), negation, questions, conditionals, modals, future tense. These elements, which have in common that they present a proposition as counterfactual, potential or hypothetical, rather than factual, set up "opaque contexts" – so called because in these contexts, on the non-specific interpretation, it is not possible to substitute for the noun phrase in question a coreferential expression. For example, in (18a) below, if the merchant banker Peter plans to marry lives next door to him, *his next-door neighbour* or *one of his neighbours* could be substituted for *a merchant banker* without affecting the truth value of the sentence; but such substitution could not be made in (18b), since the descriptive content of the noun phrase is crucial to the truth value of the sentence – only a synonymous expression, such as *someone who works in a merchant bank*, could be substituted here. We can also include here as opacity-creating expressions "intensional" verbs like *look for*, which produce the same kind of ambiguity. In the examples that follow, I give under each heading both an indefinite and a definite noun phrase affected by such ambiguity, to show that the phenomenon applies equally to both. In each example the first clause shows the relevant ambiguity, which is then cleared up by the continuation. Note that the continuation does not in all cases impose the appropriate specific or non-specific reading; but it does make this more probable, and in this way makes clear what the two readings are.

Verbs of propositional attitude
(18) a.   Peter intends to marry **a merchant banker** – even though he doesn't get on at all with her.
     b.   Peter intends to marry **a merchant banker** – though he hasn't met one yet.

(19) a.   Joan wants to present the prize to **the winner** – but he doesn't want to receive it from her.
     b.   Joan wants to present the prize to **the winner** – so she'll have to wait around till the race finishes.

Negation
(20) a.   He didn't see **a car** parked at the door – until the two men got out of it and asked him for directions.
     b.   He didn't see **a car** parked at the door – so he knew the visitors hadn't arrived yet.

(21) a.   I didn't meet **the professor** during my visit to the philosophy department yesterday morning – but I managed to get hold of him in the afternoon.
     b.   I didn't meet **the professor** during my visit to the philosophy department yesterday morning – so I began to wonder whether that chair had been filled yet.

Questions
(22) a.   Have you found **a watch**? – I'm sure I left it lying here.
     b.   Have you found **a watch**? – or can't you decide what kind you want to buy?

(23) a.   Did Fred meet **the woman of his dreams** during his trip to Poland last year? – or am I mistaken in thinking that accent is Polish?
     b.   Did Fred meet **the woman of his dreams** during his trip to Poland last year? – or is he still looking?

Semantic and pragmatic distinctions

Conditionals

(24) a.   If you've come across **a copy of the Decameron**, it's mine; I left it here.

     b.   If you've come across **a copy of the Decameron**, buy it for me; I need one.

(25) a.   If you've met **the owner of this cat**, you must know what an unpleasant person she is.

     b.   If you've met **the owner of this cat**, you'd better tell Joe, because he's convinced it doesn't belong to anyone.

Modals

(26) a.   You should go to **a film** at the Odeon tonight – it's superb.

     b.   You should go to **a film** at the Odeon tonight – don't just sit at home.

(27) a.   We may visit **John's cottage** soon – if he invites us to see it.

     b.   We may visit **John's cottage** soon – if he gets round to buying one.

Future

(28) a.   I'm going to buy **a suit** tomorrow – you'll be horrified by the colour.

     b.   I'm going to buy **a suit** tomorrow – even if I can't find one I really like.

(29) a.   I'm going to have lunch with **the president** tomorrow – I'm dreading it, he's such a boring man.

     b.   I'm going to have lunch with **the president** tomorrow – that is, if the election takes place today and we have a president.

Intensional verbs

(30) a.   Liz is looking for **a business partner** – the poor fellow disappeared last month and she suspects he's been kidnapped.

     b.   Liz is looking for **a business partner** – but it will have to be someone with plenty of experience in catering.

(31) a.   I'm still searching for **the solution to this puzzle** – and I think I'm close to finding it.

     b.   I'm still searching for **the solution to this puzzle** – though John insists it's insoluble and I think he's probably right.

In each case the noun phrase in question is understood as denoting either a particular entity, or whatever satisfies the description; that is, on one reading it is "referring" (in some sense, as discussed) and on the other it is not. There is great variety in the terminology used in the linguistic and philosophical literature for this distinction. The readings indicated in the (a) examples of (18)–(31) are termed **extensional**, *de re*, **specific** or **referential**, in contrast with the **intensional**, *de dicto*, **non-specific** or **non-referential** readings given in the (b) examples (though the four terms are in each case not, strictly, equivalent). The terms "specific" and "non-specific" tend to be used principally in relation to indefinites, but, as shown, the distinction applies equally to definites and indefinites.

The standard account of the availability of two readings of noun phrases in opaque contexts is in terms of "scope ambiguity". The element which creates the opacity is a logical operator; logicians have posited many different operators, including negation, interrogation, the modal operators of modal logic, a *belief* operator. And the definite or indefinite noun phrase has an existential entailment as part of its meaning, expressed as the existential quantification of predicate logic (for an elementary account of which see Allwood, Andersson and Dahl 1977). The ambiguity is then a matter of whether the existential quantifier is in the scope of the operator, or vice versa. The element which has scope over the other is said to have "wide scope" and the element within its scope has "narrow scope". If the existential quantifier has wide scope, this corresponds to the specific reading; if it has narrow scope the non-specific reading applies. This can be illustrated in relation to the following sentences, for which the simplified logical formulas given show the essential points of difference:

(32) a. John met a stranger.
     b. $\exists x \ (\text{stranger}(x) \ \& \ \text{met}(\text{John}, x))$

(33) a. John didn't meet a stranger.
     b. $\sim \exists x \ (\text{stranger}(x) \ \& \ \text{met}(\text{John}, x))$
     c. $\exists x \ (\text{stranger}(x) \ \& \ \sim \text{met}(\text{John}, x))$

In these formulas $\exists$ is the existential quantifier, $\sim$ is the negation operator, and x is a variable, so that (32b) may be read as: 'There is some x such that x is a stranger and John met x'. In (33) it is through its interaction with the quantifier that negation creates an opaque context, and this interaction, amounting to relative scope, is expressed in terms of relative order. In (33b), corresponding to the non-specific reading ('It is not the case that there is some x such that x is a stranger and John met x' – thus roughly 'John didn't meet any stranger'), the existential quantifier has narrow scope relative to the negation operator. In (33c), the quantifier has wide scope, representing the specific reading on which for a particular person with whom John is not familiar, John did not meet that person ('There is some x such that x is a stranger and it is not the case that John met x'). On the narrow-scope, non-specific, reading, the existential quantifier is subordinate to the operator, and there need not exist any individual corresponding to the quantified expression. Thus, on this reading, a continuation is possible in which the existence of such an individual is explicitly denied:

(34)   John didn't meet a stranger; he couldn't have, he knows everybody.

In this context the noun phrase *a stranger* in the first clause can only be meant non-specifically. On the specific reading (33c) and with the non-negated (32), on the other hand, the existence of a particular stranger is entailed.[3]

This existence entailment is often treated as a property of the article, but it, and the scope facts discussed, are in fact a property of all types of potentially referring expression, whether they contain *a*, *the*, or neither, as shown by the following examples:

(35) a.   Tom plans to bring up **three children** on his own – they're horrible brats and I wish him luck.

     b.   Tom plans to bring up **three children** on his own – but first he needs to find a woman to bear them for him.

(36) a.   The Department has decided to expand its student intake by ten this year. I don't know how we'll find classroom space for **these extra students** – but they're so well qualified we couldn't refuse to accept them.

     b.   The Department has decided to expand its student intake by ten this year. I don't know how we'll find classroom space for **these extra, students** – but the question may not arise if applications are substantially down.

(37) a.   Debbie's still waiting for **Mr Right** – he's called Mark, and she's just as crazy about him as when they first met last year; she must be to put up with his unpunctuality.

     b.   Debbie's still waiting for **Mr Right** – I wonder when she'll finally see there's no such thing and settle for Bob.

4.2.2 *Transparent contexts*

Distinctions similar to those just discussed can obtain in transparent (non-opaque) contexts, where there is no question of scope ambiguity. Let us begin by considering indefinites:

(38) a.   I haven't started the class yet; I'm missing **a student** – Mary's always late.

     b.   I haven't started the class yet; I'm missing **a student** – there should be fifteen, and I only count fourteen.

---

[3] Scope ambiguities occur with quantifiers as well as with the kinds of operators discussed above. Consider the following:

(i)   **All** the students had read **a novel by Flaubert**.

(ii)   **A train** passes here **every** half hour.

The students may have, but need not have, read the same Flaubert novel, and it may be the same train that passes each time, but is probably not. But on both readings the existence of a Flaubert novel or train is entailed. This reflects the difference between the universal quantification in these examples and the intensional operators in (18)–(31).

(39) a.   **A dog** was in here last night – it's called Lulu and Fred always lets it sit by the fire on wet nights.

     b.   **A dog** was in here last night – there's no other explanation for all these hairs and scratch marks.

On the (a) reading of (38) and (39), the speaker has a particular individual in mind. On the (b) reading this is not the case; the identity of the student or dog is beside the point. The terms "specific" and "non-specific" are also used for this distinction, though it seems to be distinct from the one illustrated in (18)–(31) in that there is no opacity-creating operator involved. The most common account of the facts exemplified in (38)–(39) is that the distinction is pragmatic rather than semantic. That is, there is no ambiguity in the sense of each such sentence having two semantic representations (differing either lexically or in structure). Rather, the expression is vague between readings on which the speaker either has or does not have a particular referent for the indefinite noun phrase in mind.

A similar distinction is also found with definites. Here there is a tendency in the literature to use different terminology – "referential" versus "attributive" rather than "specific" versus "non-specific" – but the distinction may well be the same and require the same explanation. The major discussion is Donnellan (1966), whose much repeated example is (40):

(40)   Smith's murderer is insane.

(Notice the definite possessive structure; the more overtly definite *the murderer of Smith* would serve equally well.) On one reading of (40), the referential one, *Smith's murderer* refers to a particular individual, who might just as well have been described in other ways (*Joe Bloggs, Annie's boyfriend, the fellow in the pinstripe suit*); the description only serves to pick out the individual. On the attributive reading, on the other hand, the description used is crucial to what is stated or conveyed; (40) is a statement not about a particular individual believed to have murdered Smith, but about whoever murdered Smith – the murdering of Smith or something associated with that deed being the grounds for the attribution of insanity. If it should turn out that Smith was not murdered, then on the attributive reading there is no person to whom the utterer of (40) can be said to have attributed insanity. But on the referential reading, insanity was still attributed to someone (the person the speaker thought had murdered Smith).

Notice that, by contrast with the scope ambiguity cases, the existential entailment does not seem to be suppressed in these cases. The existence of a person or thing to whom the description applies is assumed by the speaker and cannot be denied in the continuation:

(41)   ??I haven't started the class yet; I'm still waiting for a student – there's no one missing though.

(42)   ??Smith's murderer is insane – even though no one has murdered Smith.

The following example can be compared with (38) to show further the parallelism with indefinites:

(43) a.   We can't start the seminar, because **the student who's giving the presentation** is absent – typical of Bill, he's so unreliable.

b.   We can't start the seminar, because **the student who's giving the presentation** is absent – I'd go and find whoever it is, but no-one can remember, and half the class is absent.

The correspondence between the different readings of definites and those of indefinites in transparent contexts may, however, be more complex, because in each case there may be more than two readings to distinguish. Ludlow and Neale (1991) and Larson and Segal (1995), following ideas developed in Kripke (1977) and elsewhere, distinguish a "referential" use from a "specific" use, for both definites and indefinites. In the former the speaker intends to communicate something about a particular individual and intends the hearer to realize which individual is intended. In the latter the speaker has a particular individual in mind corresponding to the description but does not expect the hearer to pick out any individual; that is, there is no intention to communicate something about the individual which provides the grounds for the assertion. These uses are both distinct from the attributive or nonspecific use, which is purely quantificational, involving no individual "referent" at any level. These writers thus distinguish, in addition to the literal meaning (always quantificational according to Kripke), the proposition the speaker wishes to communicate, and the grounds the speaker has for the assertion. On this taxonomy of uses, it may be that both referentiality and specificity are common with definites, but that the former is somewhat marginal with indefinites.

I will not pursue these questions further. For more detailed discussion of the issues involved in specificity, see, in addition to the references given above, Enç (1991), Rouchota (1994), and Jaszczolt (1997).

4.2.3   A unified account of specificity?

It appears from the above discussion that there is no reason to posit an ambiguity relating to specificity in the articles themselves, or to suppose that specificity is hyponymous to either definiteness or indefiniteness (as anaphoricity may be); the ambiguities discussed in 4.2.1 and 4.2.2 apply to all types of potentially referring expression, and involve semantic or pragmatic distinctions which cut across the definite–indefinite one. To distinguish the two kinds of ambiguity discussed I shall henceforth use the labels **wide-scope** and **narrow-scope** for the pairs of readings arising in opaque contexts, and **referential** and **non-referential** for those appearing in transparent contexts. Bear in mind that this is a deliberate simplification for expository purposes, glossing over, among other things, the likelihood that there are more than two readings to be distinguished in a given case. The purpose is merely to distinguish the phenomena we have observed in opaque contexts and those seen in transparent contexts. In the two types of context the difference in interpretation seems similar, and I shall use **specific** and **nonspecific** as informal cover terms to embrace both distinctions; thus narrow-scope readings and non-referential readings are both types of non-specificity.

There have been attempts to reduce both kinds of ambiguity to a single specific versus non-specific distinction, though they are generally held to be distinct. One might try to unify them by taking the pragmatic concept of the speaker having a particular referent in mind to apply to all cases.[4] On this view the vagueness between specific and non-specific is in principle always present. It is simply that certain contexts, where the description is in the scope of some intensional element, favour a non-specific reading more than transparent contexts do. There are, in addition, contexts in which a specific or a non-specific reading is virtually obligatory, but a pragmatic explanation can be advanced for these cases. Thus, in *I bought a car yesterday*, a non-specific reading is unavailable because the speaker must have a referent in mind where she is reporting having had some interaction with it.[5] And in *Pass me a book*, a specific reading is practically impossible because if the speaker did have a particular book in mind she would want to ensure that the hearer picked out the same book; this would require a definite description (probably with an identifying relative or adjectival expression, or a demonstrative). But in fact the two parameters of scope and referentiality can vary to some extent independently. Ioup (1977) shows that wide-scope noun phrases can be referential or non-referential, and non-referential noun phrases can have wide or narrow scope; narrow-scope noun phrases, on the other hand, must be non-referential (thus non-specific in both

---

[4] In an example like the following, it seems to be a matter, not so much of the speaker, but rather of the subject (Peter) having a particular individual in mind:

Peter intends to marry a merchant banker. I wonder what she's like.

But it is arguable that, even here, the speaker does have someone specific in mind. She does not know this individual and could not identify her, but she has in mind the person that Peter intends to marry. There is in her mind a referent corresponding to the description.

[5] In fact matters are less straightforward than this. In many languages which have overt encoding of the specific–non-specific distinction, the non-specific form can occur in this context, indicating that the identity of the car bought is of no importance to the point being made. Examples will be given below. A similar observation can be made in relation to English indefinite *this* (to be discussed below), which signals specificity. *I bought this car* (with *this* understood as indefinite rather than demonstrative) invites a more specific reading than *I bought a car* needs to receive.

senses), and referential noun phrases must have wide scope (thus specific in both senses). Thus:

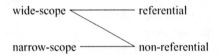

It is clear from the survey in Chapter 2 that there are many languages which, in contrast with the English data examined so far in this chapter, do have lexical or morphological encodings for specificity. Examination of these may help in identifying linguistic distinctions which English does not, or need not, make overtly. In fact a number of languages treat the two types of specificity differently, typically by encoding one but not the other. Dahl (1970) and Ioup (1977) refer to indefinite pronouns in Russian, consisting of an interrogative with a suffix *-to* or *-nibud'*. The distinction between these two forms corresponds to the concept of specificity defined in terms of scope; *-nibud'* is used only in opaque contexts and indicates that the pronoun is to be interpreted as within the scope of the opacity-creating expression, while *-to* is used both in opaque contexts when the pronoun has wide scope and in transparent contexts regardless of considerations of referentiality. Thus:

(44) a.   Ona khochet vyjti zamuzh   za kogo-to.
          she wants go in-marriage to someone
          'She wants to marry someone (a particular person).'
     b.   Ona khochet vyjti zamuzh za kogo-nibud'.
          'She wants to marry someone (anyone).'

And the subject pronoun *kto-to* in (45), which cannot be interpreted as narrow-scope, is ambiguous between referential and non-referential readings:

(45)   Kto-to ne   pojet.
           someone NEG sings
           'Someone isn't singing.'

Ioup takes this to point to the distinctness of scope ambiguities and referentiality, the former being semantic and the latter pragmatic.[6] Similar facts appear in Lakhota (Williamson 1987) and Jacaltec (Craig 1986). Lakhota distinguishes two quasi-indefinite determiners: a "realis" one *wą* 'a' with plural *k'eya* 'sm', and an "irrealis" one *wążi* with plural *'etą*; see 2.5.2 above. The latter only occurs when

---

[6] Kempson and Cormack (1981), however, argue that sentences with more than one quantifier are not ambiguous, but have a single semantic representation. This corresponds to the narrow-scope reading, because this interpretation is entailed by the wide-scope reading and is therefore common to both readings. The availability of two interpretations is seen as a matter of vagueness rather than ambiguity, the wide-scope ("stronger") interpretation being a special case of the narrow-scope ("weaker") interpretation. See also van Deemter and Peters (1996).

the noun phrase is in the scope of certain "irrealis markers" like intensional verbs, imperatives, and the irrealis mood marker *kte* – in other words, opacity-creating elements. There is also a special form *wąžini*, plural *'etąni*, occurring in the scope of the negative marker *šni*, and clearly consisting of the irrealis form plus an additional negative morpheme. Some irrealis, that is, narrow-scope, uses are illustrated in (46):

(46) a.　T'aspą wąži　wac'į.
　　　 apple　a-IRR want-1SG
　　　 'I want an apple.'
　 b.　C'ą　'etą　aku　　we.
　　　 sticks sm-IRR bring-back IMP
　　　 'Bring back sm sticks.'
　 c.　Wowapi wąži lawa　　kte　iyececa.
　　　 [book　a-IRR read-2SG IRR] be-proper
　　　 'You should read a book.'

In each case the speaker is not thinking of a particular apple etc., and there may even not be one. Replacing *wąži* and *'etą* by *wą* and *k'eya* would give the wide-scope sense. The situation is similar in Jacaltec. The quasi-indefinite article is *hune?*, which is replaced by *hun-uj*, in which *-uj* is the irrealis suffix, in opaque contexts for the narrow-scope reading:

(47) a.　X?oc' heb' ix　　say-a?　hune? munlab'al.
　　　 started PL　CLASS look-for a　　pot
　　　 'They started looking for a (specific) pot.'
　 b.　X?oc' heb' ix　　say-a?　hun-uj munlab'al.
　　　 started PL　CLASS look-for a IRR pot
　　　 'They started looking for a (non-specific) pot.'

Notice that in the three languages just discussed it is the distinction relating to scope which is indicated morphologically, and I have found no example of a language which encodes the distinction between referential and non-referential and not that between wide and narrow scope (though there are many that encode both identically). A possible exception to this generalization is pronominal forms occurring in many languages corresponding to English *one* and French *on*, which are probably non-referential and in some cases (English being such a case) restricted to a generic subset of non-referential uses; I shall return to such forms in 4.3.2 below. It is also the case in the three languages discussed above that narrow scope rather than wide scope is the morphologically marked term of this opposition; it is the narrow-scope interpretation which is encoded by the addition of an affix or by replacing a basic morpheme (like Russian *-to*) which occurs with wide-scope referential and non-referential readings. This is not universal, however, and English is one language which has a form encoding specific rather than non-specific. We have seen that in English *the* and *a* occur without modification in specific and non-specific noun phrases, but there is the optional possibility of indicating the specific reading of indefinites by means of the colloquial use of *this* in examples like the following:

(48) a.   I was walking to work yesterday morning, when **this** man came up to me and asked if I was a news announcer.

     b.   **This** woman round the corner breeds pedigree pigs.

It is clear from its behaviour in diagnostic environments that this use of *this* is indefinite:

(49) a.   Strong as **this** chap was, he couldn't lift it.

     b.   **This** house is mine.

     c.   Which of **these** women are you talking about?

     d.   Some/All of **these** people know more than I do about phonetics.   .

     e.   There's **this** strange message on the noticeboard.

All these sentences are acceptable, but the first four must be understood as anaphoric or situational demonstrative uses of *this/these* – the referent has been spoken of or is being pointed out. (49e) shows a context largely limited to indefinites, and is most naturally understood as an instance of colloquial *this*. It is also clear from (48) that *this* can be used in first mentions, which is typical of *a*.

    Colloquial *this* is a purely optional alternative to *a* and is of course stylistically limited. It is typically used when the referent is going to be talked about further, and is for this reason particularly suitable for starting stories, anecdotes, jokes etc. In this it is comparable to a number of elements appearing in other languages to be discussed in Chapter 5, elements like object markers and classifiers, which express a kind of referential prominence. It is, moreover, specific in both senses; the indefinite must be wide-scope and referential for *this* to be acceptable:

(50) a.   He didn't see **this car** parked at the door – until the two men got out of it and asked him for directions.

     b.   ??He didn't see **this car** parked at the door – so he knew the visitors hadn't arrived yet.

(51) a.   Peter intends to marry **this merchant banker** – even though he doesn't get on at all with her.

     b.   ??Peter intends to marry **this merchant banker** – though he hasn't met one yet.

(52) a.   You should go and see **this film** at the Odeon tonight – it's superb.

     b.   ??You should go and see **this film** at the Odeon tonight — don't just sit at home.

(53) a.   Liz is looking for **this business partner** – the poor fellow disappeared last month and she suspects he's been kidnapped.

b.   ??Liz is looking for **this business partner** – but it will have to be someone with plenty of experience in catering.

(54) a.   I haven't started the class yet; I'm still missing **this student** – Mary's always late.

b.   ??I haven't started the class yet; I'm still missing **this student** – there should be fifteen and I only count fourteen.

(55) a.   **This dog** was in here last night – it's called Lulu and Fred always lets it sit by the fire on wet nights.

b.   ??**This dog** was in here last night – there's no other explanation for all these hairs and scratch marks.

Colloquial *this* is interesting syntactically because, its indefiniteness notwithstanding, it is quite clearly in a paradigmatic class with definite determiners, which are in Det position; it is not a quasi-indefinite article expressing cardinality. This is evident from its co-occurrence with and position in relation to numerals in examples like:

(56)   I was just minding my own business when **these two men** came up to me.

It is not obvious what to make of this. Is it a real indefinite article, falsifying my hypothesis that no language has such an expression? Or is it after all a demonstrative, or a definite determiner at least, with odd semantics? Its unusual morphology (with the irregular number alternation *this–these*) suggests strongly that it is not a distinct lexical item from demonstrative *this*. The German demonstrative *dieser* 'this' also has the same colloquial specific indefinite use as English *this*. This could be due to borrowing, and the phenomenon is not common cross-linguistically, though Blass (1990) notes that the Sissala specificity marker *né* may be a form of the general demonstrative *né* 'this', 'that'. On English indefinite *this* see also Prince (1981).

It will have been noticed that all the languages discussed which show some morphological or lexical expression corresponding to specificity do so only for indefinites, and indeed no language appears to mark either scope or referentiality distinctions for definites, despite the fact that these distinctions apply very clearly to definites just as much as to indefinites. In fact a number of languages of the Austronesian family have an article which combines definiteness with specific indefiniteness (both wide-scope and referential). This determiner is usually described as a definite article, but it is also used for reference to something known or familiar to the speaker but not necessarily either previously mentioned or familiar to the hearer. See the discussion of Samoan and Maori in 2.2.4. In Sissala (Blass 1990), distinctions of specificity are doubly encoded, by the morphology or tonology of the noun and by an accompanying marker (possibly a determiner), non-specific *ré* or specific *né*. Thus *bál ré* 'a man (non-specific)', *báálɔ né* 'a man (specific)'.

But definites, marked by the article *ná*, always involve the specific form of the noun: *báálɔ ná* 'the man'. It is not clear which form of the noun is unmarked: if the non-specific form, then Sissala treats definites as specific; if the specific form, then specific and non-specific are only distinguished in indefinites, definites being neutral in this respect.

To summarize, the two types of specificity seem to be distinct, though there are a number of interesting mismatches between the distinctions made morphologically or lexically by languages and the semantic–pragmatic distinctions identified in 4.2.1 and 4.2.2. Scope ambiguities may be semantic (whether involving true ambiguity or merely vagueness) and referentiality pragmatic, but languages can lexicalize or grammaticalize both. There are languages which display morphological or lexical encoding of the scope distinction but not the referentiality distinction, but, equally, there are languages which show the same encoding for both. This suggests that the two phenomena, though different, are closely related (as they seem intuitively to be) and that languages can treat specificity as a unified phenomenon. The fact that specificity and non-specificity (of either kind) are overtly distinguished only in indefinites is striking, because it contrasts strongly with the semantic–pragmatic findings. It suggests that linguistically, contrary to what I stated at the beginning of this section, specificity as a lexical or morphological category may be hyponymous to indefiniteness. It also makes it very unlikely that there is a quantificational–referential ambiguity in the English definite article; if there were, we would expect to find languages in which this ambiguity did not hold, with a distinct article form for each interpretation.

There is another respect in which linguistic expressions of specific or non-specific can go beyond the distinctions of interpretation discussed in 4.2.1 and 4.2.2. I noted above that English specific indefinite *this* is optional and tends to be used where the referent is to be a significant topic in the ensuing discourse. It was also observed, in 2.5.2, that the Turkish cardinal article *bir*, essentially limited to specific indefinites, tends to be omitted when the identity of the referent does not matter. What this amounts to is that referentiality and non-referentiality are extended to embrace instances where the speaker may be in a position to identify the referent of the noun phrase but chooses to treat its identity as significant or not. We have seen other examples of this: in Samoan, where the non-specific article *se* is used where the identity of a referent may be known but is considered unimportant; and in Hausa, where the specific indefinite *wani* tends to be used, like English *this*, when the referent is likely to recur in the subsequent discourse. Nama, too, has a particle (from a verb root meaning 'exist') which can be used to signal that a referent is to play an important part in the discourse, and the Sissala specificity marker *né* has the same function. The phenomenon is common, and is discussed in more detail and with further exemplification by Givón (1982).

4.3 Generics

Generic noun phrases are those in which reference is made to an entire class, or, perhaps more accurately, which are used to express generalizations about a class as a whole – the class in question being that consisting of all the entities satisfying the description inherent in the noun or nominal. Of course a straightforward way to refer to the whole class is by means of a determiner such as *all*, *every*, *each*, *any*, which approximate to universal quantification. In fact the term "generic" is not used of these because of semantic differences; as pointed out by Lawler (1973), Smith (1975), a single exception would usually invalidate a statement with *all* etc., whereas generics admit exceptions, since they express general tendencies. It has often been pointed out that no language has noun phrases distinctively generic in form – whether with a special generic determiner, a morphological mark on the noun, etc. Perhaps not too much should be made of this point, given that lexical devices (such as the adverbs *typically*, *generally*) are available, as are determiners like *all* which come close to generic meaning – especially since not all generic expressions are generic in the same way, and some admit exceptions more readily than others, as we shall see. But the point is that genericity is typically expressed by noun phrase types which also have a non-generic use, which is arguably more basic. This leads to the suggestion that genericity is not a primitive category of semantic or syntactic description; generic noun phrases are all basically something else and are to be characterized in other terms (such as nonspecific).

We have observed that in some languages generic noun phrases are typically indefinite (if it is correct to treat "bare", indeterminate, nominals as indefinite), in others definite. But many languages show a range of available noun phrase types with generic value, definite and indefinite, singular and non-singular, as is shown by the following three, more or less synonymous, English sentences:

(57) a.   A dog has four legs.
    b.   The dog has four legs.
    c.   Dogs have four legs.

In such cases where a language has several noun phrase types capable of generic interpretation, it is not clear that they form a unified class of expressions; rather, they may get their generic value in different ways from different basic values. This is particularly probable in view of the fact that the alternatives are not all fully synonymous or interchangeable.

Some of the semantic differences most discussed relate to the nature of the reference to a class: in particular, whether it is to the class as an entity, a second-order individual; or to the class as the aggregate of its members, the generalization being about the members of the class. Which of these interpretations is appropriate is usually determined by the predicate. Expressions like *die out, disperse, be numerous, abound* are class predicates; they require a class (or group) expression as subject, and apply to the class as a whole, as a unit. Similarly, verbs like *decimate* require such an expression as object. On the other hand, predicates denoting an action or state applicable to individuals may involve a generic subject or object being treated as a collection of individuals. Compare:

(58) a.   Ostriches are rare these days.
     b.   Ostriches lay eggs.

Rarity is a property of the class as a whole, while egg-laying is something individual ostriches do. In fact it is not quite so simple, because though individuals cannot be rare (in the relevant sense), it is not so clear that only individuals, and not a set, can be seen as laying eggs. We return to this below. But the point is that these two ways of looking at a class are not equally available to all generic expressions. Another important semantic difference between generic types is the extent to which they admit exceptions, that is, the extent to which they approximate to universal quantification; some are closer in interpretation to *all N* than are others. Indeed this distinction may relate to the first one, references to a set as a second-order individual being more liberal as regards members not conforming.

Genericity in noun phrases interacts with aspectual distinctions in verbs, in that generics are generally – though not in all cases – accompanied by verb forms expressing habitual/generic/timeless aspect. This has led linguists to talk of generic sentences rather than generic noun phrases. But a distinction between generic noun phrases and generic sentences has to be made, since non-generic noun phrases can occur perfectly well in generic or habitual contexts:

(59) a.   My best friend shaves twice a day.
     b.   This kitten frightens easily.

Also, not all generics require such a context; at least those generics which treat the class as a unit can occur with punctual aspect:

(60) a.   The dodo died out in the eighteenth century.
     b.   Dodos died out in the eighteenth century.

Also, at least some generics can occur with progressive aspect (*Ostriches are/The ostrich is laying smaller eggs these days*), though it is arguable that this is a special habitual use of the progressive.

It is important to note that genericity applies equally to mass nouns and to count nouns. And mass nouns do not, strictly, correspond to sets or classes. Just as we can make a statement about ostriches in general, that is, about the class of entities satisfying the description *ostrich*, so we can about the substance matching the description *butter*, or the quality matching the description *sincerity* – as opposed to specific quantities or instantiations. One might, somewhat loosely, stretch the terms "class" and "set" to embrace such memberless "masses" as well as collections of individuals. What is really needed is a concept embracing both sets and the wholes with no atomic minimal parts corresponding to mass nouns; the term "ensemble" is introduced by Bunt (1979, 1985) for this idea, and the term "kind" is used by several writers in a similar way, as we will see below. I shall adopt the former term (as well as continuing to use "set" or "class" in relation to count nouns). On the analysis of mass nouns see also Pelletier and Schubert (1989).

The literature on generics is vast. Some important references are: Smith (1975), Nunberg and Pan (1975), Carlson (1977, 1980), Heyer (1987), Burton-Roberts (1989a), Declerck (1986b, 1991), Schubert and Pelletier (1989), and the papers in Carlson and Pelletier (1995), especially the introductory contribution of Krifka et al.[7] For a promising recent pragmatic account of the interpretation of generics, see Papafragou (1996).

4.3.1   Generics in English

Let us briefly survey English generics, since English displays a wide range of generic noun phrase types, and they are the most intensively studied. Consider the following paradigms defined on the parameters of definiteness and number:

(61) a.   **A dog** has four legs.
    b.   **The dog** has four legs.
    c.   **Dogs** have four legs.
    d.   (**The dogs** have four legs.)

(62) a.   I admire **an intellectual** when he speaks out.
    b.   I admire **the intellectual** when she speaks out.
    c.   I admire **intellectuals** when they speak out.
    d.   (I admire **the intellectuals** when they speak out.)

The definite plural is in general not available for generic use, though it can be used generically with some types of noun, such as nouns of nationality, and some nouns denoting classes of classes (for example, names of animals and plants representing groups larger than the species):

---

[7] Krifka et al. (1995) gives a very useful survey of recent thinking on genericity as well as a detailed theory of the semantics of many of the phenomena involved. The reader should approach this work with some caution, however, on the level of description and data; for example, the predicate *be numerous* is said to require a plural subject (wrongly ruling out *The family is numerous*), and *cattle* is presented as a mass noun.

(63) a.   **The Swiss** consume a lot of chocolate.
     b.   John has a soft spot for **the Finns**.

(64) a.   **The dinosaurs** dominated the earth for a very long time.
     b.   **The cats** – at least the big ones like tigers and pumas – are particularly fierce predators.

For further discussion of these see Lyons (1992a).

The distinction between generics which predicate something of each member of the class and generics which predicate something of the class as an entity is presented in Smith (1975), with the following examples:

(65) a.   **The squid** lives on seaweed.
     b.   **Squids** live on seaweed.
     c.   **A squid** lives on seaweed.

(66) a.   **The dodo** is extinct.
     b.   **Dodos** are extinct.
     c.   *__A dodo__ is extinct.

(67) a.   The lion hunts **the antelope**.
     b.   The lion hunts **antelopes**.
     c.   *The lion hunts **an antelope**.
     d.   A lion preys on **an antelope**.

(68) a.   Pollutants are decimating **the squid**.
     b.   *Pollutants are decimating **squids**.
     c.   *Pollutants are decimating **a squid**.

The picture is that all three generic types can be used for generalizing over the members of the class. But *a N* is ruled out for referring to the class as a unit, while both *the N* and *Ns* are generally possible here.[8]

This picture is criticized by Burton-Roberts (1989a), who claims there is no justification for positing a type of predicate which holds only of individuals and therefore only of members of a class; for him this kind of generic reference does not exist. Thus *the squid* is not ambiguous between "class generic" and "individual generic". It is a class generic only, and *lives on seaweed* is as much predicated of the class as is *is extinct*. This view is supported by the claim of Kempson and Cormack (1981) that sets can have actions predicated of them which are actually not performed by the set as a whole or are performed by only some of the members.

---

[8] Example (68b) points to the impossibility of indefinite plural generics as object of a class predicate, an unexplained restriction. But perhaps Smith's intuition of unacceptability here is simply wrong – I find (68b) less good than (68a), but not impossible. The impossibility of the indefinite singular generic object in (67c), by contrast with (67d), is explained by Smith in terms of a constraint on combinations of indefinite and definite singular generics in the same sentence. Smith examines in detail many other mysterious restrictions on generics.

For example, *Three examiners marked six scripts* describes several possible scenarios as regards just who did what, but Kempson and Cormack claim there is no ambiguity, the correct semantic representation being one that simply predicates the marking of six scripts to the set of three examiners. Similarly, *Six students took five papers* is true if six students took part in a raid in which only one of them actually carried the papers away; it is true because *took five papers* is predicated of the whole set of students involved. As Burton-Roberts observes, if a generic noun phrase can be ambiguous between interpretations as class qua class and class as aggregate of members, it should not be possible for both interpretations to be present simultaneously as a result of occurrence with both types of predicate in coordination, but it is:

(69)   **The dodo** lived on figs and is now extinct.

So classes can "inherit" properties, actions etc. from their members, and this is true not only of predicates like *live on figs*, which we might be able to conceive of the species as well as its members doing, but also of those which can only be understood as holding of individuals:

(70) a.   **The dodo** had two legs and is now extinct.
     b.   **Blackbirds** often re-use the same nest several times and are increasing in numbers.

Burton-Roberts introduces another distinction to explain the impossibility of **a squid is extinct*. This is ruled out, he claims, because *is extinct* is an accidental property rather than an inherent characteristic. The indefinite singular generic is alone in being a **property-generic**: it denotes not a class, nor a representative or arbitrary member of a class, but the essential property defining that class – thus not the **extension** of the noun (the set of entities satisfying the description), but the **intension** (the sense, the description itself). Generic *a dodo*, for example, denotes "dodohood". And an accidental characteristic like being extinct or numerous cannot be predicated of the intension of a noun. We shall return to this.

I have suggested that Smith's asterisk in (68b) is too strong, though this sentence is certainly less felicitous than (68a). I believe the same can be said (if not to the same degree) of generic subjects with class predicates. *The dodo is extinct* is considerably better than *Dodos are extinct*, though both are possible. On the other hand, *The squid lives on seaweed* and *Squids live on seaweed* are equally good. This suggests there may still be something in the distinction between a class and the members of a class. Reference to a class qua class is markedly better with *the N*; *Ns* inclines more to interpretation as the totality of members, though not as far as *a N* does. The different generic forms show a cline of acceptability in relation to the two kinds of generic interpretation.

As hinted at above, there is a link between this cline and tolerance of exceptions. The generic type that most readily accepts a class-qua-class interpretation admits exceptions most readily:

(71) a.   **The academic** likes his comfort, though I believe Professor Laserbeam is very spartan.

    b.   **Academics** like their comfort, though I believe Professor Laserbeam is very spartan.

    c.   ?**An academic** likes his comfort, though I believe Professor Laserbeam is very spartan.

The point is made more clearly when nationality terms (which allow definite plural generics) are taken into account:

(72) a.   **The Italian** drinks rather a lot, though I must say Luigi is very abstemious.

    b.   ***An Italian** drinks rather a lot, though I must say Luigi is very abstemious.

    c.   **The Italians** drink rather a lot, though I must say Luigi is very abstemious.

    d.   ?**Italians** drink rather a lot, though I must say Luigi is very abstemious.

Definite generics admit exceptions, then, more easily than do their indefinite counterparts. And the definite plural certainly accepts class predicates more readily than does the indefinite plural:

(73) a.   **The Brazilians** are twice as numerous as thirty years ago.

    b.   ?**Brazilians** are twice as numerous as thirty years ago.

Again it is a matter of degree; but this is enough to suggest that the distinction drawn by Smith between two types of generic has some validity.

How can these differences be accounted for, and how do the different types of generic expression get their generic interpretation? Let us look at the different types in turn, at the same time looking beyond English.

4.3.2 Singular generics

We begin with the definite and indefinite singular generic types exemplified by English *the squid* and *a squid*, limited to count nouns. Recall that mass nouns like *butter* or *sincerity* pattern in most respects with the plural of count nouns; not only do they not occur with *a*, but in generic use they do not occur with *the* either, but appear in "bare" form comparable to the bare plural of count nouns. I am taking mass noun phrases, like plurals, to be [− Sg]. So the two singular generic types are non-central in the sense that they are not available in principle for all nouns. They are nevertheless not an idiosyncrasy of English but are both very common in languages that have articles, French and German for example:

(74) a. *French*
     Le/Un castor construit des barrages.
   b. *German*
     Der/Ein Biber baut Dämme.
     'The/A beaver builds dams.'

And many languages that do not have articles, like Russian, can use the bare singular of count nouns with generic value:

(75)   Bogatomu   nje spitsja.
          rich-SG-DAT not sleep-IMPRS
          'A/The rich man cannot sleep.'

This is probably to be distinguished from the many languages in which a form unmarked for number and without any determiner is the central one, used both with count and mass nouns. In Turkish, for example, absence of plural marking with count nouns does not entail singularity. Rather, such a noun (or noun phrase) is neutral with respect to number, and can be used generically to denote the entire class.

As noted above, it has been claimed (Burton-Roberts 1976, 1989a) that the indefinite singular represents a "property generic", denoting the intension of the noun with no extension; for this reason this generic type can only take predicates which express inherent or defining characteristics. It is to be equated with the predicative use of a noun phrase, as in *John is a doctor*, where *a doctor* is not a referring expression; it predicates a description of the subject. (This is by contrast with *John is the doctor you met*, which expresses identity of reference between two referring expressions.) Although this analysis is presented as a claim about English only, it would obviously gain in plausibility if supported by comparative evidence. This support is largely lacking, however, since many languages which have indefinite singular generics, behaving much as they do in English, do not show identity between these and the form of noun phrases used predicatively. In French, Spanish and German, for example, the bare noun or nominal is the usual predicative form (*Jean est médecin, Juan es médico, Johann ist Arzt*), but the bare singular is not used generically; rather, the quasi-indefinite article appears as in English (*un médecin, un médico, ein Arzt*). A possible response to this fact is that while the predicative use of a property expression is non-argumental, the property generic is an argument, and that singular arguments in these languages require a determiner, while non-arguments do not.

The more common view, which I believe is correct, is that the indefinite singular generic is simply a special case of what I termed in 4.2 the "non-referential" indefinite

185

(exhibiting the kind of non-specificity found in transparent contexts); see Nunberg and Pan (1975), Krifka et al. (1995). Burton-Roberts (1989a) argues against identifying generic with non-specific on the grounds that an indefinite singular noun phrase can be ambiguous between generic and non-specific interpretations; he points out that the following sentence is three-ways ambiguous:

(76)   **An Indian** smokes a pipe every night.

On the specific reading, a particular Indian is a nightly smoker; on the non-specific reading, pipe-smoking occurs nightly, but it may be a different Indian each night; and on the generic reading, nightly pipe-smoking is a defining property of Indians – to be a real Indian you have to smoke a pipe every night. Since the second and third readings are distinct, generic cannot be the same as non-specific. But this is to consider as non-specific only the narrow-scope interpretation; on the second reading described, *an Indian* is in the scope of *every*. This still leaves the non-referential reading, in which *an Indian* has scope over *every* (as in the first reading), but the speaker does not have a particular Indian in mind and the description is crucial. It is this non-referential use which is to be equated with the generic third reading. The generic reading is in fact the non-referential use in an appropriate context; in the case of (76) the generic value is imposed by the habitual or generic aspect of the predicate. This can be contrasted with the non-generic non-referential interpretation that results from a punctual aspectual context, as when Tex finds his favourite ten-gallon hat shot through by an arrow and ruined, and exclaims: *An Indian did this!*

Many languages have a pronominal form which can be analysed as an indefinite singular generic, corresponding to English *one*, with arbitrary human reference. French *on* and, to a more limited degree, German *man* are different in that they can also be non-arbitrary (non-generic), non-referential indefinites (close in meaning to non-referential *someone*).[9] They are therefore like non-pronominal indefinites in having the possibility of both generic and non-generic reference: non-generic *On frappe à la porte* 'Someone's knocking at the door', *Ich muß gehen, man wartet auf mich* 'I must go, someone's waiting for me' (in which the non-referentiality may amount to a judgment that the identity of the person waiting is unimportant); generic *On ne pense jamais à tout* 'One can't think of everything', *Man muß alles selbst machen* 'One must do everything oneself'. But *one* is essentially limited to the arbitrary, generic use:

---

[9] With all these pronouns it is also important to set aside definite uses, like the use of French *on* as a first-person plural pronoun (*On part à six heures* 'We're leaving at six'), or the use of English *one* by some speakers as a vague first person, usually singular, form (*They told me about it yesterday; well, what could one say, one was rather embarrassed*).

(77)   *One* should always keep one's problems in perspective.

(78)   *One knocked at the door.

These languages therefore have an indefinite which is marked as non-referential, and in the case of English *one* also generic. Another indefinite "expression" is the implicit, understood subject or agent of passive and passive-like constructions. The agent of a passive with no overt agent expression (or "*by* phrase"), such as *Bill was mugged on his way home last night*, is generally equivalent to an indefinite pronoun like *someone*. But the implicit agent of the middle construction (*Cotton washes easily* or *This surface doesn't paint well*) is by definition arbitrary, equivalent to *one*, and so probably generic. In some languages, like Spanish, there is no middle construction distinct from the passive, but in others (like French and English) there is, and it is restricted to the same habitual or generic aspectual contexts that indefinite singular generic noun phrases are constrained to occur in. These overt and implicit items encoding non-referential and limited to generic contexts are discussed in Lyons (1995a), and we return to them in Chapter 5.

The definite singular is the most difficult generic form to account for, and I will here suggest an explanation based on a proposal of Burton-Roberts (1989a). It is well known that noun phrases can be used to refer to kinds or varieties, and sets of these, as well as to (sets of) individuals; thus *a whale* can denote not only an individual animal but also a variety or species of whale. This possibility is available for all determiner–noun combinations:

(79)   We're studying the migration habits of **a whale** that may be on the verge of extinction. Unfortunately I can't remember the name of **the whale** that we're studying. Jill says she finds **this whale** pretty boring since she read about **three other whales** that have much more interesting habits, and she's asked if she can work on **these whales** instead. I can't remember the names of **the whales** she's interested in either. I just think **whales** are fascinating whichever ones you do.

All the highlighted noun phrases in (79) are most naturally interpreted as denoting species of whale (except the last one – see below). Burton-Roberts refers to this as the "class-generic" interpretation – misleadingly, because on the usual understanding that generic means reference to the whole class constituting the extension of the noun, it is not generic, but merely reference to varieties, or pluralities of varieties, rather than individuals. In Chapter 1 I termed this use the "variety interpretation". We can of course use it to refer generically to the whole class of varieties just as we can refer generically to a whole class of individuals:

(80)   We've been investigating fluctuations in the populations of different whales, and it seems that **the whale/a whale/whales** increase(s) in numbers when the sun shines.

In this sentence the bold *a whale* must be interpreted as a generic over species, while *the whale* and *whales* can be read either as generic over individual whales or over species of whale, as is the case also with *whales* in the last sentence of (79).

Now consider the definite singular *the whale* in (79). Burton-Roberts's proposal is that, in the absence of qualifying information (such as the relative clause here) to identify the variety, the reference is taken to be not to a variety, but to the "super-class", the set of all varieties or species of whale. Thus it is like the generic-over-varieties interpretation of (80), though Burton-Roberts considers it to be a simple specific singular reference to a unique class of classes. This is the definite singular generic. I want to modify this account slightly, to say that the reference here is not to the "super-class" or class of varieties, but to the class of individuals perceived as a unique variety. What I mean by this apparent contradiction is that generic *the whale* is the variety use, but the class of all individual whales is taken as consisting of one single variety. I make this modification because there are instances of *the N* where one would not normally think of the class having obvious subclasses. For example, *The dodo ate figs* and *The Londoner is spoilt for choice as regards theatre* are generalizations about dodos or Londoners, not about varieties of dodo or kinds of Londoner. So what we have with the definite singular generic is entities on the varieties level which are treated as unique, and therefore definite – like *the sun*, *the equator* on the individuals level.

The variety interpretation of count noun phrases which underlies the account given above is presumably related to the use of normally mass nouns as count. When mass nouns are recategorized in this way, it is either on the individuals level (*Give me a beer*, *Another hot whiskey please*) or on the varieties level (*a great wine*, *an expensive perfume*). But, interestingly, the latter does not normally involve kinds of the former. The individuals are usually portions, so *a beer* means a glass or bottle of beer; but on the varieties level, *a beer* means a type or brand of beer, not a kind of glass/bottle of beer. And in the case of recategorization on this varieties level, there is apparently no possibility of a definite singular generic of the type in *The squid lives on seaweed*, in which the variety is viewed as unique, standing in this case (*the beer*) for all beer.

Krifka et al. treat the definite singular as the central nominal generic (or "kind-referring" expression), because, unlike the bare plural and other forms, it only occurs with generic value with nouns or nominals denoting "well-established kinds": thus *the lion* or *the Coke bottle*, but not *the green bottle. The assumption is that only with such kinds can noun phrases be themselves generic (as opposed to getting generic value from being in the scope of a generic operator, as happens with indefinite singulars in generic aspectual contexts). Since, by contrast with the definite singular, a bare plural like *green bottles* can have generic value, this value is also taken to come from the generic sentence context, the noun phrase itself being a non-generic (presumably non-referential) indefinite. It is not certain, however, that the notion of well-established kind provides a valid diagnostic for nominal genericity; it may be that the restriction noted is a peculiarity of definite singular generics rather than of generics generally. For a discussion of generics in French, concentrating on the definite singular, see Kleiber (1990).

4.3.3   Non-singular generics

Plural count noun phrases form a natural class with mass noun phrases, both differing from singular count noun phrases in denoting non-atomic parts of a totality rather than individuals and for this reason being compatible with certain quantifiers and cardinality expressions (*sm/all/a lot of books/water/*book*). I assume this can be captured in terms of number by seeing both as [− Sg]. Plural and mass generics are typically indefinite in some languages, like English, and definite in others, like French. These are the central or canonical generic forms in that they are available for both count and mass nouns in these languages.

A widely accepted view is that the indefinite type, consisting of the noun or nominal with no determiner, is semantically the same whether used generically or not. Carlson (1977), limiting himself to plurals, what he terms the "bare plural", argues that the generic and non-generic uses are in complementary distribution, and that their distribution is wholly determined by the linguistic context. This entails that bare plurals are never ambiguous in context; any ambiguity lies elsewhere in the sentence, in the verb for instance. The following are his examples:

(81) a.   **Dogs** bark.
   b.   Mark really loves **puppies**.
   c.   The man over there believes **Texans** to be friendly.
   d.   **Frogs** are clever.

(82) a.   **Plumbers** stormed into the convention demanding longer lunch breaks.
   b.   Alice personally knows **actresses**.
   c.   **Frogs** are awake.

(83)   **Dinosaurs** ate kelp.

The bold noun phrases in (81) admit a generic reading only, and those in (82) only a non-generic reading. Where the predicate reports an event or a non-essential state, it selects the non-generic reading; a predicate which posits a characteristic or property selects the generic reading. (83) is ambiguous between generic and non-generic readings, but this is because the verb *ate* is ambiguous between characteristic and event interpretations, the English simple past systematically representing both habitual and punctual aspect.[10] As support for the non-distinctness of generic and non-generic bare plurals, Carlson shows that a generic instance can serve as antecedent for a pronoun understood non-generically, and vice versa:

(84)   **Lemmings** are protected by law, but Mick goes ahead and traps **them** anyway.

(85)   Mick traps **lemmings**, even though he knows full well that **they** are protected by law.

Carlson's descriptive claims are not unproblematic, however. Consider the following:

(86) a.   I know **actresses** – and I can tell you there's no more neurotic group of people.
    b.   I know **actresses** – I've got a couple coming for dinner tonight.

(87) a.   **Lions** live in Africa – so if you want to see lions, that's where you have to go.
    b.   **Lions** live in Africa – in fact there are more lions in Africa than any other continent.

The highlighted noun phrases in (86a) and (87a) seem to be generic, and those in (86b) and (87b) to be non-generic – though the predicate is the same. This appears to cast doubt on the claim that it is the predicate that imposes a generic interpretation on a bare plural. There are probably grounds for positing an ambiguity in the verb *know* in (86), and one might argue that there is some property–state ambiguity in the verb in (87). Notice that a difference in intonation is likely between (87a) and (87b), corresponding to a difference in information structure; the first is likely to occur in a discussion about lions, the second in a discussion about Africa. Thus *lions* in (87a) is the **topic** of the sentence, while in (87b) the same noun phrase is part of the **comment**; these elements of discourse structure will be discussed in Chapter 6. It appears that the position of a bare nominal in relation to the discourse structure of a sentence can play a role in its interpretation as generic or non-generic. Further examples make it clear that, if a generic or non-generic interpretation of a bare plural is selected by other elements in the sentence, it is not enough to consider the aspect of the verb. The following examples show that other parts of the predicate that can vary for generality are relevant:

(88) a.   **Cats** mess in loose soil.
    b.   **Cats** mess in gardens other than their own.
    c.   **Cats** mess in the open air.
    d.   **Cats** mess in my garden.

---

[10] This is also true, in fact, of the simple present in (81a). As part of the text of a play, describing what happens at a certain point in the drama, this sentence would be non-generic.

The verbal aspect is habitual in all four sentences, but while (88a–c) seem necessarily generic, (88d) is most naturally understood as non-generic. The generality of the locative expression seems to play a central role. See also Burton-Roberts (1976) for similar observations.

Despite these difficulties, Carlson's claim that bare plurals have a constant semantic representation is supported by the possibility of coordination between generic and non-generic instances (reinforcing his argument from anaphora):

(89)   **Hedgehogs** are shy creatures but often visit my garden.

This should be impossible if the generic and non-generic uses were semantically distinct; compare (90), where different senses of the word *bank* fail to coordinate acceptably:

(90)   ****Banks** are good places to keep your money and to picnic.

To treat bare plural generics as non-referential indefinites, like indefinite singulars, is problematic, since their distribution is different from that of indefinite singular generics, as seen in 4.3.1. Carlson's proposal is that bare plurals are proper names of sets or "kinds", these being abstract individuals, unanalysable wholes. He gives detailed arguments to show that bare plurals pattern very much like phrases such as *this kind of animal*, which also can have both generic and "indefinite plural" readings:

(91) a.   **This kind of animal** is a vertebrate.
     b.   **This kind of animal** is tall.

(92) a.   **This kind of animal** is likely to win the race.
     b.   **This kind of animal** is in the room.
     c.   Harriet caught **this kind of animal** yesterday.

The non-generic indefinite plural reading arises when the predicate is one that selects, not the set or kind as a timeless whole, but a realization of the kind at a particular time and place. This kind of realization or instantiation is termed a "stage" by Carlson. Stages are instantiations not only of kinds (denoted by bare common nouns) but also of individuals (denoted by proper nouns). So one stage of Fred might be a particular three-hour stretch of his life; one stage of the kind denoted by *cats* would be a particular group of cats at a given point or period in time. There are then stage-level predicates and individual-level predicates – the latter selecting also whole kinds because these are for Carlson second-order individuals. And since proper names like *Fred* denote individuals, bare plurals, which denote kinds, are also proper names – proper names of kinds. Carlson supports this treatment by pointing to similarities in behaviour between bare plurals and proper nouns.

A difficulty for this analysis is that bare plural generics in English are more general than definites, which suggests they represent generalizations over the members of a class rather than over the class as an individual; see (72c,d) and (73) above. Moreover, my impression is that kind-expressions on their generic rather than indefinite plural reading, as in (91), are closer to the definite plural generic than to the bare plural:

(93) a.   ?*Italians* are musical, though a few of them are tone-deaf.
     b.   *The Italians* are musical, though a few of them are tone-deaf.
     c.   *This nationality* is musical, though a few of them are tone-deaf.

A further problem is that the analysis does not extend straightforwardly to other languages. There are many languages (such as French and Spanish) in which proper nouns are typically bare but generics are not. If common nouns are names of kinds in these languages too, one would expect that bare plurals could be used generically. But they cannot, the central generic in these languages being (for count nouns) the definite plural. In Spanish bare plurals do occur, but only with the indefinite plural reading, thus with stage-level predicates. Despite these problems, the analysis of bare nominals as names of kinds, in both their generic and non-generic uses, has a lot of explanatory power (though Carlson seems to backtrack on this claim in more recent, collaborative, work; see Krifka et al. (1995)).

The non-singular definite is the central generic form in many languages, and I will illustrate it here from French. It can probably be analysed as a special case of the non-generic use of the same form. The obvious account would be to relate the generic interpretation to the inclusiveness element in definiteness; thus in some languages the context within which inclusiveness applies may be the universe, so *les livres* (the books) may refer to the totality of books in some pragmatically determined domain or to the totality of books without this pragmatic limitation. An interesting contrast with English bare plurals is that the linguistic context does not select the interpretation of a non-singular definite noun phrase in the same way. It is true that an event context sometimes imposes a non-generic reading, as on the object noun phrases in *J'ai bu le vin* 'I've drunk the wine', *J'ai perdu les oeufs* 'I've lost the eggs'. But both readings tend to be available in non-event contexts:

(94) a.   J'adore **le vin**.
            'I love (the) wine.'
     b.   J'adore **les huîtres**.
            'I love (the) oysters.'
     c.   **Le vin** est délicieux.
            '(The) wine is delicious.'
     d.   **Les huîtres** sont délicieux.
            '(The) oysters are delicious.'

In fact the generic interpretation is the unmarked one here; the tendency would be to use a demonstrative to convey the non-generic sense (*ce vin* 'this wine', *ces huîtres* 'these oysters'). A non-generic interpretation is possible however. Notice the contrast with the corresponding English bare non-singulars, which can only be understood generically: *I love wine/oysters, Wine/Oysters is/are delicious.* Non-singular definites in English pattern in this respect in the same way as in French:

(95) a. Mary admires **Russians**.
     b. **Bolivians** have a subtle sense of humour.

(96) a. Mary admires **the Russians**.
     b. **The Bolivians** have a subtle sense of humour.

The indefinites in (95) can probably only be understood as generic, but the definites in (96) admit both generic and non-generic interpretations. The non-availability of the non-generic reading with the indefinites is, on Carlson's theory, due to the fact that they name the kind, and are thus generic in principle. The non-generic reading is only possible when induced by a stage-level predicate. On another view, this constraint on the interpretation of the bare or indefinite non-singulars would be linked to the availability of the cardinality quasi-article *sm*, which would be required in (95) (probably necessarily in unreduced form) if a non-generic interpretation were intended.

While English has non-singular definite generics for only a limited class of nouns, French does not seem to have non-singular indefinite generics at all. No language appears to permit both definite and indefinite non-singular generics freely – an interesting contrast with the singular.

4.3.4 *Generics and proper nouns*

Proper nouns have traditionally been viewed as almost the exact opposite of generics, denoting individuals as opposed to classes, and as being fundamentally different from common nouns. They are supposed to designate an individual entity directly, rather than via a description which that entity satisfies (thus being a member of the class of entities satisfying it). They therefore have reference but not sense. In logic, proper nouns (or proper names, the logician's preferred label) are usually treated, following Kripke (1972), as "rigid designators", expressions which denote the same individual in all possible worlds. Thus full noun phrase descriptions like *my next-door neighbour* or *Smith's murderer* may apply to one individual or another, depending on who in a particular world (that is, in a particular scenario or version of reality) lives next door to me or murdered Smith. And the same is true even more obviously of individual common nouns; a given person may or may not be accurately described by the noun *student* or *fool*. But *Fred Bloggs* denotes Fred Bloggs whatever else happens.[11] One consequence of this is that proper nouns are said not to be subject to scope ambiguities. Compare the ambiguities in (97), where common noun phrases, definite and indefinite, may be understood as specific or non-specific in the opaque context created by the verb *want*, with the lack of such ambiguity in (98):

(97) a.   Bill wants to meet **a bishop**.
    b.   Bill wants to meet **the winner**.

(98)   Bill wants to meet **Mary**.

There is another logical tradition, going back to Russell (1905), of seeing proper names as disguised definite descriptions, but this is rejected by most logicians today. This Russellian treatment parallels a linguistic view of proper nouns as a peculiar kind of definite noun or noun phrase – peculiar in that in most languages they show no encoding of [+ Def]. A further distinction between proper nouns and common nouns is that the referent of the former is always an individual (though it may be a collective individual), never a plurality or a mass, as can be the case with the latter.

The contrast between proper and common nouns is perhaps no longer quite so clear given the proposals of Carlson (1977) for treating bare plurals as proper names of classes ("kinds"), following suggestions in the philosophical literature by Kripke (1972) and others. In their generic use, bare plurals do resemble proper nouns in a number of ways, and they can be thought of as directly denoting, and rigidly designating, an entire class in the same way as proper nouns do an individual. But there still appear to be differences between names of classes and names of individuals. For one thing, in a generic the noun does describe a class or ensemble, it has descriptive semantic content; this is supposedly not the case with proper nouns. I want here to advance a proposal which I believe has the merit of integrating proper nouns into the general system of nouns; that is, it abolishes the proper–common distinction. This account inverts the claim of Carlson that generics are names of ensembles, these being second-order individuals. Rather, proper nouns are a kind of generic; they do denote ensembles (or better in this case, kinds), but always generically, because these "ensembles" consist of only one entity. This analysis is presented in more detail in Lyons (1995c), and I outline only the main points here.

The familiar count–mass distinction is central to the argument. As pointed out above, proper nouns only have individual entities as referents, never pluralities or masses; for this reason, it is generally assumed that the count–mass distinction applies to common nouns only. The following traditional schema would, therefore, be generally accepted as a categorization of nouns:

---

[11] For an outline of possible-world theory, see Cann (1993: chapter 9).

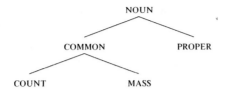

My claim is that the category of proper noun is of the same order as count and mass, so that a more accurate categorization would show a three-way count–mass–proper contrast, as follows:

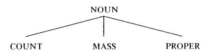

There are two main reasons for making this claim. The first is that proper nouns are not distinguished from common nouns by having reference but no sense; they are in principle no more devoid of sense (descriptive content) than are common nouns. It is reasonable to say that typical names of persons or places (like *John* and *Paris*) have no sense. But the same is true of names given by a deliberate act of christening to kinds of things; commercial brand names or model names are a case in point:

(99)   Peter has sold his **Astra** and now drives a **Golf**. He's owned three **Golfs** before.

(100)   I bought a 10-kilo box of **Persil** to deal with all these dirty clothes. I've never used so much **Persil** for one wash.

These names have no more descriptive content than typical proper names. One might claim that they are proper nouns. But they take articles and other determiners (unlike normal proper nouns in English); they can (in the case of the car model names in (99)) be singular or plural (without it being a matter of the kind of recategorization occurring in *three beers* or *sm apple*); or they can (as with the detergent brand name in (100)) be uncountable and denote a mass or substance. Their syntactic behaviour is exactly that of common nouns, count in (99) and mass in (100). And semantically, they do denote an ensemble – a class of car in (99) and a substance in (100). If proper nouns denote individuals, directly, then *Golf* and *Persil* here are common nouns. But, while denoting an ensemble, they lack sense. The converse of this is that there are true proper nouns – bare one-word forms in English designating individuals – which do have sense:

(101) a.   I'm dining in **Hall** this evening.
   b.   **Senate** has decided to abandon the scheme.
   c.   This measure must be put before **Parliament**.

These nouns can be used as common count nouns (*a high-ceilinged hall, the senate of your university, most modern parliaments*). But here, as a result of the familiar process of recategorization, they appear as proper nouns, denoting an individual entity (such as an institution) and requiring no determiner. But they have the same sense as when used as common nouns. Their extension is simply treated as being reduced to one object.

The second reason follows from these observations and is to do with the process of recategorization. I have been using this term to label what is happening when a noun which is normally mass is used as count and vice versa; thus mass to count in *three beers, a good wine*, and count to mass in *a piece of lamb, sm apple*. In fact it may well be the case that nouns are not lexically marked as count or mass, and that any noun can in principle be used either way. But most nouns are probably typically used as one or the other, and the concept of recategorization is a useful one for expository purposes. But notice that this process seems to underlie the uses in (101), normally common count nouns being turned into proper nouns (assuming the common use of these nouns is the basic one; the argument would still work, with some modification, if the recategorization were taken to be in the opposite direction). So common count nouns can be recategorized as mass, or as proper. This suggests strongly that proper, count and mass are categories on the same level.

If, then, we assume such a three-way distinction in nouns (at least in principle – not all languages necessarily show all three types), we can define the three categories on the basis of the type of ensemble or kind constituting a noun's extension. A count noun denotes a kind with subparts (non-atomic instantiations) and individual members; we can refer to the whole ensemble (generic use: *I love dogs*), to a subpart (plural non-generic: *I like those dogs*), or to a member (singular: *A dog bit me*). A mass noun denotes a kind with subparts, but no atomic members; we can refer to the whole (generic: *I love butter*), or to a subpart (non-generic: *I've bought sm butter*). A proper noun denotes a kind with neither subparts nor members, being made up of one entity; reference is always to the whole and is therefore always generic (*I admire John/Paris/Parliament*). And there are nouns with descriptive content and nouns without it in all three categories.[12]

---

[12] It will be noticed that on this picture count and mass nouns do have something in common distinguishing them from proper nouns: the possibility of reference to a subpart. But this is quite different from the traditional assumption of a radical proper–common dichotomy, with proper nouns regarded as marginal to the nominal system. On the account offered here the difference lies in the possibility or not of cardinality modification, and, in terms of cardinality, mass nouns differ as much from count nouns as from proper nouns.

This analysis would lead us to expect proper nouns to have the same form as other generics. And this expectation is borne out for many languages, including English, where the typical generic is the bare noun or nominal (plural if count), and where proper nouns too are bare. In other languages, like Greek and Catalan, both "common" generics and some proper nouns take definiteness marking. But there are also languages in which this correspondence does not hold. In French generics are typically definite in form (*le vin* 'wine', *les chiens* 'dogs') but proper nouns typically bare. But in at least some such languages there is evidence for the proper noun itself to be in Det position, itself taking the part of the definite article; we saw this for Italian in 3.2, following Longobardi (1994).[13] I assume that the definite article or equivalent (noun in Det position) characterizing proper nouns and "common" generics in Italian, Catalan and Greek is the full definite article and not some empty pleonastic article restricted to these uses. Count and mass generics and proper nouns are definite in these languages, and indefinite (typically) in languages such as English. But both definite and indefinite proper nouns are generic – except that, as said in 3.1, it could be that definite proper nouns in languages like Greek are merely a special case of uniques like *the sun*.

The apparent definiteness of all proper nouns follows from the fact that generics generally, whether [+ Def] or [– Def], show much of the behaviour and distribution of definites. This can be shown by reference to some of the diagnostics used earlier.

(102) a. Big as **the/*a boy** was, he couldn't lift it.
   b. Big as **an elephant** is, we'll find room for Nellie here.
   c. Big as **elephants** are, you'll never get one to lift that load.

(103) a. **The/?A house** is mine.
   b. Surely **a letter** is mine if it's addressed to me.
   c. '**Vengeance** is mine' said the president.

(104) a. Is there **a/?the dictionary** in the house?
   b. Is there **a lion** in Africa?
   c. Are there **dolphins** on the verge of extinction?

(102) and (103) show indefinite generics patterning like non-generic definites; in (104) the (b) and (c) examples are good but the indefinites cannot have a generic

---

[13] Longobardi claims that proper nouns (and generics) in English too move to the Det position, but at the abstract level of "logical form" (the level of analysis at which many relations of an essentially semantic nature are explicated). This is because he assumes that all argumental noun phrases must have a Det, and this can only be null if indefinite. A universal principle assigns an indefinite interpretation to any null Det; this would apply to non-generic bare nouns, which are thus seen (in contrast with Carlson's view) as quite distinct from bare generics. I take the view, with Carlson, that a unified treatment of bare nouns, generic and non-generic, is correct. It is not self-evident that arguments need a Det. I return to this in Chapter 8.

reading. The fact that all generics pattern with definites in these contexts may be due to the fact that, since their reference is to a whole ensemble, they can be characterized as inclusive. They can perhaps also be said to be familiar, and therefore to meet the criterion of identifiability. For while a hearer may fail to identify the referent of a noun phrase like *a/the pencil*, the ensemble denoted by generic *pencils* is familiar to us all. Generics are thus semantically definite, though not necessarily grammatically definite.

4.4 Concluding comments

What emerges from this chapter is that there is no evidence for ambiguity in the definite article relating either to the various uses of definites distinguished in Chapter 1 or to specificity. There is hyponymy, however. I have suggested a primary division of definiteness between what I term textual–situational ostension on the one hand and all other uses on the other. The former of these itself divides into anaphoric and immediate situation uses. Languages may represent these finer distinctions within definiteness morphologically or lexically, but need not. The different types of specificity seem to be treated by some languages as hyponymous to indefiniteness, but (strikingly in view of the semantic and pragmatic research findings) never to definiteness.

There is also no reason to posit special generic articles. Noun phrases used generically never have a specifically generic form, and even noun phrase types claimed to be kind-referring also have non-generic uses. Both "ordinary" generics and proper nouns, which I have suggested are a kind of generic, can be definite or indefinite in form. They behave much like definites, because they apparently meet both the basic semantic/pragmatic criteria for definite reference (inclusiveness and identifiability), but it does not follow that languages must represent them grammatically as definite.

5

Interaction with other grammatical phenomena

A number of grammatical processes appear to refer to the feature [+ Def], in the sense that they only apply when this feature is present. An example is object marking, which, as we have briefly observed, only takes place in some languages for definite objects. An alternative way to view such phenomena is that definiteness is only encoded in certain grammatical contexts; thus, for some languages, definiteness is only marked in object position. Apart from restrictions of this kind, some grammatical categories interact with definiteness in that they are encoded together on the same formative – number and gender on the French definite article for example. There are also certain grammatical structures in which a definite element may be inherent; in this connection we will consider the relevance of definiteness for the theory of empty categories.

5.1 Direct object marking

We saw in 2.4.1 that some languages have adpositional object markers which are restricted to occurring with definite noun phrases. On the face of it, it is debatable whether these adpositions are "articles" (encoding definiteness) or object markers. There is good reason to believe the latter is the correct conclusion, in part because it is not always, if ever, strictly or only definiteness that is the decisive factor in their appearance. In fact the phenomenon is not limited to such adpositional markers, but extends to what appear to be accusative case morphemes.

In this section we will examine a number of instances, grouped, somewhat arbitrarily, under three headings: first, languages in which the accusative is restricted to definite objects, indefinite objects appearing in a different (but also non-subject) case; second, languages in which accusative case, or an object marker, is restricted to definite objects, other objects being unmarked, or in a case form not distinct from that of subjects; third, languages in which accusative case, or a simple unmarked form, is restricted to indefinite objects, definites taking some oblique case or a marker basically associated with some other function.

5.1.1   Differential case marking

We have seen in 2.5.4 how in Finnish direct objects can appear in the accusative or in the partitive case, and that this correlates partly with the definite–indefinite distinction. The distinction expressed by this case variation is usually treated as one between total and partial affectedness; the referent of the object noun phrase is completely affected (accusative) or partially affected (partitive) by the action expressed by the verb. But the choice of case can also indicate completed versus incompleted action, or even alter the time reference or express emphasis; see Whitney (1956) and Chesterman (1991). It is clear that the case variation does not directly express variation for [± Def].

Similar facts are found in Hungarian (Moravcsik 1978), the accusative being used if the object is fully involved, the partitive if it is only partially involved:

(1)   Ette   a   süteményt.
         ate-3SG-OBJ the pastry-ACC
         'He/She ate the pastry.'

(2)   Evett   a   süteményből.
         ate-3SG the pastry-PART
         'He/She ate some of the pastry.'

The variation in the verb form between *ette* and *evett* is due to agreement of verbs with definite direct objects, a matter we will return to. It is interesting because agreement does not take place with a partitive object, even when this is definite as here. This fact suggests that such partitive noun phrases are not actually direct objects; perhaps they are rather partitive complements of a null indefinite head in object position. Hungarian is also interesting in having a definite article, unlike Finnish. This means that it is possible to see the definiteness or indefiniteness of the object noun phrase independently of its case. It can be seen that the partitive construction is used in Hungarian where the domain of partitivity is definite; Finnish would use the contrast between elative and partitive to distinguish definite and indefinite domains (see 2.5.4). What this means is that in Hungarian, even more clearly than in Finnish, partitive case expresses genuine partitivity, not indefiniteness. Indeed, the accusative can be used where the object is indefinite. Moravcsik also cites Kabardian (data from Knobloch 1952), an ergative language showing a state of affairs very similar to that of Hungarian and Finnish; if the patient of a transitive verb is totally involved or affected it takes the absolute case, but if only partially involved it takes the locative:

(3) a.   ḥăm   q°ópśḥăr   yeʒàqe.
          dog-ERG bone-ABS chews
          'The dog chews up the bone.'

b.   ħăr   qʿə́pṣħăm yóȝàqe.
       dog-ABS bone-LOC chews
       'The dog is chewing (on) the bone.'

Notice that 'dog' in (3b) is in the absolutive, not the ergative, suggesting that the construction here is an intransitive one (since the general pattern of ergative languages is that ergative is the case of subjects of transitives, and absolutive the case of objects of transitives and subjects of intransitives). If this is so, the locative case patient, *qʿə́pṣħăm*, is not grammatically a direct object, but is rather in some adjunct, oblique, position. This may be support for the suggestion above that partitive objects in Finnish and Hungarian are not true direct objects. And notice that this locative object, like the partitive object in Finnish and Hungarian, need not be indefinite.

Languages making use of a partitive or other oblique case to express indefiniteness or partial affectedness often use this case for indefinites, and in some cases also for definites, in the scope of negation. The following examples illustrate this process in Russian:

(4) a.   Ja nje khochu   khljeba.
           I not want-1SG bread-GEN
           'I don't want (any) bread.'
    b.   Ona nikogda nje vidjela   morja.
           she never   not saw-F-SG sea-GEN
           'She has never seen the sea.'

There is, however, a growing tendency in Russian for genitive case in negative contexts to be restricted to indefinites. This use of an oblique case for (mainly) indefinites within the scope of negation occurs in many languages where this case is not otherwise used for indefinite or partially affected arguments. One such language is Gothic (Wright 1910):

(5)   jah ni was im   barnē
        and not was them-DAT child-PL-GEN
        'and they had no children'

In summary, the pattern of accusative case alternating with an oblique case is widespread. The temptation to view it as a unified phenomenon is very strong, despite variation in precisely what triggers the appearance of the oblique case. But both this variation, and the complexity of the trigger within individual languages, make it clear that if we are dealing with a single phenomenon, then it cannot be correlated directly with the definite–indefinite distinction, though definiteness does play a part in what is happening.

5.1.2 *Definite object marking*

A distinct, though possibly related, phenomenon is that of languages in which accusative case, or some other marker of direct objects, is used only with definite objects (or, again, a subset of objects characterized in some other way). Direct objects which lack the determining feature are in an unmarked form; that is, they are not distinguished formally from subjects.

Turkish illustrates this phenomenon in terms of case morphology. Turkish has a system of six cases, realized by agglutinative suffixes. The case form used for subjects is the unmarked one morphologically, distinguished by absence of a suffix.[1] It is in fact sometimes termed "absolute" or "absolutive" rather than "nominative" in traditional grammars, because it is the form used also for indefinite direct objects. The accusative, realized by -*i* (and its vowel harmony variants) is limited to definite direct objects. The following examples are from Lewis (1967):

(6) a.　　Bilet satıyorlar.
　　　　　ticket sell-3PL
　　　　　'They are selling tickets.'
　　b.　　Bir mavi kumaş istiyor.
　　　　　a　blue　material want-3SG
　　　　　'She wants a blue material.'

(7) a.　　Mavi kumaş-ı　　　seçti.
　　　　　blue　material ACC chose-3SG
　　　　　'She chose the blue material.'
　　b.　　Bu gazete-yi　　　okumadım.
　　　　　this newspaper ACC read-NEG-1SG
　　　　　'I have not read this newspaper.'
　　c.　　Biz-i　selâmladı.
　　　　　us ACC greeted-3SG
　　　　　'He greeted us.'
　　d.　　Hasan'-ı　hemen　　　tanıdım.
　　　　　Hasan ACC immediately recognized-1SG
　　　　　'I recognized Hasan immediately.'

Sentence (6a) illustrates the "incorporation" construction: the use of a noun unmarked for number, with no commitment as to the cardinality of what is denoted; (6b) shows an indefinite with the cardinal article. Both these types of indefinite normally occur as direct objects without the accusative suffix. As illustrated in (7), this suffix is used with direct object noun phrases interpreted as simple definite, as well as demonstratives, personal pronouns, and proper nouns.

The situation is similar in Persian, though this language shows major differences in overall pattern from Turkish. Both are SOV, but Turkish is archetypally

---

[1] Nominative is in this sense the unmarked case in a great many, though not all, languages.

so, while in Persian nominal modifiers follow the head and there is little inflection; in particular, Persian has no morphological case system. But definite direct objects take a suffix *-rā*, the status of which is unclear. The following examples are from Mace (1971):

(8) Man pūl   gereftam.
     I   money took-1SG
     'I took (sm) money.'

(9) a. Man pūl-rā   gereftam.
        I   money OBJ took-1SG
        'I took the money.'
    b. Ān ketāb-rā   khānd.
        that book OBJ read-3SG
        'He/She read that book.'
    c. Mard mā-rā   dīd.
        man us OBJ saw-3SG
        'The man saw us.'
    d. Hasan-rā   dīdand.
        Hasan OBJ saw-3PL
        'They saw Hasan.'

Persian also makes the distinction observed in Turkish between singular indefinites and incorporated indefinites consisting of the unmarked noun, neutral with respect to number:

(10) a. Nāme-ī   minevise.
         letter ART write-3SG
     b. Yek nāme minevise.
         one letter write-3SG
         'He writes a letter.'

(11) Nāme minevise.
      letter write-3SG
      'He writes letters/a letter.'

But Turkish *-i* and Persian *-rā* must be analysed as accusative or object markers rather than definite articles restricted to object position (or morphemes encoding simultaneously [+ Def] and accusative case). This is because they do sometimes appear on indefinite direct objects. Persian examples (Windfuhr 1979) are:

(12) a. Kas-ī-rā   ferestād.
         person ART OBJ sent-3SG
         'He sent someone.'
     b. Khāne-ī-rā   ātesh zadand.
         house ART OBJ fire struck-3PL
         'They burned a house.'

Here the indefinite objects are interpreted as specific; the addition of *-rā* is optional, and serves to make the specificity of the reference prominent. It works similarly in Turkish, where the accusative suffix can co-occur with the quasi-indefinite article *bir*:

(13)   Her gün bir gazete-yi   okuyorum.
         every day a newspaper ACC read-1SG
         'Every day I read a newspaper.'

Here the implication is that the speaker reads one particular newspaper every day.

Comrie (1978, 1981a: 128–9) argues that the use of the "definite object marker" in Persian and "definite accusative case" in Turkish can suggest that the reference of the noun phrase, while not known to the hearer, is important, perhaps because it is to recur in the discourse – a concept we have encountered in several languages. Comrie still treats this as definiteness, but a more plausible conclusion is that these morphemes do not relate directly to [+ Def]. Rather, they convey "referential prominence" – a concept to be interpreted pragmatically, which embraces definites and some specific indefinites, while leaving room for subjective choice.

A third language showing the phenomenon, and one where object marking correlates more strongly with definiteness, is Modern Hebrew (Rosen 1962, Borer 1984). The direct object marker is a preposition *'et*;[2] but Hebrew also has a prefixal definite article, and indefinites are typically recognized by absence of this:

(14)   Ra'iti   xatul.
         saw-1SG cat
         'I saw a cat.'

(15)   Ra'iti   'et ha-xatul.
         saw-1SG OBJ DEF cat
         'I saw the cat.'

The correlation between appearance of *'et* and definiteness of the object is very close, though Moravcsik (1978), following Cole (1975), notes that *'et* can occur with indefinite pronouns.

In many languages accusative or object marking is limited to a subset of direct objects characterized by other properties, such as animacy or pronominality. For example, accusative case is restricted to animates in Thargari, personal pronouns, proper nouns and kin terms in Gumbainggir; Hindi uses an object marker *ko* with

---

[2] Borer claims *'et* is a case marker rather than a preposition, but without substantiation. Prepositions in Hebrew inflect for the features of pronominal complements, which are then null (thus *l-i* (to-1SG) 'to me'), and *'et* shows precisely the inflectional behaviour of prepositions. "Object pronouns" are in fact inflected forms of *'et*.

all human, definite non-human animate, and (usually) definite inanimate direct objects (Comrie 1981a, Croft 1990). Cross-linguistically, definiteness is just one of a complex array of properties which may trigger object marking. In Khalkha Mongolian (Poppe 1970) accusative case is used with personal pronouns, numerals, substantivized adjectives, proper nouns, human nouns, and nouns modified by a genitive or with a possessive suffix. All other object noun phrases take the unmarked, absolutive, case form, the one used also for subjects, but only when immediately followed by the governing verb. When separated from it by other material, such as the subject in sentences like (17) with atypical word order, they too take accusative morphology:

(16)   Šinə barilgə   baribə.
        new building-ABS built-3SG
        'He built a new building.'

(17)   Šinə barilgəiig   nutəgiiŋ arəduud baribə.
        new building-ACC local   people built-3SG
        'The local people built a new building.'

5.1.3   Oblique direct objects

In some languages, direct objects which are distinguished by definiteness or other features differ from others in being marked by a case form, preposition, or other marker, which is otherwise associated with some "oblique" function, typically that of indirect object. Croft (1990, following Shackle 1972) cites Punjabi. Indirect objects are indicated by the postposition *nũ* 'to', and this form is also used for direct objects which are personal pronouns or animate common nouns; an inanimate direct object can also take *nũ*, but only if it is definite:

(18)   Éo nili kitāb nũ mezte   rakkho.
        that blue book to table on put
        'Put that blue book on the table.'

(19)   Koi   kitāb mez te rakkho.
        some book table on put
        'Put some book on the table.'

Another frequently mentioned case is that of Spanish, which is worth examining in some detail. This case is an interesting one because, though definiteness does not appear to be involved at all, specificity is, together with features relating to humanness and animacy. But again, the complexity of the data makes impossible any clear correlation with any one grammatical or semantic category. Spanish does not distinguish nominative and accusative cases morphologically, except in clitic pronouns; nouns are unmarked for any case distinctions, and strong pronouns simply lack direct object forms. Indirect objects are generally marked by the preposition *a* 'to', which also occurs with some direct objects (when it is traditionally termed "personal *a*"). The basic rules for the occurrence of the personal *a* are as follows. It must be used with direct objects referring to specific human beings:

(20)   Conozco   a ese chico.
         know-1SG to that lad
         'I know that lad.'

Where the direct object is non-specific, for example after opacity-creating verbs like *buscar* 'to look for', *a* is not used:

(21)   Busco   a un policía.
         look-for-1SG to a policeman
         'I'm looking for a policeman (a particular one).'

(22)   Busco   un policía.
         look-for-1SG a   policeman
         'I'm looking for a policeman (any policeman).'

But when the direct object is a pronoun like *alguien* 'someone', 'anyone', or *nadie* 'no one', with human reference, *a* must be used, even when the object is non-specific:

(23)   ¿Conoces   a alguien   en esta ciudad?
         know-2SG to someone in this city
         'Do you know anyone in this city?'

(24)   No veo   a nadie.
         not see-1SG to no one
         'I don't see anyone.'

Also, *a* is never used after *tener* 'to have'; it may be that this verb most commonly takes a non-specific object, as in (25), but (26) makes it clear that this is not necessarily the case.

(25)   Tienen   dos hijos.
         have-3PL two children
         'They have two children.'

(26)   Tengo   una hermana muy lista.
         have-1SG a   sister   very clever
         'I have a very clever sister.'

So the correlation between appearance of *a* and specificity is only partial. And the relationship with humanness is only partial too. There is a great deal of flexibility in the use of the personal *a*, the speaker's attitude to the referent and stylistic factors playing a complex role. *A* is often used with animate non-human nouns:

(27)   Vi   a tu   perro en el   coche.
         saw-1SG to your dog   in the car
         'I saw your dog in the car.'

It can also be used with any direct object, even an inanimate one, to avoid ambiguity, resulting for example from the relatively free word order of Spanish:

(28)   El artículo precede al   nombre.
         the article   precedes to-the noun
         'The article precedes the noun.'

Pronominal objects in Spanish are represented by clitics attached to the verb. And just as full noun phrase objects vary between those with and those without *a*, so the clitic corresponding to a direct object is sometimes dative, sometimes accusative (though the two case forms are only distinct in the third person). But, oddly, the use of *a* with full noun phrases and the use of dative clitics for pronominal objects do not correspond. In the standard language (as described for example in Ramsden (1959)), the dative clitic is used only for human referents, and only in the masculine singular; for the masculine plural and feminine, the accusative clitic is used. There is in fact much variation in this matter; many speakers use dative forms beyond this narrow limit, but also in many dialects the accusative form is used for the masculine singular. For a fuller discussion see Lyons 1990.

5.2   Verb agreement

The definiteness of objects may also be indicated by marking on the verb; this is the phenomenon introduced in 2.4.2 of verb–object agreement restricted to definite objects. This too is part of a wider phenomenon, that of the verb showing agreement with objects which are specified for properties only one of which is definiteness. Of course the direct object is not the only argument with which verbs may agree, and it is interesting to look at verb–subject agreement, and agreement with indirect objects, in the light of what we see in agreement with direct objects. What emerges is that agreement with these arguments too is often limited to a subset of them, defined by the same sort of properties as characterize those direct objects triggering agreement.

5.2.1   *Direct object agreement*

Transitive verbs in Hungarian show distinct "indefinite" and "definite" conjugations, the latter being used when there is a definite direct object, the former otherwise. Intransitive verbs have only the indefinite conjugation. This can be interpreted as meaning that verbs agree for definiteness with direct objects, or that they agree only with definite direct objects. But this agreement indicates only that there is such an object – there is no encoding of its person, number etc.

Interaction with other grammatical phenomena

Verbs also agree with their subjects (both definite and indefinite) for person and number, and the agreement features corresponding to subject and object are fused together into a single agreement morpheme. This is illustrated in the following partial paradigm (Bánhidi, Jókay, and Szabó 1965) and examples:

	indefinite	*definite*
'I read'	olvas-ok	olvas-om
'you read'	olvas-ol	olvas-od
'he/she reads'	olvas	olvas-sa

(29) Olvas-ok   egy könyvet.
      read 1SGSUBJ a   book-ACC
      'I read a book.'

(30) Olvas-om   a   könyvet.
      read 1SGSUBJ-OBJ the book-ACC
      'I read the book.'

The definite conjugation is also used with a null pronominal object: *Olvassa* 'He/She reads it'.

Verb–object agreement is often considered to be less common than verb–subject agreement. But it too may be very widespread if object clitics are taken into account. In French *Pierre le voit* 'Pierre sees him', it is a controversial question whether the clitic *le* is a pronominal element attracted to the verb or an affix generated as such. It is in fact often very difficult to distinguish clitics from agreement affixes, and the syntactic processes underlying the two are not clearly distinguished. Let us consider the case of Macedonian (Lunt 1952, de Bray 1980, Berent 1980, Lyons 1990), in which, as in French, clitics can occur in association with an empty object position – they thus arguably represent agreement with the null pronominal *pro*:

(31) Marija **go**   poznava.
      Marija 3SG-M-ACC knows
      'Marija knows him.'

But, by contrast with French, clitics in Macedonian can be associated with an overt object, full or pronominal. This "clitic doubling" is, however, limited to (and obligatory with) definite objects:

(32) Marija **go**   poznava nego.
      Marija 3SG-M-ACC knows   him
      'Marija knows him.'

(33)   Fatete   **ja**   mačkata.
          catch-IMP 3SG-F-ACC cat-DEF
          'Catch the cat.'

(34)   **Go**   vidov   Grozdana.
          3SG-M-ACC saw-1SG Grozdan
          'I saw Grozdan.'

The clitic encodes agreement in person, number, case and, in the third person, gender.

On this analysis Macedonian closely resembles Hungarian in having verb agreement with definite direct objects only (though with much fuller encoding of agreement features). In French verb–object agreement only occurs with *pro*; note, however, that *pro* is definite (see 5.5 below), so object agreement in French is with a subset of definite noun phrases. Another language showing verb–object agreement in the form of a clitic is Welsh (Sadler 1988). Here agreement is only with personal pronouns, both overt and null – and thus again with a subset of definites (and in fact is only obligatory with non-finite verb forms in periphrastic constructions):

(35)   Gwnaeth Emrys werthu y   llyfr.
          did   Emrys sell   the book
          'Emrys sold the book.'

(36) a.   Gwnaeth Emrys **ei**   werthu ef.
          did   Emrys 3SG-M sell   it
     b.   Gwnaeth Emrys **ei**   werthu.
          did   Emrys 3SG-M sell
          'Emrys sold it.'

Spanish has data superficially similar to that of Macedonian. It is often described as having clitic doubling, varying in extent from one dialect to another, but appearing in some degree in all dialects. In the standard language, direct object doubling is limited to, and obligatory with, strong personal pronoun objects:

(37)   La   quiero   a ella.
          3SG-F love-1SG to her
          'I love her.'

In some other, principally South American, dialects, doubling is available with full noun-phrase objects:

(38)   Lo   vi   a tu   hijo.
          3SG-M saw-1SG to your son
          'I saw your son.'

This doubling differs, however, from what we have seen in Macedonian in the obligatory presence of the preposition *a* before the direct object. Since *a* only occurs with a subset of direct objects (human, specific etc. – see above), clitic doubling is restricted to this same subset.[3] So for (non-standard) Spanish the same parameters which determine object marking also determine verb–object agreement. It has been argued, however, that Spanish does not have clitic doubling – and thus verb agreement with overt objects. Lyons (1990) claims that the clitic in (37) and (38) represents agreement with *pro*, the following prepositional phrase *a ella*, *a tu hijo* being an adjunct or modifier, reinforcing, or clarifying the reference of, the null object argument.

This digression is important because many apparent instances of clitic doubling involve a preposition. But the fact remains that there are many clear cases of true doubling. One of these, Macedonian, shows a strong correlation between doubling and definiteness (provided proper nouns are treated as definite in Macedonian). There is a further complication however; it may be that some apparent instances of object agreement, where the putative agreement morpheme is not especially clitic-like and where no pre-position is required before the associated noun phrase, are nevertheless not true agreement. This is argued to be the case in Chiwewa and other languages by Bresnan and Mchombo (1987), who claim that, while the Chiwewa subject agreement marker represents true agreement, the object marker is an incorporated pronoun. This pronoun is itself the object argument, and the noun phrase associated with it is a topic (see 6.1 below); in other languages this noun phrase may be an adjunct, as suggested above for the Spanish clitic doubling construction.

Finally, there are languages showing object agreement limited not just to definites. Givón (1976) points to Swahili, where the verb agrees with all human objects and definite non-human ones:

(39) a.   Ni-li-mw-ona   yule mtu.
             1SG PAST OBJ see this person
             'I saw this person.'

       b.   Ni-li-mw-ona   mto   mmoja.
             1SG PAST OBJ see person one
             'I saw one person.'

(40) a.   Ni-li-ki-soma   kitabu.
             1SG PAST OBJ read book
             'I read the book.'

       b.   Ni-li-soma   kitabu.
             1SG PAST read book
             'I read a book.'

---

[3] In fact clitic doubling is slightly more restricted than the personal *a*, since it does not occur with pronouns like *alguien* 'someone', *nadie* 'no one', while *a* does.

5.2.2 Indirect object agreement

French, Spanish and Macedonian have, in addition to the direct object clitics discussed above, dative clitics, which can be taken to encode agreement with indirect object arguments. The indirect object, like the direct object, may be null, as in the following examples:

(41)   *French*
         Je lui   enverrai   ce   document.
         I   3SG-DAT send-FUT-1SG this document
         'I will send him/her this document.'

(42)   *Spanish*
         Le   hablábamos   de ese asunto.
         3SG-DAT speak-IMPF-1PL of that matter
         'We were speaking to him/her about that matter.'

(43)   *Macedonian*
         Mu   dadov   edno penkalo.
         3SG-M-DAT give-PAST-1SG one   pen
         'I gave him a pen.'

In Spanish a dative clitic may also co-occur with an overt expression of the indirect object, which, however, requires the preposition *a*. Indirect object *a* is not limited in what noun phrases it may occur with as direct object ("personal") *a* is, so as a result indirect object doubling is not restricted either. But more striking is the fact that indirect object doubling is possible with all noun phrase types in all dialects; thus examples like the following are as acceptable in standard Spanish as in any variety:

(44)   Le   di   un libro al   estudiante.
         3SG-DAT gave-1SG a   book to-the student
         'I gave a book to the student.'

(45)   Le   di   un libro a ella.
         3SG-DAT gave-1SG a   book to her
         'I gave her a book.'

(46)   Le   di   un libro a una vecina.
         3SG-DAT gave-1SG a   book to a   neighbour
         'I gave a book to a neighbour.'

Again, it may be that this is not true clitic doubling – that agreement is with the null pronominal *pro*, which is duplicated by an overt PP. But the fact that this "quasi-doubling" is less constrained for indirect objects is interesting, and probably not unrelated to the fact that, cross-linguistically, agreement of the verb with indirect objects is frequently more prominent than with direct objects. Givón (1976) observes that in Zulu, as in other Bantu languages, dative agreement takes precedence over accusative agreement:

(47) a.   U-**yi**-nige   intoombi isiinkwa.
           3SG-M-NOM 3SG-F-DAT gave girl   bread

     b.   *U-**si**-niga   intoombi isiinkwa.
           3SG-M-NOM 3SG-INAN-ACC gave girl   bread
           'He gave the girl the bread.'

Agreement is only possible with one object, and this must be the indirect object if one is present. Facts like this may relate to the greater prominence given, as we have seen, to animate and human arguments, since indirect objects are much more likely to be human or animate than not, and more likely than direct objects.

Macedonian has genuine indirect object doubling with strong pronouns (a subset of definites). Its limitation to strong pronouns is due to the fact that these are the only overt noun phrase type having dative case forms:

(48)   Mu   dadov   nemu   edno penkalo.
           3SG-M-DAT gave-1SG him-DAT one   pen
           'I gave him a pen.'

With non-pronominal indirect objects, the preposition *na* 'to' must be used, but again, as in Spanish, a clitic may (and in Macedonian must) also occur:

(49)   Mu   dadov   edno penkalo na eden učenik.
           3SG-M-DAT gave-1SG one pen   to one pupil
           'I gave a pen to a pupil.'

As in Spanish, this is arguably not true clitic doubling, given the preposition; but, also as in Spanish, this duplication of a clitic by a PP adjunct is freer than direct object doubling, in that the noun phrase in the PP may be indefinite.

5.2.3 Subject agreement

     Verb–subject agreement is more widespread than verb–object agreement. And in most of the languages so far mentioned it is not constrained by definiteness, animacy etc. But in some languages subject agreement is limited. In Welsh and Irish it is restricted to a subset of definite subjects. Subject agreement in Welsh shows the same limitation as object agreement – to pronominal arguments (overt and null):

(50)   Agoron   (hwy) y   drws.
           opened-3PL they   the door
           'They opened the door.'

(51)   Agorodd y   dynion y   drws.
         opened   the men   the door
         'The men opened the door.'

Irish has almost complete complementary distribution between agreeing ("synthetic")
verb forms and overt subjects; agreement is thus only with *pro* (like object agreement in French). The situation is complicated by the defectiveness of the Irish verb,
as observed in 3.4.2. In each tense paradigm, only some verb forms are synthetic
(showing agreement), and only with these forms is *pro* possible. Otherwise an "analytic" (non-agreeing) form must be used, and the subject must be overt. In the
past tense, for example, there is only one synthetic form, corresponding to first
person plural:

(52) a. Nigh   mé mo bhróga.
         washed I   my shoes
         'I washed my shoes.'
     b. Nigh   sí   a   bróga.
         washed she her shoes
         'She washed her shoes.'
     c. Nigh   na cailíní a   mbróga.
         washed the girls their shoes
         'The girls washed their shoes.'

(53)   Níomar   ár mbróga.
         washed-1PL our shoes
         'We washed our shoes.'

In these languages it is not clear whether definiteness plays a part in the limitation of agreement. The constraint may refer to a subset of definites (a different
subset in each case), or simply to pronominality (Welsh) and non-overtness
(Irish). The latter solution would fail to express the unity of the phenomenon, if
it is one phenomenon.

5.3 Definiteness and animacy

Facts like those discussed in 5.1 and 5.2 have led to the formulation
of the so-called "animacy hierarchy" – a name which is somewhat misleading.
The idea is that different kinds of noun phrase can be ranked in a hierarchy such
that those in a higher place are more favoured by certain grammatical processes
(like agreement and case marking). The principal positions on this hierarchy as
it commonly appears in the literature are as follows (Silverstein 1976, Comrie
1981a, Croft 1990):

First- and second-person pronouns
Third-person pronouns
Proper names
Common nouns with human reference
Non-human animate nouns
Inanimate nouns

Apart from the processes already discussed, number marking offers a good illustration of the significance of the hierarchy (Comrie 1981a, Croft 1990). In many languages only noun phrases which are relatively high in "animacy" show a number distinction; the actual cut-off point varies from one language to another. In Guaraní only first- and second-person pronouns show number marking, in Mandarin Chinese only pronouns (and a few human nouns), in Tiwi pronouns and human nouns, and in Kharia pronouns and animate nouns; in Chukchee all noun phrases show number in the absolutive case, but in other cases it appears obligatorily only on pronouns, proper nouns, and some kinship terms, and optionally on other human nouns, but not on non-human nouns.

Phenomena like object marking and agreement suggest that definiteness needs to be taken into account too, since it often combines with animacy, humanness etc. Either it complements the animacy hierarchy, or it needs to be combined with it to form a more general hierarchy. The operation of the hierarchy in some processes (most notably object marking and verb–object agreement) has been accounted for functionally, in terms of a natural tendency for the subject or agent to be more animate and more definite than the object or patient. Deviations from this natural pattern are then marked morphologically. Hence the morphological marking, either on the noun phrase or, by agreement, on the verb, of objects high in animacy or definiteness. However, the observation that subject agreement too is sometimes limited to noun phrases high on the hierarchy poses a problem for this account.

The concept of the hierarchy is in fact problematic in a number of respects. It is not obvious why proper names and kinship terms should rank higher than human common nouns; *Mary* and *sister* are no more human than *woman*. Similarly, while first- and second-person pronouns nearly always have human referents, third-person pronouns may have too, and third-person pronouns are not in principle any more human/animate/definite than simple definite full noun phrases. It appears that the distinction between pronouns and non-pronominal noun phrases is distinct from, and cuts across, those between human and non-human, animate and non-animate etc. Comrie and Croft say that the animacy hierarchy is actually a complex clustering of distinct parameters: person, noun phrase type, animacy proper, and probably definiteness, with first- and second-person pronouns as the link between at least some of them, since they are pro-nominal, human and definite. It is in fact

yet more complex, since the definiteness sub-hierarchy these writers propose –
definite : specific indefinite : non-specific indefinite – is not uncontroversially a
single continuum. As we saw in 4.2, [± Spec] is arguably an independent parameter cutting across [± Def], so that there are non-specific definites as well as non-
specific indefinites.[4]

Despite the difficulties, particularly that posed by the heterogeneity of the properties grouped together, the notion of a hierarchy, stated informally, does seem to
express some real cross-linguistic generalizations. The question is how to interpret
these generalizations – because the hierarchy is itself merely a presentation of them,
not an explanation. My inclination is to suggest that what we are dealing with is
the subjective prominence or salience, in some sense, of entities in the domain of
discourse. It can be argued that human referents are, in general, more salient in
human perception than non-human ones; definite referents are more to the fore in
our minds than indefinites because, by definition, they are familiar; the referents
of pronominal noun phrases are more salient because the very fact of their being
pronominal means that the speaker takes their referents to be accessible to the
hearer without even the need for description. Languages will then differ as
regards what kinds of noun phrase conventionally count as prominent. But the fact
that there is a considerable amount of flexibility and subjectivity suggests that it is
largely a pragmatic matter and not fully specified in grammars. For more detailed
discussion of the concept of salience in pragmatic analysis see Lambrecht (1994).
Whatever may be the correct approach, it is clear that definiteness and specificity
play a major role in the phenomenon.

5.4   Articles and nominal feature marking

We observed in Chapter 2 a striking divergence among languages as
regards the morphological behaviour of free-form articles. In many languages which
show inflectional material (such as for agreement) on modifying words in the noun
phrase, the definite article is invariable. In other languages the definite article does
carry inflectional material, and in some cases seems to bear the major burden of
it in the noun phrase. The latter state of affairs is worth examining, especially for
languages where article inflection contrasts with a relative lack of such morphology elsewhere in the phrase.

---

[4] The point here is that work in the semantic and pragmatic literature on noun-phrase interpretation seems to show that both definites and indefinites can reveal narrow-scope and non-
referential readings. On the other hand, we have also seen that there is reason to believe languages work as if [± Spec] were hyponymous to indefiniteness; non-specificity (of one or both
types) is morphologically encoded for indefinites in many languages, but apparently never
for definites. Given this, the apparent implication of the proposed sub-hierarchy that [+ Def,
– Spec] ranks higher than [– Def, + Spec] may not be a problem if [+ Def, – Spec] is never
actually a category in languages.

Two languages in which article inflection assumes considerable importance are German and French. In German, genitive singular and dative plural are the only cases normally marked on the noun, and even these are not always encoded:

	'child'	'eye'	'hand'
SG, GEN	Kind-es	Auge-s	Hand
SG, all other cases	Kind	Auge	Hand
PL, DAT	Kind-er-n	Auge-n	Händ-e-n
PL, all other cases	Kind-er	Auge-n	Händ-e

And adjectives only show the full range of cases in the absence of a determiner. In noun phrases of the form determiner–adjective–noun (for certain determiners, including the definite article, demonstratives, and a few others), the adjective shows only a two-way case–number distinction: *-e* indicating nominative singular for masculine nouns and nominative–accusative singular for feminine and neuter nouns, and *-en* for all other cases singular and plural. With some other determiners (including the cardinal article and possessives) which are defective for inflection in the nominative or nominative–accusative singular (depending on the gender), the adjective encodes these case–number combinations in addition. But only the determiner can encode the full range of cases (with some syncretism). An illustrative pair of paradigms follows (with a masculine noun):

	'the little tree(s)'	'my little tree(s)'
NOM SG	der kleine Baum	mein kleiner Baum
ACC SG	den kleinen Baum	meinen kleinen Baum
GEN SG	des kleinen Baumes	meines kleinen Baumes
DAT SG	dem kleinen Baum	meinem kleinen Baum
NOM PL	die kleinen Bäume	meine kleinen Bäume
ACC PL	die kleinen Bäume	meine kleinen Bäume
GEN PL	der kleinen Bäume	meiner kleinen Bäume
DAT PL	den kleinen Bäumen	meinen kleinen Bäumen

In French, although nouns and adjectives are inflected for number, the usual orthographic plural affix *-s* is only pronounced when liaison occurs with a following vowel-initial word, and liaison is limited to certain contexts where the two words involved are syntactically closely linked. Compare *bons livres* [bɔ̃ livr] 'good books' and *bons élèves* [bɔ̃z elɛv] 'good pupils'; only in the second phrase, where the noun is vowel-initial, is the *-s* of the adjective *bons* pronounced. And in neither case is the *-s* of the noun likely to be directly followed by a vowel-initial word sufficiently closely bound to the noun phrase to trigger its pronunciation. What this means is that, apart from irregular plurals (*oeil* [œj] 'eye', plural *yeux* [jø]), and regular plurals formed otherwise than with -*s* (*cheval* [ʃval] 'horse', plural *chevaux* [ʃvo]), number is not in general effectively indicated on nouns and adjectives. Only determiners consistently indicate the number of the noun phrase: *le livre* [lə livr] 'the book', *les livres* [le livr] 'the books'; *la maison blanche* [la mɛzɔ̃ blɑ̃ʃ] 'the white house', *les maisons blanches* [le mɛzɔ̃ blɑ̃ʃ] 'the white houses'. It is a similar story with gender, a category inherent in nouns, and carried to other noun phrase constituents by agreement. Adjectives typically add orthographic -*e* when in agreement with feminine nouns, but this affix is not normally pronounced; with many adjectives its addition causes a preceding "silent" consonant to be pronounced (or, more accurately, it blocks deletion of an underlying consonant), or triggers some other phonological process which effectively distinguishes masculine from feminine: masculine *grand* [grɑ̃] 'big', feminine *grande* [grɑ̃d]; masculine *blanc* [blɑ̃] 'white', feminine *blanche* [blɑ̃ʃ]. But in many other cases, -*e* has no effect: masculine *fier* 'proud', feminine *fière*, both [fjɛr]. The article, however, makes a clear gender distinction between masculine *le* [lə] and feminine *la* [la].

Observations like these have motivated the suggestion that, in some languages, what is usually taken to be a definite article is really a semantically empty bearer of agreement features. This proposal has a long history particularly in relation to French, where the fact that the definite article is used in the usual, unmarked generic construction as well as in simple definites has given the impression that its presence is frequently semantically unmotivated. Foulet (1958) argues that the article has become in Modern French (by contrast with earlier stages of the language) a mere nominality particle, accompanying all nouns except in certain fixed expressions. This idea is taken up by Harris (1977, 1980), who claims that the demonstrative *ce* is in the process of developing into a new definite article, the traditional article *le* serving now as a carrier of inflectional categories for the noun phrase. The proposal is an interesting one, and I will return to discussion of its more general implications in Chapter 9.

There is a second way of interpreting the facts we are considering. The centrality of determiners in the expression of inflectional categories in German and French assumes a particular importance in the context of the DP analysis, without the need to claim that articles are semantically empty. If the article is the head of the phrase, it is natural that it should be the main focus of agreement, attracting the inflectional features of its dependents. This interpretation is consistent with demonstratives being as rich in agreement as the definite article, since demonstratives too are Dets, and therefore heads.

I believe both these interpretations of the inflectional importance of the articles in some languages are mistaken. I reject the second because I do not accept that the category Det is the head of the noun phrase, for reasons we will come to. As for the first interpretation, I have already made the point that the impression that French uses its definite article in a much wider range of contexts than does, for example, English, is due entirely to the fact that the standard generic construction in French is definite.[5] Since definite generics are no more odd than indefinite ones, I take French *le* to be no less semantically motivated generally than English *the*. There is in fact good reason to consider that the centrality of articles in the expression of nominal inflectional features has been overstated. Starting with French, it should first be noted that certain other determiners carry as much inflectional material as the definite article does. The three-way distinction between masculine singular, feminine singular, and general plural, expressed by *le*, *la*, *les*, also appears with the demonstrative *ce*, *cette*, *ces* (as well as with the cardinal article *un*, *une*, replaced by the partitive *des* in the plural). This is not a problem for the DP interpretation, which would see all Dets as possible heads of DP; but it is a problem for the view that *le* is an inflection-bearer rather than a true article. Second, while it is the case that the article (or the determiner more generally) is the principal indicator of the number of a noun phrase, this is not always so of gender. Articles and demonstratives only distinguish gender in the singular, whereas those adjectives that indicate gender (and they are numerous) do so also in the plural: *pendant les grands froids* 'in the cold season', *pendant les grandes chaleurs* 'in the hot season'; *ces pulls blancs* 'these white pullovers', *ces maisons blanches* 'these white houses'. Moreover, in the singular too gender is neutralized with both *le* and *ce* pre-vocalically; *le* and *la* are both replaced by *l'*, and masculine *ce* is replaced by *cet*, with the same pronunciation as feminine *cette*. Gender neutralization also takes place with many adjectives pre-vocalically, but a fair number maintain the distinction. I would conclude that the undeniable importance of determiners in the realization of inflectional categories is simply an incidental consequence of the fact that, since generics are standardly definite in French, it is very rare for noun phrases to occur without a determiner of some kind, whereas adjectives are a purely optional component. But this does not justify the claim that the expression of number and gender is the principal function of the article.

---

[5] Foulet (1958), in common with many writers, makes a distinction between nouns used generically and abstract nouns – the article appearing with both in Modern French: *le beurre* 'butter', *la douleur* 'pain'. In Old French the article would have been used with neither. In the case of *beurre*, the article would only have occurred in simple definite, not generic, use, as in English. In the case of *douleur*, Old French would have used the article when reference was being made to a particular instance of pain, and it is in such use that the article in Modern French is thought of as "semantically motivated"; thus *la douleur de mon coeur* 'the pain of my heart'. Foulet regards this as a "concrete" use of a normally abstract noun. But the point is that the "abstract" use of *la douleur* is simply its generic use; the "concrete" use is just as abstract, but simple definite rather than generic. So what are seen as different uses of *le*, over and above the simple definite use, are really only one – the generic one.

Turning to German, there are two points to make. First, in the sequence determiner–adjective–noun, if the determiner is the cardinal article *ein*, *kein* 'no', 'not a', or a possessive, it is the adjective which shows inflection in the nominative singular masculine (*ein klein-er Baum* 'a little tree') and in the nominative and accusative singular neuter (both *ein klein-es Kind* 'a little child'). Second, in the absence of a determiner, the adjective shows the full inflectional paradigm, with the same affixes as appear on definite determiners: *gut-er Stoff* 'good material' (nominative singular masculine), *voll-er Flaschen* 'full bottles' (genitive plural). The correct descriptive generalization is that the inflectional material appears on the leftmost modifying element, whether it be a determiner or an adjective, except that *ein* etc. cannot accept certain inflections, which then appear further to the right. This means that articles have no special status in the realization of inflectional features.

5.5 Null and implicit noun phrases

The concept of **empty category**, or phonologically null expression, is central to much work in syntax. The empty categories most intensively studied correspond to nominal expressions, that is, they are null noun phrases. As sketched in 1.2.5, three types of noun phrase are distinguished in terms of their behaviour in relation to the binding theory, which establishes one kind of referential dependency: **anaphors** (principally reflexives and reciprocals like English *ourselves* and *each other*), **pronominals** (that is, personal pronouns), and **referential expressions** or **R-expressions** (full noun phrases). Anaphors and pronominals show a rough complementary distribution, in that the former must be bound (have their reference determined) by an antecedent in a certain domain, typically the clause, while the latter may also be bound, but not in this domain. R-expressions are not bound. Now, it is claimed that there is an empty category corresponding to each of these noun phrase types (Chomsky 1981, Aoun 1985). An interesting question is whether the [± Def] distinction applies to them, and if so, whether any of them are inherently [+ Def] or [− Def]. Let us first identify the various types of null noun phrase which have been distinguished.

We have already mentioned *pro*, the null pronominal assumed to appear in the "empty" subject position of null-subject languages, as well as other positions. **NP trace**, the null element assumed to be left behind by NP Movement, is a null anaphor. It occurs, for example, in passive structures, occupying the vacated position of an underlying object which has moved to subject position, and is bound by the moved expression. **Wh-trace**, or **variable**, is a null R-expression. It is the trace left behind when a noun phrase moves through Wh-Movement, not to another argument position, but to the non-argument specifier of CP (complementizer phrase) position. This is the case, for instance, with interrogatives, which are moved to initial position in their (or a higher) clause. The moved expression binds the trace, but since the binding theory is, at least in its earlier versions (though see Aoun 1985), a theory only of "A-binding" – binding by an expression in an argument position – this does not count. The fourth empty category is **PRO**, which is never bound. It is the empty subject of non-finite clauses, as in *Mary wants [PRO to go home]* (where it has *Mary*, in the higher clause, as antecedent). The distribution of *PRO* is accounted for by the theory of "control". For discussion of all these empty categories see Haegeman (1994).

A phenomenon distinct from that of empty categories, but for our purposes worth considering in conjunction with them, is that of **implicit arguments**. These too are nominal "expressions" lacking overt form, but, unlike empty categories, they are usually assumed not to have any syntactic representation; while empty categories are abstract elements present in syntactic structures, implicit arguments are only semantically present (though see Roberts (1987) for the claim that they are also syntactically present). They correspond, for example, to the understood agent of passives with no *by* phrase; so in *Fred was expelled from school at the age of seven*, the implicit argument is the agent of Fred's expulsion.

5.5.1 Pro

In languages where rich agreement morphology licenses a *pro* subject, this null element is nothing more nor less than a personal pronoun, distinguished only by being phonologically empty. It has the interpretation of and is used under the same conditions as personal pronouns, and carries the same features, for person, number etc., these features determining the form of the agreement morpheme. Since, typically, *pro* may correspond to any overt pronoun, it represents the full range of pronominal feature values; for example, in Latin *pro amo* 'I love', *pro* is first person singular, and in *pro amant* 'they love' it is third person plural. Personal pronouns are inherently [+ Def], so *pro* must be definite too. *Pro* can be assumed to occur as direct object in Hungarian *Olvasom* 'I read it'; as complement of an inflected preposition in Irish *orainn* 'on us'; as possessor identified by a personal (possessive) suffix on the noun in Turkish *köyüm* 'my village'. In all these occurrences, the null argument identified by agreement material on the head governing it is understood as a definite pronoun.[6]

In most null-subject languages agreement is with all overt subjects, definite and indefinite, and the same is true of verb–object agreement in many languages. Yet

---

[6] I am assuming here (as suggested in 3.4) that null arguments not identified by agreement are probably not *pro*, though this may be an oversimplification. While Huang (1984) and Raposo (1986) argue that unidentified null arguments in Chinese and Portuguese are variables, Cole (1987) claims that some languages (including Korean) have unidentified *pro*. But unidentified *pro* is not constrained to be definite.

when the argument triggering agreement is null, it is interpreted as a definite pronoun. Consider the following examples of subject–verb agreement in Spanish:

(54)   **Estos hombres** pasa**ron** la mañana en la fábrica.
         'These men spent the morning in the factory.'

(55)   **Cincuenta hombres** pasa**ron** la mañana en la fábrica.
         'Fifty men spent the morning in the factory.'

(56)   *Pro* pasa**ron** la mañana en la fábrica.
         'They spent the morning in the factory.'

In all three sentences the verb morphology (*-ron*) encodes a third-person plural subject. It is triggered by, respectively, definite and indefinite overt subjects in (54) and (55). But in (56), where the subject is null, it can only be interpreted as definite – 'they', not 'some'. This makes it clear that the agreement morpheme on the verb is neutral with respect to definiteness; [+ Def] is inherent in *pro*, not in agreement.

5.5.2 *Traces*

The situation is less obvious with traces, since in general they do not correspond to any overt form as close to them in meaning as are overt pronouns to *pro*. But there is evidence that they are inherently definite. It seems reasonable that they should be; since they are bound by an antecedent, they are anaphoric in the traditional sense that their reference is established from the preceding discourse. This applies as much to wh-trace as to NP trace, a fact recognized most clearly by Aoun's (1985) "generalized binding theory" which disregards the distinction between argument binding and non-argument binding. Being anaphoric in this sense, traces meet the criterion of familiarity.

A number of languages make use of "resumptive pronouns" – overt forms appearing, especially in relative clauses, in the positions where traces appear in other languages. These pronouns are typically the same as personal pronouns, and therefore definite. This strategy exists marginally in many languages, including English, most notably in contexts where a trace is ruled out. This is the case with the subject trace in (57), by contrast with the object trace in (58):

(57)   *This is the man that I was wondering if *t* knew you.

(58)   This is the man that I was wondering if you knew *t*.

But examples like (57) can be rescued by the use of a resumptive pronoun:

(59)   This is the man that I was wondering if **he** knew you.

221

Interaction with other grammatical phenomena

This strategy would be judged substandard by many, but it is widely used. Resumptive pronouns are less acceptable (though they do occur) in contexts where a trace is not ruled out:

(60)   This is the man that I was wondering if you knew **him**.

In many languages in which resumptive pronouns are normal, they only occur, or are only obligatory, for objects of prepositions, not for subjects and direct objects. Persian is an example:

(61)   kitāb-ī   ke kharīdīd
        book ART that bought-2
        'the book that you bought'

(62)   mard-ī   ke shomā bā **ū** sohbat kardīd
        man ART that you   with him talk did-2
        'the man that you spoke with'

But in other languages the distribution is different; in Vata (Koopman 1984), resumptive pronouns only occur (and are obligatory) in subject position after wh-movement:

(63)   àlɔ́ ɔ̀ lē sâká lâ
        who he eat rice WH
        'Who is eating rice?'

(64)   yī   Kòfí lē lâ
        what Kofi eat WH
        'What is Kofi eating?'

Further evidence is provided by languages in which verbs show object agreement with definite objects only. Basri and Finer (1987) discuss Selayarese, in which transitive verbs show prefixal subject marking and suffixal object marking, but only for definite objects:

(65)   la-ʔalle-i doeʔ-iɲɟo i   Baso.
        3 take 3 money DEF ART Baso
        'Baso took the money.'

When the object is indefinite, the verb shows no object agreement and subject marking is suffixal; the verb also takes what the writers term an "intransitive" prefix:

(66)   (a)ŋ-alle-i doeʔ i   Baso.
        INTR take 3 money ART Baso
        'Baso took (sm) money.'

Topicalization of the objects in (65) and (66) gives the following results:

(67)   doeʔ-iɲɟo la-alle i   Baso
        money DEF 3 take ART Baso

222

(68) a.　　*doe?　(a)ŋ-alle-i　i　　Baso
　　　　　　money INTR take 3 ART Baso
　　　b.　　doe?　la-alle i　　Baso
　　　　　　money 3 take ART Baso

The verb now shows the same marking regardless of whether the fronted object
is definite or indefinite, and this marking is that appropriate to a definite object.
There is no object agreement morpheme, but the subject agreement marker is prefixal
and the intransitive marker is suppressed. The conclusion is that the gap left by
movement of a definite or an indefinite noun phrase is treated as a definite object,
though without the person feature to trigger agreement.[7]

5.5.3   PRO

The empty subject of infinitival and gerundive clauses is defined as
a "pronominal anaphor", but appears not to be inherently definite, because it does
not always have an antecedent. It does have in the following examples, where it
is "controlled" by either the subject or the object of the higher clause (depending
on the verb of this clause):

(69) a.　　Jill expects [PRO to arrive late].
　　　b.　　Mary asked me [PRO to wait for her].
　　　c.　　Joe always enjoys [PRO playing the piano].

PRO can also be pragmatically controlled; that is, its reference is fixed not by an
argument in the matrix clause, but by the context. This is the case in:

(70)　　　It wasn't easy [PRO changing the wheel in the dark].

It may be that PRO is definite in these uses, but there is another use where PRO
is not controlled and has a non-specific or generic indefinite interpretation similar to that of the pronoun one. In this use it is known as "arbitrary PRO", or PROarb,
and is limited to non-event contexts:

(71) a.　　It isn't easy [PROarb to learn to ski].
　　　b.　　[PROarb cycling at night without lights] is very dangerous.

5.5.4   Implicit arguments

Perhaps the most general feature of the passive cross-linguistically is
that the agent of the event or action described is not expressed by an argument in
subject position. Passive structures vary in regard to whether the agent may be

---

[7] In a discussion of these data, Hukari and Levine (1989) ask why the gap should be definite,
and claim this must be a language-specific fact since not all languages have a feature [+ Def]
in their syntax. This is begging the question however.

expressed by an adjunct phrase such as is introduced by *by* in English (*Your letter was posted by Fred*), but where such an adjunct is possible it is probably always optional (*Your letter was posted yesterday*). In the absence of a *by* phrase, there is still understood to be an agent, though this has no expression in the sentence, overt or null; this is the implicit argument. Another construction involving an implicit argument is the middle, where, again, it is the expression of the agent that is suppressed. Consider the following examples of the English passive, in (72), and middle, in (73):

(72) a.   That old tree was cut down last week.
      b.   Ann's new novel is widely read.
      c.   The police are frequently bribed.

(73) a.   The new photocopier switches on at the side.
      b.   Ann's new novel reads well.
      c.   The police bribe easily.

In the passive sentences an agent is implied but not identified; it is understood as something like 'someone/some people, it doesn't matter who/I don't know who'. That is, it is a (possibly specific) indefinite. But in the middle sentences the implicit agent is more like 'anyone' or 'whoever wishes/tries to do it' – an arbitrary indefinite very close in interpretation to *one* and *PROarb*.

In a study of constructions involving the clitic *se* in the Romance languages, Lyons (1995a) argues that these languages have two passive constructions, one similar to the English passive, involving an auxiliary and the past participle, the other involving *se* and its variants; thus Spanish *El hierro fue descubierto hace tres mil años* and *El hierro se descubrió hace tres mil años* 'Iron was discovered three thousand years ago'. The Romance middle also involves *se*, and is argued to be simply the passive with the indefinite implicit argument interpreted as arbitrary. The middle is characterized by an aspect constraint, limiting it to non-event contexts, by the presence (generally) of a manner adverbial like *easily*, and by the impossibility of adverbs which imply an agent, like *deliberately*, and it is understood as predicating a property of the subject. Lyons argues that all these characteristics follow from the arbitrary nature of the implied agent. The English passive and the Romance participial passive can also have the agent interpreted as arbitrary, if the aspectual context is appropriate, and are then subject to the same constraints as the middle. Thus (74) has the same interpretation as (73a):

(74)   The new photocopier is switched on at the side.

The point for the present discussion is that the implicit arguments of passive and middle constructions are interpreted as indefinite. In principle, this indefinite has the freedom of indefinites more generally to be either specific or non-specific (assuming an appropriate context), though in languages having a middle construction distinct from the passive it can be constrained to be non-specific.

5.6 Classifiers

Many languages have classifiers as a component of noun phrases. These are related in function to gender systems in that they group nouns into semantic classes, but differ in degree of grammaticalization, being discrete items in contrast with the inflectional agreement categories which frequently encode gender. There are several different types of classifier system, the most common probably being that of numeral classifiers, so called because they occur with numerals, to which they may be affixed. This is the case in Japanese: *Hon no san-satu kaim-asita* (book OBJ three-CLASS bought) 'I bought three books'. Another type is that of noun classifiers, which accompany nouns and do not depend on the presence of a numeral. They are found, for example, in Dyirbal (Dixon 1972), where they distinguish four classes and also encode deictic distinctions, and in Jacaltec (Craig 1986), with twenty-four classes.[8]

In languages having noun classifiers it is generally possible for nouns to occur without them, and Craig considers the possibility that the Jacaltec ones encode definiteness. At first sight this appears plausible, because a common pattern is for a classifier to be used in second and subsequent mentions, the first-mention noun phrase taking the cardinal article *hune?* (also 'one') instead of the classifier. (75) and (76) represent successive sentences in a single discourse:

(75)   Scawilal tu? xil naj hune? ñach'en tz'ulik.
        near   there saw he a   cave   small
        'Near there he saw a cave that was small.'

(76)   Maẍtic'a ch'illax naj yu tz'ulik ch'en   ñach'en.
        never   was-seen he for small CLASS cave
        'He was never seen because the cave was small.'

But classifiers can also appear in indefinite noun phrases. While the typical singular indefinite is *hune?* + noun, a marked alternative is *hune?* + classifier + noun.[9] Craig argues, on the basis of findings by Ramsay (1985), that a referent introduced by

[8] The Jacaltec classifier system is evidently a fairly recent development, since it is lacking in other languages of the Mayan family and most of the forms are either identical to existing nouns (e.g. *ix* 'woman') or reduced forms of existing nouns (*naj* from *winaj* 'man'). They are, however, unstressed when used adnominally.

[9] There is also a third indefinite structure, used for non-specific indefinites in opaque contexts. Here no classifier occurs, and the cardinal article takes a suffixal irrealis marker:

(i)   X?oc' heb' ix   say-a? hun-uj munlab'al.
       started PL CLASS look-for a IRR pot
       'They started looking for a (non-specific) pot.'

the marked indefinite construction is more likely to recur in the following discourse. The use of this construction indicates, then, that the referent is important and is to be paid particular attention. This recalls the English indefinite *this* and a number of other similar phenomena we have encountered. We have also seen that referential prominence or importance for the discourse may be the main factor determining the appearance of a direct object marker in some languages. But like these markers, noun classifiers do not encode definiteness.

5.7 Concluding point

It will no doubt have struck the reader that this chapter has a somewhat negative flavour. It has shown that definiteness plays a part in a wide range of grammatical phenomena, but frequently in a rather imprecise manner. While a number of non-overt syntactic elements can be claimed to be inherently definite (*pro*, trace) or indefinite (implicit arguments), articles have no special role in carrying nominal inflection, and definiteness apparently only comes into verb–argument agreement and object marking as part of a wider, and vague, concept of "prominence". This subsuming of definiteness under prominence may look especially disappointing, since it relegates definiteness to a subsidiary role in phenomena which, widespread as they are, promised to endow it with considerable importance in grammar. But this finding is of major importance in clarifying the nature of definiteness, and will help us identify the real significance of this category in grammar; I think this significance will turn out to be greater than generally suspected.

A distinction is sometimes drawn between semantic and grammatical definiteness, and I have suggested that generics, for example, may be formally or grammatically indefinite in some languages and yet behave in certain ways like definites because they are in some sense semantically (or, better, pragmatically) definite. More generally, the fact of the referent of a noun phrase being familiar, identifiable, or inclusive may not have any formal place in the grammar of a given language; but it may play an important role in language use, perhaps as part of a larger concept of prominence, and function as a trigger for certain grammatical choices. But then there is a grammatical category of definiteness – the grammaticalization of the pragmatic concept, but distinct from it – and it is this category (expressed so far by the feature [+ Def]) which is probably not involved in object marking and agreement. Further evidence for the claim that definiteness is a grammatical category, though based on a discourse or pragmatic concept, will be presented in Chapter 6, and the idea will be developed in Chapter 7 and subsequently.

6
Definiteness effects

At various points in the discussion so far I have observed that certain positions or contexts within sentences or utterances require a noun phrase occurring there to have a particular value of [± Def] (or to be interpreted as having such a value). Restrictions of this kind, termed "(in)definiteness effects", provide the diagnostics for definiteness introduced in Chapter 1. They relate, moreover, to the suggestion that definiteness plays a role in guiding the hearer through the organization of information in discourse, interacting therefore with other concepts and distinctions in the structure of communication. The behaviour of definiteness in its discourse and sentence context is examined in the present chapter.

6.1   Discourse structure

We begin by looking at the place of definiteness in that area of pragmatic theory which has been variously termed "discourse structure", "information structure", "thematic structure", among other labels. It is concerned with the ways in which sentences package the message conveyed so as to express the relationship between this message and its context or background. For discussion see Lambrecht (1994), Vallduví and Engdahl (1996).

6.1.1   The organization of information

The oppositions **topic–comment**, **theme–rheme**, **given–new**, **presupposition–focus** figure prominently in this literature. But the variation in the use of these pairs of terms is considerable. To a large extent they are used interchangeably, though for some writers one opposition closely overlaps with another rather than being equivalent to it; and with each opposition there is variation over whether the terms are taken to denote linguistic expressions or the referents of these expressions. The following remarks represent a synthesis, glossing over much of this variation.

Many sentences (or utterances) can be said to consist of two parts, a **topic** and a **comment**. The topic, typically but not exclusively a noun phrase, represents what the sentence is about. The comment is what is said about the topic. For example:

(1)   The burglar climbed out through a window.

This sentence may be understood as a statement about the individual identified by the description *the burglar*, in which case this is the topic. What is said about the burglar, that he climbed out through a window, is the comment.[1] For more detailed discussion of the notions of topic and "aboutness", see Strawson (1964), Dik (1978), Reinhart (1981).

In the usual case, the comment carries the main informative burden of the sentence. The topic is the point of departure for the message. For this reason the topic is likely to be something the speaker can assume to be in the hearer's present consciousness, having already occurred in the discourse or being part of more general knowledge related to the material in the discourse. As Strawson (1964) puts it, making statements involves giving or adding information about what is a matter of standing current interest or concern. The topic is therefore often characterized as what is **given**, as opposed to the comment which is **new** information. In fact topic–comment and given–new do not coincide exactly, since there can be given material which is not topical. Consider the following sentence:

(2)   The burglar climbed in through the window Jean had forgotten to close.

Taking *the burglar* to be the topic, then the rest of the sentence is the comment. But this comment, while new information, contains a definite noun phrase *the window Jean had forgotten to close* which has perhaps been mentioned before in the discourse and would therefore be given.[2] The important point, however, is that topics are generally given. The topic expression foregrounds something already in the consciousness of the participants in order to make it the point of departure for some new information.

Another concept overlapping with given and topic is **presupposition**. Declarative sentences such as those used so far for illustration in this section can be thought of as answers to implicit *wh*-questions (such as *What did the burglar do?*). In such questions, the part which is not subject to interrogation is presupposed (here, that there was a burglar and that he or she did something). What is not presupposed is in **focus**; the *wh*-expression represents the focus. This presupposition–focus

[1] Note that in this instance the topic is the subject of the sentence, and in the older grammatical and philosophical tradition **subject** and **predicate** were commonly defined as I have defined topic and comment. Indeed the term **predication** is used in something like this sense in much current syntactic work, but "subject", in its usual modern usage as a grammatical concept, is not the same as topic, though the two frequently coincide.

[2] Note that givenness is distinct from the familiarity or identifiability which may underlie definiteness, though again there is considerable overlap. As Chafe (1976) points out, the object noun phrase in *I saw your father yesterday* almost certainly denotes a person well known to the hearer, but if this person is only now being introduced into the discourse then *your father* counts as new information.

partition then carries over to the declarative sentence which answers the question. So the topic, *the burglar*, is presupposed and the comment, *climbed out through a window* for example, is the focus. If, on the other hand, this declarative sentence is thought of as answering an implicit question *Where did the burglar climb out?*, then only *through a window* is in focus, and *the burglar climbed out* is all presupposed and (for some writers at least), topical. The presupposition–focus or given–new partition largely determines the prosodic structure of the sentence/ utterance in many languages, including English, so that new information is stressed and given information less prominent. In fact "focus" is sometimes defined as that part of a sentence which carries the main stress. This lesser prominence characterizing topical, and, more generally, given, content also shows up in the fact that noun phrases of this kind show a strong tendency to be pronominal, provided that their referents are sufficiently salient to permit recovery of their descriptive content.

As well as the possibility, noted above, of the comment containing given information, it is important to observe that the topic need not be given. New information can be made topical, though this possibility is rather constrained (and ruled out in many languages). Consider the following:

(3)   **A man I work with** has won the pools.

The subject noun phrase here may well refer to an individual completely new to the discourse, yet it seems to be a topic. But this is made possible by its considerable descriptive content due to the relative clause. The relative, which links (or **anchors** – a concept discussed by Prince (1979) and Löbner (1985)) the referent to an individual present, the speaker, increases the current interest of the referent. Compare the following:

(4)   **A pensioner** has won the pools.

(5)   **A man** has phoned several times.

Here the subject noun phrases are much less likely to be topics. Indeed there may well not be an element with topic status, the whole sentence being in focus. Not all sentences divide into topic and comment. Particularly in the case of sentences beginning a discourse or section of discourse, there need not be a point of departure expressed. In such cases the implicit question that the sentence can be thought of as an answer to would have minimal presuppositional content (thus something like *What's happened today?* or *Anything to report?*). Certain presentational verbs, which can be used to express the introduction of a new referent into the discourse, particularly favour a non-topic interpretation of their subjects:

(6)   **John** appeared at the window.

(7)   **A surprising event** then occurred.

(8)   **Three strangers** arrived this morning.

A strong tendency has been observed cross-linguistically for topics to be also subjects, comments therefore to coincide with predicates. This is by no means a necessity. In the sentence *Mary drove over the flower bed*, the subject *Mary* could be but need not be topical. If the sentence is taken to respond to the question (implicit or explicit) *Who drove over the flower bed?*, then *Mary* is comment or focus, and this would normally be clear from the prosodic pattern of the sentence. But the point is that in the absence of some indication to the contrary (such as focal stress on *Mary*), the sentence would normally represent a comment on Mary that she drove over the flower bed. This topic–subject identity as the unmarked situation is extremely widespread and probably universal. In some languages, as we will see below, this common tendency is taken further and subjects are largely required to be topics. Some languages, indeed, are "topic prominent" in the sense that topic–comment structure is more evident, superficially at least, than subject–predicate structure, though it is unlikely to be correct that such languages lack a category of subject as some linguists have claimed (Li and Thompson 1976).

It is tempting to relate this subject–topic correlation to the statistical predominance cross-linguistically of sentence-initial subjects. If the topic is the point of departure for the message it is natural that it should come first. Syntactic processes which have the function of singling out the topic frequently involve fronting; this is the case in English with topicalization (*That friend of yours I really don't like*) and left-dislocation (*That friend of yours, I really don't like him*), as well as with topic-introducing frames like *as for, as regards, as far as . . . is concerned*. One might also mention here passivization, in which an underlying complement advanced to subject position is commonly the topic of the sentence. These fronting processes are extremely common in languages, serving either to place non-subject topics in the prominent sentence-initial position or to give additional prominence to a subject topic (for example because it did not figure in the immediately preceding discourse). But care is needed here, and the simple identification of topic with initial position is untenable, for several reasons. First, the numerous subject-second languages show the same tendency for subjects to be topics as do subject-initial languages. Second, it is common (in English for example) for focussed constituents to be placed initially, and indeed the "topicalization" and left-dislocation constructions can be used to give positional prominence to a focussed element as well as a topic. Thus, the examples above might express a reaction to a person recently mentioned or recently present, in which case *that friend of yours* would be a topic; but if they were part of a discussion of who one liked, *that friend of yours* would be the focus. The stress pattern would distinguish the two, but the linear order is the same. Third, topics can also be picked out by right-dislocation structures, in which they occur finally. This is very common in English: *I rather like him, that friend of yours, It's far too expensive for me, this car*. The dislocated expression is certainly not an afterthought, and it is clear from the great frequency and evidently unmarked nature of this construction for many English speakers that its function is not to give the topic the degree of prominence achieved by left-dislocation. The same is true of the similar construction used in colloquial Turkish (Lewis 1967): *Evi büyük, çiftçinin* (house-3SG big farmer-GEN) 'His house is big, the farmer's'). The correct generalization is that subjects, whether or not initial, show a strong tendency to be topical, but that topics, subject or not, can also be picked out by a range of syntactic devices which place them in a peripheral position, with initial position affording greater prominence. See Kiss (1995) for discussion of a type of language, termed "discourse configurational", in which there is a particular structural position for the topic (or for the focus, or for both).

In English, a dislocated topic is picked up by a pronoun (marginally a pronoun possessive) in the main body of the clause: ***That friend of yours, I really don't like him***, ?***Mary, I'm impressed by her car***. This means that the clause is grammatically complete without the dislocated expression, which stands outside it. In topicalization (*That friend of yours I don't like*), by contrast, the fronted expression is integral to the clause, which would be incomplete without it. Topicalization almost certainly involves movement to an initial position, while dislocation (despite this misleading label) does not, the peripheral expression being generated outside the clause. But the resumptive pronoun ensures that the dislocated topic is construed as an argument or other element of the clause; in this connection see Bresnan and Mchombo (1987). In many topic-prominent languages, however, a dislocated topic is not so construed, because it is not picked up in the clause by a resumptive pronoun. It is construed pragmatically as being related to the clause, indeed as being its point of departure, but the clause is semantically as well as grammatically complete without it. Mandarin is usually taken as typifying this phenomenon (Li and Thompson 1976):

(9)   Nèike shù yèzi   dà.
        that tree leaves big
        'That tree has big leaves.'
        'The leaves of that tree are big.'

A more-or-less literal rendering, keeping the dislocation structure, would be hardly acceptable in English: ??*That tree, the leaves are big.*[3] Chafe (1976) characterizes the function of this kind of topic as being to "limit the applicability of the main predication to a certain restricted domain", to set "a spatial, temporal, or individual framework within which the main predication holds", rather than to

---

[3] It could be improved by introducing a resumptive possessive, making the structure conform to the English pattern of left dislocation: *That tree, its leaves are big.* But there is no possessive in the Chinese example (9), and the relationship between the topic and the clause it precedes is by no means always one that can be expressed by a possessive.

say what the sentence is about. Dik (1978) uses the term "theme" for this type of topic as well as dislocated ones and those presented in a frame like *as for*, limiting the term "topic" to expressions forming part of the main predication; so a sentence like *As for Paris, the Eiffel Tower is really spectacular* has both a theme (*Paris*) and a topic (*the Eiffel Tower*). There is probably no need to draw a fundamental distinction between these "Chinese-style" topics and the English type as Chafe and Dik do. Rather, languages vary in the looseness they tolerate in the relationship between the dislocated topic and the sentence. But an important point which the Chinese dislocation structure brings out is that sentences may have more than one topic. For subjects are as likely in Chinese as in other languages to be topics, and since a dislocated topic is additional to a semantically complete subject–predicate structure, the subject in this structure can be a second topic.

Many languages have morphological marking of topic noun phrases. I exemplify from Japanese (Dunn and Yanada 1958) and Korean (Sohn 1994), in which a particle (*wa* and *(n)un* respectively) is postposed to the topic constituent. Both languages also have a subject or nominative particle (Japanese *ga*, Korean *ka*) which cannot co-occur with the topic marker; it thus marks non-topical subjects only, and therefore tends to be associated with focus noun phrases.

Japanese
(10) Koko ni **wa** pen **ga** arimasu.
      here LOC TOP pen SUBJ is
      'There is a pen here.'

(11) Enpitu **wa** asoko ni arimasu.
      pencil TOP there LOC is
      'The pencil is there.'

Korean
(12) Ku totwuk-**un** nay-**ka** cap-ass-ta.
      that thief TOP I SUBJ catch PAST DECL
      'I caught that thief.' 'That thief, I caught him.'

(13) Khal-lo-**nun** ppang-ul ssel-ci mal-ala.
      knife with TOP bread OBJ cutting stop IMP
      'Don't cut bread with a knife.' 'With a knife, don't cut bread.'

Notice the strong tendency in both Japanese and Korean for the topic to be sentence-initial; this is particularly clear in the contrast between (10) and (11).

6.1.2 Information structure and definiteness

Given that topics almost invariably represent given information, it is to be expected that topic noun phrases will frequently be definite. Definiteness and givenness are by no means the same. As already noted, a definite noun phrase can represent new information in that its referent has not already figured in the discourse or is otherwise not salient in the consciousness of both participants; and an indefinite can be given in that its descriptive content has occurred in the discourse, as in: *Would you care for a scone? – I'd love **a scone**, thanks.* Nevertheless, the identifiability which characterizes many definites is often a matter of occurrence in the preceding discourse, and the "familiarity" of many situational or general knowledge definites is often sufficient to afford the mental salience needed for givenness. So the overlap between definite and given is remarkably strong. It is this overlap, and the resultant tendency for topics to be definite, which makes it possible to say that definiteness serves partly to guide the hearer in working out how the information in an utterance is organized. Thus definiteness marking, though probably only where it is accounted for in terms of identifiability, overlaps in function with topic marking. For this reason the two tend not to co-occur in languages; a language will usually have one or the other. For example, Japanese and Korean, with topic markers, do not have definite articles, while English, French, Arabic, with definite articles, do not have morphological marking of topics (though they may have other devices, like prosodic structure, to indicate topic–comment structure). On the other hand, Tzotzil has both, so that a topic noun phrase nearly always has topic marking and a definite article (Aissen 1992). It is important to observe, however, that, in languages with definiteness marking, there is one type of indefinite which occurs readily as topic: indefinite generics. This is presumably because generics are identifiable and readily represent given information. Generics refer to entire ensembles, and these are likely to be familiar to a hearer even though particular instantiations of them might not be.

What is a strong tendency in some languages is obligatory in others, so that many languages require topics to be definite or generic. In Japanese a noun phrase marked with *wa* can only be rendered into English as definite or generic; noun phrases marked with *ga*, on the other hand, can in principle be construed as definite or indefinite. It does not follow, of course, that *wa* is a definite article, or even that a category of definiteness exists in Japanese. Since *wa*-marked noun phrases can be generic, and generics are commonly grammatically indefinite (that is, indefinite in form) in languages that have definiteness marking, the generalization is probably that a topic in Japanese is required to be identifiable – thus pointing to a dissociation of identifiability (or "semantic/pragmatic definiteness", as used in 5.7) and definiteness.

The tendency for topic and subject to coincide is equally a requirement in many languages. In Mandarin and Cantonese, subjects (in the unmarked pre-verbal position) are always topics in the absence of left-dislocation of some non-subject noun phrase, and topics must be definite or generic in interpretation (Li and Thompson 1976, 1981, Matthews and Yip 1994); (14) and (16) show left-dislocated non-subject topics, and (15) and (17) sentence-initial subjects:

Definiteness effects

Mandarin
(14)   Gǒu wǒ yǐjing kàn-guo le.
               dog I   already see EXP ASP
               'The dog I have already seen.'

(15) a.   Nèi-suǒ   fángzi hǎo guì.
               that CLASS house very expensive
               'That house is very expensive.'
       b.   Māo xǐhuān hē   niú-nǎi.
               cat like   drink cow milk
               'Cats like to drink milk.'

Cantonese
(16)   Nī dī   yéh móuh yàhn sīk ge.
               this CLASS stuff no   person know PRT
               'No one knows this stuff.'

(17) a.   Ga   chē jó-jyuh   go   chēut-háu.
               CLASS car block CONT CLASS exit mouth
               'The car is blocking the exit.'
       b.   Māau hóu   jūngyi sihk yú ge.
               cat   much like   eat fish PRT
               'Cats like to eat fish.'

With presentational verbs it is possible to place the subject in post-verbal position, in which case an indefinite interpretation is possible (and more likely), as shown in 2.4.4. To achieve an indefinite interpretation of the agent of a non-presentational predicate, this predicate has to be subordinated to an existential ('there is/are') structure, involving in Chinese the verb 'have':

(18)   *Mandarin*
               yǒu rén   gěi nǐ dǎ-diànhuà.
               have person to you hit telephone
               'Someone telephoned you.'

(19)   *Cantonese*
               Yáuh (yāt) ga   chē jó-jyuh   go   chēut-háu.
               have one CLASS car block CONT CLASS exit mouth
               'A car is blocking the exit.' 'There's a car blocking the exit.'

Where a left-dislocated non-subject topic occurs in these languages, a following pre-verbal subject is still constrained to be definite or generic. This may mean that this subject is a secondary topic, and that the subject position generally is a topic position in Chinese. In fact, direct objects in Mandarin, normally post-verbal and definite or indefinite in interpretation, can be placed pre-verbally (yielding an SOV structure), and then show a strong tendency to be definite or generic:

234

(20) a. wǒ zài mǎi shū le.
   I CONT buy book ASP
   'I am buying the/a book.'
 b. wǒ bǎ shū mǎi le.
   I OBJ book buy PRF
   'I bought the book.'

(The particle *bǎ* accompanies pre-verbal definite or specific objects which denote entities affected by the action of the verb, thus with a theme θ-role.) Again, given that sentences may in principle have more than one topic, it may be that pre-verbal objects are also topics.

A similar state of affairs is found in Lango, with some differences (Noonan 1992). The unmarked constituent order is SVO, and order is rather rigidly fixed, by contrast with Chinese; but any non-subject may be left-dislocated and constitute the topic. The loose linking between topics and the clause found in Chinese does not occur in Lango. A dislocated topic must be construed with some position in the clause, typically a null position (possibly to be analysed as filled by a resumptive *pro*, though only when human is a null verbal object identified by agreement morphology, and then not necessarily if it is third person). Again the topic is constrained to be understood as definite or generic. Where there is no left-dislocated non-subject, the subject is the topic, and clause-initial subjects are definite or generic in the absence of specific marking to the contrary:

(21) àbwòr rwòt támô   nî ènékò.
   lion king 3SG-think-HAB that 3SG-kill-PRF
   'The lion, the king thinks that he killed it.'

(22) dákô òtèdò   rìŋó.
   woman 3SG-cook-PRF meat
   'The woman cooked (the) meat.'

But, by contrast with Chinese, this definiteness requirement applies only to clause-initial subjects, so that a subject following a fronted non-subject topic can be interpreted as definite or indefinite:

(23) lócɔ̀ dákô òmìò   búk.
   man woman 3SG-give-PRF book
   'The man was given a book by the/a woman.'

Moreover, in the absence of left-dislocation or topicalization, a subject, though not having the freedom to occur post-verbally as in Mandarin, can be indefinite, but only if it is accompanied by the indefiniteness marker *-mɔ́rɔ́* (subject to assimilation of the initial consonant to a noun stem-final consonant):

(24)   twòllórô   òkàò   àtîn.
         snake-INDEF 3SG-bite-PRF child
         'A snake bit the child.'

Even the subjects of presentational verbs must be pre-verbal, and since they are almost invariably indefinite in Lango they too usually take -*mɔ́rɔ̂*:

(25)   gwók'kɔ́rɔ̂ tíê   ì ɔ̀t.
         dog-INDEF 3SG-be-HAB in house
         'There's a dog in the house.'

Note that there is no definite article in Japanese, Mandarin, Cantonese or Lango. In the last three languages, which do not make regular, obligatory use of morphological topic marking, demonstratives are used in many instances where English would have *the*. More extensive use of demonstratives is normal in languages with no definite article, but it still represents demonstrative use. Simple definiteness is not marked in these languages, and the constraints on interpretation of topics and subjects outlined relate to what I have termed "semantic/pragmatic definiteness". It is clear that this notion plays a significant part in many languages which lack formal marking of definiteness, but, as pointed out, it seems to be broader than the grammatical definiteness associated with lexical or morphological marking by an article, since it embraces all generically interpreted noun phrases. For further discussion of the interaction of definites, demonstratives, and other forms of reference with aspects of discourse structure, see Fraurud (1990), Gundel, Hedberg and Zacharski (1993), and the papers in Fretheim and Gundel (1996).

6.2   Existential sentences

It is in relation to existential sentences that the term "definiteness effects" is most commonly used, following the major study of them by Milsark (1977, 1979). In its narrowest sense the label "existential sentence" denotes the *there is/are* construction (as in *There is a fly on the wall* or *There are sm flies on the wall*) and its equivalents in other languages. I shall refer to these as the "central" existential construction. The crucial observation, made long ago in descriptive grammars and studied in detail by Milsark and other recent writers, is that the noun phrase following *there is/are* is usually indefinite. It is important to distinguish the *there* of this construction from the deictic locative adverb *there* (meaning 'in/to that place'). The latter is a fully meaningful expression, it typically carries (like demonstratives, to which it is semantically related) a non-zero degree of stress, and it has a full (commonly diphthongal) vowel – a normal RP pronunciation being [ðɛə]. Deictic *there* accompanying the verb *be* readily accepts a post-verbal definite noun phrase or proper noun: *There's the man you're looking for, behind those bushes, As she turned the corner she froze; there was Joe, staring straight at her.* Existential *there*, by contrast, is not obviously meaningful, and is usually taken to be a pleonastic, a semantically empty filler of subject position. It is typically unstressed, can undergo phonological reduction (with pronunciations like [ðəz] for *there is* and [ðərə] for *there are*), and it does not readily admit definites or proper nouns in post-verbal position. To make clear the distinction between these two items, I will henceforth follow the practice already adopted for the *some–sm* distinction, and represent the existential pleonastic as *thr*.[4]

The *thr be* construction alternates with a structure without *thr* in which the noun phrase itself appears in subject position: thus *A man is at the door* corresponding to *Thr is a man at the door*. This construction, unlike *thr be*, readily accepts definites; indeed it is indefinites that seem somewhat less felicitous in this case. *Thr is a man at the door* is generally preferred to *A man is at the door*, though *The man is at the door* is perfectly good. Notice that the preference for a definite argument in this construction without *thr* amounts to a preference for a definite in subject position, and it seems natural to relate this to the similar preference, even requirement in many languages, discussed in 6.1.

There is an extended sense of the term "existential sentence", embracing sentences with "presentational" verbs – mostly verbs which introduce an entity into the discourse. Examples of presentational verbs are: *appear, occur, emerge, arise, ensue, arrive, come, follow, remain*. These verbs can also take pleonastic *thr* as subject in English, and the post-verbal argument also shows the definiteness effect:

(26) a.   The captain appeared at the door.
     b.   ?There appeared the captain at the door.

(27) a.   A disturbance occurred soon afterwards.
     b.   There occurred a disturbance soon afterwards.

The analysis of existential sentences and of the definiteness effect holding in them has been central to accounts of definiteness since Milsark's discussion, and this effect has even been widely regarded as defining for definiteness. Only a small selection of the large literature can be examined here; some major discussions are: Rando and Napoli (1978), Safir (1985), the papers collected in Reuland and ter Meulen (1987), Lumsden (1988).

6.2.1 The phenomenon

There is a certain amount of cross-linguistic variation as regards the verb appearing in the central existential construction. Many languages are like English

---

[4] French distinguishes 'there is/are' and 'thr is/are' as *voilà* and *il y a*.

in using the copula 'be': German *es ist/sind*, Italian *c'è, ci sono*, Russian *jest'*.[5] Others use 'have': French *il y a*, Cantonese *yáuh*; Spanish uses a form of the auxiliary *haber*, descended historically from the possessive verb but now otherwise mainly used to form the perfect tense. Other verbs too occur; German has *es gibt*, with 'give', as well as *es ist/sind*. The argument noun phrase is frequently in subject or nominative form where the verb is 'be' (though commonly instrumental in Russian), but with other, apparently transitive, verbs, it is generally in an object or accusative form; in a single language, German, compare *Es ist ein Mann* (with nominative) and *Es gibt einen Mann* (with accusative) 'There is a man'. It appears, therefore, that the single argument is a complement, making the structure an unaccusative one. In languages like English and French which require overt subjects, the subject pleonastic is overt. It is null in null-subject languages, as would be expected. Other factors may intervene here, as in German where the pleonastic is only obligatorily overt where this is necessary to ensure that a main clause meets the requirement that the verb be in second position. As well as the possible pleonastic subject, there occurs in some languages in the existential construction an additional particle of locative origin, like French *y* 'there' in *il y a* (and the similar Spanish *-y* occurring only in the present tense form *hay*).

The complement noun phrase is itself commonly followed by a further expression which seems to be predicated of it. This may be a locative prepositional phrase (*Thr's a dog **on the lawn***) or a non-finite verb phrase (*Thr's a man **waiting to see you***), among other possibilities. This phrase together with the noun phrase is termed the "coda" by Milsark. The question of its structure, including whether it is a constituent, has been much debated. Williams (1984) claims the coda is an NP. Safir (1985) argues that it is a "small clause" and complement of the existential verb.[6] It may be that the status of the coda in fact varies cross-linguistically; Chung (1987) claims that it is NP in Chamorro because this language does not have small clauses, while Huang (1987) argues against an NP analysis for Mandarin. The structure as a whole may express a variety of things: presence in a location, existence (especially where the coda is a noun phrase alone, as in *Thr is a God*), or whatever predication is expressed by the post-nominal phrase in the coda. A further contentious issue is whether the verb, *be* etc., has semantic content, especially where there is a predicate in the coda.

---

[5] Russian also commonly uses a null form in the present tense, in keeping with the fact that the copula *byt'* 'be' is usually null in the present and that Russian does not have overt pleonastics.

[6] A small clause is a clause-like constituent comprising subject and predicate, but with no tense element. It is usually taken to have the category status of its predicate, so that if the predicate is PP, as in *a dog **on the lawn***, the whole small clause is a PP. See Radford (1988, chapter 6) for discussion.

An alternation corresponding to that noted in English between *Thr is a man at the door* and *A man is at the door* is probably limited to languages in which the central existential verb is 'be', but even in such languages it is not general. In languages using 'have' or 'give' or some other verb, the central existential construction may alternate with a structure in which the argument appears as subject of a clause with 'be' as verb (Spanish *Hay un hombre a la puerta* 'Thr is a man at the door', *Un hombre está a la puerta* 'A man is at the door'). What the definiteness effect amounts to, for languages with articles and therefore clearly possessing a category of definiteness, is that a noun phrase subject of 'be' may be allowed to be definite or indefinite (in languages that allow indefinite subjects), but the complement noun phrase of the existential verb is normally indefinite.

But the complement noun phrase is by no means invariably indefinite. It is recognized that definites and proper nouns are readily accepted with what is termed a "list reading":

(28) A: What have we got to eat?
     B: Well, thr's the chicken, the bacon, and that cheese you bought.

In this sense a list can be of one item:

(29) A: Is thr anyone still in the garden?
     B: Thr's Fred by the pond.

There are other specialized uses of the existential construction which accept definites and proper nouns easily, such as the colloquial French *Y a Jean qui t'attend* 'Jean's waiting for you' (literally 'Thr's Jean who is waiting for you').

In fact the prohibition on definites in non-list uses in English is far from categorical, and is subject to considerable variation between dialects and individuals – a point neglected in most of the literature, which presents the data as far more certain than they are. For many speakers the following are perfectly good:

(30) a.   Thr's John waiting at the door for you.
     b.   Thr's that man on the phone again.
     c.   Go and open the door; thr's the postman coming up the drive.

It is indeed often hard to decide whether a particular acceptable occurrence of a definite is a list use or not, since this use is not clearly defined; is (31) a list use?

(31) A: I'm starving.
     B: I'm afraid thr's only the cheese in the fridge.

There is certainly a tendency against the use of definites in the existential construction, and this tendency (like that against indefinite subjects observed above) is stronger in some languages and varieties than in others.

The same tendency (or, in many languages, constraint) is to be observed in languages lacking definiteness marking. Huang (1987) shows that in Mandarin' proper nouns and nouns modified by a demonstrative are excluded in the complement of the existential construction, and bare noun phrases are interpreted as indefinite and non-generic. The definiteness effect is, in this form, very general in languages lacking articles. This means either that these languages do have the feature [± Def], or that the constraint is about semantic/pragmatic definiteness. The latter is more likely, since even in English this definiteness effect relates not only to grammatically definite expressions, but also indefinite generics; bare noun phrases (which I claim are not definite) and singular indefinites must normally be interpreted non-generically after *thr is/are*.

Turning to the non-central existential sentences, there are several classes of verbs involved in English, not all clearly presentational, and not all showing the same behaviour. Milsark distinguishes an "inner verbal" structure in which the argument noun phrase stands directly after the verb and before any predicate in the coda, and an "outer verbal" structure in which the argument follows the predicate:

(32) a.   Thr appeared a policeman at the door.
     b.   Thr arrived a bus in front of the house.
     c.   Thr rose a great cheer from the crowd.

(33) a.   Thr walked into the room a tall man.
     b.   Thr jumped from the wall three children.
     c.   Thr sat in the doorway a huge dog.

The clearly presentational verbs illustrated in (32) occur readily in the inner verbal structure (and in the outer verbal one: *Thr appeared at the door a policeman*). Verbs of movement and location like those in (33) are better in the outer verbal structure, though location verbs work considerably better in the inner verbal structure than do movement verbs:

(34) a.   ?Thr sat a huge dog in the doorway.
     b.   ??Thr walked a tall man into the room.

The behaviour of the different classes of verb in these frames shows considerable uncertainty; see Lumsden (1988) for discussion. The verbs which occur easily in the inner verbal structure (32) are unaccusatives; their single argument is non-agentive, whether in subject or complement position, and there is no use with an additional, agentive, argument (by contrast with ergative verbs like *break*):

(35) a.   Three students arrived.
     b.   Thr arrived three students.
     c.   *We arrived three students.

Verbs of motion like *walk*, which are barely, if at all, possible in the inner verbal structure, are true intransitives, with an agentive argument. The inner verbal structure seems to require a non-agentive verb. Again, the distinctions drawn here are not absolutely clear, but they seem to be valid in essence. The outer verbal construction is said to admit a definite argument provided it is "heavy":

(36)   Thr walked into the room the man I had spoken to earlier.

The assumption here is that *the man I had spoken to earlier* is generated in subject position (in keeping with its agentive status) and moved because of its heaviness, probably to adjoin to VP. In the unaccusative inner verbal construction, the single argument, being non-agentive, is not an underlying subject but is generated in complement position. This structure is much more strongly subject to the definiteness restriction. Again this is equally true of languages lacking definiteness marking, such as Zulu (Ziervogel, Louw and Taljaard 1967). In (37a) the verb shows agreement with the argument in subject position (which is ambiguously definite or indefinite), but in the unaccusative structure (37b) the verb is in impersonal form and the post-verbal argument must be understood as indefinite:

(37) a.   Isalukazi   sihlala lapha.
           old-woman lives   here
           'The/An old woman lives here.'
     b.   Kuhlala isalukazi   lapha.
           live   old-woman here
           'An old woman lives here.'

Given the close similarity, the central existential construction is also plausibly analysed as unaccusative (though there may be problems with this treatment for the 'have' and 'give' verbs used in some languages, given that these also have a transitive use like ergatives).

6.2.2 *Explanatory accounts*

In the first major study of the phenomenon, Milsark (1977, 1979) proposed an explanation in terms of semantic incompatibility between a definite complement and the existential structure. The claim is that *thr be* is an existential quantifier which requires a variable to bind.[7] But definites are themselves

---

[7] This is on the basis of the following contrast:

(i)   Thr were three men believed to have been in the garden.
(ii)   Three men were believed to have been in the garden.

The truth of (i), in which *thr be* occurs, unlike that of (ii), is claimed to depend on the existence of three men. So *thr be* makes a claim of existence about the entity described by the complement noun phrase.

quantificational, so a definite noun phrase complement does not provide a variable free for binding. Indefinites, on the other hand, are not necessarily quantificational, so may provide a variable that the existential quantifier can bind. Milsark classifies determiners and noun phrases, or at least occurrences or uses of them, as "strong" and "weak", on the basis of their behaviour in the existential construction. The strong ones, excluded from existential sentences, are quantificational, and include definites like *the* and *that*, universals like *all*, personal pronouns, generics, and quantifiers like *most*. They thus come close to the range of "semantic/pragmatic definites". The weak ones, essentially non-generic indefinites, which are acceptable in existential sentences, involve cardinality rather than quantification. As cardinals, they are compatible with the quantifier in *thr be*. But certain cardinality determiners, notably the vague ones *some/sm* and *many*, also have a quantificational use, in which they express not simply a quantity, but a vague proportion of some already given set. For example:

(38)   About a dozen students and three or four lecturers turned up for the discussion. **Some students** wanted to move to a smaller room.

Some students here means some of the students already mentioned; the determiner (which in this use must be *some* as opposed to *sm*) expresses a partitive relationship between two sets rather than simply the cardinality of one set. Indefinites used in this way are therefore strong and, interestingly, behave like definites in relation to the existential construction; in *Thr were some/many students in the street outside*, the indefinite determiner can only be interpreted as cardinal. The definiteness effect in existential sentences is for Milsark, therefore, a "quantification restriction". As for the list use, which permits strong noun phrases, Milsark suggests the list itself counts as the argument of *thr be* for semantic purposes, so the quantificational nature of any members of this list is irrelevant.

Safir (1985) offers a syntactic account, within the theory of binding outlined in 1.2.5 and 5.5.[8] Safir takes the post-verbal noun phrase in the English *thr be* construction to be in nominative case (as we have seen is typical of 'be' existential constructions). But since nominative case is assigned to subject position by the inflectional element of the clause, this post-verbal noun phrase must be assumed to be associated with subject position. This association is expressed by "co-indexation" between the noun phrase and the pleonastic subject *thr*. Nominal expressions linked

---

[8] Recall that the binding theory consists of three principles. Principles A and B specify, respectively, that **anaphors** must be and **pronominals** may not be bound within a particular syntactic domain; **R-expressions** (full noun phrases essentially, which are referentially independent) are accounted for by Principle C, which says they may not be bound at all. The syntactic domain involved (typically the minimal clause) is termed the "governing category" of the expression in question. Binding, while accounting for referential dependence, is itself a configurational concept: the binder is co-indexed with and c-commands the bound expression.

in this way constitute a "θ-chain": they share a single θ-role and form in effect a single discontinuous argument. But, unusually, in this case the lexical element, the semantically full noun phrase, is c-commanded by the semantically empty element *thr*. This makes the pleonastic the "head" of the chain, when normally the semantically full expression should be the head. Safir terms such a chain "unbalanced". The noun phrase is in effect bound by the pleonastic (since binding is formally defined in terms of co-indexing and c-command), and, moreover, bound within its governing category. The noun phrase is therefore apparently behaving like an anaphor, when in fact it is an R-expression, subject to Principle C of the binding theory. To put this in non-technical terms, the full noun phrase is in a syntactic configuration which should require it to be interpreted as referentially dependent on the (semantically empty) pleonastic, when in fact full noun phrases are not so interpreted. This violation of Principle C should render the structure ungrammatical, but in fact it is perfectly good as long as the noun phrase is indefinite. Safir's explanation is that, at S-structure, indefinites are optionally exempt from Principle C. They may, therefore, be bound like anaphors; this is because indefinites are essentially predicative, and "less referential" than definites. In later work (Safir 1987) he proposes replacing Principle C of the binding theory (which says that an R-expression is free, that is, not bound) by a "Predication Principle", which says that a potential referring expression is a predicate or else free. This permits the indefinite noun phrase in the existential construction to be bound, because, Safir argues, it is predicative rather than argumental.

There are many difficulties with this account. As Lumsden (1988) notes, specific indefinites are perfectly good in existential sentences, though they are fully referential rather than predicative. The account offers no explanation for the definiteness restriction in languages where the complement noun phrase of the existential construction is accusative rather than nominative (essentially languages where a verb other than 'be' is used, like German and Spanish). Accusative case should be assigned directly to the complement noun phrase by the verb, and there is therefore no obvious reason to assume co-indexing with the pleonastic subject to produce the crucial unbalanced chain; for discussion see Reuland (1983). A further problem is the non-absoluteness of the data, with definites occurring in the construction much more readily than is usually acknowledged. It is widely accepted that English *be* is ambiguous between a "predicational" sense (as in *John is a fool* or *Ann is very clever*) and an "identificational" sense expressing identity of reference between two arguments (*John is the president, Ann is the author of this book*). Safir claims that the list reading of *thr be* involves identificational *be*, and that only the predicational *thr be* construction is subject to the definiteness effect. But, as noted above, definites are often acceptable in *thr be* sentences that are not obviously list uses. In this connection, the discussion in Huang (1987) of the

complexities of the definiteness effect in existential sentences in Mandarin is interesting. Huang shows, for example, that non-central existentials with unaccusative
verbs show the definiteness effect in main clauses and assertive contexts, but not
in non-assertive subordinate clauses. Central existentials, with *you* 'have', show
the definiteness effect when the subject is null (presumably with a null pleonastic) but not when an overt topic occupies subject position:[9]

(39)   *You-mei-you zheben shu zai zheli?
             have not have this   book at here
             'Is thr this book here?'

(40)   Zheli you-mei-you zheben shu?
             here have not have this   book
             'Is thr this book here?'

Moreover, the complement noun phrase in (40), while formally definite in that it
has a demonstrative modifier, must be understood as semantically indefinite, with
a "variety" reading; that is, the question in (40) is not about the presence of a particular book, but about the presence of a copy, any copy, of a particular book. But
this indefinite, variety interpretation does not suffice to rescue (39).

Perhaps the major difficulty facing a syntactic account is that of attempting to
characterize the definiteness effect data in syntactic terms. The acceptability of
(40) depends on the indefiniteness of one interpretation of a kind of noun phrase
that would normally be treated as definite. But definiteness (at least simple definiteness) is not encoded morphologically or lexically in Mandarin, and versions of
the definiteness effect in existentials hold in many languages lacking definiteness
marking. And in languages that do have definiteness marking, the definiteness effect
excludes certain noun phrases indefinite in form, like indefinite generics in
English. The definiteness effect constrains the occurrence of a class of noun phrase
characterized in semantic or pragmatic, not syntactic, terms.

Higginbotham (1987) proposes a semantic account, and Lumsden (1988) a mainly
pragmatic one. Higginbotham takes the noun phrase following *thr be* to have the
interpretation of a sentence, in which the determiner applies to a propositional
function represented by the descriptive portion of the noun phrase. Thus, in the
example *Thr is no justice* the quantifier *no* combines with the propositional function
provided by *justice*. It is the truth of this propositional function that is at issue in
the interpretation of the sentence, rather than *justice* being the expression that
limits the domain of the variable bound by the quantifier. There is in fact no propositional function specifying the domain of this variable, so the quantifier must be

[9] I follow Huang's transcription, in which tones are not shown, in his examples. Huang assumes
that the subject position is underlyingly empty in both (39) and (40), but that a fronted locative topic such as *zheli* in (40) is moved into subject position.

"unrestricted"; see McCawley (1981) for explanation of the distinction between restricted and unrestricted quantification. Higginbotham hypothesizes that only indefinite determiners, which are adjectival, can be unrestricted. The proposal that the noun phrase is interpreted as a sentence rules out "singular terms" such as proper names, since these are taken not to have a quantifier-variable structure; and definite descriptions are ruled out by the hypothesis that definite determiners cannot be unrestricted quantifiers. Higginbotham proposes, moreover, that sentences contain an "E-position" in their logical representation, where *e* is a variable ranging over events and states. This variable satisfies the single argument of the verb *be*, which is claimed to be a predicate true of everything. The analysis is straightforwardly extended to existentials with unaccusative verbs by treating these too as being predicated of *e*.

Lumsden (1988) takes the coda of existential sentences to be typically a small clause, and thus to have propositional status. He argues that the *thr be* construction represents existential quantification over this, and that the small clause proposition is interpreted as a "neutral description" rather than a "predication"; by "predication" he means a sentence with topic–comment structure, and a neutral description is a sentence which does not have this structure. Following Burton-Roberts (1984), Lumsden claims that definite, and, more generally, strong noun phrases in subject position are necessarily topics. This means that a strong noun phrase in the subject position of the small clause would impose a predication interpretation, which is incompatible with the requirement that the construction consist of quantification over a neutral description; this is the definiteness effect. Lumsden regards the list use as semantically the same as the standard use, the special interpretation, in which a definite is acceptable, being derived by implicature. The list use involves a coda with noun phrase rather than small clause status. The noun phrase cannot be interpreted as a predication, so its definiteness does not produce a violation of any semantic constraint and the sentence is well-formed. But the nominal coda presupposes the existence that *thr be* asserts, so the sentence is, if taken literally, uninformative. This leads the hearer to derive the list interpretation.

Holmback (1984) also takes an interpretative, pragmatic approach to the list use, rejecting any syntactic or semantic definiteness effect. She regards the existential construction as having the function of introducing a new entity into the discourse. This means that if the new entity is introduced in the form of a definite noun phrase, the inclusiveness which she takes to characterize definiteness must not be relative to the preceding discourse or the immediate situation. Provided the referent is inherently unique or meets the condition of inclusiveness relative to some other pragmatic domain, so that it can still count as new to the discourse, a definite is acceptable. She claims that this is the case with list uses.

In summary, existential sentences show, on the face of it, a definiteness effect, and various attempts have been made to account for it in syntactic and semantic terms. Other writers argue that there is no restriction on the occurrence of definites in the existential construction, only constraints on their interpretation stemming from the meaning of *thr* + verb. But whatever kind of constraint is at work, it is not based on definiteness in the limited sense of a noun phrase with definiteness marking, even if one takes "strong", quantificational determiners like *all*, *every*, *most* to be definite. Cardinal determiners like *many*, *three*, when used with a partitive implication, count as strong for this definiteness effect, as do bare nominals like *dogs* and simple indefinites like *a dog* used generically. There are even some clearly definite noun phrase types which do not always trigger the definiteness effect, like the Mandarin example (40) with a variety reading and certain uses of superlatives in English to be considered below in 6.3. The definiteness effect, whatever it is, applies to some semantic or pragmatic grouping of noun phrase types or uses which largely includes but also overlaps with those marked as grammatically definite in some languages. Given this, it is more likely to be a semantic or pragmatic constraint than a syntactic one. It has much in common with the constraint on indefinite subjects or topics examined in 6.1; that too is a strong cross-linguistic tendency, stricter in some languages than in others, and also involving something broader than grammatical definiteness.

6.3 Other definiteness effects

A great many putative definiteness effects have been pointed to in the literature, and some, such as the diagnostics for definiteness used in Chapter 1, have been mentioned in the present work. Some of these, and the extent to which what is at issue really is definiteness, are examined here.

6.3.1 Superlatives

It is a general fact that languages which have definiteness marking use it with superlatives: *the cleverest boy*, **a cleverest boy*. And it is clear that what is involved here is definiteness in the narrow, grammatical sense, as indicated by the obligatory presence of the definite article, not the broader notion of strong noun phrase nor a semantic/pragmatic concept of definiteness. In fact not only are strong determiners like *all*, *most*, and cardinal determiners like *some* in their quantificational use, excluded with superlatives (**all/every/most/some/many cleverest boy(s)*), but so too are demonstratives (**that cleverest boy*). Apart from the definite article, only possessives among the definite determiners are possible (*my cleverest student*), presumably because the definiteness of DG possessives is that of the definite article, "simple" definiteness. Some other modifiers, notably

246

first and *next* in English, share much of the behaviour of superlatives, and it can be no accident that these forms are of superlative origin.

Superlatives are discussed in detail by Hawkins (1978), who claims that a uniqueness or inclusiveness element in their meaning accounts for the definiteness effect they display. Superlativeness means having some property to an extent to which no other objects have it. For example, (41) means that no individuals other than Sarah and Elinor satisfy the description *prettiest girl at the party*:

(41)   Sarah and Elinor were the prettiest girls at the party.

An indefinite determiner, or indeed one of the strong determiners which do not entail inclusiveness, with a superlative would imply that there are other entities with the same degree of the property in question, and a logical contradiction would result.[10] But this account does not seem to be fully adequate. In relation to (41), Elinor can be described as *one of the prettiest girls at the party*, but then why not as **a prettiest girl at the party*? Similarly, given that one can say *I talked to a/one student who was cleverer than all the others*, why not **I talked to a/one cleverest student*?

It is well known that English superlative forms with *most*, as opposed to *-est*, can have a non-superlative sense, equivalent to *very* or *extremely*, and in this use they can be indefinite: *I met a most intriguing girl at the party*. But even with the definite article, both *most* and *-est* superlative forms can be used fairly readily in existential sentences:

(42) a.   Thr is the most intriguing girl in the garden.
     b.   Thr is the strangest man in the drawing room.

This possibility, apparently violating the definiteness effect found with existential sentences, is usually taken to be due to the superlative having the *extremely* reading. But this does not explain it. As just pointed out, *most* with this sense accepts the indefinite article, and in (42a) *the* has been chosen over the alternative *a*; if *the most intriguing* in this sentence is not fully superlative, it is certainly fully definite. Consider further the following:

(43) a.   Thr's the strangest man I've ever met in the drawing room.
     b.   Thr was the biggest frog you can imagine sitting beside the pond.

Even if these are not meant to be taken quite literally, they can only be interpreted as superlative uses of *-est*, and this suggests that the adjective phrases in (42),

---

[10] Hawkins notes that there are some non-inclusive uses of superlative forms, like *a best buy* and *a first course in German* (which allow the existence of other best buys and first courses in German), which can be indefinite.

Definiteness effects

with *the* rather than *a* (equally possible in (42a)), are also in fact superlative rather than *extremely* uses. But these examples contrast with the following:

(44)   ?Thr's the brightest student in the class leading the seminar today.

It appears that superlatives, though formally definite, only behave like definites in existential sentences when they are intended literally. For discussion see Rando and Napoli (1978) and Lumsden (1988: 176–9). If the non-literal ones are semantically indefinite, it is clear that a distinction must be made between grammatical and semantic definiteness, and that the definiteness effect in existential sentences is about the latter.

6.3.2   PP-extraposition and *any* opacity

Safir (1985) discusses two tests for definites which are particularly interesting in the context of the existential construction, because, he claims, they draw exactly the same distinction among types of noun phrase. It follows that the "definiteness" relevant to the definiteness effect of existential sentences is a genuine, independently motivated semantic category.

The first test, from Guéron (1980), involves PP-extraposition; the noun phrase left behind by this process must be indefinite. Safir uses the following sentence frame to illustrate:

(45)   X was/were sold on linguistic theory.

The position X here may be filled by *a book, three books, many books, more books* etc., but not *the book(s), John's books, all (the) books, most books* etc.

The second test involves *any* in the scope of negation. Construal of *any* with a negative outside the noun phrase is claimed to be blocked in the case of definite noun phrases; these are thus opaque for polarity *any*, while indefinites are transparent. Safir's illustrative sentence frame, designed to abstract away from certain complications, including one posed by a possible generic interpretation of the noun phrase, is the following:

(46)   John didn't expect X with any fresh eggs in it/them to arrive at 3.00 today.

X may be replaced by *a basket, three baskets, many baskets* etc., but not *the basket(s), Bill's baskets, every basket* etc.

Safir does not explain these distributional differences between definite and indefinite (or strong and weak) noun phrases beyond suggesting a link with the "more referential" nature of the former. But the tests are interesting if, as claimed, they closely complement the existential construction. The main difficulty, as more generally in discussions of definiteness effects, is the reliability and firmness of some

248

of the grammaticality judgments. But to leave this aside, Safir makes the important point that bare nominals interpreted generically count as definite on these tests, and demonstrates the point as follows. He shows that noun phrases like *men with any sense*, in which *any* is not in the scope of negation, must be understood generically, and then applies the PP-extraposition test to such generics:

(47) a.   Whenever there are jobs like these available, secretaries usually apply with good credentials.

     b.   *Whenever there are jobs like these available, secretaries usually apply with any ambition.

While *secretaries with good credentials* is ambiguous between a generic and a non-generic indefinite reading, extraposition as in (47a) imposes the latter reading. But *secretaries with any ambition* can only be understood generically, so extraposition as in (47b) is not possible. But notice that the same applies to overtly indefinite noun phrases with the same *any*, also necessarily understood generically, such as *a secretary with any ambition*:

(48)   *Whenever there are jobs like these available, a secretary usually applies with any ambition.

Again the point is clear that the class of noun phrases characterized as definite by these effects is a semantic class, and that grammatical definiteness, as expressed by articles, is something distinct.

6.3.3 *Property predication*

Milsark (1977) notes that indefinite or weak noun phrases can occur as the subjects of predicates that assign states, but not of predicates that assign properties:

(49) a.   A man is injured.
     b.   A man is drunk.

(50) a.   *A man is intelligent.
     b.   *A man has red hair.

A man here must, of course, be interpreted non-generically. Strong noun phrases are not restricted in this way: *The/Every man is drunk, The/Every man has red hair*. Again the classes of noun phrase distinguished by this effect correspond closely to those distinguished by existential sentences. The (apparent) problem is that many weak determiners, like *many, three, several*, work perfectly well in the environment (50), but Milsark claims that this represents quantificational use of cardinal determiners. He proposes that properties can only be predicated of strong noun phrases. Lumsden (1988) also discusses this material in detail, claiming that states (and events) are stage-level predicates while properties are individual-level (see

4.3.3). He accounts for the property predication restriction in terms of a treatment of weak noun phrases as quantifying over stage-level entities.

6.3.4   Internal-head relatives
Consider the following sentence containing a relative clause:

(51)   I've just bought the book which you recommended.

The relative *which you recommended* modifies the noun *book*, which is usually termed its **head**. More technically, the relative is part of the noun phrase of which *book* is the lexical head. This noun phrase as a whole functions as direct object of the main clause, while its head is also construed as having a function in the relative clause, again as direct object; thus the book is both the thing bought and the thing recommended. The function of the head in the relative clause is expressed in that clause by the relative pronoun *which*, generally taken to undergo transformational movement from its underlying object position after the verb *recommended* to a position at the left periphery of the clause. But an alternative form of the relative in this sentence would be *that you recommended*, and there is reason to believe that *that* is not a relative pronoun here but simply the general complementizer or subordinating particle, which means that there is no expression inside the relative clause of the direct object of this clause. A third alternative is to omit even the complementizer (*I've just bought the book you recommended*), making the point yet clearer that the position or role within the relative clause with which the head is construed can be unexpressed. See Radford (1988: chapter 9) for discussion.

There is considerable cross-linguistic variation in the syntactic strategies used for relative clause formation, though the pattern just exemplified of the role of the head within the relative being expressed in a reduced form (by a relative pronoun, or a resumptive pronoun in the relevant position) or not at all predominates. But another pattern is the "internal-head" type, in which the head (*book* above) appears inside the relative clause, in the position appropriate to its function there, and is not separately represented outside the relative. The relative clause absorbs, as it were, the bulk of the noun phrase (though not necessarily determiners and other grammatical markers) which it is interpreted as modifying. See Comrie (1981a) for discussion. The following example is from Bambara (Bird 1968, Comrie 1981a):

(52)   Tyɛ be   [n ye   so   mìn ye] dyɔ.
          man PRES I PAST house REL see build
          'The man is building the house that I saw.'

Bambara marks relative clauses with the morpheme *mìn*, postposed to the noun which is the head, but many languages with internal-head relatives use no such

250

marker. I noted in 4.1.2 that the internal-head relative structure is used in Lakhota, and in this language it displays a definiteness effect, examined in detail by Williamson (1987). Consider (53):

(53)   [[Joe wowapi wą owa] kį] wac'į.
         Joe book   a   wrote the want-1SG
         'I want the book that Joe wrote.'

The head inside the relative clause takes the form of a complete noun phrase including determiner, *wowapi wą* 'a book'. But there is a second determiner modifying the relative clause as a whole, *kį* 'the' in this example; in this connection recall from 2.2.5 that articles can modify clauses in Lakhota. This higher determiner can be definite or indefinite, and determines the interpretation with respect to definiteness of the noun phrase modified by the relative[11] – thus whether it is 'the book that Joe wrote' or 'a book that Joe wrote'. But whatever the higher determiner, the internal head itself must be indefinite or weak in form. If it is a full noun phrase with determiner as in (53) this determiner cannot be definite or strong. A range of indefinite pronouns are also permitted.

Williamson argues that relative clauses are treated in the semantics as propositional functions with a free variable. This makes a quantified head impossible. Following Heim (1988), Williamson regards simple definites as non-quantificational, but argues that the familiarity they express would be at variance with what is conveyed by a restrictive relative clause, rendering this uninformative. Whether or not this explanation is correct, it is striking that the range of noun phrases ruled out as internal heads is again apparently the same as that excluded from existential sentences. Williamson predicts that this definiteness effect should apply generally to languages with internal-head relatives.

A further striking point, exemplified by (53), is that where the higher determiner is definite and the lower one is the cardinal article, this does not produce a semantic clash. The higher determiner makes the phrase definite and the lower one is neutral in this regard. This is very strong evidence for my thesis that "quasi-indefinite" articles are cardinality determiners and do not encode indefiniteness.

6.3.5 *Concluding remarks*

The reader is invited to turn back to the remaining definiteness diagnostics of Postal (1970) introduced in 1.2.1, and work out where they divide the range of noun phrase types. What we have seen here is that most definiteness effects identify a definite or strong class which is considerably broader than the class of noun phrases in which definiteness is encoded. If we recognize quantifiers like

---

[11] Williamson assumes the overall relative structure, represented by the outer brackets in (53), is a noun phrase; the inner brackets represent a clause structure, sister to the higher determiner.

all, *most* etc. as definite determiners on a par with *the* and demonstratives (and by extension personal pronouns), that still leaves indefinite generics, proper nouns (if these are indeed indefinite bare nominals), and cardinals used quantificationally. The one construction which is limited to definites in the narrow, grammatical sense is superlatives, and here the restriction is in fact to a narrow subset of definites, even demonstratives being excluded.

These definiteness effects clearly do identify a genuine semantic class, but the narrower class of noun phrases overtly marked as definite is equally real, though it seems to be defined morphologically or structurally rather than semantically. This is clear from the phenomenon of DG possessives, which appears to depend on the possessive being in a particular "Det position", is always paraphrasable by a noun phrase with *the*, and seems to occur only in languages which have definiteness marking. These two notions of definiteness will be discussed further in the next chapter.

7
Defining definiteness

The informal attempt in Chapter 1 and subsequently to reach a general definition of definiteness ran into a puzzle. Definiteness seems empirically to be a unified phenomenon, on the evidence of the way languages represent it, but it is not straightforwardly characterized. Two characteristics are prominent, but neither is apparently fully adequate as the defining feature. Identifiability is particularly attractive for referential uses, especially where the referent is a physical entity locatable in a physical context, and inclusiveness is particularly attractive for non-referential uses. Indeed many uses are readily handled by either one of these concepts. But neither works for all uses. In this chapter we survey attempts to analyse definiteness within various theoretical frameworks. As will be seen, writers have variously argued for versions of identifiability or of inclusiveness, or have simply assumed one or the other, as the basic descriptive insight. The general tendency is for logicians and semanticists to prefer inclusiveness (or, very often, uniqueness – thus limiting themselves to accounting for singular definites), and pragmatists to prefer identifiability. But this is by no means a general rule; some have indeed sought to combine the two.

After outlining some major approaches I will argue (following up hints dropped in preceding chapters) that the attempt to find a fully unified characterization of definiteness in semantic or pragmatic terms is misguided. I will propose an account of definiteness as a grammatical category which, like other such categories, cannot be completely defined in semantic or pragmatic terms, though it represents the grammaticalization of some category of meaning.

7.1 The grammatical, logical and pragmatic traditions

Work by descriptive grammarians on definiteness (or on the meaning and use of articles) has long been dominated by the kind of discourse approach characteristic of current work in pragmatics, with versions of familiarity–identifiability at its centre. This hypothesis goes back to ancient times, occurring in Apollonius Dyscolus (second century AD) who distinguishes presence and absence of the definite article in Greek in terms of whether or not the referent has already been mentioned or is otherwise known (Householder 1981). The development of this view in the present century is due to Christophersen (1939), who argues that the use of *the* in English directs the hearer to the referent of a noun phrase by indicating that this referent is familiar to hearer as well as speaker; see 1.1.2. Christophersen was certainly influenced by the descriptive work of the great nineteenth-century German grammarian Maetzner (1880, 1885), who anticipates a large part of this account, and Christophersen in turn strongly influenced the account appearing in Jespersen's great grammar, the relevant volume of which appeared in 1943, and which is based squarely on the familiarity hypothesis.[1] Jespersen's account consists essentially of a theory of "stages of familiarity", familiarity being defined as "knowledge of what item of the class denoted by the word is meant in the case concerned". Stage I is complete unfamiliarity, and corresponds to indefiniteness. Stage II is "nearly complete familiarity", when the referent is to be found in the linguistic context or the non-linguistic situation, and corresponds to the use of *the* with any common noun. Stage III is complete familiarity, which renders the use of the definite article redundant, and corresponds to proper nouns, vocatives, and a few other cases. In elaborating on stage II, Jespersen discusses the sources of the "nearly complete familiarity", and here his categories are based closely on those of Christophersen. There may be an "explicit contextual basis", where the referent has been introduced in the previous discourse. An "implicit contextual basis" would be where the reference is to something connected with an entity already mentioned – that is, the associative anaphoric use. The "situational basis" is where the identity of the referent is clear from the non-linguistic context – the immediate situation (in a particular room, *the door*, *the table*), or the wider situation (in a particular town, *the gasworks*). Jespersen points to a close relationship between the implicit contextual basis and the situational basis, the difference being that with the latter there is no overt mention of the thing providing the contextual basis. Finally there is the "constant situational basis", in the case of uniques like *devil* or *sun*, which always take the definite article – though Jespersen dismisses the characterization "unique", claiming there is no such thing in human thought as an essentially singleton class; for him such nouns denote concepts fixed in the minds of speakers. A major failing in Jespersen's account is that he takes familiarity or unfamiliarity to be to the speaker – misunderstanding Christophersen who makes it clear that (un)familiarity to the hearer is what is crucial.

The logical or formal semantic analysis of definite noun phrases (or definite descriptions) goes back to Russell (1905), who was building on, and reacting to, the earlier work of Frege (1892) on the sense–reference distinction. In develop-

---

[1] The sections of Jespersen's grammar dealing with the articles were actually written by Haislund after Jespersen's death on the basis of a plan he dictated.

ing his celebrated theory of descriptions Russell limits himself to singular definite expressions, examining sentences such as:

(1)   The King of France is bald.

Russell claims that this sentence represents a conjunction of three propositions:

(i)   There is a King of France.
(ii)   There is only one King of France.
(iii)   This individual is bald.

All these propositions are of equal status in that all three are asserted. It follows that each of them is a logical entailment; thus if one of them is false, the whole conjunction is false.

Of these three conjoined propositions, the first two – the existential clause and the uniqueness clause – characterize the definite description *the King of France*, and these two elements are assumed in nearly all logical work on definites. Indeed in many accounts which replace uniqueness by familiarity or identifiability, the existential clause is still taken to be a constituent of the meaning of definite noun phrases (as also of indefinites). What is not so generally agreed on is the status of these clauses in relation to the third proposition, the assertion that the individual in question is bald. Russell's account runs counter to a strong intuition that only clause (iii) is actually asserted by use of the sentence (1), while (i) and (ii) (taking them to be descriptively correct) are felt to be background assumptions. This in fact was Frege's position, which Russell rejected; discussing a version of the existential clause only (as have most writers on this issue), Frege held that referring expressions **presuppose** a reference to something, and that such presuppositions must hold true for the sentence as a whole to be either true or false. For Frege the reference of the expression *the King of France* to some individual would not be part of the sense of (1); it is a necessary background assumption to the sentence, the sense of which is that the person referred to is bald. Much later, Strawson (1950, 1952) criticizes Russell's account and proposes in effect a return to Frege's theory, though in a more elaborated version. He argues that in (1) only Russell's (iii) is asserted; the existential clause (i) is a presupposition, a precondition for the truth or falsity of the statement presupposing it. So if (i) is false, the statement (1) lacks a truth value, because the definite description contained in it fails to refer.

Strawson insists that it is not sentences or propositions which presuppose, but individual uses of these. Thus a sentence like (1) may be used to make a particular statement or assertion, and it is this, not the sentence, which is true or false (since one may correctly assert at one point in history that the King of France is bald, but not at another), and which therefore carries the preconditions for truth or falsity. This does not make Strawson's account of presupposition a pragmatic one (like later accounts, to be discussed below), since for him all questions of truth (generally taken to be fundamental to semantics) relate to statements rather than sentences. Strawson's position is not obviously distinct from that of a number of semanticists working within the generative semantics paradigm in the early 1970s who developed a clearly semantic concept of presupposition as a property of sentences, since proponents of a truth-based theory of sentence meaning recognize that the truth or falsity of a sentence is usually relative to a particular context of utterance; the contribution to the sentence's truth value of tense morphology, deictic expressions and personal pronouns could only be assessed given a specification of the time and place of utterance and the identity of speaker and hearer etc. Presupposition as a semantic concept is in contrast with the longer established and fundamental concept of **entailment**: a sentence A entails a sentence B if whenever A is true B must be true, whereas A presupposes B if whenever A is true B is true and whenever A is false B is true. As noted above, the presuppositional account of the existence implication of referring expressions (and of the uniqueness implication of definites if one accepts this) captures the intuition that these implications are less to the fore than the central assertion of a sentence. There is a problem, however, since, as already recognized by Russell, the existential implication of definite descriptions does not necessarily survive under negation of the sentence. Consider (2), the negation of (1):

(2)   The King of France is not bald.

The most natural reading of (2) is that there exists an individual who is King of France and that this individual is not bald; here the existential implication is preserved. But there is a second possible reading, in which the existence of the King of France as well as his baldness is denied. This interpretation can in fact be imposed by adding a continuation which explicitly denies the existential implication:

(3)   The King of France is not bald – because there is no King of France.

This fact was part of Russell's motivation for rejecting Frege's presuppositional account of reference. By treating the existential clause as an assertion on the same level as the foreground assertion of the sentence, Russell was able to account for the two readings of (2) in terms of differing scope of the negation. Negation can have narrow scope, applying only to the predicate (clause (iii)); or wide scope, so that the entire proposition is negated. This is shown in the following logical representation (where *K* stands for *King of France* and *B* for *bald*):

(4)   The King of France is bald.
        $\exists x \, (Kx \ \& \ {\sim}\exists y \, ((y{\neq}x) \ \& \ Ky) \ \& \ Bx)$

256

(5)   The King of France is not bald.
   a.   *narrow-scope negation*
       $\exists x \ (Kx \ \& \ \sim\exists y \ ((y{\neq}x) \ \& \ Ky) \ \& \ \sim Bx)$
   b.   *wide-scope negation*
       $\sim(\exists x \ (Kx \ \& \ \sim\exists y \ ((y{\neq}x) \ \& \ Ky) \ \& \ Bx))$

Strawson has no account of these facts; for him, presuppositions are preserved under negation, so that the only interpretation of (2) is the one corresponding to Russell's narrow-scope analysis. Strawson's position is that there is no wide-scope reading, and (3) is simply odd; there being no King of France at the present time is no valid reason for asserting that the King of France is not bald. And indeed this view has some intuitive appeal; the narrow-scope reading of (2) is by far the more natural, and (3) – while speakers admittedly do say such things – does strike us as odd. In other instances, however, for example where the definite description is in complement position, the wide-scope interpretation works better:

(6) A: I've just heard that Mary got married last week to the King of Paraguay.
    B: Nonsense. She certainly didn't marry the King of Paraguay – Paraguay doesn't have a king.

Moreover, we saw above in Chapter 4 that the existential implication may fail to hold in a wide range of opaque contexts, where it can be argued to fall within the scope of some counterfactual or hypothetical operator. In the absence of negation or some other such operator creating an opaque context the existential implication always holds and cannot be explicitly denied (??*Mary has married the King of Paraguay, though there is no such person*), and this fact suggests that this implication may in fact be an entailment of the sentence – Russell's position. It now looks as if both Russell and Strawson are right: the existential claim is an entailment because it necessarily holds in positive non-opaque sentences, but may fall within the scope of the operator in negative and opaque contexts; but it is presupposition-like in that it may survive under negation etc., and typically does.

This led a number of writers in the mid-1970s to propose that the existential implication (along with other putative presuppositional phenomena) is both entailed (in positive transparent contexts) and pragmatically presupposed – to some extent a conflation of the accounts of Russell and Strawson (Stalnaker 1974, Kempson 1975, Wilson 1975). This view combines semantic and pragmatic elements in the account, treating the presupposition as a conversational implicature of the sort proposed by Grice (1975). The crucial point about these pragmatic presuppositions (by contrast with earlier semantic definitions) is that they can be cancelled, and this is what happens in the cases where they fail to be preserved under negation and in opaque contexts. But the pragmatic theory characterizes the cancellation of such implicatures as a marked option, and this accounts for the observation that survival of the existential implication under negation is more natural than its suppression. For criticism of this approach see Kleiber (1981), and for more recent work on presupposition see van der Sandt (1988), Burton-Roberts (1989b), Chierchia (1995).

As the discussion so far has implied, this debate concerning the status of the putative elements of the meaning of definite descriptions was concentrated on the existential implication. The uniqueness implication attracted less attention partly because a familiarity or identifiability account was more to the taste of linguists pursuing an analysis involving Gricean pragmatic elements, partly because for many writers the point at issue was the correct treatment of presupposition-like phenomena in general rather than the analysis of definiteness, and partly because this element, Russell's clause (ii), whether correctly described as a uniqueness implication or an identifiability implication, behaves differently from the existential one. The treatment of clause (ii) is crucial to understanding definiteness, however, since it is this implication which is taken to distinguish definites from indefinites; the existential implication is common to both. In fact Strawson (1950, 1952) paid considerable attention to this question, rejecting Russell's uniqueness implication on the grounds that the referent of singular indefinites is just as unique as that of singular definites. He sees the essence of definiteness as identifiability, which he discusses in pragmatic terms: we use *the* to signal reference to something previously referred to, or to signal that features of the context or background knowledge should enable the hearer to single out the referent. Kempson (1975) also treats this question in some detail, and argues that definites and indefinites are semantically (truth-conditionally) identical, the distinguishing clause being (except in the sentence-anaphoric use) a conversational implicature. She claims that the definite article implies, not that the referent is unique, but that it is "uniquely identifiable" by the hearer. This is because she regards the sentence-anaphoric use (where the definite noun phrase picks up a previous mention of the referent in the same sentence) as basic, providing the model for the interpretation of other uses. In this use Kempson has a syntactic rule of definitization, which assigns the feature [+ Def] to the second of two coreferential noun phrases, this feature then being spelled out as *the*. And it is his knowledge of this rule that enables the hearer to identify the referent of the definite noun phrase with the referent of the earlier mention; this is considered sufficient to constitute knowledge of the referent on the part of the hearer.[2] But, Kempson argues, neither this identifiability implication nor the rival Russellian uniqueness implication can be an entailment, because it can be false

[2] Hintikka (1970) argues that knowing who or what an object is amounts to knowing that that object is the same as some existing object.

without the truth of the sentence being affected. Thus *The glass has fallen on the floor* would not be rendered false either by there having been more than one glass or by the hearer being unable to identify the glass in question. It is not certain that Kempson is right here; although it is unacceptable to say *It is not true that the glass has fallen on the floor because there were eight glasses* or *It is not true that the glass has fallen on the floor because I don't know which glass you mean*, consider the following:

(7) A: The glass has fallen on the floor.
    B: No – *the* glass hasn't fallen on the floor; *one of the* glasses has – there were eight.
or B: No – *the* glass hasn't fallen on the floor; *a* glass has – there were eight.

(8) A: The glass has fallen on the floor.
    B: ?No – *the* glass hasn't fallen on the floor; maybe *a* glass has, but I don't know which glass you mean.

It does seem possible to deny a proposition on the basis of the falsity of the uniqueness or identifiability implication of a definite noun phrase within it provided the article is stressed – not surprisingly since the failed implication is what defines this article. In fact the denial in (7) seems to work considerably better than the one in (8), suggesting that a uniqueness implication would be an entailment but an identifiability implication would not be. This distinction is reinforced by examples such as (9) (based on inclusiveness rather than uniqueness), and by Kempson's (10) and (11), which show how identifiability can be cancelled both in negative and in positive non-opaque sentences:

(9) A: I've washed the dishes.
    B: No, you haven't washed the dishes; you've only done half of them.

(10)   The King of Ruritania never showed up at my exhibition, though I don't suppose you knew there was such a person, did you?

(11)   The King of Ruritania came to my exhibition, though I don't suppose you knew I was having one, let alone that there was a King of Ruritania – did you?

Kempson takes identifiability to be pragmatically presupposed in positive transparent sentences as well as negative and opaque ones. Sentence-anaphoric definites get this presupposition from a syntactic rule of definitization. In other uses, where *the* spells out an instance of [+ Def] not inserted by rule, the presupposition is a conversational implicature derived from the presence of this feature, which has no semantic interpretation. Principles of communication ensure that the hearer infers that the speaker must be intending to convey some extra

259

information by the optional use of the feature [+ Def], and since this feature is semantically empty, this extra information can only be that implication of identifiability which necessarily accompanies [+ Def] in the sentence-anaphoric use where it is obligatory.

Kempson's syntactic mechanism would not be acceptable today, but her account in many ways foreshadows the discourse semantics of Heim (1988) as well as more recent pragmatic work in relevance theory, and we will examine her own later work under this heading. What is clear more generally from the discussion in this section is that none of the three traditions in the period considered came to grips with the issue of inclusiveness (uniqueness as it then was) versus identifiability, but each chose whichever of these best suited its own purpose – reasonably enough perhaps. But it is interesting to see that the status of a uniqueness implication and that of an identifiability implication, as entailment or pragmatic presupposition, would probably be different – though I am not aware that anyone noticed this at the time.

Finally in this section, mention should be made of the grammatical tradition following Gustave Guillaume, within which a great deal of work has been devoted to definiteness. This paradigm is still very influential in the French-speaking world, but almost unknown beyond this (for good reasons – although it has produced many worthwhile ideas). The problem is that the Guillaumian literature tends to be highly metaphorical and obscure. Guillaume's major work on definiteness has been reissued as Guillaume (1975), and a good recent study, where most other important references can be found, is Pattee (1994).

7.2 Hawkins: inclusiveness and location

In terms of descriptive breadth, the most substantial body of work on definiteness is probably that of Hawkins, starting with his 1974 thesis, revised and condensed as his 1978 book. Hawkins does engage with the inclusiveness–identifiability issue, coming down firmly on the side of the first – in fact the term "inclusiveness" is his. He does, however, make a significant concession to the traditional criterion of familiarity in his concept of "location".

7.2.1 *Shared sets, inclusiveness and exclusiveness*

Hawkins (1978) gives the most detailed account to date of the range of uses of *the* and *a*. My own informal classification in 1.1.2 is a simplified version of Hawkins's, and the reader is referred to his book for a more detailed (and highly readable) presentation. Hawkins's typology of uses of *the* points to the generalization that the referent of a definite noun phrase must be part of a **shared set**, that is, the entities known by speaker and hearer to constitute either the previous discourse, the immediate or larger situation, or an association set.

The definite article instructs the hearer to infer which shared set is intended and **locate** the referent in it (that is, understand the referent to be part of it).

Hawkins has an additional usage type of "unexplanatory modifiers", in which certain modifiers, including *same, only* and superlatives, require *the*, even though they do not seem to identify an antecedent, situation or association to permit location; these are illustrated in 1.1.3. The modifier in these cases does not serve to identify the shared set, which is established in some other way. The point is that the fact that we can associate a noun phrase with a shared set does not by itself make definiteness obligatory. Consider the following:

(12)   Pass me **a bucket**, please.

(13)   Have you heard the news? **A cabinet minister** has just resigned; I didn't catch which one.

(14)   [At a wedding]
         Have you seen **any bridesmaids**?

(15)   Fred picked up a book, and tore out **some pages**.

These look like examples of Hawkins's visible or immediate situation, larger situation, general situation, and associative anaphoric use, respectively. But in each case the noun phrase in bold, which is readily related to a shared set, is indefinite. This is where **inclusiveness** comes in. In (12)–(15) the reference is to one bucket or cabinet minister, or a number of pages or bridesmaids, among several more. But with definites the reference is to the only entity or all the entities in the shared set satisfying the description used. And the reason that definiteness is obligatory with *same, only* and superlatives is that the semantics of these modifiers imposes a unique or total reading on the noun phrase, and this is incompatible with the exclusiveness which would be implicit in an indefinite reference. See the discussion in 6.3.1.

To summarize Hawkins's account of the use of the definite article, it (a) introduces a referent to the hearer, (b) instructs the hearer to locate the referent in some shared set of objects, (c) refers to the totality of the objects or mass within this set which satisfy the referring expression. It is essentially the third of these clauses which distinguishes definites from indefinites. Indefinites refer exclusively, but are neutral with respect to the pragmatic restriction of the domain of reference embodied in the idea of location in a shared set. We have seen with (12)–(15) that indefinites may be locatable, but now consider the following:

(16)   Fred bought **a car** last week, and then he sold **some tyres** to his friend.

(17)   Fred sold **a car** to one friend, and bought **some tyres** off another.

(18)   **A prime minister** has just died.

261

Defining definiteness

In (16) *some tyres* could be an associate of the trigger *a car* – that is, the tyres Fred sold could be from the car he bought – but it need not be. In (17) *some tyres* is almost certainly not associatively anaphoric to *a car*. And in (18) the referent of *a prime minister* is almost certainly not to be located in a larger situation shared set; that is, it is not to be understood as referring to the present prime minister of this country. In this last case the reason is that such location would violate the exclusiveness requirement. Since the country has only one prime minister at a time, the use of a noun phrase *Det prime minister* to refer to this individual is necessarily inclusive; it must therefore be definite. The referent of an indefinite noun phrase is only locatable in a shared set if the reference can be understood as being to a proper subset (that is, less than the whole) of the entities in that set satisfying the description. If there are in the putative shared set no entities of the right kind which can be understood as excluded from the reference, then the reference must be construed as not relating to that shared set. What we have then is a standard first-mention indefinite.

7.2.2 Subsequent developments

Hawkins (1978) has been the starting point for much subsequent work, including further developments in Hawkins's own thinking. I begin with Lyons (1980), who criticizes two aspects of the above account. One of these points has already been discussed in chapter 1, but I return to it here briefly because it is central to the issue of the nature of definiteness. I repeat the relevant examples:

(19)   [In a room with three doors, one open and two closed]
         Close **the door**, please.

(20)   [In a hallway with four doors, all closed, the speaker stands dressed
         for a journey, a suitcase in each hand]
         Open **the door** for me, please.

These are immediate situation uses of *the*, and likely to involve successful reference. But in neither case does inclusiveness apply. Some factor in the sentence or the situation makes it clear which object among several satisfying the description is intended, and this is enough. Lyons takes this to argue for identifiability rather than inclusiveness.

The second point is that there is an important distinction to be drawn in the acceptability data for definites, not clearly discerned by Hawkins. In general, the speaker who uses a definite description is appealing to knowledge on the hearer's part of a relationship between the referent and a shared set. For example, at a wedding one can refer to *the bridesmaids* because one can assume that the hearer knows that weddings tend to involve bridesmaids. Hawkins notes, however, that

262

this knowledge can be dispensed with in immediate situation uses like the following (where the hearer does not know of the presence of a dog):

(21)   Don't go in there. **The dog** will bite you.

In such examples the hearer is being informed of the existence of the referent in the appropriate shared set (the physical vicinity). According to Hawkins this possibility is only available in immediate situation uses, but in fact it is much more pervasive, and Lyons gives examples corresponding to all the other usage types. I repeat some here:

(22)   *Immediate situation*
         I'll get **the butler** to show you out.

(23)   *Larger situation*
         Meet me at **the horse-trough** tonight.

(24)   *Establishing relative* (Hawkins's example)
         What's wrong with Bill? Oh, **the woman he went out with last night**
         was nasty to him.

(25)   *Unexplanatory modifier*
         The first person to swim the Irish Sea was a Cossack.

In each of these examples, the locatability of the referent in the appropriate shared set (the fact that this household has a butler, the existence of a horse-trough in this village, the fact that Fred went out with a woman last night, the fact that the Irish Sea has been swum) may be complete news to the hearer, and the reference yet be successful. This success depends on the hearer's cooperation; he must reason that since he is unaware of the connection implied, he is being informed of it, and he must accept the definite reference as thus informing him. But the greater looseness of this usage compared with instances where the speaker is appealing to the hearer's prior knowledge of the required connection is evident from the fact that it is open to the hearer not to cooperate and to reject the definite reference with a reply such as *The what?* or *What horse-trough?* or *I didn't know the Irish Sea had been swum.*[3] All this applies too to cases where the description in the definite noun phrase is new to the hearer:

(26)   When you arrive in Mexico City, make your way to the zócalo.

The hearer may have no idea what a zócalo is, and has the choice of either saying so, or accepting that it is probably a major feature of Mexico City, or of Mexican cities, which he will manage to find. The examples of definite usage which form

---

[3] An *I didn't know . . .* response like this does not necessarily imply rejection of the reference. The hearer may accept the information and still indicate that it is new to him.

the core of Hawkins's account, in which the hearer's existing knowledge enables him to locate the referent, are straightforward; the reference can be guaranteed to be successful. But in addition we have a kind of use in which this knowledge is quite absent, and indeed in which the hearer may not even recognize the descriptive content of the definite noun phrase. And these uses may or may not succeed as references, depending on the indulgence or cooperative effort of the hearer. It is not certain that the distinction between these two kinds of use can be explained by Hawkins's account.

Hawkins (1991) updates his theory and introduces some modifications, at the same time reacting to various criticisms. He dismisses counterexamples to inclusiveness like (19)–(20) as marginal, claiming that *the door* in (19) is shorthand for *the door which is open* – but see Larson and Segal (1995: chapter 9) for discussion of the weaknesses in this ellipsis treatment. He again rejects identifiability as a criterion for definiteness, claiming however that it does hold of demonstratives and personal pronouns – implying that these are not related to the definite article.

He frames his account now in neo-Gricean pragmatics, claiming that much of the meaning of the articles is a matter of pragmatic inference, as expressed in the concept of **implicature** (Grice 1975, Levinson 1983, 1987). Implicatures are of two kinds. **Conventional implicatures** are a fixed element in the meaning of an expression, while **conversational implicatures** differ in being "defeasible" – that is, they can be cancelled, for example by overt denial of their import. Hawkins's concept of "shared set", which remains essentially the same, he now labels "pragmatic set" or "P-set", and characterizes it in terms borrowed from Sperber and Wilson (1986) as a "mutual cognitive environment" – a set of facts manifest equally to the individuals concerned; a fact is "manifest" at a given time to a person if he/she is capable at that time of representing it mentally and accepting its representation as true or probably true.

Now, *the* entails existence and uniqueness,[4] and carries a conventional implicature that there is some P-set accessible to speaker and hearer within which existence and uniqueness hold. *A* entails only existence and conventionally implicates non-uniqueness; it carries in addition other conversational (cancellable) implicatures, to account for (among other things) the fact that membership of a P-set sometimes holds with indefinites but not always. With first mentions, in particular, the referent is commonly not in any P-set. But Hawkins argues there is a preference for interpreting indefinites as involving "P-membership" where possible. Thus:

(27)   I didn't buy *the house*, because *a window* was broken.

---

[4] Hawkins (1991) partly backtracks on the inclusiveness claim of his earlier work, and limits his discussion to singular count cases so he can speak of uniqueness.

The most natural interpretation is that the window belongs to the set activated by *the house*, equivalent therefore to *one of the windows*. With this interpretation *a* implicates non-uniqueness in the P-set. It is possible, however, to cancel this implicature by adding something like *not one of the windows in the house in question, but one in an identical house on the estate*. Thus *a* can conversationally implicate P-membership provided the referent is non-unique in the P-set (and *the* therefore inappropriate). Where the referent is unique in a P-set, *the* must be used; *a* in this case would implicate non-P-membership.

Other work using Hawkins's framework or sharing many of its assumptions includes: Clark and Marshall (1981), Holmback (1984), Declerck (1986a), Chesterman (1991).

7.3 Definiteness and quantification

We saw in 7.1 above that the traditional logical view of definite descriptions takes them to imply the existence of a referent and the uniqueness of this referent. We have also seen that the uniqueness clause can be reformulated as inclusiveness or totality, with the desirable consequence that plural and mass definite descriptions are accounted for as well as singular ones. Given this, the two implications can be treated in terms of the logical concept of **quantification**. The logical notation of the **predicate calculus** provides the two operators usually symbolized ∃ and ∀, representing respectively **existential quantification** and **universal quantification** (of which we have already had some discussion in 4.2 and 6.2). For clear introductory discussions of the predicate calculus and of quantification the reader is referred to Allwood, Andersson and Dahl (1977), McCawley (1981) and Cann (1993). Neale (1990) is a good discussion and defence of the quantificational approach to definite descriptions, developing the claims of Russell (1905) outlined above.

The existential quantifier is traditionally taken to be part of the representation of indefinites (at least specific indefinites) as well as definites, so on this view, it is the universal quantifier which distinguishes definites. This idea has given rise to a huge literature on the relationship between definiteness and quantification. The starting point is the work of Milsark (1977, 1979).

7.3.1 Milsark and the quantification restriction

The nature of definiteness is not Milsark's central concern. But if definiteness is one of several phenomena important for understanding existential sentences, this sentence type has since Milsark been taken as central to understanding definiteness. Behaviour in existential sentences is often taken as criterial for definite or indefinite status. In fact, as seen in Chapter 6, Milsark breaks with most earlier logical analyses in claiming that only definites (and some uses of indefinites) are quantificational, indefinite determiners being cardinality expressions.

For many writers since, "strong", "quantificational", "definite" are synonymous. But this would mean that not only *all* and *most*, but also *some* and *many* when used quantificationally (in the sense of expressing a proportion), are definite. If behaviour in existential sentences is criterial, this is correct, but it seems counter-intuitive. But note that the criterion of quantification that defines "strong" does not just apply to universal quantification – *most* is not universal, nor are strong uses of *some, many*.

To summarize the relevant portion of Milsark's findings, determiners fall into three groups with respect to the quantificational–cardinal distinction. The first group is those which are clearly quantificational: the overt universal quantifying terms *the, each, all, every, both*; the non-universal quantifier *most*; complex partitives like *ten of the*. The second group is those which are ambiguously quantificational or cardinal: *few, some/sm, many*; the two readings can generally be distinguished by stress, and often only one reading is available in a particular syntactic context (like existential sentences). The third group is those which are cardinal only: *a*, and perhaps numerals. My feeling is that numerals belong rather in the second group. The sentence *Three men were shot* could imply that others were not. If this is correct, it may be that only *a* is purely cardinal, and this may be related to its always being weak morphophonologically; the corresponding strong form is *one*, which can be quantificational. On the other hand, *a window* in (27) above seems to be quantificational too, so perhaps there are no purely cardinal determiners.

7.3.2   *Generalized quantifiers*

The theory of generalized quantifiers represents a major departure from the assumptions of the predicate calculus, dominant since the work of Frege, which makes available only two quantifiers, the existential and the universal. The major presentation of generalized quantifiers is Barwise and Cooper (1981), developing work by Mostowski (1957) and Montague (1974). Outlines are also given by Cann (1993) and McCawley (1981). The initial claims of the theory are, first, that the quantifiers expressed by many natural language determiners (like *most*) cannot be expressed in terms of $\exists$ and $\forall$, and, second, that the logical structure of natural language quantified sentences does not correspond to that of the predicate calculus; it is in fact much closer to their syntactic structure.

In generalized quantifier theory, words like *all, most, the* are not quantifiers, but determiners; quantifiers correspond directly to noun phrases, consisting of a determiner plus a set expression, so that *all men, most people, the girl* are, semantically, quantifiers. A quantifier can be thought of as making an assertion about sets. Thus, universal quantification, $\forall x \phi(x)$ (corresponding to, for example, *All men are mortal*), says that the set of things satisfying $\phi(x)$, that is, having property ϕ (the set of mortal things), contains all individuals; existential quantification,

$\exists x\phi(x)$ (*Some men are bald*, for example), says that the set having property ϕ (baldness) is not empty. This assertion may be true or false. Thus the sentences *All men
are mortal* and *Some men are bald* will be true if the set of mortals and bald people, respectively (the set constituting the denotation of the VP in each case), contains all men or some men. The VP sets which, when combined with a quantifier,
yield a true assertion are taken to constitute the denotation of that quantifier. Put
another way, a quantifier denotes the "family" of sets (that is, set of sets) for which
it yields the value *true*. All noun phrase types, including proper names, are taken
to be uniformly quantificational; thus *Harry has a cold* is true if the VP set of
things having a cold contains Harry, and the denotation of *Harry* is the family of
sets containing Harry. If noun phrases are thus generalized quantifiers, determiners
are functions from noun denotations (which are sets) to noun phrase (or generalized quantifier) denotations (families of sets). Generalized quantifiers are said to
"live on" the sets representing the denotations of their constituent nouns.

Barwise and Cooper distinguish "strong" and "weak" determiners, these corresponding closely to Milsark's strong and weak but defined differently. The test
is a sentence of the form *Det N is a N* or *Det Ns are Ns*. For a given determiner,
if the sentence is necessarily true the determiner is "positive strong" (*every, all,
the, both, that*). If it is contradictory, necessarily false, the determiner is "negative strong" (*neither*). If its truth is contingent on the "model" (the domain of discourse), the determiner is weak (*many, some, three, a, no*). Thus *Every man is a
man* is tautologous, true in every model; *Neither man is a man* is false in every
model; *Many men are men* is true only in a model in which there are many men.
Definite determiners are considered to be a subset of the strong set, recognized
by their ability to occur in the diagnostic partitive environment *all/most/some/
many of –*.[5] Barwise and Cooper regard *the*, demonstratives, and *both* as definites.
More formally, they are the determiners which form quantifiers which are always
"sieves". I have said that the denotation of a quantifier is taken to be the family
of VP denotations which combine with it to yield a true sentence. The quantifier
can be said, therefore, to "sift" VP denotations into those for which it gives the
value *true* and those for which it gives the value *false*. With some quantifiers it
is possible for the family of VP sets corresponding to the value *true* to be empty
(*many men, some men* in those domains where there are, respectively, not many,
or not any, men) or to be all sets (*every man* or *most men* in those domains where
there are no men). A quantifier which does not allow either of these possibilities,

---

[5] This is not unproblematic, since it is not certain that, for example, *all of many men* is impossible as Barwise and Cooper claim. They also note with puzzlement the impossibility of **one
of both men*, contrasting with the acceptable *one of the two men* – an unexpected contrast since
they take *both* to be definite and equivalent to *the two*. The answer is surely that *both* does not
mean 'the two' but rather 'all two'.

thus with which the two families of sets separated are both non-empty, is termed a "proper quantifier" or a "sieve". Some quantifiers can fail to denote any set in a given domain (which is distinct from denoting the empty set), that is, they can be "undefined". Thus *the man*, given that Barwise and Cooper assume a uniqueness account of the meaning of *the*, is undefined unless there is a unique man in the domain; *both men* is only defined if there are exactly two men. But when defined, *the N* and *both N* are always sieves. This is the definition of definite quantifier, intended to capture the idea that definites presuppose the existence of the referent; so *the* and *both* are definite determiners.

As noted, Barwise and Cooper treat *the* in terms of uniqueness, in accordance with the logical tradition, so that it is restricted to use in singular count noun phrases. This is inadequate of course. But they also state that corresponding to any determiner which can be undefined there is always another determiner which is its "completion", which is semantically equivalent to it but is always defined. The completion of *the* and *both* is *every*. This suggests that Barwise and Cooper (like Hawkins) take uniqueness to be a special case of inclusiveness.

Some important studies making use of generalized quantifier theory are de Jong and Verkuyl (1985), Keenan and Stavi (1986), and a number of the papers in Reuland and ter Meulen (1987).

7.3.3 *Discourse semantics: Heim*

A very different approach to definiteness is proposed in the very influential "file-change semantics" of Heim (1988). This is a formal semantic account incorporating many pragmatic aspects of interpretation, closely related to the "discourse representation" theory of Kamp (1984). Heim argues that neither definites nor indefinites are quantificational. She characterizes definiteness in terms of the traditional concept of familiarity: a definite is used when the referent is familiar at the current stage of the discourse, and an indefinite is used to introduce a novel referent.

To circumvent the major problem facing accounts of definiteness based on notions like familiarity and identifiability, namely that many definites and indefinites are non-referential, Heim appeals to Karttunen's (1976) concept of "discourse referent". Consider the following:

(28)   Joe wants to catch **a fish** and eat **it**.

(29)   Everybody found **a cat** and kept **it**. **It** ran away.

In (28), *a fish* is most naturally understood as non-specific, within the opaque context set up by the verb *want*. Yet the definite pronoun *it* is able to relate back anaphorically to *a fish*, which should be impossible if anaphora is about having the same reference. Karttunen's explanation is that *a fish*, though not referring, sets up a "discourse referent" which can then act as antecedent for *it*. The first sentence of (29) is similar. If *everybody* is taken to have wide scope in relation to *a cat*, the latter is then interpreted as a variable bound by the universal quantifier and does not refer; but *a cat* introduces a discourse referent, and this discourse referent is familiar by the time it is picked up anaphorically by *it*, so the definite pronoun is appropriate. But notice that the *it* of the second sentence of (29) cannot relate back anaphorically to *a cat* (or to the first *it*). This is because the discourse referent created by *a cat* ceases to exist at the end of the first sentence and is no longer available to be picked up by the second *it*. The generalization is that if a discourse referent is set up within the scope of a quantifier, then its existence does not extend beyond the scope of this quantifier; in terms of syntactic configuration, a quantifier has scope over its c-command domain. It is clear that discourse reference is something quite distinct from real-world reference, with different patterns of behaviour, but this abstract concept does appear to be needed to explain instances of apparent anaphora as in (28) and (29) where there is no real-world reference. It is essentially this concept that Heim takes up and develops, using the metaphor of a "file" to express the information built up in the course of a discourse.

The idea is that understanding a discourse is like keeping a file in which each discourse referent is represented by a numbered file card. When a new discourse referent is introduced into the conversation a new card is added to the file, and on this card is entered whatever is said about this discourse referent. If the same discourse referent is mentioned again, whatever new is said is added to the same card. Definites and indefinites are claimed to affect the growth of the file in different ways, as expressed in an "appropriateness condition" to the effect that the hearer must add a new card for each indefinite, and update an old card for each definite. But it is file cards, not real referents, that are novel or familiar/old; like Karttunen's discourse referents, Heim's file cards can fail to correspond to referents, or two file cards can correspond to the same referent, and so on. Heim does, nevertheless, pay considerable attention to the nature of the relationship between file cards and referents in the world. Files, representing the information generated in discourses, are characterized as true or false, depending on whether or not they accurately represent the real-world facts. Establishing the truth of a file involves setting the sequence of file cards against a sequence of actual individuals in such a way that each individual matches the description given on the corresponding card. Such a sequence of real individuals is said to **satisfy** the file, and the file is true if a sequence can be found to satisfy it.

Heim assumes a grammatical level of logical form, essentially as advanced in work on government-binding theory; it is at this level of representation that many relations traditionally thought of as semantic, like scope of operators, are explicated. At logical form, expressions which have the status of logical operators, including quantificational determiners, are raised to an adjoined position in which they are sisters to their arguments, the expressions over which they have scope. For example, in the case of *every man*, the quantifier *every*[6] is raised out of the noun phrase to become its left sister. The indeterminate noun phrase remaining is then treated as an argument in the scope of the operator *every*.[7] But this quantifier raising does not apply in the case of *the* and *a*, which are not operators. They do not quantify, and indeed have no semantic content at all; the rules of semantic interpretation simply ignore them. Their role is to mark noun phrases as definite or indefinite, for the purposes of the appropriateness condition mentioned above. Somewhat more formally, this condition says that for a sentence with a given logical form (which includes the referential indexing of all noun phrases) to be appropriate with respect to the current file, the index of every definite noun phrase in the sentence must be already in the file, and the index of every indefinite noun phrase must be new to the file. These non-quantificational noun phrases contain a free variable, which can subsequently be bound by a quantifier having scope over the noun phrase, by a quantificational adverb like *usually*, *often*, or by a default implicit quantification which provides the clause with "existential closure" (since the truth of a file depends on the existence of referents satisfying it). So Heim does not deny that, in particular, specific indefinites are understood as existentially quantified, as traditionally supposed by logicians. Her point is that the existential quantification is not inherent in the noun phrase (or the determiner).

Heim extends her treatment to include definite reference to visible entities in the immediate situation; these are in effect treated as being in the file. But other definite uses are more problematic. For associative uses, she introduces an accommodation mechanism which connects via "bridges" the new file cards created to other cards already present in the file. In this respect Heim's account of definiteness has much in common with the earlier one of Kempson (1975), discussed above. Both take discourse-anaphoric uses of definites to be central, and other uses (principally situational and associative) to be derived.

An important sequel to Heim's work is that of Diesing (1992). This will not be considered closely here because it is largely limited to the analysis of indefinites,

---

[6] Heim uses the term "quantifier" in the traditional sense, corresponding to the syntactic notion of determiner, not in the generalized quantifier sense in which it corresponds to noun phrase.

[7] A quantificational noun phrase is itself raised out of its clause and adjoined to it, leaving a trace behind. So a sentence like *Every man left* would involve two raising and adjoining processes: the subject *every man* out of the clause, and the quantifier *every* out of the noun phrase. The result is a tripartite structure with the quantifier *every*, the rump subject *man*, and the rump clause *e left* (where *e* is the trace of the raised subject) as sisters to each other.

but a few words are in order. Diesing is concerned to establish the role that syntactic representations play in the formation of the kind of logical representation
Heim proposes (with the tripartite structure noted for quantified sentences). In the
course of this, Diesing claims that indefinites are not uniformly represented as
variables, as argued by Heim, but that some are inherently quantified. This partition of indefinites corresponds to the distinction between cardinal and quantificational indefinites drawn by Milsark (1979). For discussion of definite descriptions
in the framework of discourse representation theory, see Kamp and Reyle (1993).

7.4 Relevance theory

The most influential development in pragmatics in the last few years
is relevance theory, based on Sperber and Wilson (1986) and represented in a large
volume of subsequent work. For general accounts of the theory see Sperber and
Wilson (1987, 1995). There is not a great deal of published work on the nature
of definiteness in the relevance theory framework, but what there is merits attention. Kempson (1988) gives a relevance theoretic account of a range of types of
simple definite noun phrase and personal pronoun, and Wilson (1992) discusses
the assignment of reference to definite noun phrases. I will look at these two studies below.

In brief, relevance theory is an account of how we interpret utterances. This is
claimed to be a process of construction of mental representations, in the form of
propositions. The idea is that the grammatical form of a sentence uttered encodes
a logical form which considerably underdetermines what the speaker actually wishes
to communicate. The hearer's task is to access further, background assumptions
(the **context**) and combine these with the logical form encoded by the utterance
to yield the proposition or propositions which constitute the intended interpretation. The interaction of the newly given information with the context may amount
to confirming an existing assumption, contradicting and therefore eliminating it,
or combining with it to yield an implication not derivable from either context or
new information alone. These three possibilities are **contextual effects**, and an
utterance is said to be relevant to the extent that it achieves contextual effects. But
the relevance of an utterance is reduced by the mental effort required of the hearer
in deriving these contextual effects; the amount of effort is determined by the complexity of the utterance, the accessibility of the context, and the complexity of the
inferencing required to reach the intended implications. An utterance, then, is opti-
mally relevant if it leads to substantial contextual effects and causes the hearer no
gratuitous effort in achieving those effects.

A basic claim of the theory is that the concept of relevance is central to human
cognition. We expect relevance in utterances we have to interpret, so that, in effect,
utterances come with a guarantee of their own optimal relevance. It follows from

the requirement of minimal processing effort that the first interpretation to occur to the hearer as satisfying his expectation of relevance in a way the speaker could manifestly have foreseen is to be taken as the correct interpretation.

Wilson (1992) argues that a hearer's task of establishing the reference of definite noun phrases is part of the process just described. Assigning reference involves constructing or retrieving a mental representation of the referent, and this representation is included in the representation of the proposition expressed by the utterance. Wilson looks at anaphoric uses like (30), where there is more than one potential antecedent for the definite; bridging cross-reference (associative anaphoric) cases like (31), where the referent is not already given at all and has to be inferred; and combined instances like (32), where not only does the referent have to be inferred by bridging or association, but there is more than one potential bridge or trigger for the association.

(30)   The room had three doors, one of which was open. I closed the door.

(31)   I walked into the room. Both windows were open.

(32)   I switched from linguistics to geography. The lectures were less boring.

In the cases exemplified by (30), it may be that one potential antecedent representation is more accessible (that is, salient or prominent) than the other(s), and hence examined first; in (30) the mental representation of the open door would certainly be more accessible because it has already been singled out and more said about it than the others. But whether or not this is the case, the hearer has to find a maximally accessible context which will combine with one representation to yield worthwhile effects and an acceptable interpretation at no unjustifiable processing cost. In (30), optimal relevance is achieved by taking the open door to be the antecedent of *the door*. In bridging cases like (31), the most easily inferred representation is the most accessible (here, the two windows of the room mentioned, by way of the encyclopedic knowledge that rooms can have windows) and this will be accepted as the correct referent if it meets the requirement of relevance (as would be the case here). The mixed case (32) involves the same process of inference, but the correct bridge, too, has to be inferred. The two bridges available are the propositions (derived from encyclopedic knowledge) that studying linguistics involves attending lectures and that studying geography involves attending lectures. The second of these would be the correct choice as trigger for *the lectures*, because the resultant interpretation, that the geography lectures were less boring than the linguistics ones, would achieve relevance either by explaining why the speaker switched subjects or as an account of what she found after switching subjects.

272

Wilson's view of definiteness is a version of identifiability: interpreting a definite noun phrase means retrieving or constructing a conceptual representation which uniquely identifies the intended referent. Kempson (1988) presents a similar view more fully. Definiteness amounts to a guarantee of accessibility; a speaker uses a definite noun phrase to indicate that a conceptual representation corresponding to the noun phrase is easily accessible to the hearer. The most straightforward cases are immediate situation and anaphoric uses, in which the relevant easily accessible information consists, respectively, of the hearer's perception of the scenario in which the utterance occurs and the content of the preceding discourse. Where the situation and the explicit content of the discourse do not provide the representation required, the hearer must assume that this representation can be easily inferred by way of the context. The concepts expressed by words are claimed to be stores of information, including associated information, and such information contributes to the context. This is what is involved in bridging cross-reference. In (31), for instance, the concept 'window' consists in part of the information that windows are a feature of rooms, so the definite *both windows* must be taken as a guarantee of accessibility of a contextual premise such as 'The room had two windows'.

As already noted in 1.2.5, Kempson establishes that many of the distinctions found in pronoun uses apply equally to full definite noun phrases. In particular, the bound-variable use of pronouns, as in (33), is paralleled by examples such as (34):

(33)   **Every boy** worries that **he**'s inadequate.

(34)   Of **every house** in the area that was inspected, it was subsequently reported that **the house** was suffering from subsidence problems.

Quantifier–variable dependencies are subject to configurational requirements, which are specified at some syntactic level (S-structure or logical form). Specifically, a quantifier must c-command a variable in order to have scope over it. This requirement is claimed to be met in (34) as in (33). But Kempson observes further that bound-variable anaphora can interact with bridging cross-reference:

(35)   **Every singer** complained that **the accompanist** played too loudly.

(The relevant interpretation is that each singer complained about his or her own accompanist, possibly a different one for each singer). Again the configurational requirement is met. But the dependency between *the accompanist* and *every singer* also depends on the construction of the additional premise 'Every singer had an accompanist', derived from the contextual knowledge that singers may have accompanists; this is clearly a pragmatic matter. It seems that bound-variable anaphora is not always fully determined by grammatical principles. On the basis of this,

273

Kempson argues that it is, in fact, a pragmatic phenomenon. That is, the construction of the proposition to be conveyed by an utterance, including the binding of variables within this proposition, is a pragmatic matter. But the representations accessible to the hearer in this process include the logical form specified by the grammar, and this contains the quantifier and an associated variable. The latter is also a representation, and is constrained by the logical form to be accessible only within the c-command domain of the quantifier. The grammar can thus impose restrictions on the pragmatic process of proposition construction. To account for examples like (35), it is necessary to assume that a quantifier can bind not only the variable assigned to it in logical form, but also additional, pragmatically added variables. In this example it quantifies over ordered pairs of singer and accompanist. This type of non-referential use of definites is thus claimed to involve the same process of interpretation – the accessing of a representation – as the straightforward situational and anaphoric uses.

For an application of these ideas to definiteness in a particular language other than English, see Blass (1990) on Sissala. Blass sees determiners generally as having the function of guiding the hearer towards appropriate conceptual addresses so as to establish the intended interpretation of an utterance. The Sissala definite article *ná* behaves essentially like English *the*, and is used whenever the speaker has reason to suppose the hearer is in a position to access a conceptual representation corresponding to the intended referent.

7.5   Well, what is definiteness then?

It is clear from the foregoing survey of accounts of definiteness from various theoretical perspectives that versions of the two basic criteria introduced in Chapter 1, identifiability and inclusiveness, keep recurring. These concepts have undergone considerable mutation, perhaps most radically in the case of the relevance theory account which, though obviously derived from identifiability, is very different from the simple version of this we started with. But, in so far as we can still say that identifiability and inclusiveness have persisted, writers almost invariably choose one or the other of them and claim that this one gives the correct account. The reality, however, is that no one has shown conclusively that a version or mutation of either identifiability or inclusiveness accounts adequately for all definite uses. Some uses still seem to yield to only one or the other characterization. The question with which we began the chapter – identifiability or inclusiveness? – is, therefore, still unresolved.

In this section I propose a solution to this problem, based on the suggestion made earlier that there is a distinction to be made between grammatical definiteness and semantic/pragmatic definiteness, and on the concept of grammaticalization. The proposal is that definiteness *stricto sensu* is not a semantic or pragmatic notion as assumed by almost all writers on the subject,[8] but rather a grammatical category on a par with tense, mood, number, gender etc. But, like these, it is the grammaticalization (that is, the representation in grammar) of some category of meaning. And the crucial observation here is that the correspondence between a grammatical category and the category of meaning it is based on is never one-to-one.

Let us, therefore, examine the concept of grammaticalization, and then discuss how this can be applied to definiteness. The remaining chapters of this book will then be largely devoted to developing the proposal.

7.5.1 *Grammaticalization*

I am using the term "grammaticalization" in a sense somewhat different from, but related to, that most common in the literature; see Hopper and Traugott (1993) and the studies in Traugott and Heine (1991). The term is used mainly in diachronic studies to refer to the process by which lexical items are reduced to grammatical status. This typically involves lexical items undergoing "semantic bleaching", loss of part of their meaning, and coming to express instead some grammatical concept. This semantic reduction is usually accompanied by morphophonological reduction, so that the words affected develop into grammatical forms such as affixes or inflections, or perhaps free-form but non-lexical words. In some cases it is a matter of open-class items coming to form a closed class, usually with accompanying phonological reduction. Examples are: the creation in English of a closed class of modal auxiliaries (*will, would, can, must* etc.), usually unstressed and showing further reduced forms like *'ll, 'd*, from what were originally lexical verbs expressing modal concepts; the development in the Romance languages of a future tense paradigm with endings like Spanish *-é* and French *-ai* in the first person singular, derived from Latin *habeo* 'I have', via a stage at which the reflex of this verb was an auxiliary; the evolution in some languages of nouns used in counting (like English *head* in *three head of cattle*) into non-lexical classifiers, and perhaps further into gender morphemes. The grammatical category or concept which comes to be expressed by a grammaticalized form may already be present in the language with a different exponent (which is perhaps ousted by the new form), or it may be new to the language. A third possibility is that something of what the new grammatical form expresses was already conveyed lexically, either by other items or by the reduced item itself before its grammaticalization; this is the case with the English modals mentioned above. The second and third of these possibilities, that a concept which is not

[8] A recent exception is Lambrecht (1994), whose view of definiteness is close to that advanced here.

grammatically encoded in a language, though it may be (partly) expressed lexically, comes to be expressed by one or more grammatical morphemes, make the link with my use of the term "grammaticalization".

I use the term essentially in a synchronic sense, to denote the representation by a grammatical form or forms (and thus with the status of a grammatical category) of some concept of meaning. But note that the situation described by this use of "grammaticalization" commonly comes into being through the diachronic process described. I will therefore also use the term in a diachronic sense to denote the development whereby a concept of meaning comes to be represented as a grammatical category.

It is generally the case that grammatical categories are not direct expressions of the semantic/pragmatic concepts which they can be said to be the grammaticalizations of. When a concept comes to be represented grammatically it takes on a new life, with the result that the grammatical category created is not limited to expressing that concept. The original concept is likely, however, to continue to be the prototypical value of the grammatical category, so that the category can still be seen as expressing that concept in its central uses. This is what makes it possible to speak of the category as synchronically the grammaticalization of the concept. A few examples will make this clear.

Tense is usually thought of as the grammatical category which expresses time distinctions. Thus, in a language which distinguishes past, present and future tenses, one might expect the present to be used in describing events or states simultaneous with the utterance, the past and the future to be used in describing events or states anterior and subsequent, respectively, to the utterance. And for the most part this is likely to be the case. This simple picture is complicated by what might be thought of as secondary temporal relationships; thus, in a classic study of tense, Reichenbach (1947) points to the possibility of reference points distinct from, but themselves defined in relation to, the moment of utterance. For example, a pluperfect form like *I had left* describes an event anterior to a reference point which is itself past (that is, anterior to the utterance). Another complication is that many languages, including English, make only a two-way basic tense distinction, past and non-past rather than past, present and future. But these complications do not counter the basic point. However, much more serious difficulties confront any attempt to account for tense in terms of the expression of relative time distinctions. In many languages, it is possible for a past tense form to be used in describing a present or future event, for example in conditional contexts where unreality is to be conveyed. In English, *If I meet John tomorrow he'll be surprised* and *If I met John tomorrow he'd be surprised* both relate to some possible meeting yet to occur. The difference between *meet* and *met* has nothing to do with any temporal difference. Rather, the choice of past *met* (followed by past *'d* rather than present *'ll*) expresses (something like) the view that the meeting is unlikely to occur. So while it may be fair to say that tense is the grammaticalization of relative time distinctions, and prototypically expresses these, there is clearly much more to tense than this.[9]

Subjunctive mood is often said to indicate that the action or state expressed by a verb is being presented as hypothetical or virtual rather than factual. Again, this characterization works to a large extent; it captures, for example, the contrast in Spanish between *aunque* + indicative 'although' and *aunque* + subjunctive 'even if'. But languages vary greatly in the use of the subjunctive. In formal registers of German it is used for reported speech – a striking difference from Spanish and other languages. And in French the subjunctive is obligatory after *bien que* 'although', though there may be no element of hypotheticality in the clause: *Bien qu'il soit malade, il est déjà arrivé* 'Although he **is** ill, he has already arrived'.

To take a nominal grammatical category, consider number. In singular–plural systems, this category grammaticalizes the distinction between 'one' and 'more than one'. But there are complications, such as that presented in English by *pluralia tantum* nouns of the type *trousers*, *scissors*, which are plural even when used to refer to single objects. Thus *John's trousers are grey* could be a statement about six garments John owns or about a single garment he is wearing at present.[10] Moreover, mass nouns like *water*, *mud*, *sugar* occur in a morphologically singular form though not denoting single discrete objects; in other words, though grammatically singular, they are not semantically "singular". Finally, recall from the discussion of number in the personal pronoun systems of Carib and Lakhota in 3.1.1 and 3.4.1 that these languages have a grammatically singular first-person inclusive pronoun, with the meaning 'you and I' – thus semantically dual.

7.5.2 *Grammaticalization and definiteness*

Definiteness is, I suggest, a grammatical category like those just discussed. Given this, we can expect that, like most grammatical categories, it is

---

[9] It might be argued that the English past tense has a very general core meaning of "remoteness", of which remoteness in (past) time and factual remoteness are manifestations. This idea is discussed and rejected by Palmer (1974) and Huddleston (1984).

[10] Of course the origin of this phenomenon lies in the fact that trousers and scissors have a two-part structure, but this does not affect the point. If nouns for garments with two legs, like *trousers* and, better still, *overalls* (which have a substantial trunk section as well as legs) are plural, why not those for garments with two sleeves (*shirt*, *pullover*)? And note that we cannot use **a trouser* to speak of half of a pair of trousers, as should be possible if *trousers* really expressed 'more than one'. A good case could be made for regarding nouns of this type as semantically mass, though grammatically count and plural (like *oats*).

not present in all languages. I shall assume that it is only present in languages which show overt definiteness marking, a definite article of some kind – though I will develop below the qualification that many languages have definiteness in pronominal, but not full, noun phrases. Definiteness is the grammaticalization of what I have informally termed "semantic/pragmatic definiteness". The point here is that this semantic/pragmatic concept occurs widely in languages which lack the corresponding grammatical category. This is clear from the discussion in Chapter 6, where it was seen that a "definite" interpretation plays an important part in many languages which show no formal marking of definiteness. Thus in Mandarin a noun phrase in subject position must be a topic and therefore "definite", while a noun phrase in the existential construction must be understood as "indefinite". But what is a definite or indefinite interpretation? It appears that in these languages with no definiteness marking it is, as an element of discourse organization, to do with whether or not a referent is familiar or already established in the discourse – thus identifiability rather than inclusiveness. This assumption is bolstered by the observation that demonstratives, which cannot be characterized as inclusive, are invariably treated as definite in interpretation in (in)definiteness effect contexts. Taking this as the clue, let us say that definiteness is the grammaticalization of identifiability. It may be that identifiability is an element in interpretation in all languages, but in many languages it is not grammaticalized.

In languages where identifiability is represented grammatically, this representation is definiteness; and definiteness is likely to express identifiability prototypically. But it is to be expected that there will be other uses of definiteness which do not relate to identifiability – inclusive uses for example. Putting this point in diachronic terms, when identifiability comes to be grammaticalized as definiteness, this category will go on to develop other uses. There may also be some instances of identifiability (generics for example) which are not treated in a given language as definite. The effect of these possibilities is that (as with the subjunctive) there will be considerable variation between languages in the use of the category. Thus some languages will require generics to be definite while others do not; in some languages definiteness will be optional even in noun phrases clearly interpreted as identifiable, as was seen with Hausa in 2.2.1. In languages like Maori which, as seen in 2.2.4, show an article combining obviously "definite" (identifiable) uses with something akin to specificity, this article too can be treated as encoding definiteness; in this case certain types of noun phrase occurrence which in other languages are treated as indefinite are grammatically definite. The range of variation is considerable, but no greater than that found with many other grammatical categories. What justifies us in identifying the same category cross-linguistically despite this variation is that there is always a large central core of uses relatable directly to identifiability.

278

7.5.3 Simple and complex definiteness

The proposal just outlined gives an answer to the question whether definiteness is universal or not: while identifiability, presumably a pragmatic concept or an element of information structure (see Lambrecht (1994) for detailed discussion), may play a role in all languages, definiteness does not. Treating definiteness as a grammatical category seems fairly straightforward for simple definites, where the category is encoded by affixes, clitics or morphophonologically weak free forms – typical grammatical or "functional" morphemes. But what consequences does this treatment have for complex definites, where the article which encodes the category is in many cases not present? Let us consider demonstratives, personal pronouns, and DG possessives in turn.

In languages showing definiteness marking (thus having the category of definiteness), there is no doubt that noun phrases with a demonstrative modifier are definite. In fact, in many such languages, the demonstrative either must or can co-occur in the noun phrase with the definite article, as was shown in 3.1.3. In other cases demonstrative and article do not co-occur, but the demonstrative is a Det like the article and takes its place; it therefore itself, by its position, indicates definiteness as well as demonstrativeness. Less straightforwardly, there are also languages, typically with bound articles, in which articles and demonstratives do not co-occur, despite their not occupying the same slot in the noun phrase. These cases can only be accounted for when we come to examine the DP analysis in Chapter 8, where I will argue that the demonstrative is in a specifier position associated with the head position normally occupied by the article.

But demonstratives occur in all languages, including those lacking definiteness, and here we must come back to the tentative suggestion made in 3.1.3 that demonstratives are not lexically specified as [+ Def]. Suppose they are marked [+ Dem] and that this feature is interpreted as meaning that the speaker is pointing out or otherwise providing sufficient information for the hearer to pick out the referent. It follows that the referent is identifiable, so demonstratives bring the pragmatic concept underlying definiteness into play. This is enough to ensure that in languages with definiteness this category is triggered by the presence of a demonstrative. But in other languages only the pragmatic concept of identifiability is involved and there is no definiteness with demonstratives.

I have claimed that strong personal pronouns are demonstratives. It may be, moreover, that the forms functioning as personal pronouns in some languages, like Japanese, where they have considerable phonological substance, are actually full noun phrases. But weak personal pronouns (including null *pro*) are the pronominal correlate of simple definite noun phrases. Indeed I have argued, adapting the analysis of Postal (1970), that they are definite articles. The problem here is that weak pronouns do occur in languages which otherwise lack definiteness marking.

Defining definiteness

Russian *on* 'he', *ona* 'she' are an example; much more common is the phenomenon of languages, apparently without definiteness as a category, displaying
pro identified by agreement morphology. If *pro* is simply a null weak personal
pronoun, then it is in effect a null definite article. And this does seem to be
the correct characterization, as shown in 5.5.1. In all languages in which a null
argument is identified by agreement, it is interpreted as definite. Thus Spanish *pro*
canta (*pro* sings) can be 'he is singing', 'she is singing' or 'it is singing', but not
'one/someone is singing'. Importantly, this is not the case with null arguments not
identified by agreement. These occur freely in, for example, Korean (see 3.4.2),
and in a more limited way in other languages, as in object position in Latin *Habeo*
(have+1SG) 'I have it/one/some'. In these languages the null argument is probably
not *pro* (but see the reservation noted in 5.5.1 following Cole (1987)). Assuming
this, we can say that *pro* (at least when associated with agreement morphology)
is definite, since if it were not, it should allow an indefinite (non-identifiable) interpretation in appropriate contexts, given that it has no demonstrative content. And
pro appears in a great many languages which otherwise have no definite article.

To account for this, I propose that many languages have the category of definiteness in pronominal noun phrases only. We can therefore set up a typology of languages as follows:

Type I: no definiteness
Type II: definiteness available only in pronominal noun phrases
Type III: definiteness available in pronominal and full noun phrases

Languages of Type II certainly represent an odd phenomenon, but it is not
unusual for pronouns to differ radically in structure from full noun phrases. In
many Australian languages, for example, they are organized on a different case
system, as discussed by Dixon (1980, chapters 9–11). I shall return to this phenomenon in Chapters 8 and 9.

DG possessives, which (as one would expect) probably only occur in languages
which have definiteness, commonly displace the definite article, like demonstratives. Unlike demonstratives, they are frequently affixal, so may displace affixal
articles as well as free-form determiner articles; see 3.3.4. But, again like demonstratives, they may also occupy a different position from the article, yet not co-
occur with it. Again I will return to this in connection with the DP analysis of the
noun phrase.

I have made the point several times that possessives, unlike demonstratives, are
not inherently definite, even pragmatically. One may wonder, therefore, where the
DG phenomenon comes from. I suggest it has its origin in the phenomenon of
inalienable possession. Recall that many languages (with and without definiteness)
make a structural distinction between alienable and inalienable possession, the

280

latter usually involving a closer syntactic association between possessor and possessum. Recall also that in languages with definiteness, including English, nouns of the inalienable type show a strong preference for occurring in definite possessive structures, even when the usual conditions for definite occurrence do not strictly apply; thus *my hand, Mary's sister* when it is not contextually clear which of my hands or Mary's sisters is intended. My suggestion is that when a language acquires the category of definiteness, the structure used for inalienable possession comes to be interpreted as a definite structure, with the possessor treated as being in definite Det (or a related) position. This structure, involving either a free-form possessor or an affixal possessor in a position which could be that of a free-form or affixal article, is then eventually extended to other, non-inalienable, head nouns.

If definiteness is a grammatical category it is important to consider how it is represented in grammatical structure. This is the topic of the next chapter, where the syntactic structure of the noun phrase is examined in greater detail.

8
Definiteness and noun phrase structure

I have argued that definiteness is a morphosyntactic category, grammaticalizing a pragmatic category of identifiability. With this in mind, we will now consider the representation of definiteness in syntax. This means discussing recent developments in the theory of phrase structure according to which definite and indefinite determiners do not, as traditionally assumed, modify nouns, but rather themselves head noun phrases. This view, the DP hypothesis, is part of a more general theory of "functional heads", and I shall in fact argue that the category of definiteness is itself such a functional head. Almost all current work on the noun phrase assumes the DP analysis, but since much still important less recent work on definiteness is cast within the NP analysis, I begin by examining the syntactic representation of definiteness in this older framework.

Other questions to be considered along the way include: What is the category status of articles and other determiners? Are there constraints on the positions in which definite determiners may occur in the noun phrase? Are certain determiners, including definite articles, specified in the lexicon as [+ Def], or does definiteness arise in a noun phrase in some other way? How can the range of article types occurring in languages be accounted for? How does the analysis of definite pronouns relate to that of definite full noun phrases? These are fairly obvious questions arising from our earlier discussion, particularly from the comparative survey of Chapters 2 and 3. We will also look more closely at the phenomenon of non-configurationality, attempting to relate it to the theory of functional heads.

Finally, the treatment of definiteness as a grammatical category will be taken a step further, by examining how it relates to another such category, that of person. Specifically, I will propose that the relationship between definiteness and person is so intimate that it justifies treating the two as a single category.

8.1 The noun phrase as NP

Before the recent challenge of the DP hypothesis, it was assumed that the noun phrase was projected from the category N(oun), being therefore NP. The reader is at this point referred back to the outline in 1.4 of what this, combined with the claims of X-bar theory, means for noun phrase structure. The essential points for present purposes are that N heads the structure, with an intermediate level N' between N and NP (or N''), and that at least some determiners (of category Det) occupy the specifier position which combines with X' to form the maximal or phrasal projection NP. Linear order may vary across languages, but the overall structure given in 1.4, defined in terms of what is sister to what and what dominates what, is taken to be applicable to configurational languages generally. In this section we will discuss definiteness and definiteness marking in relation to this conception of noun phrase structure before going on to examine the rival DP analysis.

8.1.1 The specifier position and definite Dets

In many traditional grammars the term "specify" is used synonymously with "determine", and in more theoretical work the specifier was first conceived of as the position in NP where articles, other determiners and indeed possessives occur (*the house, this house, Ann's house*) – items thought of as delimiting or defining the reference of the NP. This is essentially the function assumed for the specifier in a lot of work in formal semantics. The specifier c-commands the rest of the phrase, and this structural relationship is assumed to be involved in the binding of variables by a logical operator. Therefore determiners which express quantification, including in some treatments, as we have seen, both definite and indefinite articles, are taken to be specifiers binding a variable in the semantic representation of N'.

In current work in syntax the specifier (of phrases generally, not just of NP) is seen as having three further roles. First, in a phrase headed by a θ-role assigner, VP for example, the specifier position is the target for the external θ-role (that of Agent, for instance, which is typically assigned to the subject). Second, it is a position expressions may move into from positions deeper inside the structure, for example because they cannot receive grammatical case in their original position; moreover, it may act as an "escape hatch", a position from which items can move further on, out of the immediate phrasal projection. It follows from these two functions that specifiers are commonly occupied by arguments, that is, NPs, and this fact is part of the attraction of the DP hypothesis, which treats determiners as heads. It is not necessarily ruled out, however, on either the NP or the DP analysis, that the specifier is a position where determiners may be generated as well as being one which arguments may arise in, move into or pass through. The third role of the specifier is to close off the phrasal projection. The intermediate X' level may, on some views, recur to allow multiple modification by adjunction, but the specifier must be daughter to the maximal projection, so it completes the phrase.[1] This third role relates to the semantic function referred to, since it entails the specifier

---

[1] Recent proposals by Chomsky (1995), however, allow multiple specifiers in a single phrase.

being in a c-commanding position in relation to the rest of the phrase. An important concept in recent research is a process of Specifier–Head Agreement, in which specifier expressions of various kinds enter into an agreement relationship with their head – ensuring, for example, that agreement morphology on verbs does not clash with the subject (which is a specifier) in person and number, and that interrogatives in specifier of CP (complementizer phrase) do not co-occur with declarative complementizers.

We saw in Chapter 2 that one of the most common devices occurring in languages for encoding definiteness is an item appearing in a peripheral position in NP, most commonly on the left. It is frequently phonologically weak, and may or may not carry inflectional morphology. We can hypothesize that such definiteness markers will generally have the same basic analysis (though bearing in mind that this treatment cannot be simply assumed for a given case without serious analysis of the language in question): that they are of category Det and occupy the NP specifier position. We have also seen, in Chapter 1, that in English demonstratives and possessives occupy the same slot in NP as *the*, and that NPs like *this shop*, *my car* are definite. The quantificational determiners *all*, *both*, *every*, *most*, also generally taken to be definite, either can or typically do occur in this position too. With *all* and *both* there is also the pre-determiner use in which, like a partitive, they express a proportion of the whole denoted by the complete NP following: *all the girls*, *both your friends*. But in *all three defendants* and *both lawyers*, synonymous with the alternative pre-determiner structures *all the three defendants* and *both the lawyers*, the quantifiers are almost certainly in specifier position. It should be mentioned that there are occurrences of *all* where the analysis is less clear:

(1)   **All cats** like milk.

(2)   **All pupils** must assemble in the courtyard at noon.

Given the lack of a second determiner, *all* may be in specifier position in these examples. But it is arguable that *cats* and *pupils* here are complete bare plural generic NPs with *all* as pre-determiner; *pupils* in (2) represents a generalization over a more limited domain than *cats* in (1) (a particular school rather than the world), but this is perfectly possible with generics. Yet even treating these noun phrases as "bare" plural generics it may still be that *all* is within the NP, in specifier position; as Lyons (1995c) argues, generics of this kind are not incompatible with Dets (as the description "bare" implies they should be), since they may contain a demonstrative, interpreted as non-restrictive and expressing emotional distance, and demonstratives only occur in the specifier in English:

(3)   I'm all in favour of people cycling more, but **those mountain bikes** are a nuisance in the country.

We noted in 1.4 the complication that *every* can appear not only in Det position (the normal case), but also in some more interior position in the presence of a possessive and with a restricted set of head nouns: *the king's every whim, the every whim of the king*. But this use is quite marginal. Summarizing, the general picture for English is that definite Dets occur typically, though not invariably, in the specifier of NP.

This generalization does not, however, hold for all languages. Recall first that AG possessives are in a distinct position from the definite article: Spanish *el amigo mío* 'my friend'. This is not surprising since possession does not imply definiteness, and indeed an indefinite interpretation is possible in AG languages if the definite article is not included: *unos amigos míos* 'sm friends of mine'. So possessives need not be definite determiners, and in many cases they are probably adjectives; in Spanish the adjectival inflection and position of the AG possessive contrasts with the more limited inflection of the alternative Det-like DG possessive (*mi amigo* 'my friend'), and it is plausible to suppose a difference of category between the two (though I shall question this supposition below). But demonstratives too, which do entail definiteness, are often found in some position other than the specifier: Irish *an leabhar sin* (the book that) 'that book', Catalan (optionally) *els detalls aquells* (the details those) 'those details'. The same is true of other definite determiners. Corresponding to English *all*, German has *all*, close in behaviour and position, but also *ganz*, appearing further inside the NP and possibly adjectival: *all die Frauen* or (colloquially) *die ganzen Frauen* 'all the women'. *Meiste* 'most' and *beide* 'both' are similar in position to *ganz*: *die meisten Leute* 'most people', *die beiden Kinder* 'both (the) children'. The same holds of a range of determiners in Hungarian (Szabolcsi 1994), where possessive expressions (in nominative case form) can follow the definite article and be themselves followed by demonstratives or other definite determiners: *a Peter minden/ezen kalapja* (the Peter+NOM every/this hat) 'every/this hat of Peter's'. All these observations are made more fully in Chapter 3.

Facts like these seem to tell against the hypothesis that the specifier position has a special relationship to definiteness. But two further facts must be considered here. First, the definite article itself is not subject to this kind of variation in position. In all the languages just examined, the article occupies a peripheral position which is likely to be the same as that of English *the*,[2] and cannot occur lower in the NP. And this is more generally true; in all languages in which the definite article

[2] Szabolcsi (1994) argues that the Hungarian noun phrase has a structure closer to that of the clause than has that of English, and that the Hungarian definite article occupies a position corresponding to the complementizer, a position more peripheral than that of English *the*. Lyons (1994a), however, offers a different analysis, in which the Hungarian and English articles do occupy the same position.

is a free form as opposed to an inflectional morpheme or clitic, it appears in such a peripheral position. Second, in the languages considered above in which various determiners associated with definiteness occur deeper in the NP structure (or outside this structure), the definite article (or some other definite Det) must also appear, in what I am taking to be specifier position. That is, whereas in English definite possessives, demonstratives and quantifiers replace *the*, in these other languages where such determiners occupy a different position they do not replace the definite article but co-occur with it (or with some other specifier definite Det). Thus Catalan *detalls aquells* 'those details', German *meiste Leute* 'most people'. The point about some other definite Det in the specifier is important; German, for example, permits, as well as *die beiden Kinder* 'both (the) children', also *diese beiden Kinder* 'both these children' and *meine beiden Kinder* 'both my children'. The essential thing is not simply that the definite article must be present, but that some Det must be present in specifier position. It is likely that the definiteness of the NP, which may be required by the presence in it of certain determiners, depends on the expression in the specifier; the demonstrative or quantifier lower down, which requires the definite interpretation, is not itself able to impose it when not in the right position.

I have argued that quasi-indefinite articles like English *a* are cardinality expressions, like the numerals and *much/many* which clearly occur in a post-specifier position, as shown by *the one problem, these many letters*. While *a* and *the* do not co-occur, *a* is in fact just as complementary to the numeral *one*, and *the* and *one* unquestionably occupy different positions. The likelihood that *a* belongs in numeral position is all the greater in the many languages where the cardinal article and the singular numeral are identical in form, and I shall take this to be the correct analysis. Assuming cardinality position to be daughter to N′ (and adopting the arbitrary category label Q, recalling Bresnan's (1973) QP analysis referred to in 1.4) would give *the three blue cars* and *a blue car* the following structures:

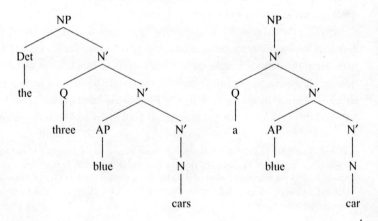

Given this analysis, and the doubt I have expressed that any language has a true indefinite article though many have a cardinal article, then not only is the specifier the position of the definite article and, in some languages, at least some other definite Dets. It is plausible to claim that it is a position *only* definite Dets may occupy.

8.1.2   *Affixal articles*

The second commonly occurring type of definite article is the affixal one, and the obvious way to relate this type to the present discussion is in terms of a relationship between the affix and the specifier position. Where the affix is attached to the head noun, this might involve invoking Specifier–Head Agreement, so that the affix is seen as a marker of agreement between N and a null (in most cases) [+ Def] Det in the specifier. Alternatively, it might be a matter of movement, a specifier article cliticizing to its head or elsewhere. Which of these approaches is the more appropriate could only be determined through analysis of the facts of individual languages, and both processes may occur. The phenomenon would be parallel to possessive agreement, where an affix occurs on a head noun, either showing agreement with an overt possessive expression, or itself being the only possessive expression. Given that free-form DG possessives occur in the specifier, this latter phenomenon (where it has a DG interpretation) is probably to be seen as a relationship between a possessive agreement affix and a null pronominal possessive in the specifier – exactly like the relationship between an agreement inflection on a verb and a null pronominal subject. In both cases the relationship may be seen as true agreement or cliticization, depending on the individual language and on the theoretical position adopted. Subject–verb agreement and possessive agreement both involve a relationship between an affix and an argument in the specifier. What I am suggesting for affixal articles, on the other hand, is a relationship between an affix and a Det in the specifier. This difference by no means rules out the idea, but it should be pointed out that a lot less is known about agreement and cliticization processes involving categories other than NP. Let us examine the relevant facts of one language, which give some support to the proposal.

Danish has both an affixal article and a free-form article. The basic rule is that the free-form article is used when the noun is preceded by an adjective or other modifier. Thus *hus* 'house', *huset* 'the house', *det store hus* 'the big house'. The position of the lexical article *den/det/de* in relation to other pre-nominal modifiers shows it to be closely comparable to English *the*, as a specifier Det: *de tre børn* 'the three children'. The first pointer to a relationship between the two article forms is that they are in complete complementary distribution in simple definite NPs. This suggests that they may well be, at some level, the same thing. One possible analysis is that there are two specifier definite articles, one overt and one null, and the null form triggers agreement on the noun; this agreement has the function of "identifying" the null Det, and is comparable to the subject–verb agreement morphology of Irish, which is also only available when the subject is null. The other analysis is the cliticization one, on which again there are two specifier articles, but both are overt; one is *den/det/de*, a lexical item, the other is the clitic *-(e)n/-(e)t/-(e)ne*, which must move to attach to the noun. I will not attempt to choose between these analyses; the important thing is that both involve a syntactic relationship between specifier and head. The evidence goes further. Pre-nominal possessives and genitives in Danish are of the DG type, occupying specifier position (*dine tre børn* 'your three children', *mandens tre børn* 'the man's three children') and imposing a definite interpretation. The lexical article cannot co-occur with a possessive, as expected, because they occupy the same "slot"; but nor can the affixal article, despite the definiteness of the NP: **dine børnene* 'your children', **mandens børnene* 'the man's children'. This is less expected, but would follow from the assumption that the affixal article is syntactically related to the specifier position. Since this relationship involves the specifier being phonologically null on the surface (either because agreement is only with a null Det or because a clitic Det moves from there, whether or not some kind of empty category remains), it cannot hold if the specifier is occupied by a possessive.

The account would be more complex for a language such as Swedish, where there is not complete complementarity between the affixal article and specifier Dets. But the point is that for some languages there is a clear case for taking an affixal article to stand in a syntactic relationship with the specifier position, and it is legitimate to hypothesize that a similar analysis can be extended to other languages. Given this, we may suppose that the proposal of a special relationship between the specifier and definiteness is valid not only for languages in which the definite article is a lexical item, but more generally.

8.1.3   The definite constraint

This generalization gives rise to a question: what is the nature of the association between NP specifier and definiteness, and why is it that only definite Dets occupy this position? An answer has been offered by Lyons (1985, 1986a), who suggests that definite Dets are not, in fact, lexically specified as [+ Def]; there is no such feature, and definiteness or indefiniteness is determined by syntactic structure.

The starting point for this claim is the observation in 8.1.1 that demonstratives and other definite determiners in languages where they are in some non-specifier position have to be supplemented by the definite article or some other specifier Det to give a well-formed definite NP (in languages having a definite article). It seems that, although NPs modified by certain determiners must be definite, the lexical content of the determiner itself is not sufficient to guarantee this definite value. So the suggestion is that the "inherent definiteness" of such determiners lies in their having a lexico-semantic content which is incompatible with indefiniteness in the modified NP; an indefinite NP with a modifier like *that, most, both* would be semantically anomalous. But definiteness itself, expressed as a feature [+ Def], is not part of their meaning or grammatical content. This suggestion accounts straightforwardly for the necessity of the article in Irish *an fear sin* (the man that) 'that man', German *die meisten Leute* (the most people) 'most people' etc. In languages like English where demonstratives and definite quantifiers are in the specifier, no further marker of definiteness appears, suggesting that these determiners are [+ Def] in these languages. But then why are they lexically definite only in those cases where they occur in specifier position, and not otherwise? There is a redundancy here. A better account is to say that such determiners are not marked [+ Def] in any language; English *this* is not different in meaning from Spanish *este*, nor English *most* from German *meiste*. Rather, the definiteness (which the determiner requires but does not itself impose) comes from the filling of the specifier, and it may be the demonstrative or quantificational determiner itself which fills this position, or something else, typically the definite article.

AG possessives differ from demonstratives in that the modified NP can be indefinite; the definiteness or indefiniteness of the NP has nothing to do with the possessive. So we would not even consider marking such possessives [+ Def]. But DG possessives are like definite determiners. Again, however, the apparent [+ Def] value of these possessives correlates invariably with specifier position, and can therefore be argued to follow from this. It is possible to make the attractive claim that specifier possessives do not differ in meaning from adjectival possessives, and moreover that the two types do not necessarily differ in category. Spanish has both DG *mi* 'my', *tu* 'your', apparently definite Dets, and AG *mío, tuyo*, post-nominal adjectives, showing a clear morphological difference. But several commonly occurring adjectives in Spanish appear in a reduced form when pre-nominal; examples are *buen* 'good', *gran* 'great', *primer* 'first', reductions of *bueno, grande, primero*. So the morphological difference does not necessarily point to a difference of category; *mi* and *mío* may well both be adjectives. Lyons proposes that English *my car* and Spanish *mi coche* are definite because the specifier is filled, by the possessive as it happens. But if the possessive is elsewhere, a definite interpretation can still be achieved by putting some other item, such as the definite article, in the specifier; thus Spanish *el coche mío* 'my car', or *este coche mío* (this car my) 'this car of mine'.

The possessive facts make it clear that what occupies the specifier to yield a definite reading need not be a "definite determiner". This points to a general principle of interpretation, that definiteness in an NP arises from the filling of the specifier, by anything at all. This principle is termed by Lyons the "definite constraint". Definiteness is thus seen as being determined structurally, not lexically. In the works referred to, Lyons leaves open the question whether indefinite NPs simply have their specifier empty, whether they have no specifier position, or, more radically, whether they lack the specifier because they are not maximal projections. This last possibility is closely comparable to the proposal of Rothstein and Reed (1984) that indefinites are N″ and definites N‴. An important consequence of the definite constraint, if it is correct, is that, since the expression inducing definiteness in the NP merely by its presence in the specifier need not be a definite Det, there is no need even for the definite article to be [+ Def]. And since the definite article frequently has no semantic or grammatical content apart from [+ Def], this means it can be semantically and grammatically empty. It is a meaningless filler, with the role of occupying NP specifier in the absence of any contentful item to fill that position. It is thus a pleonastic Det, comparable to the pleonastic pronoun *it* in *It seems that . . .*

The ideas discussed in this section will be reinterpreted below in terms of the DP framework, which offers a way of explaining why the filling of a particular structural position induces definiteness.

8.2 The DP hypothesis

The idea that the noun phrase is projected from Det rather than N arises out of the distinction, which has grown in importance, between lexical or substantive categories like N, V, A and P, and "functional" categories, whose role is essentially grammatical and which are often realized as inflectional morphemes. A currently influential view is that phrases projected from lexical categories occur as complements in higher phrases projected from functional heads. Thus for a time the clause was taken to be headed by a category I(nflection), expressing tense and "subject–verb" agreement; more recently I has been split into separate T(ense) and Agr(eement) heads, and the lexical projection VP is relatively low in the tree structure. The DP hypothesis represents the extension of such ideas to the noun phrase, argued to be headed by Det (or D), paralleling I (or one of its components T and Agr, or perhaps C(omplementizer)), and with NP, headed by N, lower down in a place in the tree parallel to that of VP in the clause. And just as the number of functional heads in the clause has multiplied, there are now numerous proposals in the literature for functional heads additional to D in the noun phrase. The major presentation of the DP hypothesis is Abney (1987), and some basic discussions for a number of languages are: Hellan (1986), Szabolcsi (1987), Haider (1988), Ritter (1988), Radford (1993). For critical discussion see Payne (1993). The reader is invited to turn back at this point to 1.4 for the essentials.

The DP analysis is attractive on a number of grounds. First, it makes the noun phrase closely parallel in its structure to the clause. The desirability of this has long been evident, since it captures the many similarities in behaviour between the two, exemplified by the relationship between nominalizations like *the army's destruction of the city, the city's destruction* and the corresponding clauses *The army destroyed the city, The city was destroyed.* In these expressions the position of the noun *destruction* corresponds to that of the verb *destroy*; both these lexical heads may take a complement, *(of) the city*, which in both cases may undergo a passivization process; and both nominalization and clause can have a subject, taken to occupy the specifier of the functional head. A second advantage afforded by the DP hypothesis is that it makes the theory of phrase structure much more general, since now all categories, not just the major lexical ones, have full phrasal projections. And thirdly, the analysis of pronouns becomes more straightforward. On the NP analysis pronouns are arguably anomalous in lacking an overt noun head – unless pronouns are taken to be a kind of noun, a problematic view given that they cannot in general be modified by Dets (**this him, *the me*). Within the DP framework pronouns can be treated as Dets (following Postal 1970) which lack an NP complement.

8.2.1 Movement processes in DP

A central assumption of current syntactic theory is that constituents may move from their underlying position. A major movement process is Head Movement, whereby a head moves, invariably upwards, to another head position where it combines in some way with the head already in that position. For discussion of the theoretical issues involved see Haegeman (1994: chapter 2). It is proposed in much research that N raises in many languages, in some cases all the way to D, in others only as far as some intermediate head position. This is to account for the fact that languages vary in the surface position of N relative to modifying constituents like APs and PPs. For example, in English APs generally precede N and PPs follow; in most Romance languages some APs precede N while most APs and all PPs follow. On the assumption that the position of most modifying expressions is relatively fixed, and that they mostly originate pre-nominally, the varying surface patterns can be accounted for by movement of N over varying distances. Movement of N all the way to D would be taken to occur in languages where the definite article is an affix on the noun, representing merging of N and D. But a complicating factor is that some modifiers can also move, again mostly upwards. This applies particularly to possessives.

Possessives (such as *John's, my*) are widely assumed to originate in NP specifier position, following Fukui (1986), but to move, at least in some languages, to a higher specifier position in order to be case-marked, since no case is assigned to NP specifier. A difficulty for this analysis is that this movement applies not only to nominal possessives (noun phrases and pronouns in the genitive), but also to apparently adjectival ones. But it may be that some factor other than case assignment underlies this process. The reason for taking the D-structure position of possessives to be within the NP projection is that they frequently represent arguments of the head noun (in examples like *John's arrival, her disgust at his behaviour, the town's destruction*) and therefore must receive their θ-role from N. But it is assumed that a head can only θ-mark arguments within its own projection (thus, here, within NP).[3] The same reasoning is used to argue that subjects of clauses originate in VP specifier (the "VP-internal subject hypothesis") and then raise to the specifier of some functional projection where they can receive nominative case. With phrases like *John's car, her house* it is less clear that the possessive gets its θ-role from the noun, which does not seem to have an argument structure, but some writers at any rate treat these cases in the same way as those above. A further reason for believing that possessive expressions originate rather low in the structure is that some, particularly prepositional ones like that in English *a painting of Ann's*, appear superficially to the right of N despite the · fact that in the languages concerned the leftward movement of N is thought to be rather short. But some possessives surface well to the left, as in English *Ruth's first great publishing success*, indicating movement. Let us term this process Poss Movement.

Just as a head can only move to another head position, a specifier expression (which must itself be a complete phrase) can only move to another specifier. For English and many other languages Poss Movement is taken to be to DP specifier – thus, in terms of linear order, just to the left of D. On one view (most fully presented in Radford (1993)), the *'s* which occurs with full noun phrase (DP) possessives like *John's, my friend's* is the D. On another (adopted by Abney (1987) among others), the *'s* is a genitive case morpheme or postpositional case transmitter or some such particle forming part of (or attached to) the possessive DP, and the head D is null. These two variants can be shown by the following S-structures, with *t* representing the trace left behind in the D-structure position of the possessive, and with intermediate projections between DP and NP omitted:

---

[3] Note that the possessives in *John's arrival* and *the town's destruction* have theme or patient θ-roles, and probably originate as complements rather than specifiers of the head nominalization. *John's arrival* is an unaccusative structure and *the town's destruction* is passive-like. So possessives originate in NP, but not necessarily in NP specifier; it may be, however, that they pass through NP specifier before moving out of NP.

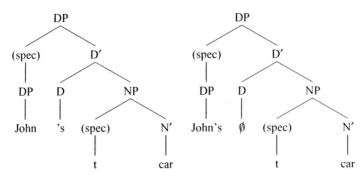

But in many other languages, like Italian, Catalan and Portuguese, pronoun possessives, while clearly higher in S-structure than specifier of NP, are still to the right of (and therefore lower than) D, as is shown by the presence of the definite article or some other determiner before the possessive: Italian *i miei tre bei quadri* (the my three beautiful pictures) 'my three beautiful pictures'. It must be that in these languages the possessive raises only as far as some specifier between that of NP and that of DP. Let us term this "partial Poss Movement" by contrast with the "full Poss Movement" assumed for English. Notice that this difference in the distance of Poss Movement correlates with the AG–DG distinction.

These AG languages with partial Poss Movement and DG languages with full Poss Movement differ in another respect. The definite article or some other recognizable determiner may occur in Poss Movement structures in the former (Italian *i miei quadri* 'my pictures', *dei/quei miei quadri* 'sm/those pictures of mine'), but not in the latter (English **Peter('s) the/these pictures*, **your a plate*). As noted above, the D position in the English structure is taken to be either null or occupied by *'s* (which is therefore a Det), and no other Det can appear there.[4] The reason assumed for this is that the D head in the English DG structure has to be able to assign genitive case to the possessive in its specifier, and the familiar Dets do not have this property. So a special Det (in form *'s* or zero) which is a genitive case assigner occurs in D only in the Poss Movement structure. To avoid commitment to whether *'s* is this special possessive Det, let us represent it as D^{POSS}. There are arguments in the literature for D^{POSS} having overt form in other languages as well as English, for example Olsen (1989) for German, but these are mostly unconvincing,[5] and D^{POSS} seems to be null in most, if not all, DG languages. In

---

[4] This is on the assumption that cardinality expressions are not D in phrases like *Peter's three/many pictures*. Of the definite determiners, it is, moreover, arguable that *every* is an exception to the generalization made here in *Peter's every whim*. But this is the only possible exception.

[5] Olsen claims that only a limited range of noun phrase types (principally proper nouns) can occur in DP specifier in Modern German, and that the *-s* inflection they take is D^{POSS}. But *-s* is one of a range of realizations of genitive case in German, and the assumption that it is

the AG languages mentioned, the possessive is not in DP specifier, because partial Poss Movement does not carry it that far, so there is nothing to prevent an ordinary Det appearing in D.

Notice that the DP hypothesis, in its standard form, differs from the NP analysis in the following crucial respect. According to the latter, free-form definite articles, at least some other determiners, and DG possessives all occupy the same slot (NP specifier), while affixal articles are in a different position (typically attached to N). This is essentially the distribution I have taken for granted up to now. But the DP analysis takes both free-form and affixal definite articles (as well as, for most writers, other determiners too) to be D heads. And DG possessives are taken to be (after Poss Movement) DP specifiers – thus in a position distinct from that of the article and other Dets. I will claim below that these two assumptions of the DP paradigm are misguided.

8.2.2   *Other functional categories in the noun phrase*

As observed above, many more functional projections have been hypothesized in the literature than were originally envisaged, both in the clause and in the noun phrase. The clause was for a time seen as having only IP and CP above the lexical VP, but, as well as I being split into separate T and Agr heads, other clause-level categories like negation, aspect and mood have been claimed to project functional phrases. Similarly, while the DP analysis of the noun phrase originally envisaged only one functional projection above the lexical NP, there have since been numerous proposals for functional categories other than D projecting phrases, principally between DP and NP. Functional categories have been suggested corresponding to all the different classes of determiner (article, demonstrative, quantifier etc.) and to all the grammatical categories associated with nominal expressions. Let us briefly examine a few of these.

Abney (1987) and Kornfilt (1991) discuss a possible Agr(eement), heading AgrP, to represent possessive agreement in languages such as Hungarian and Turkish. Thus in Turkish *ev-imiz* (house-1PL) or *biz-im ev-imiz* (us-GEN house-1PL) 'our house', the agreement morpheme *-imiz* would be the Agr head, attached to the noun as a result of Head Movement of N to Agr. The possessive (null *pro* or overt *bizim*) would be in AgrP specifier and enter into Specifier–Head agreement with the head Agr. Notice that this proposal means that there are both clausal and nominal AgrP projections. Num and NumP, representing grammatical number, are proposed for

D fails to account for DG structures in which it does not occur, like *der Welt größtes Saurierskelett* 'the world's biggest dinosaur skeleton'. A similar argument for not taking *'s* to be D[POSS] in English is that this form does not occur when the possessive in the specifier is pronoun-derived: **my's car*. If *'s* is seen as a genitive case morpheme, the possessive forms of personal pronouns, *my, your, his* etc., can be simply taken to involve idiosyncratic genitive allomorphy. On the other hand, Radford (1993) claims that *my* etc. are Ds like *'s*.

Hebrew by Ritter (1991, 1992), and this proposal has been taken up by several writers for other languages. Lyons (1995c) argues that NumP is present in English only in plurals, where the plural morpheme (-*s* etc.) is the Num head. Since number morphology appears on the noun in many languages like English which appear to have only short movement of N, NumP must be rather low in the overall structure. Even grammatical gender, though arguably a property of individual nouns and therefore to be represented in their lexical entries, has been claimed to constitute a functional head (Picallo 1991). If it does, then this category, Gen, is still lower than Num, given its intimate association with the noun. Picallo describes Gen as a "word marker", which assigns the noun in its complement to a class of the kind distinguished in gender systems. Finally Travis and Lamontagne (1992) argue for a functional head K corresponding to case and showing properties in common with clausal C. Unlike the other possible functional categories mentioned, KP would be a peripheral projection above DP, so that the overall nominal structure is of category KP. Laughren (1989) similarly treats the noun phrase in Warlpiri as KP, with its case morpheme as head. And the KP analysis is adopted more recently by Bittner and Hale (1996), with the difference that only "marked cases" are considered to be realizations of K; nominative is regarded as "unmarked", so that a nominative noun phrase is caseless and therefore not KP. Some other writers claim that case is realized in D rather than in a separate category (Giusti 1992, Cornilescu 1992). This implies a relationship of some kind between case and referential properties like definiteness. There is some evidence for such a relationship, and it has been used to explain the diachronic emergence of definiteness marking in terms of changes in case systems; I shall take this up in Chapter 9. But, anticipating the discussion there, I here take case to be represented as a separate K head.

Taking all these categories, and the hierarchical relationships generally assumed among them, to be valid would give the following overall schema (omitting X′ levels for brevity):

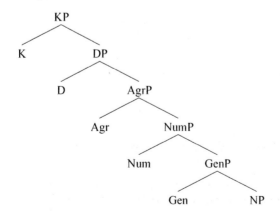

Each phrasal category (except the highest, KP) is the complement of the next higher head (which is its sister). And note that each phrase has a specifier position (not shown in the above schema), daughter to XP and sister to X'. Note also that the categories shown here are not all claimed to occur in all languages; for example, languages lacking determiners, possessive agreement, and grammatical number would be taken not to have, respectively, DP, AgrP and NumP.

Cinque (1995) makes the more radical proposal that adjectives and other attributive modifiers are generated in the specifiers of a series of functional projections between NP and DP. The evidence for this is that in various languages the number of non-coordinated attributive APs occurring in a noun phrase is limited to around six, and that the different classes of adjective (ordinal, quality, size, colour etc.) tend to show a specific serialization cross-linguistically. Take, for example, the phrase *a lovely little white cat*; any variation in the ordering of the three APs would be marked and probably require a marked intonation contour. And the same pattern, as regards which semantic classes of modifier are generated closest to the head noun, is found in many other languages (though upward Head Movement of N may interfere, causing some or all modifiers to be superficially post-nominal rather than pre-nominal, and further from or closer to N than in D-structure). Functional projections corresponding to each of these modifier classes offer an attractive account of these observations. Thus the AP *little*, for instance, would be generated in the specifier of a "SizeP" projection, which would be slightly more peripheral than the "ColourP" within which *white* arises as specifier. This means, however, a considerable expansion of the number of functional projections assumed to figure in the noun phrase. Among these additional projections proposed by Cinque, one of the highest in the overall structure is one relating to cardinality; the assumption is that numerals would be specifiers of this. Now given the claim I have made at various points in the present discussion that the "indefinite article" is a cardinality term in a paradigmatic relationship with numerals and modifiers like *many*, it would be natural to take this article too to be generated here. The usual assumption in work on DP structure is that *a* is a D, but I believe this is incorrect. I will come back to this point below.

8.2.3 *Weaknesses in the DP analysis*

Despite its attractions, the DP hypothesis in its standard form is problematic in a number of ways. It will suffice here to outline just two of these problems.

The first has already been discussed briefly in 2.3.4. Double determination as it occurs in Swedish (*den långa resan* 'the long journey') and Norwegian (*den nye boken* 'the new book') is difficult to account for. This is ironic, because affixal articles attached to the head noun, implying Head Movement of N to D (or possibly lowering of D to N) with amalgamation of these two categories, should be among the strongest evidence for the DP hypothesis – because these processes are only possible if D, like N, is a head; but there should not be an additional free-form article. One solution, implicit in Taraldsen (1990) for Norwegian, is that there are two DP projections, one above the adjective with the free-form article as head and one below with the affix as head. This is unattractive because it means postulating two co-occurring functional heads with the same semantic content. Another way out, proposed by Giusti (1994), is to say that only the free-form article is a head D and the affix is an agreement morpheme on the noun. This is better, but there are two difficulties with it. The first is that, as discussed in 2.3.2, the affixal article of all the Scandinavian languages has the morphological structure of an inflected formative attached to a separately inflected noun. It therefore looks much more like a case of amalgamation of D and N after movement. The second is more technical. A widespread current view is that inflectional categories on lexical heads are indeed generated there rather than resulting from movement of lexical heads into functional head positions. But then the lexical head has to raise to the appropriate functional head, either overtly or at the abstract level of logical form (LF), for the inflectional category to be "checked"; see Chomsky (1995) for discussion. This is Giusti's analysis; the definite affix on N is checked in D at LF. But in such cases the functional head where checking takes place should normally be empty prior to LF Head Movement; this at any rate is the case in other instances of this process. The reason assumed for D being already overt in this case, in the form of the free-form article, is that this overt Det is necessary to license the immediately following AP by governing it. But the result is that [+ Def] (or whatever the content of the article is) will be overtly encoded twice in the same head position at LF. A further observation is that, on this analysis, the overt D in Swedish and Norwegian (by contrast with Danish) shows a greater propensity to trigger agreement on the noun than does the null D – the opposite of what one tends to find in agreement systems.

The second problem posed by the DP hypothesis relates to the definite constraint on full Poss Movement structures – thus the DG phenomenon. The suggestion advanced in 8.1.3, in terms of the NP framework, is that what makes *the car, those people, Ann's car, a neighbour's car* definite is the mere filling of a particular position, whether by a Det or a possessive or anything else. But the DP analysis has Dets and possessives in different positions, the former in the D head position and the latter in the specifier of this head, and the complementary distribution between them is taken to be only apparent. On this view what makes *Ann's car* or *a neighbour's car* definite is that D^{POSS} is a definite Det – lexically specified as [+ Def] like *the*. Now two questions arise. First, it seems to be universally the case that semantically contentful Dets like demonstratives and quantifiers, assuming they are of category D, are not case assigners and there-fore cannot replace D^{POSS} in the possessive structure. Why should this be so in all languages? Second, D^{POSS} is, again apparently universally, identical in essential con-tent to the definite article except that it can assign case to its specifier (abstract-ing away from the deictic marking and agreement morphology sometimes occurring with articles). In English for example, D^{POSS} (whether realized as *'s* or null) is completely synonymous with *the*, differing only in its genitive-case assigning property which guarantees that it is the only Det occurring in the Poss Movement construction. Given this, we would expect that in at least some lan-guages D^{POSS} would be non-distinct morphologically from the definite article; that is, the equivalent of *the* should also serve as D^{POSS}, the distinction English draws between the two being a language-specific peculiarity. But the definite article (in languages having one) and D^{POSS} appear to be always distinct, and this surprising fact is unexplained.

8.3 A modified DP analysis

The literature of the last few years contains numerous proposed modifications of the basic DP framework, and it is possible to amend the DP analy-sis outlined above so as to solve the difficulties just discussed. The proposals I present in this section summarize the account given in more detail in Lyons (1994a, 1995b). The crucial claims of this analysis are, first, that free-form definite arti-cles like *the* are, as in the NP analysis, specifiers rather than heads, but specifiers of DP rather than NP; and second, that D represents not the word class of Det, but the grammatical category of definiteness.

8.3.1 D as definiteness

The arguments presented in 8.1 and earlier chapters for believing that definite determiners are associated with a position higher in the noun phrase struc-ture than cardinality or quasi-indefinite determiners are equally valid in the DP framework. Given the widely accepted assumption of multiple functional projec-tions, it is reasonable to suggest that only definite determiners are associated with D and its projection DP, other determiners being associated with some lower func-tional head. The DP projection, then, is the place to look for the definite "Det position" hypothesized earlier. But if determiners in general are not associated with D it makes little sense to see this head as representing the class of Det; in fact the whole original point of the DP hypothesis, that the noun phrase is really "deter-miner phrase", collapses. Rather, D is definiteness (and by a happy coincidence serves just as well in this role!) and DP is definiteness phrase. So the grammati-cal category which I have claimed definiteness is has its representation in syntax in the form of this functional head. This claim fits in well with the fact that nearly all other proposed functional heads correspond to grammatical or semantic categories rather than to word classes.

Free-form definite articles and other definite determiners are generally not D heads, however. They are specifiers, as are noun phrase modifiers more generally, following Cinque's (1995) treatment discussed above. D itself is most commonly null, again as must be true of most functional heads on Cinque's analysis. But affixal definite articles are realizations of D, surfacing after the operation of various movement processes as inflections on N or second-position clitics, among the possibilities discussed in 2.3. See Giusti (1993) for an account of how the Wackernagel position of the Romanian affixal article comes about. In a noun phrase with the underlying form *[-ul [batrin [om]]]* (the old man), N may raise to D, to combine with the article suffix there: *[om-ul [batrin [t]]]*; or the AP may raise from its intermediate specifier to specifier of DP, in which position the article cliticizes to it: *[batrin-ul [t [om]]]*. The assumption of specifier articles and head articles immediately provides, in a rather natural way, the two positions needed to account satisfactorily for double determination. The affixal article in Swedish and Norwegian is the head D which combines with N (or, perhaps better, it is initially an affix on N which is checked in D after raising of N at LF), while the free-form article is generated in DP specifier; see Lyons (1995b) for the details of the analysis. I do not rule out the possibility of D heads being free-standing rather than affixal in some languages. In particular, the post-nominal definite article *la* of many French-based creole languages, probably a free form, may be a head (see Ritter 1992). This is because it is thought that creoles have very few movement processes, and affixation is assumed to arise usually from Head Movement (or at least to be associated with Head Movement, which may be abstract, as in the checking account). It may be that heads in such a language must be capable of standing alone. And other languages too may have D heads not needing the morphological support of a lexical host. This is a matter for investigation of individual languages. I assume here, however, partly to simplify the exposition, that free-form articles are typically specifiers.

These assumptions also offer a more natural account of DG possessive structures. In particular, the special Det D^{POSS} with its attendant problems can be dispensed with. Possessives fail to co-occur with free-form articles and other definite Dets, in languages like English, because they occupy the same position, DP specifier. And these structures are definite because Poss Movement to DP specifier means DP and D have been projected – and D is definiteness. This is why only definite Dets are associated with DP (as specifiers if free-form, heads if affixal) and quasi-indefinite Dets appear lower in the structure. It follows from this analysis that only definite noun phrases will be DPs; indefinites can have no D, therefore no DP projection. It is, however, still possible to regard definite and indefinite noun phrases as of the same category if both have KP as their highest functional projection; but K selects a DP complement only optionally. Apart from KP, the projection of indefinites stops one level below that of definites. As for the position occupied by cardinality Dets like *a*, *sm*, *one*, *many*, there are two obvious possibilities to consider. One is that they are specifiers of NumP, headed by the category of grammatical number. But this is unlikely, since NumP appears to be not far above NP, and cardinality modifiers tend to occur well to the left in terms of linear order. Also, NumP must be present in bare plurals to account for their number morphology, but bare plurals cannot be accompanied by cardinality Dets, and it is not obvious how to rule these out if they are specifiers of a projection which is present. It is more probable that they are specifiers of the cardinality projection, call it CardP, identified by Cinque (1995) as one of the highest functional projections. For more detailed discussion of this see Lyons (1995c).[6] Parallel to my treatment of the definite article, I propose that the cardinal article too, where a free form, is in this specifier along with numerals. Affixal cardinal articles can be taken to be Card heads.

I argued in 7.5 that the pragmatic concept of identifiability may play a role in communication in all languages, but that definiteness as a grammatical category is more limited. On the hypothesis advanced here, what characterizes languages in which definiteness is not found is that they lack DP. I shall say more about this in 8.4 below.

The usual indication that a language does have a DP projection is that it has a definite article – because the essential function of this is to express the projection, a point I develop below. For this reason, definite articles are normally overt forms. But there are languages which probably make it necessary to suppose that a definite article can be null, and DP therefore non-overt. These are languages like Mam, Sinhalese, and probably Turkish, in which definiteness is signalled not by a definite article, but by absence of a quasi-indefinite article. I exemplify from Sinhalese (Masica 1986), which has a suffixal cardinal article (a phrasal clitic, in fact, suffixed noun phrase-finally) *-ek/-ak* (derived from the numeral *eka* 'one', with which it can co-occur). This article attaches to nouns only in the singular, and a singular noun lacking it is understood as definite: *pota* 'the book', *potak* 'a book'; *lamayā* 'the boy', *lamayek* 'a boy'. The definite–indefinite distinction can also be made in the plural by attaching the cardinal article to a numeral: *lamay dennā* 'the two boys', *lamay dennek* 'two boys'. I assume the article suffix is a Card head, but this does not account for its expressing indefiniteness. It seems Sinhalese has a DP and a null definite article. As is the case with overt definite articles, the presence of this in a noun phrase excludes the overt appearance of

---

[6] For Lyons (1995c), absence of CardP is definitional of bare nominals; a noun phrase may have NumP and even DP and still count as "bare".

the cardinal article – see below. In this way, the cardinal article indirectly signals indefiniteness, exactly as in languages with overt definiteness marking.

8.3.2 The content of determiners

If D is definiteness and DP is definite noun phrase (under KP), it follows that no definite Det need be lexically specified [+ Def]. And, as already suggested in 8.1.3, this applies even to the definite article. Affixal articles realize the D head, and free-form articles are the default or minimal Det which is required to occupy DP specifier position in the absence of any contentful expression there. Apart from any agreement or deixis features, definite articles have no semantic or other lexical content; they are lexically empty pleonastic Dets, with the function of indicating by their presence that DP is projected. The same analysis can be extended to cardinality Dets. Just as demonstratives, for example, may occur in DP specifier, but can also appear elsewhere provided DP is projected (and shown to be projected by a default definite article), cardinality Dets such as numerals are associated with specifier of CardP, but we should not exclude the possibility that they too can be adjectival and generated lower in the noun phrase. The cardinal article, however, appears only in CardP, either to realize the head if affixal or as a pleonastic specifier. Lyons (1995c) argues that in English *a* or *sm* always appears in CardP specifier in indefinites if no meaningful Det is generated there; bare plural and mass indefinites, where *sm* does not occur, have no CardP projection. This pleonastic or default function is what defines articles, and the fact that definite and cardinal articles do not both appear in definites is due to some constraint (perhaps phonological) which permits only one article to introduce a noun phrase, as suggested in 1.3.1.

Note that this treatment of the articles is incompatible with the claim of Vergnaud and Zubizarreta (1992) and Longobardi (1994), referred to in Chapter 4, that "substantive" and "expletive" uses of definite articles must be distinguished; in the former the article genuinely expresses definiteness, and in the latter it is semantically empty and has a merely grammatical function. On my analysis, free-form definite articles are always expletive, but they can only appear in DP, of which the head is definiteness, so they always signal definiteness while not encoding this. Related to the substantive–expletive claim is the further assumption made by many writers that a noun phrase must have a Det in order to function as an argument. This is in fact taken to be one of the main roles of the expletive article. But again, this assumption cannot stand on my analysis – and is, I believe, unnecessary. In particular, English bare plural and mass generics, if they have neither DP (typically) nor CardP (necessarily) as suggested above, are determinerless; but they are certainly argumental. What argumental nominal expressions have in common is not D, nor even a broader notion of determiner, but K.

I have observed that substantive definite determiners like demonstratives may be in DP specifier or in some other position (such as an adjectival position deeper within the noun phrase), and that in the latter case a definite article must also appear (in languages which have DP). In some languages both these possibilities are found, and this has given rise to the suggestion that demonstratives can originate in a lower specifier and then (optionally in some languages, obligatorily in others) raise to DP specifier – somewhat like DG possessives. This is proposed by Giusti (1993) for Romanian (*omul acesta* and *acest om* 'this man'), and by Lyons (1995d) for Spanish (*la casa esta* and *esta casa* 'this house'). Whether or not this raising applies the noun phrase must be definite, whence the definite article accompanying the non-raised demonstratives. This is presumably because the semantic content of demonstratives, [+ Dem], entails identifiability of the referent by the hearer, which is what underlies definiteness. Lyons proposes that the fact that a demonstrative requires the projection of DP should be expressed syntactically by a require- ment that unraised demonstratives be linked by co-indexing to the DP specifier position. This amounts to binding of the demonstrative by the article in Spanish (and perhaps by a null pleonastic specifier in Specifier–Head Agreement with the affixal article in Romanian), and if the demonstrative raises to DP specifier it too will bind its own trace in its original position. On this view demonstratives and other definite determiners are linked to DP specifier either by being in that posi- tion or by being bound by it.

In the Romanian example in which the demonstrative has raised to DP specifier, it is to be noted that the article, a D head, does not appear. As pointed out in 7.5.3, it is common for bound articles to fail to co-occur with demonstratives and free- form DG possessives (which are also DP specifiers), and it is not obvious why this should be so. I assume it reflects a fact frequently observed in relation to other syntactic projections for many languages: that head and specifier may not both be overtly expressed. The best-known example of this is the "doubly-filled Comp filter" discussed, for example, in Chomsky (1981), and similar filters have been suggested for other structures. It may be partly a matter of avoiding redundancy, since head and specifier, on the present analysis, share the function of indicating the pres- ence and content of the projection. When a demonstrative raises to DP specifier or Poss Movement carries a free-form possessive to the same position, this serves to express the presence of the DP projection, and an overt D head becomes unnec- essary. Recall that possessives are frequently affixal; these affixes may originate in a lower Agr head. But if an affixal possessive is of the DG type, inducing a definite interpretation without the presence of any definiteness marker, the assumption is that it has raised, by Head Movement, to D – thus again signalling the projection of DP. Demonstratives too are occasionally affixal, thus heads. It may be that these originate as D heads, though it cannot be ruled out that they too raise to D from some lower head position.

8.3.3 The analysis of personal pronouns

Postal's (1970) claim, outlined in 1.2.5, that personal pronouns are definite articles has a natural attraction in a framework that takes articles to be heads, and Abney (1987) takes up and adapts this analysis; see also Radford (1993) for a similar DP account of pronouns. On this approach, *she, him, they* are D heads which differ lexically from *the* in being subcategorized for no NP complement, while *we* and *you* are specified as optionally taking an NP complement. It is argued that Postal's proposal works better in the DP framework, because there is then no need to posit a head N which is abstract or gets deleted. While the DP treatment works quite elegantly, it is worth noting that the very fact that the pronouns-as-Dets analysis dates back so far, and was found compelling by many in its early days, makes it clear that it is not dependent on a view of determiners as heads. It is, moreover, ironic that some recent revisions (such as Cardinaletti (1994)) propose that personal pronouns (at least strong ones) are underlyingly nouns, which raise by Head Movement to D.

I believe this last proposal must be rejected; it misses the point that even strong third-person pronouns, though often distinct morphophonologically from the corresponding definite article, are similar to it in many languages, and often identical to a demonstrative Det. Part of Cardinaletti's motivation is that in Italian *noi linguisti* 'we linguists', *voi linguisti* 'you linguists', as in their English equivalents, only first- and second-person "pronouns" are possible: *loro linguisti '*they linguists'. Moreover, a similar constraint operates with other structures: *noi/voi/*loro con i capelli rossi* 'we/you/*they with the red hair', and Cardinaletti draws the conclusion that pronouns cannot be Dets underlyingly; *noi/voi linguisti* must be an apposition structure. But this is to miss the point that there is suppletion and that the "personal determiner" in the third person, in Italian as in English, takes the form of the definite article or, crucially, a demonstrative: *i linguisti* 'the linguists', *quei linguisti* 'those linguists'. The impossibility of *loro* before a modifying PP is also paralleled in many languages, including standard English, and is not explained by the apposition proposal; here too *loro* would be replaced by a demonstrative.

Cardinaletti analyses clitic pronouns as Abney does all personal pronouns, as D heads with no NP complement. This captures the close morphophonological similarity between clitic pronouns and the definite article in many languages. Clitic pronouns differ from full pronouns in attaching to some host, typically but not invariably the verb, rather than appearing in argument position. This "clitic placement" is often analysed as an instance of Head Movement to the host head position, and this analysis depends on the treatment of clitics as D heads. In an important recent version of this analysis, Uriagereka (1995) claims pronominal clitics are the head of a DP with null (but present) NP complement; this head raises by Head Movement through the various phrasal projections of a clause to adjoin to a special clitic-hosting head.

The analysis I want to propose, derived from my account of definite articles, is that weak non-clitic pronouns like English unstressed *you*, *he* are DP specifiers like free-form articles, and clitic pronouns are D heads like affixal articles. Personal pronouns are DPs (under KP) like full definite noun phrases except that they contain no NP. If weak (in the very general sense discussed in 3.4.2 in which weakness may be manifested in a variety of ways), they contain a definite article either in DP specifier or in D; the former is realized as a free-form pronoun, the latter as a clitic. This article is the only overt material in the DP; it may express features (such as for gender in English *he*, *she*) not carried by the non-pronominal article, presumably because the lack of the descriptive content of NP gives more importance to such features in referent identification. Where this overt material is in D (thus affixal), it can undergo Head Movement and climb through higher heads to its eventual placement position, as described by Uriagereka. Strong definite pronouns are, like weak non-clitic pronouns, DPs with their overt content in DP specifier, but this content is demonstrative. The same analysis can be applied to pronominal occurrences of cardinality modifiers (like *one*, *three*, *some*), though complex indefinite pronouns like *something* presumably do involve an NP of which the head raises to a higher, functional head where it cliticizes to a determiner.

The essential point of this account, for personal pronouns, is that the distinction between free-form and bound pronouns corresponds exactly to that between free-form and bound articles. A definite pronoun, whether strong, weak free-form, or bound (clitic) has the same structure as the corresponding full DP, except that it lacks the NP complement. There are in addition morphological differences, partly but not entirely accountable for in terms of the need for more content where the descriptive part of the noun phrase is lacking. Notice that in English the morphologically poorer *the* occurs rather than the fuller *he*, *she* etc. not only in the presence of NP, but where any post-D material is present: *the book*, *the red one*, *the three*.[7] But if the three types of definite pronoun distinguished correspond structurally to definite Det types, there is a mismatch in individual languages. Many languages have a free-form definite article but bound weak pronouns (though, interestingly, the reverse is less common); an example is French, where the same

[7] Other determiner–pronoun pairs show the same distribution, for example *my book*, *my red one*, *my three*, but, where no material follows in the noun phrase, *mine* (both pronominally and predicatively).

third-person forms, *le, la, les*, serve as the (almost certainly) free-form article and as clitic pronouns. There is a second, more profound, mismatch, already discussed in 7.5.3. Many languages seem to have a category of definiteness in the personal pronoun system but not in full noun phrases; this is apparent from the fact that, in Latin and Russian respectively for instance, *pro* and weak personal pronouns can only be interpreted as definite, despite the lack of definiteness marking in full noun phrases. I shall discuss the latter of these two mismatches further in 8.4, and come back to both in Chapter 9, where I will suggest that they are connected.

8.4 Configurationality and definiteness

The discussion in this chapter has been based on languages which show fully configurational noun phrase structure, and we must consider how the proposals advanced apply to non-configurational languages. It should be borne in mind that the issues of whether there are in fact any truly non-configurational languages, which languages are to be so characterized if there are, and what non-configurationality actually amounts to, are highly contentious. A further complication, yet to be investigated in detail, is posed by the development of the theory of functional categories. It is not clear what would be meant by a "flat structure" within the current highly elaborate conception of clause and noun phrase with their multiple functional heads. The resolution of these matters is beyond the scope of the present study, but it is important to pursue the question of configurationality a little way because it has considerable bearing on the issue of definiteness. It is striking that the languages most frequently taken to be, at least in the noun phrase, non-configurational (Japanese and Warlpiri for example) lack definiteness marking. As indicated in 3.9, Gil (1987) proposes that absence of definiteness marking is a typical characteristic of languages with non-configurational noun phrases because definiteness (and, for him, indefiniteness too) is expressed by a Det in NP specifier, a position missing in such languages (because N is projected only as far as N'). This view fits in well with the account of the relationship between definiteness and syntactic structure outlined in 8.1, in which definiteness arises from the filling of NP specifier. It is not, however, compatible with the DP account of noun phrase structure, either in its standard form or in the modified form proposed here. It should be perfectly possible for a language which has D but only projects it as far as D' to express definiteness.

I have argued that languages which do not encode definiteness lack the category D; their noun phrases may be projections of a different functional head, or they may be NPs. It may be fruitful to consider whether these languages are the ones that have been thought to be non-configurational in the noun phrase, and whether the properties giving rise to this supposition might follow from the lack of one or more functional projections. Recall Gil's observation that the languages with the most strongly non-configurational noun phrase structure (his type B) not only lack definiteness marking; they are also characterized by the use of numeral classifiers and absence of number marking – features he attributes to the absence of the count–mass distinction in such languages. But another possible explanation for these characteristics is absence of such functional categories as Num and Card. Num is the locus for the singular–plural distinction (as well as more elaborate number oppositions in many languages), and numerals normally occur in specifier of CardP. In the absence of CardP some other device is required to enable numerals to appear, and a classifier system is one possibility. The absence of Num in a language may perhaps also be taken to have the direct consequence that all nouns are mass, classifiers then being needed to provide units for enumeration. More generally, it may be that a number of features taken to be characteristic of non-configurationality in fact follow from the absence of certain functional categories.

Japanese, Gil's paradigm non-configurational language, has neither definite article nor number marking, and uses numeral classifiers for enumeration:

(4) a.　　Hon o　　ni-satu　　　kaimasita.
　　　　　book ACC two CLASS bought
　　or
　　b.　　Ni-satu　　　no　　hon o　　kaimasita.
　　　　　two CLASS POSS book ACC bought
　　　　　'I bought (the) two books.'

If Japanese lacks D, Num and Card, the two specifier positions typically filled by definite Dets and numerals are unavailable. The status of the classifier (of which Japanese has several dozen, the one appearing depending on the noun) is unclear; it could be one of a limited class of count nouns, perhaps even an overt realization of Card, permitting numerals in its specifier – among other possibilities. What is clear is that the classifier is a device permitting numerals to occur. Similarly the lack of DP does not prevent the occurrence of demonstratives. There are languages in which demonstratives occur with classifiers, but Japanese uses the alternative device of treating demonstratives as adjectives: *kono tegami* 'this letter', *ano hako* 'that box'.

Another language widely assumed to be non-configurational is Dyirbal (data from Dixon 1972). Dyirbal has a system of classifiers, noun class markers rather than numeral or demonstrative classifiers; they occur in most noun phrases and indicate the noun's membership of one of four classes (roughly: masculine, feminine, neuter, and edible vegetable). These markers, which usually precede the noun and agree with it in case, also specify the location and visibility of the referent of the noun phrase; thus they are based on three deictic roots, the forms of which are given above in 3.1.1. Suffixed to these roots are the case inflection and a class morpheme. A Dyirbal noun phrase generally consists of a noun marker, a noun, and possibly one or more adjectives, usually in that order; but ellipsis is so prevalent that not only may the marker be omitted, but a marker may occur without the noun, or an adjective may occur alone, etc. Dyirbal has no definiteness marking, but is not without number marking, though this is purely optional in non-pronominal noun phrases; the bare noun is the unmarked form to refer to one or more: *ḏugumbil* 'woman' or 'women'. But plurality (three or more) may optionally be indicated by reduplication: *ɲalŋga* 'girl(s)', *ɲalŋgaɲalŋga* 'girls'; dual number may be expressed by a suffix -*ḏaran* attaching to either the noun or the noun marker: *bayi baŋguy-ḏaran* (CLASS frog-DU) or *bayi-ḏaran baŋguy* (CLASS-DU frog) 'two frogs'; and half a dozen nouns (all with human reference) have obligatory plural inflection: *naɲi* 'girl (past puberty)', plural *naɲinba*. This may mean that Dyirbal has a category Num which is not generated in the unmarked case. But again, this does not prevent numerals occurring in such unmarked noun phrases, and in this language without the support of numeral classifiers. Numerals are simply adjectives: *bayi yaṛa bulay* (CLASS man two) 'two men'. The single demonstrative *giɲa-* is in complementary distribution with the noun class markers, suggesting that these markers are determiners and occur in some specifier: *bayi yaṛa* (CLASS man) 'the/a man', *giyi yaṛa* 'this man'. That this may be NP specifier, so that this position is a possible locus for demonstratives in languages lacking DP, is suggested by the following. In the inalienable possession construction, the possessed noun cannot be accompanied by a marker, while the possessor can: *balan ḏugumbil mambu* (CLASS-F woman back) 'the/a woman's back'. This suggests that the position of the possessor phrase *balan ḏugumbil* in the matrix noun phrase is the same as that of a noun marker. On the plausible assumption that the possessor is in NP specifier in this construction, it follows that the class markers and the demonstrative are NP specifier determiners.

The hypothesis is, then, that one or more of the functional heads connected with definiteness and cardinality, D, Num and Card, may be missing in a language, and that this may correlate with properties taken by Gil to indicate some degree of noun-phrase non-configurationality. Determiners such as demonstratives and numerals which have independent semantic content are not dependent for their appearance on these functional categories in whose specifiers they often occur in configurational languages. They can occur elsewhere: in a classifier construction, in a different specifier such as that of NP, or in an adjectival position (possibilities that exist more marginally in configurational languages too). But no definite article is possible in languages lacking DP, since when an article is not itself a realization of D it has no semantic content, signalling definiteness only indirectly by filling a position which shows DP to have been projected. The quasi-indefinite article, similarly, should be unable to appear in a language lacking the category

Definiteness and noun phrase structure

Card. If this is correct, the observations on Cantonese in 3.9 suggest that the numeral classifiers of this language are realizations of Card.

The situation with pronouns is more complex, as already noted in 7.5.3. Dyirbal has first- and second-person singular, dual and plural personal pronouns (noun markers serving the pronominal function in the third person). Phonologically, these pronouns are fully stressed words of between two and five syllables (*ɲaḍa* (1SG+NOM), *ɲubalaḍingu* (2DU+DAT)). This suggests strongly that they correspond to strong rather than weak pronouns in other languages. And if strong pronouns are demonstratives, and these need not be definite, we can maintain the position that Dyirbal has no category of definiteness, because no DP. I assume the Dyirbal personal pronouns, while not DPs, are like strong DP pronouns in other languages' in that their overt content consists of a specifier demonstrative. But the specifier concerned is that of some other projection – perhaps the same specifier that demonstratives occupy in full noun phrases in this language. A similar situation obtains in Japanese, where personal pronouns are equally strong phonologically: *watasi* (1SG), *watasitati* (1PL), *anata* (2SG), *anatatati* (2PL). The situation is particularly clear in the third person, where no real pronoun exists and 'he' and 'she' are rendered by a full noun phrase with demonstrative determiner: *ano hito* 'that person'. Japanese also permits pronominal arguments to be null, but these are not identified by any agreement morphology; a non-overt argument has to be identified pragmatically from the context. This seems to be a very different phenomenon from the *pro* of null-subject languages, whose content is identified by agreement morphology. Japanese may have genuine gaps in sentence structures, the missing arguments being supplied pragmatically, not grammatically. If this approach is correct, then Japanese, like Dyirbal, has only strong pronouns.

The difficulty arises with languages in which a non-overt argument, interpreted pronominally, is identified by agreement morphology. This is the case in many Australian languages including Warlpiri, for many linguists the paradigm non-configurational language. The Warlpiri system is illustrated by the following sentences (adapted from Hale 1983 and Laughren 1989):

(5) a.   (Ngajulurlu) ka-rna-ngku   (nyuntu) nyanyi.
          I-ERG   IMPF 1SG-NOM 2SG-ACC you-ABS see
          'I see you.'

    b.   Malikijarrarlu ka-pala-jana   marlu   wajilipinyi.
          dog-DU-ERG IMPF 3DU-NOM 3PL-ACC kangaroo-ABS chase
          '(The) two dogs are chasing (the) kangaroos.'

Every Warlpiri sentence includes an auxiliary complex which contains a clitic cross-referencing each argument of the sentence. Thus in (5a) the clitics *rna* and *ngku* cross-reference free-form pronouns; in (5b) *pala* and *jana* cross-reference' full noun phrases – and in the second case partly identify the content of this

308

argument, since the object noun phrase here is not itself overtly specified for number. Notice that the clitics are case-marked on a nominative–accusative system, whereas the noun phrases (including free-form pronouns) they "agree" with are organized on an ergative–absolutive case system. But otherwise the characterization of the auxiliary as an agreement element is accurate enough. Its cross-referencing of all arguments makes it possible to dispense with the noun phrases themselves: as indicated in (5a), the free-form pronouns can be omitted – and they typically are omitted, unless it is desired to express emphasis on a pronominal argument. Similarly, the full noun phrases in (5b) could be omitted, with the result that the two arguments identified by the clitics would be interpreted pronominally:

(6)   Ka-pala-jana   wajilipinyi.
        IMPF 3DU-NOM 3PL-ACC chase
        'They (the two of them) are chasing them.'

A standard analysis of this phenomenon is that, in sentences like (6), the subject and object are realized as *pro*, the content of which is identified by the corresponding clitic in the auxiliary. An alternative, advocated for Warlpiri-type non-configurational languages by Jelinek (1984), is that the clitics themselves have pronominal status and represent the arguments; there are no null pronouns in (6), and in sentences like (5), where overt noun phrases occur, these are not arguments but adjuncts, supplementing the arguments in the auxiliary. For recent arguments against this view see Austin and Bresnan (1996). For our purposes it does not matter which of these treatments is preferred. What does matter is the following. Overt free-form pronouns, as in (5a), clearly represent the strong-pronoun option, arguably with demonstrative value. The pro-nominal interpretation resulting from the omission of overt noun phrases corresponds to the weak-pronoun option, that of non-demonstrative definite pronouns. On the *pro* analysis, *pro* is the weak pronoun; on the argumental clitics analysis, the clitic is the weak pronoun. On either view, the crucial point is that the interpretation is that of a weak *definite* pronoun (Hale 1983, Bittner and Hale 1996); (6) could not be glossed 'They are chasing some', 'Two are chasing them', or 'Two are chasing some'. Clitics cross-reference all overt nominal arguments, including noun phrases for which an indefinite gloss would be appropriate. It is natural that the absence of an overt noun phrase should lead to a pronominal interpretation, but one might reasonably expect in this case that the clitic could identify a null pronoun, or itself be construed as a pronoun, without reference to definiteness, and that in some instances an indefinite gloss could be appropriate; but it is not so (and, as pointed out in 7.5.3, this is always the case with identified null arguments). What this means is that the grammar of Warlpiri must make reference to definiteness – though only, it seems, for pronouns. And if definiteness is universally a function of the occurrence of D, then this category must exist in Warlpiri, weak pronouns (at least) being DPs. Note also that, in both Warlpiri and Dyirbal, pronouns, unlike full noun phrases, obligatorily encode number.

We have identified two groups of languages lacking a definite article. There are those, like Warlpiri, in which agreement morphology makes possible the omission of argument noun phrases, the result being a weak definite pronoun interpretation. This weak pronoun is of category DP. Full noun phrases, including perhaps the demonstrative free-form personal pronouns, do not involve a DP projection, and are neutral with respect to definiteness. The second group consists of languages in which either there are no null arguments (like Dyirbal) or null arguments are not identified by agreement morphology (Japanese). In Dyirbal non-pronominal noun phrases are neutral with respect to definiteness, and the "pragmatic definiteness" of personal pronouns derives from their being demonstrative. In Japanese an unexpressed argument may be interpreted pragmatically, and the interpretation is not necessarily definite. These languages have no syntactic category D and hence no definiteness.[8]

8.5 Definiteness and person

Here I develop the claim that definiteness is to be assimilated to the well-established grammatical category of person, so that DP, which I have argued is definiteness phrase, is actually person phrase. This claim has been advanced in Lyons (1994b and 1995e), and the discussion here is based on this work.

8.5.1 *Personal determiners and pronouns*

The reader is at this point referred back to the cross-linguistic survey of personal pronouns and personal determiners (as in *we linguists*) in 3.4, and the treatment of these forms in 1.2.5, 8.3 and 8.4. Recall that I am taking personal pronouns and personal determiners to have the same source. Expressions of the type *we linguists* are full noun phrases in which the personal form *we* is a definite – and in this case demonstrative – determiner. This determiner is a DP

---

[8] See Baker (1996) for discussion of the absence of definiteness marking in the polysynthetic subgroup of non-configurational languages. Baker explains this in terms of the lack of a functioning system of determiners in these languages. He proposes that determiners modify, in some sense, a special "R(eferent)" argument of NPs (representing the entity described by the nominal). This R argument commonly takes the form of a free variable – the variable taken in many semantic treatments to be bound by determiners. But in the polysynthetic languages this argument is assigned as a θ-role to the specifier position of NP, and is in this way discharged or "saturated". This blocks its modification by a determiner outside NP. Baker allows that some polysynthetic languages may still have determiners, but these are degenerate, typically meaningless and attaching to nouns as a mere formal requirement; they do not include genuine articles. Degenerate determiners of this kind are also discussed by Greenberg (1978) as deriving historically from earlier fully functioning determiners; see 9.3.2 below.

specifier Det in English; Nama *siĭ kxòe-ke* (we person-1PL+M) 'we men' probably involves a demonstrative Det *siĭ* in DP specifier and a person-marked D head *-ke*. In languages lacking DP structure, it may be that a demonstrative encoding person distinctions occurs as part of some other projection (functional or lexical) as modifier of the noun phrase. Personal pronouns (in common with other types of pronoun) are noun phrases of the same kind except that they lack the lexical head noun and other descriptive material. Their overt content typically consists of a specifier Det (for free-form pronouns) or a head D (for pronominal clitics) in DP languages, and may consist of a determiner in some other projection in languages lacking DP. Strong pronoun forms involve a demonstrative element, and weak pronouns are simply definite articles.

But if personal pronouns and personal determiners are essentially the same thing, there are differences between them. The pronouns show complete person–number paradigms, whereas the pre-nominal determiners tend to show gaps. Interestingly, these gaps are cross-linguistically rather consistent: in many languages non-demonstrative argument use is only possible in the third person, and in a fair number of languages demonstrative and non-demonstrative argument use is excluded in first and second persons singular. But in addition many languages show more severe constraints, for example disallowing any first- or second-person pre-nominal forms. I have also argued that many languages only have DP structure in personal pronouns, and in some cases perhaps only in weak or null pronouns.

Both personal pronouns and personal determiners express grammatical person, but they are one of two principal expressions of this category, since it is also commonly encoded in an agreement morpheme (standardly analysed as a functional head Agr) appearing on the verb or as part of an Aux(iliary) constituent. In fact person tends to be more fully and consistently expressed in Agr, which does not show the constraints seen in the noun phrase (where person is often only fully represented in pronouns, and not then, overtly at least, in the case of *pro*). The discrepancy between the noun phrase and Agr in the encoding of person is considerable, and is due, first, to the null subject/object phenomenon, in which a rich Agr makes possible a pronoun encoding nothing overtly, and, second, to the fact that the relationship between a noun phrase and Agr is often not quite one of "agreement". They may disagree, in limited ways so that semantic compatibility is maintained, with Agr encoding either more material or different features in comparison with the noun phrase argument (the apparent source of the "agreement"). The categories encoded may be organized differently in the noun phrase and on Agr; this is true of case, for example, in Warlpiri, where the noun phrase shows an ergative–absolutive pattern and the auxiliary a nominative–accusative pattern. More important for person is where Agr makes more distinctions than do non-pronominal noun phrases and compatibility rather than strict agreement is required.

This is the case in Spanish and Warlpiri examples like the following:

(7)   *Spanish*
        Los estudiantes trabajáis   mucho.
        the students   work-2PL much
        'You students work hard.'

(8)   *Warlpiri*
    a. Ngarka ka-rnalu   purlami.
        man   AUX 1PL shout
        'We men are shouting.'
    b. Ngarka njampu ka-rna   purlami.
        man   this   AUX 1SG shout
        '*I man am shouting.'

The subject noun phrase in such sentences (which may be definite or indefinite in Spanish, while Warlpiri has no definiteness marking in non-pronominal noun phrases) seems to be third person. This functions as the unmarked person and is compatible with first- or second-person marking on Agr. Note that the subjects are also unmarked for number in Warlpiri, while Agr may encode singular or plural; subject and Agr must agree for number in Spanish, however, where in fact this "non-agreement" for person is only permitted in the plural. Other languages require strict agreement between arguments and Agr – including English, though Agr is very impoverished in English. But English does show an intriguing agreement phenomenon, comparable to the Spanish and Warlpiri facts, in sentences containing a partitive; here the agreement or non-agreement is not with Agr but with an anaphoric expression which takes the partitive structure as its antecedent:

(9) a. **Some of us** like **our** beer chilled.
    b. **Some of us** like **their** beer chilled.

(10) a. **Some of us** disgraced **ourselves** last night.
     b. **Some of us** disgraced **themselves** last night.

The head of the partitive structure is *some*, which is not first person, but an anaphoric expression dependent on it (and required in English to agree for person with its antecedent) may be first or third person. It seems anaphor agreement may be either with the head or the complement (*us*) of the partitive; this might be captured by saying that the person feature of the complement can optionally percolate up to the head. But the (a) and (b) variants are not synonymous; the former, with first-person agreement, imply that the subset defined by *some* includes the speaker, while the latter, with third-person agreement, imply that it does not. This suggests that, as with the Spanish and Warlpiri subject–Agr relationship, it may be a matter of semantic compatibility between third-person *some* and the first-person possessive or reflexive. But this anaphor-non-agreement is only possible in English where the first-person interpretation of the partitive is rendered probable explicitly by a first-person partitive complement, whence the impossibility of *Some lecturers disgraced ourselves* and *Some of us disgraced yourselves.*[9]

8.5.2 Person and definite determiners

Having established some important background facts, I now wish to argue that definiteness and person should be conflated. There are two observations favouring this analysis: first, the fact that person is incompatible with indefiniteness, and second, a certain complementarity between person and definiteness. These two arguments are developed here.

In languages that have definiteness, a noun phrase in which person is encoded must be definite – DP therefore. More specifically, the person features are always encoded either on a definite Det (which may be the definite article or a demonstrative) or on D. This covers personal pronouns and personal determiners. Languages lacking DP, like Dyirbal and Japanese, do nevertheless have strong personal pronouns (or forms functioning in an equivalent manner) which express person distinctions. These appear in many cases to be demonstrative; recall that demonstratives, which are identifiable or pragmatically definite, are found in all languages. It is probably the case, therefore, that all languages distinguish discourse participant roles (speaker, hearer etc.) just as all express demonstrativeness, but that the expression of these roles need not be grammaticalized (that is, represented as a functional projection). Words which express participant roles lexically are, like demonstratives, characterized pragmatically as identifiable, and where identifiability comes to be grammaticalized, in the creation of a DP projection, these words must then be linked to that projection. The point is that the marking of person in a noun phrase is universally incompatible with indefiniteness. This is expected if person is always associated with D in languages having DP structure.

A reasonable assumption is that this association reflects a semantic incompatibility between person and indefiniteness, and it is interesting to consider what a person-marked indefinite would mean. A first-person plural indefinite, for example, would denote an indefinite plurality (such as might be expressed by *some*) which includes the speaker. And this does not seem nonsensical; indeed precisely this is conveyed by the following Spanish sentences:

(11) a. Dos hombres hablamos.
two men speak-1PL
b. Algunos estudiantes trabajamos mucho.
some students work-1PL much

[9] On the other hand, *Some of the team disgraced ourselves/yourselves* is perfectly possible, where the complement of the partitive does not agree with the reflexive but does not clash with it. This supports a pragmatic mechanism involving compatibility of features.

Recall that in the Spanish structure exemplified in (7), showing compatibility between a first or second person-marked Agr and a subject not showing this person feature, the noun phrase may be indefinite, as here. But the point is that the first-person feature which co-occurs with indefiniteness in (11) is not encoded in the subject noun phrase. It is only the non-agreement for person between Agr and subject in Spanish which makes possible the combination of first-person Agr and indefinite subject. The non-agreement in English between an anaphoric word and the head of a partitive antecedent, discussed above, also gives rise to the same first-person plural indefinite interpretation:

(12) a.   **Some of us** like **our** beer chilled.
  b.   **Some of us** disgraced **ourselves** last night.

As observed, the indefinite subset denoted by *some* (of the totality denoted by *us*) is understood, because of the first-person anaphoric word, to include the speaker; thus the speaker likes her beer chilled or disgraced herself. But again, though the subject is interpreted as first person plural indefinite, it does not encode first person, and I would maintain it is not grammatically first person.

But if it is universally the case that person cannot be encoded on an indefinite, the fact seems to remain that a first-person plural indefinite interpretation is possible. This is problematic, since if person and definiteness are, as I claim, the same thing, the combination of person with indefiniteness should be inconceivable; it should produce a semantic anomaly. And I believe this is the case, despite appearances. The key lies in the difference between singular and plural person values. First person singular corresponds to the speaker, but first person plural does not represent a plurality of speakers; rather it expresses a plural set which includes the speaker (or speakers). So *we* is not the plural of *I* in the same way as *these books* is the plural of *this book*. And while an encoding of the speaker role cannot be indefinite, it is perfectly possible for the speaker to be a member of an indefinite set. The issue is distorted by the fact that the concept of a definite plurality of which I am a member is represented grammatically as the plural of *I*, namely *we* – as if a group of cars of which one is mine could be referred to as *my cars*. And, crucially, the first-person indefinite interpretation discussed is only available, where at all, as a first-person *plural* indefinite – where it is, semantically, a plurality which includes first person rather than the plural of first person. Thus (13) in English and (14) in Spanish, with singular subjects, are impossible:

(13)   *One of us disgraced myself last night.

(14)   *Un estudiante trabajo   mucho.
     a   student   work-1SG much

It can be concluded, therefore, that indefinite person (as opposed to an indefinite including a given person) can neither be expressed nor occur as an interpretation. Moreover, a plural indefinite including person, while meaningful and indirectly available as an interpretation because of the phenomenon of non-agreement, as in (11) and (12), is never directly encoded in a noun phrase (in any language, I claim), because such inclusion is treated grammatically by languages as the plural of the person value.

The second piece of evidence favouring conflation of person and definiteness also involves the relationship between noun phrase arguments and Agr. Person is one of the "φ-features" figuring widely in agreement; it appears in numerous languages on Agr elements, whether on the verb or on an auxiliary component, to cross-reference a subject or object or other argument. But it differs from other φ-features like gender and number in typically not being encoded on the cross-referenced noun phrase itself. We have seen that person is encoded on personal pronouns and on non-pronominal noun phrases containing a personal determiner, though the latter are severely constrained in occurrence in many, probably most, languages. And in the case of non-pronominals without a personal determiner (*sm apples, this man, the houses, many people, a horse*), which are far more common in occurrence, it is not obvious that there is any person feature present. Noun phrases of this type are traditionally treated as third person, and on the assumption accepted here that third-person pronouns are forms of the definite article or a demonstrative, it seems reasonable to see *the houses* and *this man* as third person, but it is far from clear that there is any encoding of third person in *a horse, sm apples* and *many people*. It is only with first- and second-person determiners that one can be sure that person is encoded in a non-pronominal noun phrase, and given the restrictions found on these cross-linguistically (see 3.4.3 for details), it is fair to say that in general non-pronominal noun phrases typically do not show person marking.[10] This contrasts strongly with number and gender, which, as nominal φ-features, tend to occur obligatorily in the noun phrase in languages which have these features.

On the other hand, definiteness is regularly encoded in the noun phrase. In languages which have DP for non-pronominal as well as pronominal noun phrases, definiteness marking is usually obligatory in noun phrases meeting the conditions for its occurrence. But, curiously, definiteness is typically not cross-referenced by Agr elements; it is not one of the usual φ-features. This is not to say it never is; recall the discussion in 5.2 of the involvement of definiteness in agreement. In

---

[10] The fact that personal pronouns do encode person while non-pronominal noun phrases generally do not seems likely to be related to the fact, observed at several points, that in many languages definiteness (DP structure) is limited to pronouns.

Hungarian, for example, with definite and indefinite verb conjugations, the former amounts to the encoding in the verb's Agr morpheme of the presence of a definite object. The object clitics of Macedonian operate in a similar fashion, with the person, number, gender (for third person) and case of the object encoded in addition. But this is not very common, and even in these languages subject agreement does not take account of definiteness.

So the general cross-linguistic pattern is of a complementarity between person and definiteness. Person tends to appear in Agr but not in the noun phrase, and definiteness tends to appear in the noun phrase but not in Agr. This suggests that the two categories should be conflated, with the result that these distributional oddities vanish. It is now possible to say that in all languages that have definiteness marking, person is encoded in every noun phrase that has person – that is, in every DP. In most cases (the exception being the non-agreement phenomenon illustrated in (7)–(8)) this encoding will correspond to the person feature on a cross-referencing Agr.

This analysis has important consequences for the definition of "third person", since it treats only definites as personal. Thus *the house* and *these houses* are third person, while *a house* and *six houses* are personless, because not DPs. This distinction may seem improbable because most agreement systems would not distinguish between these two sets of noun phrases. Both third-person definite arguments and indefinites are generally cross-referenced by what looks like a third-person Agr morpheme, as in the following subject-agreement instances:

(15)   *German*
   a.   Die Frau wartet.
        'The woman is waiting.'
   b.   Eine Frau wartet.
        'A woman is waiting.'

(16)   *Spanish*
   a.   Estos estudiantes trabajan.
        'These students are working.'
   b.   Algunos estudiantes trabajan.
        'Some students are working.'

However, third person is traditionally recognized as differing significantly from first and second persons, in that the two latter relate to participants in the speech situation whereas third person does not. It is the unmarked person value, often having a default function (as when it co-occurs with Agr displaying a different person value in the Spanish construction illustrated in (7)). In keeping with this unmarked value, third person is frequently morphologically unmarked in Agr, taking zero form; I illustrate with some partial paradigms:

316

	Spanish	Biblical Hebrew (perfect aspect, non-feminine forms)	Turkish	Warlpiri
1SG	various	-tî	-m/-im	-rna
2SG	-s	-tā	-n/-sin	-npa/-n
3SG	–	–	–	–

Moreover, the morpheme which expresses person on Agr is nearly always a portmanteau morpheme, encoding other features at the same time. In particular, it almost invariably encodes number. So it is plausible to suppose that what looks like a third-person singular or third-person plural morpheme is actually encoding only singular or plural, third person having its usual zero realization. In fact, singular tends to be the morphologically unmarked number value, also frequently taking zero realization, with the result that the combined person–number form for third singular is zero, as in the paradigms above. So while I am suggesting that German -*t* in (15) represents singular number only, the point applies in many languages more clearly to third person plural, as in (16), where the proposal is that Spanish -*n* encodes only plural. If this is correct, the usual morphological identity between third-person Agr and the Agr form accompanying indefinites is unremarkable.

But just as the morphological realization of singular number is not always zero, we would expect an overt realization of third person on Agr sometimes. The effect of this would be that all three persons are overtly encoded, and person marking should then distinguish definites and indefinites in what is traditionally seen as third person. That is, we should find cases of encoding of first, second, and definite third person, contrasting with lack of marking for indefinites. This is the situation with the Macedonian object-agreement clitics, which encode person (as well as other features) and are obligatory with all definite objects, but absent with indefinite arguments:

(17) a. Marija me poznava mene.
Marija 1SG-ACC knows me
b. Marija te poznava tebe.
Marija 2SG-ACC knows you
c. Marija go poznava nego.
Marija 3SG-M-ACC knows him
d. Marija ja najde mačka-ta.
Marija 3SG-F-ACC found cat DEF
e. Marija najde edna mačka.
Marija found one cat

The conventional assumption is of two distinct categories, person and definiteness, third person differing from first and second in not relating to a participant in the discourse; and while first- and second-person forms are, for some reason, always definite, only third-person forms may be indefinite. Against this assumption I have argued that person and definiteness are the same thing. We may call this category either "person" or "definiteness"; what matters is that the traditionally recognized person distinctions are hyponymous to definiteness. And while *the car* is, like *he* and *she*, third or unmarked person (or, equivalently, definite non-participant), indefinites like *a car* or *someone* are personless.

8.5.3 *The nature of person-definiteness*

I am assuming that at least some grammatical categories are represented syntactically as functional heads, but also that distinctions within categories can be specified by features encoded on these heads (or, in some cases, on expressions in their specifiers). Thus if mood, for example, is represented by a functional head, it will still be necessary to express sub-categories of mood (indicative, subjunctive etc.) in this head or in its projection, and features are the usual way of expressing such distinctions. In the same way, person is a category under which a number of subordinate distinctions must be made, and the feature representation of these distinctions is considered next.

Third person, as the unmarked value, can be considered to be simply person with no further subordinate specification. First and second persons behave differently from third person in a number of ways, syntactically and morphologically, as observed. What distinguishes them is that they correspond to discourse participants, so let us assume a feature [+ Participant] characterizing them. What distinguishes first from second person is that only the former may (and must) include reference to the speaker.[11] We can therefore add a feature [± Speaker], giving the following hierarchy of properties:

> Person
> Participant
> Speaker

Note that, on the account assumed, only the two subordinate, hyponymous properties are represented as features; the superordinate property, person, is the category D. But we have seen that personal forms, like demonstratives, occur in all languages, including languages like Dyirbal and Japanese with no DP structure. In these languages the personal forms found are strong forms, and it seems person distinctions are expressed lexically rather than grammatically. We can hypothesize,

---

[11] Recall that the hearer may be included in the reference of a non-singular first-person form, except in the case of exclusive first-person forms in languages which have these.

however, that only the hyponymous properties in the hierarchy above, those represented as features, can be lexically expressed, not person itself. This would account for the morphophonological strength of the forms concerned in non-DP languages, since forms expressing merely person (that is, simple definites in our earlier terms) tend to be weak. It may also account for an interesting contrast between personal forms and demonstratives. Both are incompatible with indefiniteness, though both occur in non-DP as well as DP languages; and in languages with DP structure, both must be associated with D at least in the sense that they require projection of DP. But, in DP languages, a demonstrative need not be expressed in D or specifier of D; it may be elsewhere in the noun phrase, in an adjective position for example, provided there is a definite article present (to which the demonstrative may perhaps be syntactically linked by coindexing). Examples, from 3.1, are Ewondo *é mvú ɲí* (the dog this) 'this dog', Catalan *la ciutat aquella* (the city that) 'that city', Maori *te whare nei* (the house this) 'this house'. This is apparently not possible with forms expressing participant roles. It is not enough for these to be accompanied by a marker of definiteness in D or its specifier; they are always themselves in one or other of these positions. I suggest this is because the features [+ Participant, ± Speaker] are more directly subordinate to person-definiteness, thus to D, than is [+ Dem], which is merely incompatible with omission of D. Participant role features must be encoded in the locus of person-definiteness itself because this represents their own superordinate category.

It is worthwhile at this point to return to the "animacy" hierarchy (or cluster of hierarchies) discussed in 5.3. Person and definiteness (understood in a broad sense to include specificity) are two of the sub-hierarchies proposed in the literature as being involved in this complex, and the unification I have advanced here between these categories offers a significant simplification of this idea. Some of the noun phrase types argued to play a part in the animacy hierarchy (such as proper names and animates proper) will still have to be accounted for separately, but a considerable number of the properties involved can now be treated as forming a chain of hyponymy. Recall my suggestion in 7.5 that in languages like Maori where an article combines pragmatic definiteness (identifiability) with specificity, this can be treated as grammatical definiteness with merely a broader than usual range of use. This means that specificity in such languages is also part of person.

But in other languages specificity is encoded independently of definiteness, and indeed associated rather with indefiniteness. Common patterns are for a quasi-indefinite article to be limited to specific indefinite use, and for an "irrealis" marker to accompany a cardinal article with non-specific indefinites; see 2.5 and 5.2. This association of the [± Spec] distinction sometimes with definiteness and sometimes with indefiniteness is not problematic provided we keep in mind that person-definiteness is a grammatical category capable of considerable variation in what it expresses.[12] In semantic–pragmatic terms, indefinites can be specific or non-specific, and we have seen evidence that languages treat definiteness as hyponymous to specificity; specifics are thus intermediate between indefinites and definites. But indefinites are defined negatively with respect to definiteness, so that it would be more accurate to say that noun phrases are specific or non-specific, and specifics are definite or indefinite. It is then open to languages to have a grammatical category of person which embraces pragmatic definites only or which also takes in (at least some) pragmatically indefinite specifics. In the former case, [± Spec] may then be encoded for those noun phrases not covered by person.

We can therefore establish a hierarchy of properties, to be interpreted as a chain of hyponymy, part or all of which (working up from less to more general) may be embraced by person-definiteness:

> Specific
> General definite (identifiable)
> Ostensive (textual–situational: see 4.1.3)
> Anaphoric (see 4.1.2 and 4.1.3)
> Participant
> Speaker

The expression of these properties, up to but not above ostension, may also be combined with [+ Dem]. I suggest that this chain of properties may be a useful input to comparative work relating to the idea discussed of an "animacy hierarchy".

8.6 Summary of proposals

I have argued in this chapter that definiteness is represented syntactically as a functional category, and I have identified this category with the widely accepted D. So DP is definiteness phrase rather than determiner phrase. I have gone on to claim that definiteness and person are one and the same category. Thus the familiar discourse participant distinctions traditionally associated with person, as first and second person, are finer distinctions within the larger category of person-definiteness, in much the same way as past, present and future can appear as distinctions subordinate to the category of tense. This category of person-definiteness (or whatever we choose to call it) is represented as D and DP in grammar, and the subordinate distinctions are features on some expression in DP (in head or specifier position).

---

[12] If further illustration is needed of the mismatches tolerated between grammatical categories and meaning, consider the fact that in numerous languages polite pronoun forms referring to the hearer are grammatically third person.

Only definite noun phrases are DP, though both definites and indefinites are ultimately of the same category KP (which is higher than DP). Languages with no category of definiteness lack DP, but there are many languages which have DP in pronouns but not in full noun phrases. Other functional projections, like CardP and NumP, may similarly be absent in languages, either completely or only in certain (for example full) noun phrases, and this will correlate with lack of cardinal articles and number marking.

Articles may be either heads or specifiers (of DP in the case of definite articles and CardP in the case of cardinal articles). Head articles are typically bound forms and directly express the category (D or Card), while specifier articles are typically free forms and pleonastic, lexically empty fillers of a position that would otherwise be empty, indicating merely by their presence that the category is projected. Substantive definite determiners, such as demonstratives, may also occupy DP specifier, though they may also appear in a range of other modifier positions. In the latter case, they are probably syntactically linked to DP specifier in languages which have DP, and an article or other determiner in DP has to appear. In languages with no DP, demonstratives involve identifiability, the pragmatic concept underlying definiteness, but are not grammatically definite. A parallel analysis is probably appropriate for substantive cardinal determiners, like numerals. Possessives are not definite, grammatically or pragmatically, but in many DP languages they can raise into DP, to head or specifier position, and this yields the DG phenomenon in which possessives give the appearance of being definite determiners.

Definite pronouns have the same structure as definite full noun phrases, but lack the lexical element, NP. They consist essentially of a definite determiner, which is the definite article in the case of weak pronouns and a demonstrative in the case of strong pronouns. In the former case, a specifier article gives a free-form weak pronoun and a head article gives a pronominal clitic.

9
Diachronic aspects

It is appropriate to devote some attention to the emergence and development of markers of definiteness, because a great deal has been written on this topic, both from the point of view of general historical linguistics and in work on particular languages or language families. Indeed, in the course of the present study, I have repeatedly made reference to the diachronic sources of articles in other, typically demonstrative, elements. It may be too much to say that this area of morphosyntax is more prone to historical change than others, but research indicates that it is possible to trace quite radical shifts affecting definiteness and determiners, sometimes over relatively short time spans. In this chapter I will examine three aspects of this issue: first, the acquisition of a syntactic category of definiteness by languages previously lacking it; second, the emergence of articles from other, substantive, determiners; third, the subsequent development of articles and definiteness.

9.1 The emergence of functional structure

Until recently, most research on the appearance of definiteness marking in languages which had previously lacked it concentrated on the process of semantic weakening whereby a demonstrative, or other determiner, became a definite article. But the development in the last few years of the theory of functional categories, including the DP analysis of the noun phrase, has made it possible to look at the question in new ways. It is assumed that languages vary in what functional projections they have (so that, for example, a language with no number marking can be taken to lack NumP), and the absence of DP in a given language should have the consequence, on the standard DP hypothesis as outlined in 8.2, that this language has no class of determiner. The emergence of articles can thus be linked to the development of DP structure. An explanation along these lines is' problematic, however, since it implies that definiteness markers must be determiners and that a language with determiners will have definiteness marking. Apart from the fact that articles can be affixal, it is not clear why an adjectival demonstrative in a non-DP language should not weaken to express merely definiteness while

remaining adjectival; and conversely, it is not clear why a language with determiners (because with DP) should not have only demonstrative, cardinal etc.
determiners, without a marker of simple definiteness.

The modified DP analysis presented in 8.3, on which D is not the word class
of determiner but the category of definiteness, offers a clearer account. With this
framework it is possible to maintain that DP structure is necessary for a language
to have a definite article, and even that the creation of an article is a necessary
concomitant of the emergence of DP structure. This is a desirable position
because the empirical evidence is for a much closer association with D on the
part of definite articles than of other "definite determiners" like demonstratives.
We have seen (in 3.1.3, 3.5 and 8.3.2) that demonstratives and quantificational
determiners can be adjectival in languages with DP structure as well as in languages without, but definite articles are never adjectival in position. Demonstratives etc. may either occur in head D or DP specifier position, or alternatively be
linked with an expression in one of these positions, but only the former option
is open to the article. This follows from the view given in 8.3 of what a definite
article is: either a realization of D itself, particularly if affixal; or, if a free form,
a semantically empty, pleonastic DP specifier, a (usually obligatory) place-filler
of this position in the absence of some substantive occupant, serving merely to
indicate that DP has been projected. It is the projection of DP that makes a noun
phrase definite, and the article signals this projection. It is clear, therefore, that
there can be no definite article in languages lacking DP structure, and, to the extent
that it is obligatory to have some expression of a projection, languages with DP
structure must have a definite article. See also Lyons (1995d) for this account.

9.1.1 The development of DP

The diachronic emergence of definite articles, then, represents the
appearance of the category of definiteness in languages, and amounts to a change
in syntactic structure: the creation of a DP projection. The major qualification that
must be added is that in languages like Turkish and Sinhalese which signal
indefiniteness by a cardinal article but have no definite article, it may be that DP
can exist without overt realization. This is uncertain, and I shall concentrate on
the dominant pattern, that creation of DP entails creation of definiteness marking.
The obvious mechanism by which this might come about is the reanalysis by speakers of an adjectival demonstrative as an article, and I shall say more about this
below. Another possible mechanism, which might interact with this reanalysis and
encourage it, is the reinterpretation of an inalienable possession structure as a DG
structure (as suggested in 7.5.3). The idea is that inalienable constructions are readily interpreted as definite, because there is a tendency for their semantic equivalent in DP languages like English, with no special inalienable construction, to be

DG, even where the usual conditions for definiteness (identifiability or inclusiveness) do not apply, as in *I've cut my finger*. Given this, and the fact that inalienable constructions tend to be morphologically simpler than alienable ones, which often involve an additional particle, the alienable–inalienable distinction is probably easily reanalysed as an AG–DG distinction. AG possessives tend similarly to be more complex morphologically than DG ones, showing an additional marker such as a preposition.

Other possible triggers for the creation of definiteness and definite articles have been discussed in the literature. There is a tradition of linking it to a shift from synthetic to analytic structure, to changes in word-order pattern, and to the loss or reduction of morphological case systems. This last suggestion is particularly intriguing, and figures prominently in the recent literature on this topic, reinterpreted in terms of current syntactic theory. It is not at first sight obvious why a loss of case distinctions should lead to the emergence of a category of definiteness, but in some languages (such as the Romance and Germanic groups) the two developments have coincided approximately, and the idea grew out of this observation. A traditional account of this coincidence is that case morphology (as well as other nominal feature marking) is often preserved on determiners after it has been lost on nouns. The creation of articles is therefore a way of ensuring that noun phrases will generally contain an expression of their case. This suggestion relates to the view discussed (and rejected) in 5.4 that the principal function of the definite article, at least in some languages, is to carry the inflectional morphology of the noun phrase. A more recent account is based on the proposal that case has its locus in the D position, so that case morphology and an article are alternative realizations of this head (Giusti 1993). I am assuming a K head distinct from D, however. But we saw in 5.1 that case distinctions function in a number of languages to express a variety of contrasts approximating to the definite–indefinite one, and such facts have been used to support the claim of a close relationship between definiteness and case. Philippi (1997) argues, on the basis of Germanic, that case and articles are both devices for expressing the definite–indefinite distinction, so that weakening of a case system naturally leads to the creation of a definite article. But it is clear from the discussion in 5.1 that the contrast expressed by different choices of case for direct objects in languages like Finnish, Hungarian, Kabardian and Turkish is not the same as that involved in definiteness, though it may come close to it. Nevertheless, one might argue that, while case and definiteness are grammatically distinct, the pragmatic contrast expressed by the choice of direct object case in these languages is sufficiently close to the definite–indefinite distinction to encourage speakers to create a category of definiteness when the possibility of the case strategy is lost. But the evidence is lacking for the assumption that languages with articles generally used such a case strategy before. Moreover, the loss or weakening of case systems and the creation of definiteness marking do not show a particularly close correspondence cross-linguistically. Fairly substantial case systems co-exist with definite articles in Classical Greek, Icelandic and German, and Hungarian even shows the direct object case strategy discussed as well as a definite article. For these reasons I discount the claim that the emergence of definiteness is linked to the loss of case systems. I assume that the reanalysis of demonstratives (brought about by factors to be discussed below) is the principal trigger for the creation of a category of definiteness.

If a demonstrative, occurring in a position which could be interpreted as DP specifier, is reanalysed as an article, with the usual phonological weakening, and, perhaps additionally, if the possessor expression in an inalienable construction is reanalysed as being in DP specifier (rather than, perhaps, NP specifier), the result is necessarily that the structure becomes DP. But at the point at which this happens, it may well be that the language already has DP in a more limited way. Recall from 7.5.3, 8.3.3 and 8.4 that many languages apparently have DP in their pronominal system only, and perhaps only in weak personal pronouns, whether overt or null. I repeat the typology proposed in 7.5.3, representing definiteness as DP structure:

Type I: no DP
Type II: pronominal DP only
Type III: pronominal and full noun phrase DP

Type I is exemplified by Japanese, Korean and Dyirbal, in which there is no definite article in full noun phrases, and either no weak or null personal pronouns or only unidentified null arguments (interpreted pronominally but not constrained to be definite). Type II is exemplified by Russian, Latin and Warlpiri, languages with no article in full noun phrases, but with either overt weak personal pronouns or null pro-nominal arguments (probably *pro*) identified by agreement; both these kinds of weak pronoun are always definite. And Type III is represented by English and all languages with definiteness marking in full noun phrases.

These three language types give us two possible major diachronic shifts. That from Type I to Type II consists of the development of weak personal pronouns, overt or null. The shift from Type II to Type III consists of the extension of the availability of DP structure to full noun phrases. Of course it is not ruled out that a language may move directly from Type I to Type III; what is ruled out is a Type I language acquiring a definite article in full noun phrases only.[1] Interestingly, both shifts are probably typically mediated by the weakening of a demonstrative. I have

---

[1] This strong claim would be falsified by a language with unidentified null arguments but with a definite article. According to Givón (1978), Japanese is such a language; Givón claims Japanese has a definite article *sono*, a form I take to be a demonstrative.

already indicated how this is so of the second shift, but consider how the first, from Type I to Type II, might come about. Strong personal pronouns, in Type I languages like Dyirbal as well as in Type II and Type III languages, are likely to be demonstrative (except where they are full noun phrases, as may be the case in Japanese), with lexical encoding of discourse participant features. And the change to Type II consists of these demonstrative pronouns weakening semantically and morphophonologically to yield weak pronouns – which are necessarily definite, and represent the grammaticalization of the discourse participant features as person.

Weak definite pronouns may, as noted, be either overt (English, Russian) or null (Latin, Spanish, and probably Warlpiri), and the latter (*pro*) must be identified by agreement morphology (Agr). But Agr (whether on a verb as in the Romance languages or on an auxiliary as in many Australian languages) itself usually comes into being through the cliticization of weak pronouns (see Dixon (1980: chapter 11)). It may be, therefore, that the shift from Type I to Type II should be divided into two sub-shifts, of which only the first is essential. This is the formation of overt weak pronouns through the weakening of strong pronouns. This may, but need not, be followed by the evolution of these weak pronouns into clitics and eventually agreement inflections, cross-referencing *pro*. This second sub-shift, while not essential to the achievement of Type II status, more often than not does take place, as evidenced by the numerical preponderance of null-subject languages.

Personal pronouns may, then, develop DP structure before full noun phrases do, and are in this sense more "advanced" in relation to definiteness. We can speculate that this is related to the fact that pronouns exhibit discourse participant features (which underlie person-definiteness) much more readily and commonly than do non-pronominal noun phrases (because reference to speaker and hearer is usually pro-nominal). But we will see that this more "advanced" nature shows itself again at a later stage in the diachronic progression.

9.1.2 A definite article cycle

Type III, fully DP, languages may have free-form or bound definite articles, and I have argued that, generally, the former are pleonastic Dets in DP specifier while the latter are D heads. But there is a diachronic process at work here too, since bound forms commonly originate from free-standing items. Just as agreement clitics or inflections arise from weak pronouns, so free-form articles are diachronically prior to bound articles. This means that the second major shift, from Type II to Type III, can also be seen as involving two sub-shifts, with, once again, only the first being essential to reach Type III. First a demonstrative adjective comes to be reanalysed as a free-form article, and subsequently this may become a clitic or inflection. This second sub-shift consists of a specifier Det evolving into a D head. This process is well attested, and can be illustrated by the similarity between affix and free form in Icelandic, or (taking two Romance varieties) between the Romanian affix and the Italian free form:

(1)   *Icelandic*
   a.   hestur-**inn**   'the horse'
   b.   **hinn** sterki hestur   'the strong horse'

(2) a.   *Romanian* profesor-**ul**   'the teacher'
   b.   *Italian*   **il** professore   'the teacher'

In some cases, the evolution of a free-standing article into a bound form has been followed by the creation of a new free-form article, again typically from a demonstrative. This new form may complement the affix, as in Danish where the two divide up the range of definite structures or in Hausa where they are alternatives. Or it may reinforce the affix, as in the double determination structures of Swedish. See 2.3.4 for details of these distributions. It may be that the next step in the diachronic process is for the affix to be lost and for the more recent free-form article to take over as the sole exponent of definiteness. If so, this would recall recent work on the syntax of negation (Zanuttini 1991, Rowlett 1994), which revives the idea first proposed by Jespersen (1917) of a "negative cycle". Negation in this research is analysed as a functional head Neg projecting a phrase NegP, and the idea of the cycle, reinterpreted in terms of this analysis, is as follows. A negative expression in or associated with NegP specifier evolves into a Neg head; this is subsequently reinforced by a new specifier negative; the head form then drops out, leaving the more recent specifier form as the sole exponent of negation; this then in turn becomes a head; and so on. Analogous to this, I suggest there may be a diachronic "article cycle" as described, with repeated renewal of definiteness marking.

It will be recalled from 2.3 that affixal articles are of various kinds, some attaching to the lexical head of the noun phrase, others to a different host. Wackernagel forms are particularly common. I assume these are all D heads, having in common that they need morphological support from some host. The phenomenon of definite adjectives seen in the Baltic and Slavonic languages (at least in relic form) may also have arisen from the Wackernagel pattern. Adjectival modifiers are prenominal in these languages, and a second-position article would therefore attach to such a modifier where present, as it does in Amharic and with the modern Wackernagel article of Macedonian and Bulgarian (see 2.3.3). What is unclear on this account is why the older Slavonic and Baltic definiteness marking only persisted (if it ever occurred more generally) in the presence of an adjective. Another interesting case of cliticization of an article to something other than the noun is the preposition–article contractions also mentioned in 2.3. Here the combination is with an element outside the noun phrase, and it is, in some cases at least, most naturally accounted for by Head Movement of a D head to cliticize to the structurally higher P head. Let us look more closely at this phenomenon in German, which shows some intriguing distributions of article forms, and perhaps an interesting illustration of the article cycle suggested.

Preposition–article contraction in German is optional, and more common with some choices of preposition and form of article than others (Durrell 1991). Some combinations, mainly involving the masculine–neuter singular dative form of the article (like *in dem* → *im* 'in the'), are normal in all styles; others, involving the neuter singular accusative (*für das* → *fürs*), are less common in writing; others, including further masculine singular datives and all instances of the masculine singular accusative (*für den* → *für'n* 'for the') and dative plural (*mit den* → *mit'n* 'with the'), are essentially limited to the spoken language. Most prepositions take the dative, but only one contraction occurs in writing with the feminine dative (*zu der* → *zur* 'to the'). When contraction does not occur, and in contexts not involving a preposition, the article is free-standing in written and careful spoken German, though unaffected speech uses a few heavily reduced forms, also probably clitics. These are the same as those occurring in contractions. These clitic article forms, both in preposition–article contractions and elsewhere, are as follows, together with the corresponding free forms:

free	clitic
das	s
den	n
dem	m
der	r

The standard assumption concerning the diachrony of these clitic forms is that they are reductions of the corresponding free forms. Synchronically, a standard DP analysis, taking both article forms as D heads, might involve an optional reduction process triggered by stylistic factors or presence of a governing preposition. The reduced forms would be bound variants requiring morphological support from a host, which could be achieved by Head Movement of D to P or by cliticization to whatever is immediately to the right in the noun phrase. In my revised DP framework, the free-form articles are specifiers and the clitics D heads (again undergoing raising to P or cliticizing to adjacent material). And the choice between the two articles is optional but involves the same stylistic and syntactic triggers mentioned above. This analysis implies a diachronic process whereby (at some point in the medieval period) a head D article developed from a specifier article in the usual way (and with the typical reduction), but without ousting the latter, resulting in co-existence of two article types. This is somewhat similar to the situation in Icelandic, if the two articles of that language are indeed cognate. But while the synchronic characterization just offered for German may be accurate, there is reason to question the diachronic background outlined.

There are two striking points which may cast doubt on the standard view of the relationship between the two German article forms. First, while the morphophonological reductions affecting grammatical items in weak positions (like clitic articles) can be radical and idiosyncratic, the systematic loss of the entire root here is surprising, especially given that the loss of initial [d] or an earlier dental fricative is not a process known to have occurred otherwise in early German.[2] Second, the fact that clitic forms exist corresponding to only some free-standing forms, and their optionality, make them look like relic forms from an older, fuller system. The fact that the free-standing forms are always possible suggests that these may represent the more recent article rather than being the source of the clitic forms, especially given that the preposition–article contractions are attested in very early High German texts. While stressing that this differs from the standard view, I suggest that the clitic article forms could be relics of an earlier article (perhaps cognate with the A-article of Fering – see below – and even with the Scandinavian affixal article) which was largely supplanted by the *d*- article after developing into a bound D head. If so, then these forms instantiate the article cycle proposed.

I suggested above that personal pronouns tend to be more "advanced" diachronically in relation to definiteness than full noun phrases, since they often acquire DP structure earlier. A second manifestation of this characteristic relates to the article cycle outlined. Pronouns tend to travel more rapidly through this cycle; that is, a specifier definite article is likely to evolve into a D head earlier in pronominal than in non-pronominal noun phrases. I proposed in 8.3.3 that the difference between weak free-form personal pronouns and clitic pronouns is that the definite article which constitutes the overt and essential content of both is a specifier Det in the former and a D head in the latter. This head status is what enables pronominal clitics (in the Romance languages for instance) to undergo Head Movement to their placement position. It is well established that these clitics develop diachronically from free-form pronouns, so it is clear that their formation instantiates part of the article cycle, the change of a specifier article into a head. This process is, of course, the first step in the formation of agreement inflection, briefly discussed above in relation to Type II languages. In these languages it can only

---

[2] To take a somewhat parallel case, note that the English colloquial pronoun form *'em*, while no doubt synchronically a reduction of *them*, is not derived diachronically from this, but from an earlier *hem* which was otherwise supplanted by *them* in the Middle English period.

affect pronominal noun phrases because only they are DPs. But in Type III languages both pronominal and full definite noun phrases can undergo this development, so that both free-form pronouns and free-form articles become affixal. This has happened in Romanian, for example. But, as pointed out in 8.3.3, many Type III languages show a mismatch here, with clitic pronouns but free-form article. The mismatch is particularly striking in languages where the two are cognate and close in form. In French the definite article, most probably a free form, and the third-person direct object clitic pronouns are identical:

	article	*clitic pronoun*
M SG	le	le
F SG	la	la
PL	les	les

It seems the article (originally a specifier) has advanced to D status only in pronominal DP in French. I suggested above that the more advanced nature of pronouns in relation to the acquisition of DP structure can be accounted for in terms of their special relationship to the discourse participant features which underlie person, but it is not obvious why they should also be more advanced in relation to the article cycle. Perhaps this second mismatch between pronouns and full noun phrases should not be overstated; there are languages (like the Scandinavian group) which show the opposite of the French pattern, with bound definite articles but free-form personal pronouns. But this pattern is less common.

9.1.3   Indefinites and CardP

The emergence of cardinal articles is in many ways parallel to that of definite articles. They nearly always develop from the semantic weakening of the singular numeral, comparable to the weakening of a demonstrative to yield the definite article. I have proposed that both articles are to be analysed as either pleonastic specifiers or functional heads; in the case of the cardinal article this means the specifier or head of CardP rather than DP. So this article depends on the language having a projection CardP, and it may be hypothesized that the emergence of a cardinal article in many cases goes hand-in-hand with the development of this functional projection. Numerals and other substantive cardinality modifiers need not be CardP specifiers; they can for example be adjectival. But an adjectival numeral 'one' may, if in an appropriate position relative to other noun phrase constituents, undergo semantic and phonological weakening and be reanalysed as a pleonastic CardP specifier. If the language lacks this projection, the reanalysis leads to its creation.

A specifier cardinal article may subsequently undergo cliticization and develop into a Card head, though this seems to occur less readily than with definite articles. The Persian data discussed in 2.5.1 further suggests the possibility of cyclic developments of specifier and head articles.

9.2 The origin of articles

Here we look more closely at the sources of definite and cardinal articles (again concentrating on the former, which have been much more intensively studied) in the reanalysis of some substantive determiner, usually a demonstrative or numeral.

9.2.1 Demonstrative to definite article

In fact definite articles derive not only from demonstratives, but sometimes from verbs and classifiers, among other possibilities. The Sissala article *ná* has its source in the verb 'see', which still has the same form (Blass 1990). The development seems to be via the use of this verb in the ostensive sense of French *voici/voilà* (expressions which in French too are based on the verb 'see'), Latin *ecce* or archaic English *behold*: *Ná cɔlmɔ* (see spear) 'There is the spear'. In fact *ná* has developed a range of other uses, including that of a deictic particle 'there', and that of a temporal demonstrative 'that' (*tɛŋ ná* 'that time'). See J. Lyons (1977: chapter 15) for discussion of how "quasi-referential" items of the *behold* type may ontogenetically underlie demonstratives and definiteness. The Bengali definite article, affixed to the noun, is derived from a numeral classifier (Masica 1986). Interestingly, the same form is still in use as a classifier, and it is only when attached to the noun that it expresses definiteness: *ek-ṭi chele* (one-CLASS child) 'one/a child', *chele-ṭi* (child-DEF) 'the child'. In many French-based creoles the article is a form *la* derived from the French adverb *là* or deictic particle -*là* 'there'. The French definite article has in many cases been reanalysed as part of the noun stem. Thus, corresponding to French *le lit* 'the bed', Mauritian Creole has *lili la* (Baker 1984, Grant 1995). Even genitive morphemes may be a possible source for definite articles; see Bader (1993). Demonstratives are, however, overwhelmingly the most common source.

The semantic weakening or "bleaching" taken to be involved in the shift from demonstrative to article reflects a very general diachronic process of devaluation of lexical content. This process can be described in terms of loss of lexico-semantic features, and in the case we are concerned with it is essentially the feature [+ Dem] which is affected. We have seen that in some languages (like Macedonian) definite articles maintain the deictic distinctions displayed by demonstratives, so the only difference is that the latter are [+ Dem]. It is much more common, however, for articles to have no deictic content, so that their creation involves loss of deictic features as well as [+ Dem]. It is likely, though, that in many such cases there has been an intermediate stage at which the demonstrative concerned has already lost its deictic feature to become a general, deictically unmarked demonstrative. If this is so, it may be that definite articles not encoding deixis typically have their immediate source in such general demonstratives. Apart from deictic features, definite articles may carry agreement features, but they may have neither of these and be grammatically and semantically completely empty. In this case, it is the position of the item, in specifier of DP if free-form, that causes it to express anything; indeed, even if it does have deictic or agreement content, it is its position in DP which makes it a definite article. For this reason, I have argued that a demonstrative would have to be in a position in the noun phrase which permits reinterpretation as specifier (or, occasionally, head) of DP to evolve into a definite article. This development is, therefore, not just a matter of feature loss (or however else one chooses to characterize semantic weakening). It is probably a complex interaction of reanalysis and weakening, the two operating simultaneously and reinforcing each other.

I suggest the crucial fact that makes this possible is that there is a broad overlap in function between definite article and demonstrative (particularly deictically unmarked demonstrative). We have seen that there are many contexts in, for example, English where the choice of definite article or demonstrative makes little difference to the message conveyed, and I have noted that languages lacking definiteness tend to use demonstratives more extensively. This area of overlap is what I have called (in 4.1.3) "textual–situational ostension", consisting of anaphoric (and cataphoric) together with immediate situation uses. We have seen that this band of uses of the definite article can be overtly distinguished from other uses by a distinct article form. This is the case in Fering, as discussed, where the form used for textual–situational ostension, the D-article, is, though unstressed, morphologically fuller than the A-article – in keeping with the fact that it is closer in function to a demonstrative; indeed the D-article is, apart from its lack of stress, identical to a demonstrative. Fering is in fact not an isolated instance of the partition of article functions along this line; see Heinrichs (1954) for discussion of the German dialect of Amern, which also has two definite article forms, dividing up the field of definiteness in almost exactly the same way as Fering. I believe it is in the textual–situational ostensive function that demonstratives undergo phonological weakening and reanalysis as articles. As a result, a new article is likely to be restricted to this range of uses before, perhaps, generalizing to other definite uses. For further discussion of this point see Lyons (1995d).

One of the most intensively studied cases of definite article creation is that of Romance. All the modern Romance languages have a definite article, though Latin, the ancestor language, had not; Latin was a Type II language, with definiteness only in its pronoun system. Classical Latin had a rich demonstrative system, with a three-way person-based deictic contrast as well as a deictically unmarked form:

general	is
ASS1	hic
ASS2	iste
ASS3	ille

In a complex series of developments (which I greatly simplify here), late spoken Latin (or early Romance) largely dropped *is* and *hic*, perhaps in part because they were phonetically rather insubstantial and would become more so with the sound changes of the period. *Ille* took the place of *is* (while continuing in use as third-person form), while *iste* replaced *hic*. The place of *iste* as second-person form was taken over by *ipse*, originally not a demonstrative but expressing the sense of emphatic *self* (*ego ipse* 'I myself', *Caesar ipse* 'Caesar himself'); *ipse* also tended to occur as general demonstrative. This gives a system something like the following:

general	ille, ipse
ASS1	iste
ASS2	ipse
ASS3	ille

In further developments, the deictically marked forms tended to be morphologically reinforced (thus *ecce-iste* to yield Old French *cist* 'this', and *accu-ille* giving Spanish *aquel* 'that'), while *ille* and *ipse* evolved into definite articles. Almost all modern Romance varieties have an article descended from *ille*, forms from *ipse* surviving only in a few pockets. But *ipse* articles were much more widespread during the first millennium AD, and many late Latin texts of that period show *ipse* forms predominating. Much has been written on the question of when *ille* and *ipse* became articles, most estimates falling into the period between the third and eighth centuries. A major reason for the doubt is that texts during this long period show a high, and increasing, frequency of occurrence of *ille* and *ipse* in noun phrases, but that, at least in the earlier part of the period, this frequency is greater than would be expected for demonstratives (even given the tendency of these to be used more in non-DP languages) yet smaller than obtains later with the definite article. Aebischer (1948) coins the term "articloid" to label this incipient article, which is for some writers a demonstrative with very high frequency of occurrence and for others an article with a still limited range of use. More recent research (Renzi 1976, Selig 1992) indicates that *ipse* was restricted to second-mention, strictly anaphoric (not cataphoric) use, while *ille* was less constrained but mainly used cataphorically, before a restrictive relative. The point is that, between them, *ipse* and *ille* cover anaphora and cataphora, and do not go beyond this in the earlier part of the period indicated.

Given that the evidence for these early Romance developments is necessarily from texts rather than speech, we cannot expect to find much, if any, information about immediate situation reference, and this may distort conclusions. My suspicion is that, say around 400 AD, Romance had a definite article (with two forms, *ipse* limited to strictly anaphoric use), covering the same range of functions as the Fering D-article. Thus the "articloid" is an article limited to textual–situational ostension.[3] This limitation, and the further limitation on the *ipse* article, clearly relate . to the chain of hyponymy discussed in 8.5.3. The point for the diachrony is that a demonstrative does not immediately become a general definite article; the new article begins by being restricted to the area of overlap already available to the demonstrative, and expands from there.

9.2.2 Articles in competition

In early Romance, both *ille* and *ipse* articles expanded from the restrictions described to become general definite articles. Different Romance-speaking regions came to prefer one or the other, though around the end of the millennium *ille* expanded geographically to almost eliminate its rival. But the most interesting point here for general historical linguistics is that two article forms should have been introduced in the first place. The originally distinct article functions of the two forms seem to follow from their earlier senses. It is fairly common for emphatic 'self' and 'same' to be expressed by a single form (French *même*, Classical Greek *autos*), and *ipse* seems to have replaced Latin *idem* in the sense 'same'; French *même*, indeed, derives from a reinforced form of *ipse*. And it is common for the form for 'same' to function also as an anaphoric demonstrative; see the comments on Lezgian and Nama in 3.1.2. From anaphoric demonstrative to anaphoric article is then a small enough step, involving just the usual loss of the feature [+ Dem]. The demonstrative *ille*, not having the anaphoric feature, would naturally weaken initially to a more general textual–situational ostensive article. See also Vincent (1997), who argues that early Romance *ipse* is in fact further limited, to marking topic continuity, so that it would not appear with second-mention items which are not informationally prominent. Vincent also suggests a pragmatic connection between topic marking and second-person deixis, and points out that the geographical areas where *ipse* forms survived longest as an article are also areas with an [Ass2] demonstrative derived from *ipse*.

---

[3] It was probably also still optional in this function. But recall from 2.2.1 that some languages, like Hausa, do have an optional definite article, its appearance being determined by complex pragmatic factors. The widespread view that a weakening demonstrative only achieves fully fledged article status when it becomes obligatory in appropriate contexts is incorrect.

A striking feature of these Romance developments is that, while articles emerged from two substantive forms, the two first complementing and later rivalling each other, and while these same two forms also survived (without the morphophonological reduction characterizing the article, indeed in some Romance varieties with reinforcement) as demonstratives and strong personal pronouns, there is no evidence at any period of pronominal clitics derived from *ipse*. Clitic object pronouns are another Romance creation, perhaps arising about the same time as the article or slightly later; and all attested forms derive from *ille* only. This too is discussed by Vincent, who relates it to the observation that definiteness marking in full noun phrases was initially largely limited to those in subject position. In Old French, Spanish etc., and in many other languages, objects (like complements of prepositions in many languages) often appear without an article even though identifiable. This may relate to the cross-linguistic generalization that subject position is topic position and that topics are definite; if a language has a category of definiteness, it must be represented in this position but may be optional elsewhere. Vincent argues that Romance clitics, being objects and phonologically weak (therefore inappropriate for representing informationally prominent referents), did not correspond to the value of the topic-marking article *ipse*.

There are many cases of articles coming into existence in languages already possessing an article, as discussed above in relation to the proposed article cycle. The Scandinavian languages, in which a free-form article was introduced at some stage to complement or double an existing affixal article, illustrate this well. Fering may well be an instance of a language in which a free-form article has appeared to compete with an existing free-form article. It is likely that the two Fering articles are of distinct origins, and that the A-article is older, having once covered the whole range of definiteness. The younger D-article has partly replaced it, but only in textual–situational ostension, the range of functions commonly covered by a new article. The greater age of the A-article would (perhaps as well as its now being limited to uses not available to demonstratives) also account for its weaker form. If this is correct, it is an interesting illustration of how one article may replace another in stages. The same process may be at a more advanced stage in German, where I have suggested that the clitic article forms are relics of an older article (which may be cognate with the Fering A-article).

9.2.3 Numeral to cardinal article

Much of the above is paralleled in the development of the cardinal article. This also arises through semantic weakening, almost always of the singular numeral, though non-singular forms like English *sm* often derive from some other substantive cardinality item. Again the item yielding the article would have to be in a position which can be reanalysed as specifier or head of the relevant projection, CardP. And the process may be helped by an overlap in function between 'a' and 'one'. It is not unusual for languages which lack a cardinal article, particularly if they also lack number marking on nouns, to use the singular numeral more widely than other languages, for example where it is desired to indicate the non-plurality of a referent. It is important to note that these parallels between the emergence of definite articles and that of cardinal articles do not imply that the two processes are likely to occur together. This is clear from the many languages with a definite, but no cardinal, article, and Abraham (1997), discussing the origins of definiteness marking in Germanic, argues that the "indefinite" article emerged later than the definite article as a distinct development.

We have seen that cardinal articles expand their use in stages, usually being limited initially to specific indefinite function and gradually extending into non-specific uses. In this connection it is interesting to note that a number of English-based creoles have not taken over the English article *a*. Instead they have introduced a new one based on *one* – Hawaiian Creole *wan*, for example. But this article, unlike English *a*, is restricted to specific singular indefinites. For discussion see Bickerton (1981) and Janson (1984). A singular form derived from 'one' may also expand into non-singular use. See 2.5.2 and 2.5.5 for exemplification of these points.

9.3 The longer perspective

Let us now consider what can happen to an article once established (apart from elimination by a new rival article). The expansion of a definite article from an initial limited range of uses to the more general definite value of English *the* does not stop at that point. An article may even expand in use to the point where it ceases to be a definite article.

9.3.1 Expansion in article use

We have discussed the expansion of cardinal articles from singular specific use to non-specific and to non-singular use, and that of definite articles from textual–situational ostension to wider definite use. Limiting the discussion to definites, we now examine further possible expansions which do not yet take the article beyond the domain of definiteness. Languages with definiteness marking vary considerably in their use of it, as noted in Chapter 2, where it was seen that the main difference in this regard between English and French is that generics are typically definite in French but not in English. This difference is in part a diachronic fact, because Old French was much like Modern English in using bare plural and mass nouns for generic reference. The same is true of the other Romance languages, where definiteness has spread into the generic function. Plural and mass generics can be definite in English too with a limited range of nouns, as seen in 4.3.1 (*The Danes read a lot, The vertebrates have certain evolutionary advantages, I can't stand the rain*), so it may be that English is moving in the same direction.

Other languages use the definite article yet more than French. Italian and Portuguese, AG languages, use it with definite possessives, while Greek and Catalan use it with proper nouns. Interestingly, Italian and Portuguese also use the article with generics, and Greek and Catalan use it with generics and definite possessives. This gives, for these languages, a neat progression in respect of definite article use:

1 (English): simple definite
2 (French): simple definite, generic
3 (Italian): simple definite, generic, possessive
4 (Greek): simple definite, generic, possessive, proper noun

It is almost certainly too much to suggest that this represents a universal implicational scale, and by extension a series of diachronic stages languages may pass through. Examination of further languages would make the picture much less neat. But there is a diachronic progression reflected here, in that, for example, a language is only likely to start using the article with proper nouns when it already makes extensive use of it; this is true of Greek, and indeed Italian, which has limited use of the article with names.

In all the uses just discussed, the definite article does, according to the analysis I have given, represent definiteness. The point is that within the semantic/pragmatic field that definiteness may cover there is room for a language to increase the ground which the category actually covers in that language. But, as we will see next, an article can expand in use beyond this field.

9.3.2 The life cycle of definite articles

In languages like Greek and Catalan there are few potentially definite noun phrase types which do not already take the article. It could expand further to embrace what are at present in these languages specific indefinites, thus coming to resemble the articles of Samoan and Maori; I have suggested that specific reference counts as definite in these latter languages (2.2.4 and 7.5.2). But any expansion beyond this would entail the article acquiring non-definite uses, and thus becoming something other than a definite article. Greenberg (1978) argues that the normal development is for the definite article to end up as a mere marker of nominality, a noun class or gender marker, or even a case morpheme; he claims in particular that the gender affixes of many languages are derived from old definite articles. He posits three stages in this diachronic process. His Stage I would embrace all the definite article uses I have so far discussed – that is, where the article genuinely expresses definiteness, whether in the limited version of fifth-century Romance or the greatly expanded version of Modern Greek. His Stage III is that of the gender morpheme or meaningless nominality marker. At the intermediate Stage II, the article (which Greenberg terms the "non-generic article") no longer has any function relating to reference, but nor does it yet accompany all nouns. Its presence in a noun phrase is largely or wholly "grammaticalized", being determined by the construction; it tends to be absent, for example, in predicative noun phrases and in the objects of negative sentences.[4]

Greenberg illustrates from a subgroup of the Voltaic languages, in which nouns take a suffixed class marker. In Gurma, nouns may have in addition a preposed marker also encoding class membership, and this expresses definiteness. Thus *niti-ba* 'men', *ba niti-ba* 'the men'. Other languages in the group lack this preposed article, and presumably have no category of definiteness. Gangam, a further language of this group, has a preposed marker like Gurma, but this is a Stage II article; it accompanies the noun in the vast majority of occurrences, but is omitted, for example, with the object of negative sentences. Then there are other languages in the group in which nouns always carry prefixes as well as suffixes, expressing nothing beyond class membership; this is Stage III. Diachronically, there is evidence that the prefixes are younger than the suffixes, and that they have their origin in a pronoun or determiner showing class agreement; they do not originate as class markers. Greenberg points to many further instances of the phenomenon, mostly in Africa, and some involving noun classification, others not. In many of these instances the historical development from Stage I to Stage III seems to have been very rapid. In contrast with this, let us consider one more of his cases, one in which the historical development has taken several thousand years. The earliest recorded Aramaic (ninth century BC) had a definite article suffix *-ā*. By the early Christian period this had developed into a Stage II article in eastern dialects but was still a Stage I article in western dialects. Since then it has become a Stage II article in Modern Western Aramaic, while in Eastern Aramaic the earlier Stage II article is now a meaningless Stage III noun marker. One dialect of Eastern Aramaic has, moreover, developed a new, prefixed, definite article.

Greenberg's survey of languages is very wide ranging, but he gives few concrete illustrative examples and few references. His thesis is therefore hard to assess.

---

[4] Greenberg is less than clear about the Stage II article, saying at one point that it combines the uses of a definite article with those of a specific indefinite article. Put like this, the "non-generic article" seems to correspond to the definite-specific article of Samoan and Maori; but this is not what is meant. He adds that Stage II articles always appear in addition in many non-specific uses, "so that they correspond *grosso modo* to the combined uses of a definite and indefinite article". The Samoan and Maori definite (as I claim) articles do seem to be still at Stage I, that of real definiteness.

But some subsequent research does support his basic claims. Schuh (1983), in a careful study of the development of definite determiners in the Chadic languages, refines and gives detailed exemplification of Greenberg's notions of Stage II and Stage III articles. Schuh notes that in some dialects of Bade a suffix which was once a definite article and is now a Stage II article actually signals indefiniteness because of the range of grammatical contexts in which it occurs; this is similar to what I proposed for Arabic nunation in 2.5.1. He also shows how definite determiners can develop into linker morphemes in possessive constructions; we have seen this process at work in Romanian and Hausa, in 2.3.4. We can also illustrate the Stage II article from our discussion of definite adjective declensions in 2.3.5. In Serbo-Croat and Lithuanian, where it may be that the definite adjective form no longer expresses definiteness but is either merely required in certain grammatical contexts or is an emphatic alternative, it probably represents Stage II. In the case of the relic -*i*- stem extension of Macedonian, descended from the definite morpheme, it is not clear whether we have to do with a Stage II or a Stage III form.

The distinction between Greenberg's Stage II and Stage III is small and somewhat arbitrary. The Stage II "article" is clearly not an article; it is already a semantically empty marker of nominality or has acquired some other function like that of indicating gender, and has been generalized to most noun phrases except those in which it rarely occurred when it expressed definiteness. Stage III is then the analogical extension of the particle to all, or most, nominal contexts. An important point to make here relates to the steps of definite article expansion discussed in 9.3.1. These steps are all within Greenberg's Stage I, and include the article coming to be used with proper nouns. But proper nouns always appear without the "article" at Stage II in the languages investigated by Greenberg. This means that an article can move to Stage II and lose its function of marking definiteness before realizing its full potential as a definiteness marker.

It is this shift from Stage I to Stage II which is for our purposes the most intriguing point in this progression. It is far from obvious why a formative with an important discourse function should lose it, and in many cases cease to have any grammatical or semantic function. Note also that the move of an article to Stage II is in many instances not accompanied by the creation of a new definite article. This means that in these languages the category of definiteness, DP structure, is lost. The answer to this puzzle may lie in the flexibility of the category of definiteness, the fact that (in common, it must be emphasized, with other grammatical categories) it can vary considerably in the semantic/pragmatic ground it covers. When it comes to be stretched close to its maximum possible extent, as in Modern Greek and Samoan, it has such a high frequency of occurrence in noun phrases that it becomes possible for speakers to reanalyse it as a particle characterizing nouns or noun phrases but conveying nothing.

9.4 In conclusion

In this chapter I have discussed the origins and subsequent evolution of definiteness and definiteness marking in the light of the synchronic findings of the rest of the study. Central to the account offered is the claim that, while the pragmatic concept of identifiability may play a part in all languages, and discourse participant features certainly do figure in all languages, the grammatical category of person-definiteness does not. When a language acquires definiteness marking it acquires definiteness, which, formally, means it acquires DP structure. Various subsequent developments can then occur, affecting both the category and its exponent. Articles can undergo morphological modification from free form to affix (typically with concomitant syntactic change from specifier Det to D head status), and can be replaced by new forms. Definiteness itself can expand its range of application, taking in generics, specifics etc., and a point can come at which its exponent is reanalysed as grammatically and semantically empty (perhaps leading to its being pressed into service with some other function). At this point, unless a new article emerges with a reduced function to renew the category, the definite–indefinite distinction collapses. Not only can languages acquire the category of definiteness; they can also lose it.

REFERENCES

Abney, Stephen Paul 1987. The English noun phrase in its sentential aspect. PhD thesis, MIT.

Abraham, Werner 1997. The interdependence of case, aspect and referentiality in the history of German: the case of the verbal genitive. In *Parameters of morphosyntactic change*, ed. Ans van Kemenade and Nigel Vincent, 29–61. Cambridge: Cambridge University Press.

Adams, J. N. 1994. Wackernagel's law and the position of unstressed personal pronouns in Classical Latin. *Transactions of the Philological Society* 92: 103–78.

Aebischer, Paul 1948. Contribution à la protohistoire des articles *ille* et *ipse* dans les langues romanes. *Cultura Neolatina* 8: 181–203.

Aissen, Judith L. 1992. Topic and focus in Mayan. *Language* 68: 43–80.

Akmajian, Adrian and Stephen R. Anderson 1970. On the use of the fourth person in Navaho, or Navaho made harder. *International Journal of American Linguistics* 36: 1–8.

Allwood, Jens, Lars-Gunnar Andersson and Östen Dahl 1977. *Logic in linguistics*. Cambridge: Cambridge University Press.

Anderson, Stephen R. 1985. Inflectional morphology. In *Language typology and syntactic description*, vol. III: *Grammatical categories and the lexicon*, ed. Timothy Shopen, 150–201. Cambridge: Cambridge University Press.

Anderson, Stephen R. and Edward L. Keenan 1985. Deixis. In *Language typology and syntactic description*, vol. III: *Grammatical categories and the lexicon*, ed. Timothy Shopen, 259–308. Cambridge: Cambridge University Press.

Andrade, Manuel J. 1933. *Quileute*. New York: Columbia University Press.

Andrews, J. Richard 1975. *Introduction to Classical Nahuatl*. Austin: University of Texas Press.

Aoun, Joseph 1985. *A grammar of anaphora*. Cambridge, Mass.: MIT Press.

Aquilina, Joseph 1965. *Maltese*. London: English Universities Press.

Ariel, Mira 1990. *Accessing noun-phrase antecedents*. London: Routledge.

Armbruster, C. H. 1908. *Initia amharica. An introduction to spoken Amharic*. Cambridge: Cambridge University Press.

Arrigaray, C. de 1971. *Euskel-irakaspidea, o sea gramática de euskera (dialecto guipuzcoano)*. San Sebastian: Auñamendi.

References

Ashton, E. O. 1944. *Swahili grammar (including intonation)*. Harlow: Longman.

Austin, Peter and Joan Bresnan 1996. Non-configurationality in Australian aboriginal languages. *Natural Language and Linguistic Theory* 14: 215–68.

Bader, François 1993. Les génitifs-adjectifs déterminés et le problème de l'article: comparaison typologique entre l'étrusque et les langues indo-européennes. In *Indogermanica et Italica. Festschrift für Helmut Rix zum 65. Geburtstag*, ed. Gerhard Meiser, 12–45. Innsbruck: Universität Innsbruck.

Baker, Mark C. 1996. *The polysynthesis parameter*. New York: Oxford University Press.

Baker, Philip 1984. Agglutinated nominals in Creole French: their evolutionary significance. *Te Reo* 27: 89–129.

Bánhidi, Z., Z. Jókay and D. Szabó 1965. *A textbook of the Hungarian language*. London: Collet's.

Barwise, Jon and Robin Cooper 1981. Generalized quantifiers and natural language. *Linguistics and Philosophy* 4: 159–219.

Basri, Hasan and Daniel L. Finer 1987. The definiteness of trace. *Linguistic Inquiry* 18: 141–7.

Bastuji, J. 1976. *Les relations spatiales en turc contemporain*. Paris: Klincksieck.

Bauer, Winifred 1993. *Maori*. London: Routledge.

Belletti, Adriana 1988. The case of unaccusatives. *Linguistic Inquiry* 19: 1–33.

Berent, Gerald P. 1980. On the realization of trace: Macedonian clitic pronouns. In *Morphosyntax in Slavic*, ed. Catherine V. Chvany and Richard D. Brecht, 150–86. Columbus, Ohio: Slavica.

Bickerton, Derek 1981. *Roots of language*. Ann Arbor: Karoma.

Biggs, Bruce 1969. *Let's learn Maori: a guide to the study of the Maori language*. Wellington: Reed.

Bird, Charles 1968. Relative clauses in Bambara. *Journal of West African Languages* 5: 35–47.

Bittner, Maria and Ken Hale 1996. The structural determination of case and agreement. *Linguistic Inquiry* 27: 1–68.

Blackburn, Patrick 1994. Tense, temporal reference, and tensed logic. *Journal of Semantics* 11: 83–101.

Blake, Barry J. 1994. *Case*. Cambridge: Cambridge University Press.

Blass, Regina 1990. *Relevance relations in discourse. A study with special reference to Sissala*. Cambridge: Cambridge University Press.

Boas, Franz and Ella Deloria 1939. *Dakota grammar*. Washington: National Academy of Sciences.

Bokamba, E. G. 1971. Specificity and definiteness in Dzamba. *Studies in African Linguistics* 2: 217–38.

Borer, Hagit 1984. *Parametric syntax. Case studies in Semitic and Romance languages*. Dordrecht: Foris.

Börjars, Kersti 1994. Swedish double determination in a European typological perspective. *Nordic Journal of Linguistics* 17: 219–52.

342

Börjars, Kersti and Nigel Vincent 1993. On the parametrization of the clitic-affix distinction. Paper presented at the Autumn Meeting of the Linguistics Association of Great Britain, Bangor.

Bresnan, Joan W. 1973. Syntax of the comparative clause construction in English. *Linguistic Inquiry* 4: 275–343.

Bresnan, Joan W. and Sam A. Mchombo 1987. Topic, pronoun and agreement in Chiwewa. *Language* 63: 741–82.

Budiņa-Lazdiņa, Terēze 1966. *Latvian*. London: English Universities Press.

Buechel, Eugene 1939. *A grammar of Lakhota. The language of the Teton Sioux Indians.* Rosebud: Rosebud Educational Society.

Bunt, Harry C. 1979. Ensembles and the formal semantic properties of mass terms. In *Mass terms: some philosophical problems*, ed. Francis Jeffry Pelletier, 249–77. Dordrecht: Reidel.

  1985. *Mass terms and model-theoretic semantics*. Cambridge: Cambridge University Press.

Burton-Roberts, Noel 1976. On the generic indefinite article. *Language* 52: 427–48.

  1984. Topic and the presuppositions of simple sentences. Paper presented at the Autumn Meeting of the Linguistics Association of Great Britain, Colchester.

  1989a. Les paradigmes génériques en anglais. *Travaux de linguistique* 19: 17–32.

  1989b. *The limits to debate. A revised theory of semantic presupposition*. Cambridge: Cambridge University Press.

Butt, John and Carmen Benjamin 1994. *A new reference grammar of Modern Spanish*. London: Arnold.

Cann, Ronnie 1993. *Formal semantics. An introduction*. Cambridge: Cambridge University Press.

Cardinaletti, Anna 1994. On the internal structure of pronominal DPs. *Linguistic Review* 11: 195–219.

Carlson, Gregory N. 1977. A unified analysis of the English bare plural. *Linguistics and Philosophy* 1: 413–56.

  1980. *Reference to kinds in English*. New York: Garland.

Carlson, Gregory N. and Francis Jeffry Pelletier (eds.) 1995. *The generic book*. Chicago: University of Chicago Press.

Carlson, Robert 1994. *A grammar of Supyire*. Berlin: Mouton de Gruyter.

Chafe, Wallace L. 1976. Givenness, contrastiveness, definiteness, subjects, topics, and point of view. In *Subject and Topic*, ed. Charles N. Li, 25–55. New York: Academic Press.

Chesterman, Andrew 1991. *On definiteness. A study with special reference to English and Finnish*. Cambridge: Cambridge University Press.

Chierchia, G. 1995. *Dynamics of meaning: anaphora, presupposition and the theory of grammar*. Chicago: Chicago University Press.

Chomsky, Noam 1981. *Lectures on government and binding*. Dordrecht: Foris.

  1995. *The minimalist program*. Cambridge, Mass.: MIT Press.

References

Christophersen, Paul 1939. *The articles. A study of their theory and use in English.* Copen-hagen: Munksgaard.

Chung, Sandra 1987. The syntax of Chamorro existential sentences. In Reuland and ter Meulen (eds.), 191–225.

Cinque, Guglielmo 1995. On the evidence for partial N-Movement in the Romance DP. In *Paths towards Universal Grammar. Studies in honor of Richard S. Kayne,* ed. Guglielmo Cinque, Jan Koster, Jean-Yves Pollock, Luigi Rizzi and Raffaella Zanuttini, 85–110. Washington: Georgetown University Press.

Clark, Herbert H. and Catherine R. Marshall 1981. Definite reference and mutual knowledge. In *Elements of discourse understanding,* ed. Aravind K. Joshi, Bonnie L. Webber and Ivan A. Sag, 10–63. Cambridge: Cambridge University Press.

Cole, Desmond T. 1955. *An introduction to Tswana grammar.* London: Longman.

Cole, Peter 1975. An apparent asymmetry in the formation of relative clauses in Modern Hebrew. *Studies in the Linguistic Sciences* 5: 1–35.

　　1987. Null objects in universal grammar. *Linguistic Inquiry* 18: 597–612.

Comrie, Bernard 1978. Definite direct objects and referent identification. *Pragmatics Microfiche* 3.1.D3.

　　1981a. *Language universals and linguistic typology: syntax and morphology.* Oxford: Blackwell.

　　1981b. *The languages of the Soviet Union.* Cambridge: Cambridge University Press.

Cook, Eung-Do 1984. *A Sarcee grammar.* Vancouver: University of British Columbia Press.

Cooke, J. R. 1968. *Pronominal reference in Thai, Burmese and Vietnamese.* Berkeley: University of California Press.

Cooper, Robin 1979..The interpretation of pronouns. In *Syntax and semantics,* vol. 10: *Selections from the Third Groningen Round Table,* ed. F. Heny and H. Schnelle, 61–92. New York: Academic Press.

Corbett, Greville G. 1987. The morphology–syntax interface: evidence from possessive adjectives in Slavonic. *Language* 63: 299–345.

　　1995. Slavonic's closest approach to Suffixaufnahme: the possessive adjective. In *Double case. Agreement by Suffixaufnahme,* ed. Frans Plank, 265–82. New York: Oxford University Press.

Cornilescu, Alexandra 1992. Remarks on the determiner system of Rumanian: the demonstratives *al* and *cel. Probus* 4: 189–260.

Coulson, Michael 1976. *Sanskrit. An introduction to the classical language.* London: Hodder and Stoughton.

Cowan, M. 1969. *Tzotzil grammar.* Norman, Oklahoma: Summer Institute of Linguistics.

Craig, Colette G. 1986. Jacaltec noun classifiers. A study in grammaticalization. *Lingua* 70: 241–84.

Croft, William 1990. *Typology and universals.* Cambridge: Cambridge University Press.

Dahl, Östen 1970. Some notes on indefinites. *Language* 46: 33–41.

Dambriūnas, Leonardas, Antanas Klimas and William R. Schmalstieg 1972. *Introduction to Modern Lithuanian*. New York: Franciscan Fathers.

De Bray, R. G. A. 1980. *Guide to the South Slavonic languages*. Columbus, Ohio: Slavica.

Declerck, Renaat 1986a. Two notes on the theory of definiteness. *Journal of Linguistics* 22: 25–39.

  1986b. The manifold interpretations of generic sentences. *Lingua* 68: 149–88.

  1991. The origins of genericity. *Linguistics* 29: 79–102.

Dede, Müserref 1986. Definiteness and referentiality in Turkish verbal sentences. In *Studies in Turkish linguistics*, ed. Dan Isaac Slobin and Karl Zimmer, 147–63. Amsterdam: Benjamins.

Deemter, K. van and S. Peters (eds.) 1996. *Semantic ambiguity and underspecification*. Stanford: Center for the Study of Language and Information.

Delorme, Evelyne and Ray C. Dougherty 1972. Appositive NP constructions: *we, the men*; *we men*; *I, a man*; etc. *Foundations of Language* 8: 2–29.

Diesing, Molly 1992. *Indefinites*. Cambridge, Mass.: MIT Press.

Dik, Simon C. 1978. *Functional grammar*. Amsterdam: North-Holland.

Dixon, R. M. W. 1972. *The Dyirbal language of North Queensland*. Cambridge: Cambridge University Press.

  1980. *The languages of Australia*. Cambridge: Cambridge University Press.

Donaldson, T. 1980. *Ngiyambaa: the language of the Wangaaybuwan of New South Wales*. Cambridge: Cambridge University Press.

Donnellan, Keith S. 1966. Reference and definite descriptions. *Philosophical Review* 75: 281–304.

  1978. Speaker reference, descriptions, and anaphora. In *Syntax and semantics*, vol. 9: *Pragmatics*, ed. P. Cole, 47–68. New York: Academic Press.

Dunn, C. J. and S. Yanada 1958. *Japanese*. London: English Universities Press.

Durrell, Martin 1991. *Hammer's German grammar and usage* (second edition, revised). London: Arnold.

Eachus, Francis and Ruth Carlson 1966. Kekchi. In *Languages of Guatemala*, ed. Marvin K. Mayers, 110–24. The Hague: Mouton.

Ebbing, Juan Enrique 1965. *Gramática y diccionario aymará*. La Paz: Don Bosco.

Ebert, Karen H. 1971a. Referenz, Sprechsituation und die bestimmten Artikel in einem nordfriesischen Dialect (Fering). *Studien und Materialen* 4. Bredstedt: Nordfriisk Instituut.

  1971b. Zwei Formen des bestimmten Artikels. In *Probleme und Fortschritte der Transformationsgrammatik*, ed. D. Wunderlich, 159–74. Munich: Hueber.

Einarsson, Stefán 1949. *Icelandic: grammar, texts, glossary*. Baltimore: Johns Hopkins University Press.

Enç, Mürvet 1991. The semantics of specificity. *Linguistic Inquiry* 22: 1–25.

England, Nora C. 1983. *A grammar of Mam, a Mayan language*. Austin: University of Texas Press.

Evans, Gareth 1980. Pronouns. *Linguistic Inquiry* 11: 337–62.

References

Everett, Daniel L. 1987. Pirahã clitic doubling. *Natural Language and Linguistic Theory* 5: 245–76.

Feoktistov, A. P. 1966. Erzjanskij jazyk. *Jazyki Narodov SSSR* 3: 177–98.

Feydit, Frédéric 1969. *Manuel de langue arménienne (arménien occidental moderne)*. Paris: Klincksieck.

Fodor, Janet Dean and Ivan A. Sag 1982. Referential and quantificational indefinites. *Linguistics and Philosophy* 5: 355–98.

Foulet, Lucien 1958. *Petite syntaxe de l'ancien français*. Paris: Champion.

Fraurud, Kari 1990. Definiteness and the processing of noun phrases in natural discourse. *Journal of Semantics* 7: 395–433.

Frege, Gottlob 1892. Über Sinn und Bedeutung. *Zeitschrift für Philosophie und Philosophische Kritik* 100: 22–50.

Frei, Henri 1944. Systèmes de déictiques. *Acta Linguistica* 4: 111–29.

Fretheim, Thornstein and Jeanette K. Gundel (eds.) 1996. *Reference and referent accessibility*. Amsterdam: Benjamins.

Fukui, Naoki 1986. A theory of category projection and its applications. PhD thesis, MIT.

Gil, David 1987. Definiteness, noun phrase configurationality, and the count-mass distinction. In Reuland and ter Meulen (eds.), 254–69.

Gildersleeve, B. L. and Gonzalez Lodge 1895. *Gildersleeve's Latin Grammar*. London: Macmillan.

Giusti, Giuliana 1992. La sintassi dei sintagmi nominali quantificati. PhD thesis, University of Padua.

   1993. *La sintassi dei determinanti*. Padua: Unipress.

   1994. Enclitic articles and double definiteness: a comparative analysis of nominal structure in Romance and Germanic. *Linguistic Review* 11: 241–55.

Givón, Talmy 1976. Topic, pronoun, and grammatical agreement. In *Subject and topic*, ed. Charles N. Li, 149–88. New York: Academic Press.

   1978. Definiteness and referentiality. In *Universals of human language*, vol. 4: *Syntax*, ed. Joseph H. Greenberg, Charles A. Ferguson and Edith A. Moravcsik, 291–330. Stanford: Stanford University Press.

   1981. On the development of the numeral 'one' as an indefinite marker. *Folia Linguistica Historica* 2: 35–53.

   1982. Logic vs. pragmatics, with human language as the referee: toward an empirically viable epistemology. *Journal of Pragmatics* 6: 81–133.

Glendening, P. J. T. 1961. *Icelandic*. London: Hodder and Stoughton.

Goodwin, William W. 1992. *A Greek grammar*. Walton-on-Thames: Nelson.

Grant, Anthony 1995. Article agglutination in Creole French: a wider perspective. In *From contact to creole and beyond*, ed. Philip Baker, 149–76. London: University of Westminster Press.

Greenberg, Joseph H. 1978. How does a language acquire gender markers? In *Universals of human language*, vol. 3: *Word structure*, ed. Joseph H. Greenberg, Charles A. Ferguson and Edith A. Moravcsik, 47–82. Stanford: Stanford University Press.

Grice, H. Paul 1975. Logic and conversation. In *Syntax and semantics*, vol. 3: *Speech acts*, ed. Peter Cole and Jerry L. Morgan, 41–58. New York: Academic Press.

Guéron, Jacqueline 1980. On the syntax and semantics of PP-extraposition. *Linguistic Inquiry* 11: 637–78.

Guillaume, Gustave 1975. *Le problème de l'article et sa solution dans la langue française.* Quebec: Presses de l'Université Laval.

Gundel, Jeanette K., Nancy Hedberg and Ron Zacharski 1993. Cognitive status and the form of referring expressions in discourse. *Language* 69: 274–307.

Haegeman, Liliane 1994. *Introduction to government-binding theory* (2nd edition, revised). Oxford: Blackwell.

Hagman, Roy Stephen 1973. Nama Hottentot grammar. PhD thesis, Columbia University.

Haider, Hubert 1988. Die Struktur der deutschen Nominalphrase. *Zeitschrift für Sprachwissenschaft* 7: 32–59.

Haiman, John 1985. *Natural syntax: iconicity and erosion.* Cambridge: Cambridge University Press.

Hale, Ken 1973. Person marking in Walbiri. In *A Festschrift for Morris Halle*, ed. Stephen R. Anderson and Paul Kiparsky, 308–44. New York: Holt, Rinehart and Winston.

1983. Warlpiri and the grammar of non-configurational languages. *Natural Language and Linguistic Theory* 1: 5–47.

1989. On nonconfigurational structures. In Marácz and Muysken (eds.), 293–300.

Harris, Martin 1977. 'Demonstratives', 'articles' and 'third person pronouns' in French: changes in progress. *Zeitschrift für Romanische Philologie* 93: 249–61.

1980. The marking of definiteness in Romance. In *Historical morphology*, ed. Jacek Fisiak, 141–56. The Hague: Mouton.

Hartmann, Josef 1980. *Amharische Grammatik.* Wiesbaden: Steiner.

Haspelmath, Martin 1993. *A grammar of Lezgian.* Berlin: Mouton.

1997. *Indefinite pronouns.* Oxford: Oxford University Press.

Haugen, Einar 1976. *The Scandinavian languages. An introduction to their history.* London: Faber.

Hausser, R. 1979. How do pronouns denote? In *Syntax and semantics*, vol. 10: *Selections from the Third Groningen Round Table*, ed. F. Heny and H. Schnelle, 93–139. New York: Academic Press.

Hawkins, John A. 1974. Definiteness and indefiniteness. PhD thesis, University of Cambridge.

1978. *Definiteness and indefiniteness: a study in reference and grammaticality prediction.* London: Croom Helm.

1991. On (in)definite articles: implicatures and (un)grammaticality prediction. *Journal of Linguistics* 27: 405–42.

Haywood, J. A. and H. M. Nahmad 1962. *A new Arabic grammar of the written language.* London: Lund, Humphries.

Heim, Irene R. 1988. *The semantics of definite and indefinite noun phrases.* New York: Garland.

347

References

Heinrichs, Heinrich Matthias 1954. *Studien zum bestimmten Artikel in den germanischen Sprachen*. Giessen: Schmitz.

Hellan, Lars 1986. The headedness of NPs in Norwegian. In *Features and projections*, ed. Pieter Muysken and Henk van Riemsdijk, 89–122. Dordrecht: Foris.

Hewitt, Brian George 1979. *Abkhaz*. Amsterdam: North-Holland.

Heyer, Gerhard 1987. *Generische Kennzeichnungen. Zur Logik und Ontologie generischer Bedeutungen*. Munich: Philosophia.

Higginbotham, James 1987. Indefiniteness and predication. In Reuland and ter Meulen (eds.), 43–70.

Hinrichs, Erhard 1986. Temporal anaphora in discourses of English. *Linguistics and Philosophy* 9: 63–82.

Hintikka, Jaako 1970. Objects of knowledge and belief: acquaintances and public figures. *Journal of Philosophy* 67: 869–83.

Hockett, Charles F. 1966. What Algonquian is really like. *International Journal of American Linguistics* 32: 59–73.

Hoff, B. J. 1968. *The Carib language*. The Hague: Nijhoff.

Holmback, Heather K. 1984. An interpretive solution to the definiteness effect problem. *Linguistic Analysis* 13: 195–215.

Holmes, Philip and Ian Hinchliffe 1994. *Swedish: a comprehensive grammar*. London: Routledge.

Hopper, Paul J. and Elizabeth Closs Traugott 1993. *Grammaticalization*. Cambridge: Cambridge University Press.

Householder, Fred W. 1981. *The syntax of Apollonius Dyscolus. Translation with commentary*. Amsterdam: Benjamins.

Huang, C.-T. James 1984. On the distribution and reference of empty pronouns. *Linguistic Inquiry* 15: 531–74.
    1987. Existential sentences in Chinese and (in)definiteness. In Reuland and ter Meulen (eds.), 226–53.

Huang, Yan 1994. *The syntax and pragmatics of anaphora. A study with special reference to Chinese*. Cambridge: Cambridge University Press.

Huddleston, Rodney 1984. *Introduction to the grammar of English*. Cambridge: Cambridge University Press.

Hukari, Thomas E. and Robert D. Levine 1989. On the definiteness of trace. *Linguistic Inquiry* 20: 506–12.

Ioup, Georgette 1977. Specificity and the interpretation of quantifiers. *Linguistics and Philosophy* 1: 233–45.

Jaeggli, Osvaldo and Kenneth J. Safir (eds.) 1989. *The null subject parameter*. Dordrecht: Kluwer.

Jagger, Philip John 1985. Factors governing the morphological coding of referents in Hausa narrative discourse. PhD thesis, UCLA.

Jakobson, Roman 1966. Beitrag zur allgemeinen Kasuslehre. Gesamtbedeutungen der russischen Kasus. In *Readings in linguistics*, vol. 2, ed. Eric P. Hamp, Fred W. Householder and Robert Austerlitz, 51–89. Chicago: University of Chicago Press.

Janson, Tore 1984. Articles and plural formation in creoles: change and universals. *Lingua* 64: 291–323.

Jaszczolt, Katarzyna M. 1997. The 'default *de re*' principle for the interpretation of belief utterances. *Journal of Pragmatics* 28: 315–36.

Javarek, Vera and Miroslava Sudjić 1963. *Serbo-Croat*. London: English Universities Press.

Jelinek, Eloise 1984. Empty categories, case, and configurationality. *Natural Language and Linguistic Theory* 2: 39–76.

Jensen, Hans 1959. *Altarmenische Grammatik*. Heidelberg: Winter.

Jespersen, Otto 1917. *Negation in English and other languages*. Copenhagen: Host.
    1943. *A modern English grammar on historical principles*, Part 7: *Syntax*. Copenhagen: Munksgaard.

Jong, Franciska de and Henk Verkuyl 1985. Generalized quantifiers: the properness of their strength. In *Generalized quantifiers in natural language*. ed. Johan van Benthem and Alice G. B. ter Meulen, 21–43. Dordrecht: Foris.

Kadmon, Nirit 1997. On unique and non-unique reference and asymmetric quantification. PhD thesis, University of Massachusetts.

Kamp, Hans 1979. Events, instants and temporal reference. In *Semantics from different points of view*, ed. Rainer Bäuerle, Urs Egli and Arnim von Stechow, 376–417. Berlin: Springer.
    1984. A theory of truth and semantic representation. In *Truth, interpretation and information*, ed. J. A. G. Groenendijk, T. M. V. Janssen and M. J. B. Stokhof, 1–41. Dordrecht: Foris.

Kamp, Hans and Uwe Reyle 1993. *From discourse to logic: introduction to modeltheoretic semantics of natural language, formal logic and discourse representation theory*. Dordrecht: Kluwer.

Karttunen, Lauri 1976. Discourse referents. In *Syntax and semantics*, vol. 7: *Notes from the linguistic underground*, ed. James D. McCawley, 363–86. New York: Academic Press.

Keenan, Edward L. 1976. Remarkable subjects in Malagasy. In *Subject and Topic*, ed. Charles N. Li, 247–301. New York: Academic Press.

Keenan, Edward L. and Jonathan Stavi 1986. A semantic characterization of natural language determiners. *Linguistics and Philosophy* 9: 253–326.

Kempson, Ruth M. 1975. *Presupposition and the delimitation of semantics*. Cambridge: Cambridge University Press.
    1977. *Semantic theory*. Cambridge: Cambridge University Press.
    1988. Grammar and conversational principles. In *Linguistics: the Cambridge Survey*, vol. II: *Linguistic theory: extensions and implications*, ed. Frederick J. Newmeyer, 139–63. Cambridge: Cambridge University Press.

Kempson, Ruth M. and Annabel Cormack 1981. Quantification and ambiguity. *Linguistics and Philosophy* 4: 259–309.

Kennedy, Benjamin Hall 1962. *The revised Latin primer*. London: Longman.

Kiparsky, Paul 1996. Partitive case and aspect. Ms, Stanford University.

References

Kiss, Katalin É. 1987. *Configurationality in Hungarian*. Dordrecht: Reidel.
 1995. *Discourse configurational languages*. Oxford: Oxford University Press.
Klavans, Judith L. 1985. The independence of syntax and phonology in cliticization. *Language* 61, 95–120.
Kleiber, Georges 1981. *Problèmes de référence: descriptions définies et noms propres*. Paris: Klincksieck.
 1990. *L'article LE générique. La généricité sur le mode massif*. Geneva: Droz.
Knobloch, Jean 1952. La voyelle thématique -e-/-o- serait-elle un indice d'objet indo-européen? *Lingua* 3: 407–20.
Koopman, Hilda 1984. *The syntax of verbs: from verb movement rules in the Kru languages to Universal Grammar*. Dordrecht: Foris.
Kornfilt, J. 1991. A case for emerging functional categories. In *Syntax and semantics*, vol. 25: *Perspectives on phrase structure: heads and licensing*, ed. Susan D. Rothstein, 11–35. San Diego: Academic Press.
Kraft, Charles H. and A. H. M. Kirk-Greene 1973. *Hausa*. London: Hodder and Stoughton.
Krámský, Jiři 1972. *The article and the concept of definiteness in languages*. The Hague: Mouton.
Krifka, Manfred, Francis Jeffry Pelletier, Gregory N. Carlson, Alice ter Meulen, Godehard Link and Gennaro Chierchia 1995. Genericity: an introduction. In Carlson and Pelletier (eds.), 1–124.
Kripke, Saul 1972. Naming and necessity. In *Semantics for natural language*, ed. Donald Davidson and Gilbert Harman, 253–355 and 763–9. Dordrecht: Reidel.
 1977. Speaker's reference and semantic reference. In *Contemporary perspectives in the philosophy of language*, ed. P. A. French, T. E. Uehling and H. K. Wettstein, 6–27. Minneapolis: University of Minnesota Press.
Krupa, V. 1982. *The Polynesian languages. A guide*. London: Routledge and Kegan Paul. (Originally published as *Polinjezijskije Jazyky*, Moscow, 1975.)
Kryk, Barbara 1987. *On deixis in English and Polish. The role of demonstrative pronouns*. Frankfurt: Lang.
Kuipers, Aert H. 1974. *The Shuswap language. Grammar, texts, dictionary*. The Hague: Mouton.
Kurdojev, K. K. 1957. *Gramatika kurdskogo jazyka (kurmandzhi)*. Moscow: Izdatjel'stvo Akadjemii Nauk.
Lakoff, Robin 1974. Remarks on *This* and *That*. In *Papers from the 10th Regional Meeting of the Chicago Linguistic Society*, ed. Michael W. La Galy, Robert A. Fox and Anthony Bruck, 345–56. Chicago: Chicago Linguistic Society.
Lambdin, Thomas O. 1973. *Introduction to Biblical Hebrew*. London: Darton, Longman and Todd.
Lambrecht, Knud 1994. *Information structure and sentence form. Topic, focus and the mental representations of discourse referents*. Cambridge: Cambridge University Press.

Larson, Richard and Gabriel Segal 1995. *Knowledge of meaning. An introduction to semantic theory*. Cambridge, Mass.: MIT Press.

Laughren, Mary 1989. The configurationality parameter and Warlpiri. In Marácz and Muysken (eds.), 319–53.

Lawler, J. 1973. Studies in English generics. *University of Michigan Papers in Linguistics* 1.

Lee, W. R. and Z. Lee 1959. *Czech*. London: English Universities Press.

Leech, Geoffrey N. 1983. *Principles of pragmatics*. London: Longman.

Lencek, Rado L. 1982. *The structure and history of the Slovene language*. Columbus, Ohio: Slavica.

Leslau, Wolf 1968. *Amharic textbook*. Berkeley: University of California Press.

Levinson, Stephen C. 1983. *Pragmatics*. Cambridge: Cambridge University Press.

1987. Pragmatics and the grammar of anaphora: a partial pragmatic reduction of binding and control phenomena. *Journal of Linguistics* 23: 379–434.

Lewis, G. L. 1967. *Turkish grammar*. Oxford: Oxford University Press.

Li, Charles N. and Sandra A. Thompson 1976. Subject and topic: a new typology. In *Subject and Topic*, ed. Charles N. Li, 457–89. New York: Academic Press.

1981. *Mandarin Chinese: a functional reference grammar*. Berkeley: University of California Press.

Löbner, Sebastian 1985. Definites. *Journal of Semantics* 4: 279–326.

Longobardi, Giuseppe 1994. Reference and proper names: a theory of N-Movement in syntax and logical form. *Linguistic Inquiry* 25: 609–65.

Ludlow, Peter and Stephen Neale 1991. Indefinite descriptions: in defense of Russell. *Linguistics and Philosophy* 14: 171–202.

Lukas, Johannes 1968. Nunation in afrikanischen Sprachen. *Anthropos* 63: 97–114.

Lumsden, Michael 1988. *Existential sentences: their structure and meaning*. London: Croom Helm.

Lunt, Horace G. 1952. *A grammar of the Macedonian literary language*. Skopje: Drzhavno Knigoizdatelstvo.

Lyons, Christopher 1977. The demonstratives of English. *Belfast Working Papers in Language and Linguistics* 2.5.

1980. The meaning of the English definite article. In *The semantics of determiners*, ed. Johan Van der Auwera, 81–95. London: Croom Helm.

1985. A possessive parameter. *Sheffield Working Papers in Language and Linguistics* 2: 98–104.

1986a. The syntax of English genitive constructions. *Journal of Linguistics* 22: 123–43.

1986b. On the origin of the Old French strong–weak possessive distinction. *Transactions of the Philological Society*, 1–41.

1990. An agreement approach to clitic doubling. *Transactions of the Philological Society* 88: 1–57.

1991. English nationality terms: evidence for dual category membership. *Journal of Literary Semantics* 20: 97–116.

References

1992. The construct: 'VSO' genitive structures. *University of Salford Working Papers in Language and Linguistics* 15.

1994a. Movement in 'NP' and the DP hypothesis. *University of Salford ESRI Working Papers in Language and Linguistics* 8.

1994b. Definiteness and person. Paper presented at the Autumn Meeting of the Linguistics Association of Great Britain, London.

1995a. Voice, aspect, and arbitrary arguments. In *Linguistic theory and the Romance languages*, ed. John Charles Smith and Martin Maiden, 77–114. Amsterdam: Benjamins.

1995b. Determiners and noun phrase structure. Ms, University of Salford.

1995c. Proper nouns, generics, and the count–mass distinction. Paper presented at the ESRI Research Seminar, University of Salford.

1995d. The origins of definiteness marking. Paper presented at the 12th International Conference on Historical Linguistics, Manchester.

1995e. Pronombres y persona en español. Paper presented at the 21st International Romance Linguistics Conference, Palermo.

Lyons, John 1975. Deixis as the source of reference. In *Formal semantics of natural language*, ed. E. L. Keenan, 61–83. Cambridge: Cambridge University Press.

1977. *Semantics*. Cambridge: Cambridge University Press.

McCawley, James D. 1981. *Everything that linguists have always wanted to know about logic but were ashamed to ask*. Oxford: Blackwell.

McCloskey, James and Kenneth Hale 1984. On the syntax of person–number inflection in Modern Irish. *Natural Language and Linguistic Theory* 1: 487–533.

Maclaran, Rose 1982. The semantics and pragmatics of the English demonstratives. PhD thesis, Cornell University.

Mace, John 1971. *Modern Persian*. London: Hodder and Stoughton.

Maetzner, Eduard 1880. *Englische Grammatik*, vol. I: *Die Lehre vom Worte*. Berlin: Weidmannsche Buchhandlung.

1885. *Englische Grammatik*, vol. III: *Die Lehre von der Wort- und Satzfügung*. Berlin: Weidmannsche Buchhandlung.

Malherbe, Michel and Cheikh Sall 1989. *Parlons wolof, langue et culture*. Paris: L'Harmattan.

Marácz, László and Pieter Muysken (eds.) 1989. *Configurationality: the typology of asymmetries*. Dordrecht: Foris.

Masica, Colin P. 1986. Definiteness marking in South Asian languages. In *South Asian languages: structure, convergence and diglossia*, ed. B. Krishnamurti, 123–46. Delhi: Motilal Banarsidass.

Matthews, G. H. 1965. *Hidatsa syntax*. The Hague: Mouton.

Matthews, Stephen and Virginia Yip 1994. *Cantonese: a comprehensive grammar*. London: Routledge.

Matthews, W. K. 1949. The Polynesian articles. *Lingua* 2: 14–31.

Mayers, Marvin K. and Marilyn A. Mayers 1966. Pocomchi. In *Languages of Guatemala*, ed. Marvin K. Mayers, 87–109. The Hague: Mouton.

Mbassy Njie, Codu 1982. *Description syntaxique du wolof de Gambie*. Dakar: Nouvelles Editions Africaines.

Meillet, A. 1936. *Esquisse d'une grammaire comparée de l'arménien classique*. Vienna: PP Mekhitharistes.

Milsark, Gary L. 1977. Toward an explanation of certain peculiarities of the existential construction in English. *Linguistic Analysis* 3: 1–29.

1979. *Existential sentences in English*. New York: Garland.

Minassian, Martiros 1976. *Manuel pratique d'arménien ancien*. Paris: Klincksieck.

Mitchell, T. F. 1962. *Colloquial Arabic*. London: Hodder and Stoughton.

Mithun, Marianne 1984. How to avoid subordination. In *Proceedings of the 10th Annual Meeting of the Berkeley Linguistics Society*, ed. Claudia Brugman and Monica Macaulay, 493–509. Berkeley: Berkeley Linguistics Society.

Mohanan, K. P. 1983. Lexical and configurational structure. *Linguistic Review* 3: 113–41.

Montague, Richard 1974. The proper treatment of quantification in ordinary English. In *Formal philosophy*, ed. Richmond H. Thomason, 247–70. New Haven: Yale University Press.

Moravcsik, Edith A. 1978. On the case marking of objects. In *Universals of human language*, vol. 4: *Syntax*, ed. Joseph H. Greenberg, Charles A. Ferguson and Edith A. Moravcsik, 249–89. Stanford: Stanford University Press.

Mosel, Ulrike and Even Hovdhaugen 1992. *Samoan reference grammar*. Oslo: Scandinavian University Press.

Mostowski, Andrej 1957. On a generalization of quantifiers. *Fundamenta Mathematicae* 44: 12–36.

Murrell, Martin and Virgiliu Ştefănescu-Drăgăneşti 1970. *Romanian*. London: Hodder and Stoughton.

Nater, H. F. 1984. *The Bella Coola language*. Ottawa: National Museums of Canada.

Neale, Stephen 1990. *Descriptions*. Cambridge, Mass.: MIT Press.

Nespor, Marina and Irene Vogel 1986. *Prosodic phonology*. Dordrecht: Foris.

Newman, Stanley 1969. Bella Coola paradigms. *International Journal of American Linguistics* 35: 299–306.

Newmark, Leonard, Philip Hubbard and Peter Prifti 1982. *Standard Albanian. A reference grammar for students*. Stanford: Stanford University Press.

Noonan, Michael 1992. *A grammar of Lango*. Berlin: Mouton de Gruyter.

Nunberg, Geoffrey and Chiahua Pan 1975. Inferring quantification in generic sentences. In *Papers from the 11th Regional Meeting of the Chicago Linguistic Society*, ed. R. E. Grossman, L. J. San and T. J. Vance, 412–22. Chicago: Chicago Linguistic Society.

Olsen, Susan 1989. AGR(eement) in the German noun phrase. In *Syntactic phrase structure phenomena*, ed. Christa Bhatt, Elisabeth Löbel and Claudia Schmitt, 39–49. Amsterdam: Benjamins.

Palmer, F. R. 1974. *The English verb*. London: Longman.

Papafragou, Anna 1996. On generics. *UCL Working Papers in Linguistics* 8: 165–98.

353

References

Partee, Barbara H. 1984. Nominal and temporal anaphora. *Linguistics and Philosophy* 7: 243–86.

Pattee, Joseph 1994. *Le problème de l'article: sa solution en allemand.* Tübingen: Niemeyer.

Payne, John 1993. The headedness of noun phrases: slaying the nominal hydra. In *Heads in grammatical theory*, ed. Greville G. Corbett, Norman M. Fraser and Scott McGlashan, 114–39. Cambridge: Cambridge University Press.

Pelletier, Francis Jeffry and Lenhart K. Schubert 1989. Mass expressions. In *Handbook of philosophical logic*, vol. 4, ed. D. Gabbay and F. Guenthner, 327–407. Dordrecht: Kluwer.

Perlmutter, David M. 1970. On the article in English. In *Progress in linguistics*, ed. Manfred Bierwisch and Karl Erich Heidolph, 233–48. The Hague: Mouton.

Perrott, D. V. 1951. *Swahili.* London: Hodder and Stoughton.

Philippi, Julia 1997. The rise of the article in the Germanic languages. In *Parameters of morphosyntactic change*, ed. Ans van Kemenade and Nigel Vincent, 62–93. Cambridge: Cambridge University Press.

Picallo, M. Carme 1991. Nominals and nominalizations in Catalan. *Probus* 3: 279–316.

Pipa, Fehime undated. *Elementary Albanian: Filltar i shqipes.* Boston: Vatra.

Poppe, Nicholas 1970. *Mongolian language handbook.* Washington: Center for Applied Linguistics.

Postal, Paul M. 1970. On so-called pronouns in English. In *Readings in English transformational grammar*, ed. Roderick A. Jacobs and Peter S. Rosenbaum, 56–82. Waltham, Mass.: Ginn.

Prince, Ellen F. 1979. On the given/new distinction. In *Papers from the 15th Regional Meeting of the Chicago Linguistic Society*, ed. Paul R. Clyne, William F. Hanks and Carol L. Hofbauer, 267–78. Chicago: Chicago Linguistic Society.

1981. On the inferencing of indefinite-*this* NPs. In *Elements of discourse understanding*, ed. Aravind K. Joshi, Bonnie L. Webber and Ivan A. Sag, 231–50. Cambridge: Cambridge University Press.

Pustejovsky, James 1995. *The generative lexicon.* Cambridge, Mass.: MIT Press.

Radford, Andrew 1988. *Transformational grammar: a first course.* Cambridge: Cambridge University Press.

1993. Head-hunting: on the trail of the nominal Janus. In *Heads in grammatical theory*, ed. Greville G. Corbett, Norman M. Fraser and Scott McGlashan, 73–113. Cambridge: Cambridge University Press.

Ramsay, V. 1985. Classifiers and referentiality in Jacaltec. In *Proceedings of the First Annual Meeting of the Pacific Linguistics Conference*, ed. S. DeLancey and R. Tomlin, 289–312. Eugene: University of Oregon.

Ramsden, H. 1959. *An essential course in Modern Spanish.* London: Harrap.

Rando, Emily and Donna Jo Napoli 1978. Definites in *there*-sentences. *Language* 54: 300–13.

Raposo, Eduardo 1986. On the null object in European Portuguese. In *Studies in Romance linguistics*, ed. Osvaldo Jaeggli and Carmen Silva-Corvalán, 373–90. Dordrecht: Foris.

Redden, James E. 1979. A descriptive grammar of Ewondo. *Occasional Papers in Linguistics, Southern Illinois University* 4.

Reichard, Gladys A. 1951. *Navaho grammar*. New York: Augustin.

Reichenbach, Hans 1947. *Elements of symbolic logic*. London: Macmillan.

Reinhart, Tanya 1981. Pragmatics and linguistics: an analysis of sentence topics. *Philosophica* 27: 53–93.

  1983. *Anaphora and semantic interpretation*. London: Croom Helm.

Renisio, A. 1932. *Etude sur les dialectes berbères des Beni Iznassen, du Rif, et des Senhaja de Sraïr. Grammaire, textes et lexique*. Paris: Leroux.

Renzi, Lorenzo 1976. Grammatica e storia dell'articolo italiano. *Studi di Grammatica Italiana* 5: 5–42.

Reuland, Eric J. 1983. The extended projection principle and the definiteness effect. In *Proceedings of the West Coast Conference on Formal Linguistics* 2, ed. M. Barlow, D. Flickinger and M. Wescoat, 217–36. Stanford: Stanford Linguistics Association.

Reuland, Eric J. and Alice G. B. ter Meulen (eds.) 1987. *The representation of (in)definiteness*. Cambridge, Mass.: MIT Press.

Ritter, Elizabeth 1988. A head-movement approach to construct-state noun phrases. *Linguistics* 26: 909–29.

  1991. Two functional categories in noun phrases: evidence from Modern Hebrew. In *Syntax and semantics*, vol. 25: *Perspectives on phrase structure: heads and licensing*, ed. Susan D. Rothstein, 37–62. San Diego: Academic Press.

  1992. Cross-linguistic evidence for number phrase. *Canadian Journal of Linguistics* 37: 197–218.

Roberts, Ian G. 1987. *The representation of implicit and dethematized subjects*. Dordrecht: Foris.

Rosen, Haiim B. 1962. *A textbook of Israeli Hebrew, with an introduction to the classical language*. Chicago: Chicago University Press.

Rothstein, Susan and Ann Reed 1984. Definiteness and set determination. Paper presented at the Fifth Groningen Round Table on (In)definiteness, Groningen.

Rouchota, Villy 1994. On indefinite descriptions. *Journal of Linguistics* 30: 441–75.

Rowlands, E. C. 1969. *Yoruba*. London: Hodder and Stoughton.

Rowlett, Paul 1994. The Negative Cycle, negative concord and the nature of spec-head agreement. *University of Salford ESRI Working Papers in Language and Linguistics* 7.

Ruhl, Charles 1989. *On monosemy: a study in linguistic semantics*. Albany: State University of New York Press.

Russell, Bertrand 1905. On denoting. *Mind* 14: 479–93.

Sadler, Louisa 1988. *Welsh syntax: a government-binding approach*. London: Croom Helm.

Safir, Kenneth J. 1985. *Syntactic chains*. Cambridge: Cambridge University Press.

1987. What explains the definiteness effect? In Reuland and ter Meulen (eds.), 71–97.

Saltarelli, Mario 1988. *Basque*. London: Croom Helm.

Samarin, William J. 1967. *A grammar of Sango*. The Hague: Mouton.

Sandt, Rob A. van der 1988. *Context and presupposition*. London: Croom Helm.

Scatton, Ernest A. 1983. *A reference grammar of Modern Bulgarian*. Columbus, Ohio: Slavica.

Schachter, Paul 1985. Parts-of-speech systems. In *Language typology and syntactic description*, vol. I: *Clause structure*, ed. Timothy Shopen, 3–61. Cambridge: Cambridge University Press.

Schmalstieg, William R. 1987. *A Lithuanian historical syntax*. Columbus, Ohio: Slavica.

Schubert, Lenhart K. and Francis Jeffry Pelletier 1989. Generically speaking. In *Properties, types and meaning*, vol. 2: *Semantic issues*, ed. G. Chierchia, B. Partee and R. Turner, 193–268. Dordrecht: Kluwer.

Schuh, Russell G. 1983. The evolution of determiners in Chadic. In *Studies in Chadic and Afroasiatic linguistics*, ed. Ekkehard Wolff and H. Meyer-Bahlburg, 157–210. Hamburg: Buske.

Selig, Maria 1992. *Die Entwicklung der Nominaldeterminanten im Spätlatein*. Tübingen: Niemeyer.

Selkirk, Elisabeth O. 1984. *Phonology and syntax: the relation between sound and structure*. Cambridge, Mass.: MIT Press.

Shackle, C. 1972. *Punjabi*. London: English Universities Press.

Silverstein, Michael 1976. Hierarchy of features and ergativity. In *Grammatical categories in Australian languages*, ed. R. M. W. Dixon, 112–71. Canberra: Australian Institute of Aboriginal Studies.

Smith, N. V. 1975. On generics. *Transactions of the Philological Society*, 27–48.

Sohn, Ho-min 1994. *Korean*. London: Routledge.

Sommerstein, Alan H. 1972. On the so-called definite article in English. *Linguistic Inquiry* 3: 197–209.

Speas, Margaret J. 1990. *Phrase structure in natural language*. Dordrecht: Kluwer.

Spencer, Andrew 1992. Nominal inflection and the nature of functional categories. *Journal of Linguistics* 28: 313–41.

Sperber, Dan and Deirdre Wilson 1986. *Relevance: communication and cognition*. Oxford: Blackwell.

1987. Précis of *Relevance: communication and cognition. Behavioural and Brain Sciences* 10: 697–754.

1995. *Relevance: communication and cognition* (2nd edition, revised). Oxford: Blackwell.

Stalnaker, R. 1974. Pragmatic presuppositions. In *Semantics and philosophy: studies in contemporary philosophy*, ed. M. K. Munitz and P. K. Unger, 197–214. New York: New York University Press.

Stockwell, Robert P., Paul Schachter and Barbara Hall Partee 1973. *The major syntactic structures of English*. New York: Holt, Rinehart and Winston.

Strawson, P. F. 1950. On referring. *Mind* 59: 320–44.

1952. *Introduction to logical theory*. London: Methuen.

1964. Intention and convention in speech acts. *Philosophical Review* 73: 439–60.

Suárez, Jorge A. 1983. *The Mesoamerican Indian languages*. Cambridge: Cambridge University Press.

Suñer, Margarita 1988. The role of agreement in clitic-doubled constructions. *Natural Language and Linguistic Theory* 6: 391–434.

Svane, Gunnar Olaf 1958. *Grammatik der slowenischen Schriftsprache*. Copenhagen: Rosenkilde and Bagger.

Szabolcsi, Anna 1987. Functional categories in the noun phrase. In *Approaches to Hungarian*, vol. 2: *Theories and analyses*, ed. István Kenesei, 167–89. Szeged: JATE.

1994. The noun phrase. In *Syntax and semantics*, vol. 27: *The syntactic structure of Hungarian*, ed. Ferenc Kiefer and Katalin É. Kiss, 179–274. San Diego: Academic Press.

Taraldsen, Knut Tarald 1990. D-projections and N-projections in Norwegian. In *Grammar in progress: GLOW essays for Henk van Riemsdijk*, ed. Joan Mascaró and Marina Nespor, 419–31. Dordrecht: Foris.

Thaeler, M. D. and A. D. Thaeler undated. *Miskito grammar*. Managua: Board of Christian Education.

Traugott, Elizabeth Closs and Bernd Heine (eds.) 1991. *Approaches to grammaticalization*. Amsterdam: Benjamins.

Travis, Lisa and Greg Lamontagne 1992. The case filter and licensing of empty K. *Canadian Journal of Linguistics* 37: 157–74.

Tritton, A. S. 1977. *Arabic*. London: Hodder and Stoughton.

Tura, Sabahat Sansa 1986. Definiteness and referentiality in Turkish nonverbal sentences. In *Studies in Turkish linguistics*, ed. Dan Isaac Slobin and Karl Zimmer, 165–94. Amsterdam: Benjamins.

Ultan, Russell 1978. Some general characteristics of interrogative systems. In *Universals of human language*, vol. 4: *Syntax*, ed. Joseph H. Greenberg, Charles A. Ferguson and Edith A. Moravcsik, 211–48. Stanford: Stanford University Press.

Uriagereka, Juan 1995. Aspects of the syntax of clitic placement in Western Romance. *Linguistic Inquiry* 26: 79–123.

Vallduví, Enric and Elisabet Engdahl 1996. The linguistic realization of information packaging. *Linguistics* 34: 459–519.

Van Peteghem, Marleen 1989. Non spécificité, attributivité et article indéfini dans les langues romanes. *Travaux de Linguistique* 18: 45–56.

Van Valin, Robert D. 1985. Case marking and the structure of the Lakhota clause. In *Grammar inside and outside the clause: Some approaches to theory from the field*, ed. Johanna Nichols and Anthony C. Woodbury, 363–413. Cambridge: Cambridge University Press.

Vergnaud, Jean-Roger and María Luisa Zubizarreta 1992. The definite determiner and the inalienable constructions in French and in English. *Linguistic Inquiry* 23: 595–652.

References

Verkuyl, Henk J. 1981. Numerals and quantifiers in X-bar syntax and their semantic interpretation. In *Formal methods in the study of language*, ed. J. A. G. Groenendijk, T. M. V. Jansen and M. J. B. Stokhof, 567–99. Amsterdam:' Mathematisch Centrum.

Vincent, Nigel 1997. The emergence of the D-system in Romance. In *Parameters of morphosyntactic change*, ed. Ans van Kemenade and Nigel Vincent, 149–69. Cambridge: Cambridge University Press.

Wackernagel, J. 1892. Über ein Gesetz der indogermanischen Wortstellung. *Indogermanische Forschungen* 1: 333–436.

Watahomigie, Lucille J., Jorigine Bender and Akira Y. Yamamoto 1982. *Hualapai reference grammar*. Los Angeles: American Indian Studies Center, UCLA.

Welmers, W. E. 1976. *A grammar of Vai*. Berkeley: University of California Press.

Westermann, Diedrich 1960. *A study of the Ewe language*. London: Oxford University Press. (Originally published as *Grammatik der Ewe-Sprache*, Berlin, 1907.)

Whitney, Arthur H. 1956. *Finnish*. London: English Universities Press.

Williams, E. S. 1984. *There*-insertion. *Linguistic Inquiry* 15: 131–53.

Williamson, Janis S. 1984. Studies in Lakhota grammar. PhD thesis, University of California at San Diego.

1987. An indefiniteness restriction for relative clauses in Lakhota. In Reuland and ter Meulen (eds.), 168–90.

Wilson, Deirdre 1975. *Presuppositions and non-truth-conditional semantics*. London: Academic Press.

1992. Reference and relevance. *UCL Working Papers in Linguistics* 4: 167–91.

Wilson, G. 1978. On definite and indefinite descriptions. *Philosophical Review* 87: 48–76.

Windfuhr, Gernot L. 1979. *Persian grammar: history and state of its study*. The Hague: Mouton.

Woisetschlaeger, Erich 1983. On the question of definiteness in 'an old man's book'. *Linguistic Inquiry* 14: 137–54.

Wright, Joseph 1910. *Grammar of the Gothic language*. Oxford: Oxford University Press.

Yates, Alan 1975. *Catalan*. London: Hodder and Stoughton.

Young, Robert W. and William Morgan 1987. *The Navaho language. A grammar and colloquial dictionary*. Albuquerque: University of New Mexico Press.

Zanuttini, Raffaella 1991. Syntactic properties of sentential negation: a comparative study of Romance languages. PhD thesis, University of Pennsylvania.

Ziervogel, D., J. A. Louw and P. C. Taljaard 1967. *A handbook of the Zulu language*. Pretoria: Van Schaik.

Zwicky, Arnold M. 1977. On clitics. In *Phonologica 1976*, ed. W. Dressler and O. Pfeiffer, 23–39. Innsbruck: Institut für Sprachwissenschaft der Universität Innsbruck.

Zwicky, Arnold M. and Geoffrey K. Pullum 1983. Cliticization vs inflection: English n't. *Language* 59: 502–13.

INDEX

Index

Index

LANGUAGES INDEX

377

Printed in the United Kingdom
by Lightning Source UK Ltd.
99537UKS00001B/97-108